NWI0000793        CYPF

# NONPROFIT ORGANIZATIONS IN AN AGE OF UNCERTAINTY

# SOCIAL INSTITUTIONS AND SOCIAL CHANGE

*An Aldine de Gruyter Series of Texts and Monographs*

EDITED BY

James D. Wright

Larry Barnett, **Legal Construct, Social Concept: A Macrosociological Perspective on Law**

Vern L. Bengtson and W. Andrew Achenbaum, **The Changing Contract Across Generations**

Thomas G. Blomberg and Stanley Cohen (eds.), **Punishment and Social Control: Essays in Honor of Sheldon L. Messinger**

Remi Clignet, **Death, Deeds, and Descendants: Inheritance in Modern America**

Mary Ellen Colten and Susan Gore (eds.), **Adolescent Stress: Causes and Consequences**

Rand D. Conger and Glen H. Elder, Jr., **Families in Troubled Times: Adapting to Change in Rural America**

Joel A. Devine and James D. Wright, **The Greatest of Evils: Urban Poverty and the American Underclass**

G. William Domhoff, **The Power Elite and the State: How Policy is Made in America**

G. William Domhoff, **State Autonomy or Class Dominance? Case Studies on Policy Making in America**

Paula S. England, **Comparable Worth: Theories and Evidence**

Paula S. England, **Theory on Gender/Feminism on Theory**

George Farkas, **Human Capital or Cultural Capital? Ethnicity and Poverty Groups in an Urban School District**

Joseph Galaskiewicz and Wolfgang Bielefeld, **Nonprofit Organizations in an Age of Uncertainty: A Study in Organizational Change**

Davita Silfen Glasberg and Dan Skidmore, **Corporate Welfare Policy and the Welfare State: Bank Deregulation and the Savings and Loan Bailout**

Ronald F. Inglehart, Neil Nevitte, Miguel Basañez, **The North American Trajectory: Cultural, Economic, and Political Ties among the United States, Canada, and Mexico**

Gary Kleck, **Point Blank: Guns and Violence in America**

Gary Kleck, **Targeting Guns: Firearms and Their Control** (paperback)

James R. Kluegel, David S. Mason, and Bernd Wegener (eds.), **Social Justice and Political Change: Public Opinion in Capitalist and Post-Communist States**

Thomas S. Moore, **The Disposable Work Force: Worker Displacement and Employment Instability in America**

Clark McPhail, **The Myth of the Madding Crowd**

James T. Richardson, Joel Best, and David G. Bromley (eds.), **The Satanism Scare**

Peter H. Rossi and Richard A. Berk, **Just Punishments: Federal Guidelines and Public Views Compared**

Alice S. Rossi and Peter H. Rossi, **Of Human Bonding: Parent-Child Relations Across the Life Course**

Joseph F. Sheley and James D. Wright: **In the Line of Fire: Youth, Guns, and Violence in Urban America**

David G. Smith, **Paying for Medicare: The Politics of Reform**

James D. Wright, **Address Unknown: The Homeless in America**

James D. Wright and Peter H. Rossi, **Armed and Considered Dangerous: A Survey of Felons and Their Firearms, (Expanded Edition)**

James D. Wright, Peter H. Rossi, and Kathleen Daly, **Under the Gun: Weapons, Crime, and Violence in America**

Mary Zey, **Banking on Fraud: Drexel, Junk Bonds, and Buyouts**

# NONPROFIT ORGANIZATIONS IN AN AGE OF UNCERTAINTY
## A Study of Organizational Change

Joseph Galaskiewicz and Wolfgang Bielefeld

ALDINE DE GRUYTER
New York

# About the Authors

**Joseph Galaskiewicz** is a Professor of Sociology and Strategic Management/ Organization at the University of Minnesota. He is the author of several books, and coeditor with Stanley Wasserman of the volume entitled *Advances in Social Network Analysis: Research in the Social and Behavioral Sciences* (Sage, 1994). His research has focused on the role of informal social structures in explaining business organizational behavior, and more recently, organizational change.

**Wolfgang Bielefeld** is Associate Professor of Sociology and Political Economy in the School of Social Sciences at the University of Texas at Dallas. His research interests include the relations between organizations and their environments, and the dynamics of nonprofit sectors.

Copyright © 1998 Walter de Gruyter, Inc., New York

ALDINE DE GRUYTER
A division of Walter de Gruyter, Inc.
200 Saw Mill River Road
Hawthorne, New York 10532

This publication is printed on acid free paper ∞

**Library of Congress Cataloging-in-Publication Data**
Galaskiewicz, Joseph.
    Nonprofit Organizations in an age of uncertainty : a study of organizational change / by Joseph Galaskiewicz and Wolfgang Bielefeld.
      p.  cm. — (Social instititutions and social change)
    Includes bibliographical references (p. ) and index
    ISBN 0-202-30565-1 (alk. paper). — ISBN 0-202-30566-X (pbk. : alk. paper)
    1. Nonprofit organizations. 2. Organizational change. I. Title. II. Series
    HD62.6.G35 1998 98-17049
    658'.048—dc21 CIP
Manufactured in the United States of American

10 9 8 7 6 5 4 3 2 1

# CONTENTS

# Preface

Not-for-profit public charitable organizations constitute an important sector of American society. In 1994 there were 506,370 active public charities and 49,487 active private nonoperating foundations on file with the Internal Revenue Service (IRS) for a total of 555,857 active charitable nonprofit organizations in the United States [organizations exempt under section 501(c)(3)].[1] This total represented an increase of 28.5% since 1989 (Stevenson, Pollak, and Lampkin 1997:4), and there were more than twice as many charitable organizations in the United States in 1994 as in 1977 (Hodgkinson and Weitzman 1996:37–38). Together, charitable organizations and social welfare organizations [nonprofits exempt under section 501(c)(4)] employed 6.7% of all full- and part-time employees in 1994, up from 5.3% in 1977 (Hodgkinson and Weitzman 1996:44). If we aggregate all nonprofit organizations—charitable, social welfare, and other—operating expenditures totaled $499.1 billion in 1993, which was roughly 7.9% of gross domestic product (GDP). This compared to $102.7 billion in 1977, which was roughly 5.2% of GDP (Hodgkinson and Weitzman 1996:48).

People come into contact with public charities on a daily basis. The college their son or daughter attends, their hospital, HMO, or clinic, the public television station they watch in the evening, the community theater and local museums, their children's little league team, day-care center, or Boy/Girl Scout troop, and their parents' nursing home are all likely to be public charities. They also benefit from the activities of public charities with which they never interact personally but that have a major impact upon their lives and communities: community development corporations, health advocacy groups (e.g., the American Cancer Society), relief organizations, research universities, public policy institutes, and the United Way. The public charity is an important part of American life. It is almost unimaginable to think what our nation would be like without these organizations.

## THE PURPOSE OF THE BOOK

This is a study of organizational change. We use data from a panel of public charities in the Minneapolis–St. Paul metropolitan area that we

followed from 1980 to 1994 and four cross-sectional sample surveys conducted in 1980, 1984, 1988, and 1992. During this period, organizations
experienced a considerable amount of change. Some dramatically increased their revenues, employees, volunteers, and expenditures; others
declined. Some switched from being dependent upon donations to being
dependent upon fees and program service income, while others became
less reliant on government funding. Some became more "businesslike,"
while others became more political. Some changed their mission and
goals; others went to great lengths to remain faithful to their original
purpose. Some changed the services they provided and the people they
served; others continued to do the same things over the course of the
study period. Some organizations became more autocratic; others became
more democratic. In some organizations morale improved; in others it
plummeted. Finally, most organizations survived the study period, but
others either chose or were forced to close.

To understand why these charitable organizations changed, we drew
on a wide range of organizational theories, derived testable hypotheses,
and then compared what actually happened to what these theories predicted. As we shall see, researchers and practitioners have formulated
many different theories to explain organizational change, and they have
already done a considerable amount of research on these topics. Yet in the
last ten years there has been a remarkable convergence in thinking among
sociologists, management scientists, and other organizational theorists. In
explaining almost any organizational phenomenon, researchers agree
that it is necessary to examine at the macro level the institutional order
(i.e., values, norms, the law, public opinion) and patterns of inequality
(i.e., the distribution of authoritative and allocative resources across social
positions), and at the micro level informal social structures (i.e., networks), formal structures (i.e., size and age), and agency (i.e., individual
preferences and initiatives) (Coleman 1986; Sewell 1992). While it would
certainly be easier to focus on only one set of effects, e.g., agency or social
structural effects, we do not believe that one can understand organizational change by taking such an approach. Organizational scholars have
concocted a variety of theories, and all of them need to be considered.
This means that our study will be more eclectic than most and will not
advocate any one theoretical perspective. If readers are looking for the
"silver bullet" that can explain change among nonprofits, they will not
find it here. On the other hand, if they are up for a little contest among
ideas, they may find this book attractive.

Perhaps the most controversial feature of the study is that the theories
we tested and the analyses we presented were ahistorical. The book is
written as if time and place made no difference. This was a difficult

decision for us. Because all the authors lived in the Minneapolis–St. Paul metropolitan area, walked the streets, read the newspapers, and visited the organizations we studied in person, we are fully aware of the context in which this study was done. We know that the Twin Cities are "different" (although how different remains to be seen) and that the time frame for this analysis, 1980 to 1994, spanned the Reagan revolution, privatization, the New Federalism, two recessions, the AIDS epidemic, church scandals, Aramony and the United Way, a scathing indictment of the sector by the *Philadelphia Inquirer*, a complete reorganization of the health care field, Newt Gingrich, and efforts to rescind property tax exemptions in some states. It certainly has been an exciting period, and it would be foolish not to acknowledge that each of these events impacted the charitable sector in important ways—stimulating demand, raising doubts among donors, burying nonprofit managers in red tape, and giving birth to new nonprofits. Yet our analysis will ignore these contextual events.

It is important that we give our rationale for ignoring the larger context. First, our goal was to build and test organizational theory. We felt that the best way to do this was to draw a relatively large random sample of organizations, survey them with reliable instruments, and employ statistical analyses to test hypotheses. We did not think that comparative case studies nor sociohistorical analyses would be as effective. Others may disagree. Second, and more importantly, it was simply too difficult to model contextual events. Studies that take into account the larger context are mostly industry specific, e.g., Gray's (1991) study of hospitals, Alexander's (1996) research on museums, Gronbjerg's (1993) book on social service and community development organizations, and Arnove's (1980) anthology on foundations. This is the best way to study these effects. We examined different ways of coding contextual events across the industries represented in our sample and found that our sample was too heterogeneous and each industry had its own unique context. Perhaps there is a way of incorporating contextual events into the analysis, and we welcome others to reanalyze our data with this agenda in mind.

## THE PLAN OF THE BOOK

The first chapter begins by reviewing several theories of organizational change. Because of space constraints we are not able to review all the pertinent literature and research findings related to each and every theory; but we give the reader an overview of each theory, show how the different theories apply to different levels of analysis and are based on different assumptions about organizational processes, and identify different variables that can explain organizational change. We break down our discussion into three parts. The first examines selection theories highlighting the work of organizational ecologists and institutionalists in sociology. The second examines adaptation theories reviewing the work of institutional economists, institutional sociologists, and strategy theorists. Third, we discuss how formal and informal structures can affect organizational change. We call this the *embeddedness approach*, and it draws heavily from the strategy and structure and social networks literature.

The first chapter also profiles nonprofit organizations and how they differ among themselves. We make the distinction between charitable nonprofits (or public benefit nonprofits) and clubs (or mutual benefit nonprofits). Next we distinguish between nonprofits that rely on the sale of services versus those that rely heavily on donated income. Then there are nonprofits that provide ordinary private goods, trust goods, and collective or public goods. Finally, we distinguish between charities that use employees from those run by volunteers. We develop a typology of nonprofits based on the cross-classification of the last three pairs of categories. We are especially attentive to two polar extremes. On the one hand, we have utilitarian public charities, which are businesslike in nature and commercial. They sell private goods and services directly to consumers and use employees as service providers. On the other hand, we have normative public charities, which are more communitarian in style. These are the prototypical charitable organizations. The purpose of these organizations is to provide collective and/or trust goods or services; they are heavily dependent upon donations and are staffed by volunteers. We argued that both types of nonprofits are resource driven, but the way they go about acquiring resources is very different. We discuss the utility of our theories of change in explaining the behavior of both types of nonprofits.

The second chapter describes the research site and the methods we used to gather our data, and presents descriptive data on the organizations in our study. As noted above, this book used data from both a panel study of public charities and cross-sectional surveys of public charities done in the Minneapolis–St. Paul area spanning the period from 1980 to 1994. The chapter also charts changes in expenditures and funding over the years. Revenues are an important part of this research, and we need to understand how funding has changed in the sector as a whole and for our panel. We also look at changes in the composition of the sector, i.e., organizational activities, employment, and the use of volunteers, again looking at both cross-sectional and panel data.

The third chapter focuses on the growth and decline of revenues and personnel, studying the period from 1980 to 1994. Our purpose is to identify the causes of growth and decline. We examine environmental conditions, e.g., the density of an organization's niches, the level of resource concentration, and the status of others in the niches. We also look at the effects of different tactics on growth and decline. We examine managerial tactics aimed at making service delivery more instrumentally rational, political or legitimacy tactics aimed at convincing stakeholders of the organization's normative purity, and retrenchment or cutback tactics aimed at reducing the size of the organization. We also describe the effects of interorganizational network centrality, ties to the local community elite, decision-making structure, size, and activities on the growth and decline of revenues and personnel.

The fourth chapter examines tactics more closely and asks the question, Why do organizations use the tactics they do and why do organizations change their tactics and activities over time? Here tactics and activities are the dependent variables, and the period is from 1984 to 1992. Why do some organizations try to make themselves more businesslike, while others are more concerned with establishing their public credibility and trustworthiness? Why do some retrench operations while others don't? Why do organizations decide to go into new product/service lines? Is this due to conditions in their resource niches, e.g., the level of competition? Under what conditions do organizations abandon their niche and try something new? Are social influences important in selecting tactics? Do managers mimic the tactics of organizations that they perceive to be especially successful? Do ties to local elites affect the choice of tactics?

The fifth chapter addresses the question, What brings about changes in the pattern of decision-making and morale within the organization? What causes conflicts and disagreements? The period we study is from 1988 to 1994. Many would say growth and decline in revenues. We usually think that growth is "good" and decline is "bad," but shrinking may be a strategy that has very positive long-term payoffs. Another important question is whether growth and decline or the tactics employed by management affect outcomes more. This chapter also examines how managerial and political tactics affect the quality of life within organizations and how this can differ, depending upon one's funding streams.

The final chapter summarizes our findings and returns to the theories outlined in the first chapter to see which theories worked better in explaining organizational change. We also discuss findings that were unexpected and that give us clues as to how to build better theories of change in the future. We conclude by discussing the implications of our findings for the sector and the study's shortcomings and offering some suggestions for future research.

*Joseph Galaskiewicz*
University of Minnesota, Minneapolis

*Wolfgang Bielefeld*
University of Texas, Richardson

## NOTE

1.  This number is a conservative estimate since certain organizations, such as congregations, integrated auxiliaries, subordinate units, and conventions or associations of churches, need not apply for recognition of exemption unless they desire a ruling.

# Acknowledgments

Funding for this research came from many different sources. The bulk of the funds were provided by the Sociology Section of the National Science Foundation (SES 80-08570, SES 83-19364, SES 88-12702, and SES 93-20929). Other donors included the Program on Nonprofit Organizations (PONPO) at Yale University, the Nonprofit Sector Research Fund, the Northwest Area Foundation of St. Paul, the Center for Urban and Regional Affairs (CURA) at the University of Minnesota, the Graduate School at the University of Minnesota, the Rockefeller Brothers Fund, and the American Association of Colleges. Of course, we must also acknowledge the Department of Sociology, its chairs, and the College of Liberal Arts at the University of Minnesota, which provided the project with space, clerical help, copying, phones, accounting services, travel funds, and, most importantly, computer hardware, software, and Karl Krohn, the department's very own wizard of the information age. We would also like to thank the Department of Sociology at Harvard University and its chair, Peter V. Marsden, for their hospitality while we finished writing this book.

We need to thank the graduate and undergraduate students and office staff who have been so important in helping us gather, clean, and analyze data and writing reports, mailing papers to respondents, and preparing this book. Many were truly heroic, spending weekends, evenings, and early morning hours tracking down nonprofits, calling for interviews, conducting on-site interviews in homes, agencies, organizations, restaurants, bars, wherever people would meet with them, calling back for missing data, going back into files to check on data, running to the state's attorney general's office for more data, and calling back again for that one last piece of information. There was also data entry, creating files, verifying data, analyzing data, and then writing memo after memo after memo, creating an institutional memory. The work of Mark Hager, Naomi Kaufmann, Joel Pins, Alisa Potter, and Kay Schaffer is especially appreciated. In alphabetical order we acknowledge and thank Sarah Allen-Walters, Donna Bergstrom, Steve Carlton-Ford, Pitt Cheang, Insub Choi, Deborah Felt, Heidi Hanson, Laura Hutton, Yoshito Ishio, Cheryl Jorgensen, Wayne Kobbervig, Li Jin, Gretchen Lieb-Peterson, Gretchen Matteson,

Amy Miller, Patti Mullaney, Leila Nouraee, Michael O'Neal, Anneli Olila, Phuong Phan,Asha Rangin, Barbara Rauschenbach, Mary Jo Reef, Jeanne-Marie Rohland, Kim Simmons, Lisa Thornquist, Heather Vanderley, and Deborah Woodworth. I am especially indebted to the current sociology office staff including Gwen Gmeinder, Hilda Daniels, Mary Drew, Kate Stuckert, and Naaz Babvani. Many others in the front office, e.g., Gloria DeWolfe, have helped us over the years as well.

We also want to acknowledge colleagues and people in the Twin Cities and elsewhere who have been very supportive of our project and have given us assistance throughout the years in a number of different ways. In particular we want to acknowledge Tom Scott of CURA, Brad Gray formerly of PONPO, Terry Saario formerly of the Northwest Area Foundation, Sheila Fishman of the Minnesota State's Attorney Office, Jon Pratt of the Minnesota Council of Nonprofits, Jackie Ries of the Minnesota Council on Foundations, Virginia Hodgkinson of Independent Sector, and Avner Ben-Ner, David Knoke, Peggy Marini, Diane Rulke, Kathie Sutcliffe, and Andy Van de Ven at the University of Minnesota. Paul DiMaggio, Stanley Wasserman, and Burt Weisbrod have also been very supportive and given us guidance over the years. We are also indebted to the people at Aldine de Gruyter and especially our editor, Richard Koffler, who gave us the time to "do it right." Furthermore, the first author would like to thank Mariko Karatsu for being so patient and understanding throughout the writing of this book, and the second author would like to thank Patricia Donohue for her patience and encouragement throughout the course of this project. And, finally, we would like to acknowledge the executive directors, financial officers, board members, human resource personnel, and volunteers of the nonprofits in this study. They have given us days of their time in order to make our study a success. It is with genuine humility that we present our results, for it is *their* story that we seek to tell. To all of you, we say thank you.

# 1

# Organizational Change and the Public Charity

The first half of this chapter reviews theories of organizational change. First, we examine theories that look for the source of change in the environment. Barnett and Carroll (1995) label this the selection approach. Included in this camp are organizational ecology (Hannan and Freeman 1977) and later versions of institutional theory (DiMaggio and Powell 1991; W. R. Scott 1995). Next we review theories that attribute change to the actions of managers as they try to achieve certain objectives for their organization. Barnett and Carroll (1995) label this the adaptation approach. Theories in this camp include contingency theory (Lawrence and Lorsch 1967), resource dependence theory (Pfeffer and Salancik 1978), transaction cost economics (Williamson 1975), and earlier versions of institutional theory (Meyer and Rowan 1977; DiMaggio and Powell 1983). The third set of theories focuses on how organizational action is embedded in different social structures and how these modify the impact of environment on strategy formulation and the impact of tactics on organizational outcomes. This we call the structural embeddedness approach, and it draws heavily on social network analysis (Granovetter 1985).[1]

The second part of this chapter addresses the question, Can these theories be applied to nonprofit organizations and particularly public charities? Various theories assume that organizations strive to maximize resources, contain costs, and ensure their legitimacy, while achieving their goals. We conclude that all assumptions apply to nonprofits—although they vary in importance across different types of nonprofits. Some nonprofits behave in ways that are similar to business organizations, emphasizing efficiency norms and striving to reduce costs. Others behave like traditional eleemosynary organizations, paying a great deal of attention to their noneconomic goals and being legitimate. But almost all nonprofits—just like their for-profit brethren—seem interested in maximizing inputs. We will argue that the theories of organizational change

1

outlined in the first part of the chapter are applicable to studying change among nonprofits and for-profits alike.


## LEARNING FROM THE LITERATURE
## ON ORGANIZATIONAL CHANGE


Barnett and Carroll define organizational change as "a transformation of an organization between two points in time. . . . On the basis of content, major changes consist of transformations that involve many elements of structure or those that entail radical shifts in a single element of structure" (1995:219). Sometimes it is relatively easy to know when change has taken place. An organization is born or it dies. Sometimes after long periods of inertia, there are revolutionary or radical changes where deeply established structures are fundamentally transformed and the identity of the organization is altered (see Tushman and Romanelli 1985). Sometimes there are changes in decision-making patterns, the hierarchy of control, or the division of labor (Blau 1972; Lawrence and Lorsch 1967; Hage and Aiken 1967). Then there are changes in effectiveness (Haveman 1992) and size (Cameron, Kim, and Whetten 1987); the adoption of innovations (Van de Ven and Garud 1993); and goal succession (Selznick 1949). Studying organizational change is not something new, and one wonders if the concept has any utility given that it refers to so many different phenomena.[2]


### A. Selection Models


Environmental effects on organizations have been studied for many years [e.g., Selznick's (1949) study of the TVA]. However, it was only in the 1960s that organizational theory came to recognize fully the importance of environmental factors. An important part of the perspective is that organizations are not closed systems, but rather are open to environmental influences. Early studies saw more give and take in the relationship between the environment and the organization (e.g., Lawrence and Lorsch 1967). However, later writings were more deterministic. Managers do not adapt to changing conditions. Rather survival depends upon selection processes, and the degree to which there is a fit between environmental conditions and organizational forms.

According to Hannan and Carroll (1995a:23), selection refers to a change in the composition of a set of organizations as one form (e.g., the unitary divisional form) is replaced by another (e.g., the multidivisional form). One form comes to be dominated by another, because more of the latter arise and fewer fail than is the case for the former. An important part of the selection process is that firms have a very poor capacity to change themselves, i.e., they are inert and core features do not change. Stinchcombe (1965) even suggested that organizations are imprinted upon founding and are likely to retain features acquired at their beginning. Thus once born, organizations tend to retain the same form until they die and, in fact, increase their chances for failure if they try to change form (for a review of research on this topic, see Barnett and Carroll 1995). Given the importance of inertia, the impetus for birth or death, growth or decline, comes not from actions that the organization takes, but from conditions in the environment.

*The Ecological Environment.* The ecological environment is the arena where organizations live out their day-to-day lives. We equate it to the technical environment. Readers are familiar with the task environment where the actual work of an organization gets done. This includes all actors that are relevant to its goal attainment, e.g., suppliers, customers, regulators, and competitors (Dill 1958). If we aggregate these egocentric configurations along institutional lines, we derive the organizational field (Warren 1967; DiMaggio and Powell 1983). If we aggregate within some geographical area, we derive the ecological community (Hawley 1950). In both cases a multitude of organizations are procuring the factors of production and distributing their output. They sometimes cooperate with one another in strategic alliances or action sets to put pressure on institutional gatekeepers or to raise prices, and sometimes they compete against one another for inputs. We see organizations formulating goals, implementing strategies, and carrying out transactions with other organizations that are doing the same. It is a highly dynamic system, very concrete, and fraught with action. The more technically adept succeed; the less adept fail.

Over the last twenty years organizational ecology has made a major contribution to the study of organizational change, particularly in the study of population dynamics [for a review of research results, see Carroll (1984) and Singh and Lumsden (1990)]. For example, ecologists have documented a strong relationship between population density (the number of organizations with a given form) and organizational births and deaths. As the density of a population increases, the death rate falls and the birth rate soars until at a certain point births drop off and the rate of organizational death increases. In other words, the relationship between density and birth rates is nonmonotonic with the form of an inverted U, while the relationship between density and death rates is nonmonotonic with the form of a U. Ecologists argue that the first effect is due to the increasing constitutive legitimacy of a specific organizational form as the population increases, which in turn encourages more new organizations to come on board. The latter is due to population density reaching the "carrying capacity." At this point organizational death is an adjustment to the limited stock of resources in the environment and increased competition (Hannan and Freeman 1989; Hannan and Carroll 1992).

Ecologists have also looked at resource concentration. Concentration is almost always measured at the industry level and used as an indicator of intraindustry competition. The assumption is that high levels of concentration lessen competition, while low levels heighten it. According to Swaminathan (1995), however, there is not a simple negative correlation between concentration and density. He argues that in the early stages of a population's history, low density is accompanied by low levels of concentration, while later in the population's history, when density is again low, concentration should be high. Concentration has been shown to affect birth and death rates as well. For example, Carroll (1985) found that when a market concentrates, the death rate of generalist organizations increases and that of specialists decrease. With increasing concentration, generalists tend to compete vigorously for the center of the market, thus allowing specialists to thrive on the periphery. Others have focused on the effects of concentration on founding rates (Swaminathan 1995; Barnett and Carroll 1987). Industrial organization economists have looked at the effects of concentration on industry profitability. Almost always there is a strong, significant, positive relationship (for a discussion of this literature, see Burt 1983:18–19).

Recently, some ecologists have come to recognize the shortcomings of focusing exclusively on populations, and more particularly industries. Ecologists define populations in terms of shared structural forms (Hannan and Freeman 1989:Chapter 3), but not all organizations within a population compete against one another and sometimes different populations compete for the same resources (Hannan and Freeman 1977). The first point is illustrated in the case of nonprofit organizations. Even though two nonprofit organizations are providing the same service and are organized in similar ways, e.g., drug rehabilitation programs, if one is reliant on fees while the other is reliant on donations, or one has volunteers and the other employees, it is difficult to see how they are competing against one another for inputs. Furthermore, organizations, for the most part, do not compete across size categories—even in the same industries. Hannan and Freeman (1977) pointed this out in one of their earliest papers (see also Baum and Haveman 1997). Large organizations do not compete against small firms, but both probably compete against medium-size firms. That is, firms compete against others with similar capabilities. Competition is further restricted by geography and customer demographics. For example, Baum and Oliver (1996) not only distinguished between day care centers serving different age groups but day care centers that were located in different parts of the metropolitan Toronto area. It is also the case that two very different types of organizations compete against one another for the same resources (Hannan and Freeman 1977). Baum and Oliver (1996), Weisbrod (1988), and Gray (1991) showed that nonprofits often compete against for-profits for the same clients, students, or patients. Professional sports teams, casinos, and movie theaters compete for the same consumer dollars within metropolitan areas. Researchers at universities, community development corporations, health care providers, and arts organizations often compete for funding from the same foundations.

Studying niches is an attractive alternative to studying populations, because incumbents are identified relationally rather than on the basis of shared organizational traits. Niches are locations in multidimensional space defined by the distribution of resources in the environment (McPherson 1983; see also Baum and Singh 1994a, 1994b; Baum and Oliver 1996; Hannan and Freeman 1989). Niches are the sites where resources are located and where organizations compete for technology, labor inputs, customers, grants, capital, etc. Thus organizations are in the same niche if they are structurally equivalent to one another vis-à-vis valued resources (see Burt and Talmud 1993).

The niche perspective also enables us to study organizations' "microniches" and thus identify generalist and specialist organizations. We define the microniche from the perspective of the organization. It is the area in the niche space where the organization "feeds" (McPherson 1983). An organization may procure all its resources within one niche, but more likely it draws on several, crossing niche boundaries. If it procures its resources from a single niche, then we say it is a specialist. If it competes for resources in several niches, we call it a generalist. The microniche is also important because it can tell us which pairs of organizations are in competition with one another. If microniches overlap, two organizations will be feeding off the same fauna. Although this monograph will not address niche overlap and its consequences (e.g., board interlocking, strategic alliances, and joint ventures), we have begun work on these issues and have promising preliminary results (Bielefeld, Galaskiewicz, and Hudson 1998).

Recent work on microniches by Baum and his associates (Baum and Singh 1994a, 1994b, 1996; Baum and Oliver 1996) and Podolny, Stuart, and Hannan (1996) has taken research on niche effects to a new level. Building on the work of McPherson (1983), Baum et al. operationalized organizational niches in terms of the attributes of organizations' clientele. That is, organizations were in the same niche if they targeted the same customers or delivered services in the same geographical area. They were also able to operationalize niche density and found that it was correlated with organizational foundings and deaths. Using patent citations, Podolny et al. (1996) operationalized organizational niches in terms of firms' drawing on similar inventions for their own research activity and found a strong empirical relationship between crowding (or density) and organizational decline. An important contribution of this research was the recognition that each organization faced a slightly different context—it had its own microniche—due to its particular mix of products, market segments, technology, investors, etc., and the degree to which other organizations competed for the same resources.

While most ecological research has focused on for-profit organizations, ecologists have also examined a number of nonprofit forms, including trade unions (Hannan and Freeman 1988), state bar associations (Halliday, Powell, and Granfors 1987), trade associations (Aldrich, Staber, Zimmer, and Beggs 1990), cooperatives (Staber 1989), voluntary social service agencies (Singh, Tucker, and House 1986; Singh, House, and Tucker 1986), day care centers (Baum and Singh 1994a, 1994b; Baum and Oliver 1996), and membership organizations (McPherson and Rotolo 1996; Minkoff 1997). In most instances, they find strong support for their hypotheses.

*The Institutional Environment.* The institutional environment encompasses cultural patterns external to the organization and how they influence organizational behavior. Paraphrasing Meyer and Rowan (1977), Scott says:

> Modern societies contain many complexes of institutionalized rules and patterns—products of professional groups, the state, public opinion. These social realities provide a framework for the creation and elaboration of formal organizations. . . . [I]n modern societies, these institutions are likely to take the form of rationalized myths. They are myths because they are widely held beliefs that cannot be objectively tested: they are true because they are believed. . . . They are rationalized because they take the form of rules specifying procedures necessary to accomplish a given end. . . . Institutional theory emphasizes that organizations are open systems—strongly influenced by their environments—but that many of the most fateful forces are the result not of rational pressures for more effective performance but of social and cultural pressures to conform to conventional beliefs. (1992:117–18)

Following Scott (1995), we regard institutional effects as having little to do with the technical performance of organizations and more to do with defining and enforcing appropriate behaviors, i.e., conferring organizational legitimacy.

A useful way to study institutions is to differentiate among institutional effects. Scott distinguished between regulative, normative and cognitive aspects of institutions: "the models are differentiated such that each identifies a distinctive basis of compliance, mechanism of diffusion, type of logic, cluster of indicators, and foundations for legitimacy claims" (1995:60). The regulative effect is based on coercion. Conformity is expedient, because there will be material consequences otherwise. The normative effect is based on socialization into societal meanings, values, and norms. Conformity is based on actors having internalized values, social obligation, formal laws, or quasi-moral norms. The cognitive effect is based on mimetic processes. Actors comply with deeply ingrained cultural scripts, assumptions, and solutions. These are the "taken for granteds" that no one challenges. Conformity is based on membership and participation in a culture.

Both ecologists and institutionalists are interested in legitimacy. The former has done more research on constitutive legitimacy and the latter on sociopolitical legitimacy (see Baum and Powell 1995; Hannan and Carroll 1995b). Constitutive legitimacy is cognitive and describes the process whereby organizational forms come to be "taken for granted." This supposedly explains the ecologists' density dependence effects described earlier. As the number of organizations with a given form multiplies, entrepreneurs founding new organizations adopt this form, because it is "obvious," and probably could not think of another way of organizing themselves. Sociopolitical legitimacy refers to organizations being rewarded for behavioral conformity to—or punished for violation of—some law, norm, or standard by authorities, publics, or institutional gatekeepers. Rewards might be in the form of grants or contracts or simply social recognition. Punishments range from fines to penalties to ostracism.

There has been considerable research on the effects of sociopolitical legitimacy on organizational outcomes. Sponsorships and external referents of legitimation are oft-studied indicators of sociopolitical legitimacy. For example, Baum and Oliver (1992, 1996) looked at day care centers in metropolitan Toronto and their relations with community organizations and government agencies. In niches where ties were more extensive (i.e., the sociopolitical legitimacy of organizations was greater), foundings were much higher. Baum and Singh (1994a) also found that day care centers with relational ties had much lower death rates (see also Baum and Oliver 1991). Singh, Tucker, and Meinhard (1991) looked at voluntary social service organizations in Toronto and found that organizations that were listed in community directories, had a charitable registration number, and had a large board of directors had a significantly lower death rate (see also Singh, House, and Tucker 1986). Both sets of results support the argument that sociopolitical legitimacy is crucial for organizational survival.

Another approach to studying legitimacy looks at changes in the law or the passage of legislation that "cuts off" or channels funds to organizations that provide certain types of services. This is neither constitutive nor sociopolitical legitimacy. Rather something in the larger institutional environment changes that, overnight, makes some organizations more public regarding and legitimate than others (e.g., see Fligstein 1996). Singh, Tucker, and Meinhard's (1991) research on the effects of changes in government policies on the births and deaths of voluntary social service organizations in Toronto illustrates this process. Also ecologists have examined a number of populations where birth and death rates were affected by some exogenous institutional change (Hannan and Carroll 1995b).

Institutional theory relies heavily on selection to explain organizational behavior and survival, and this is reflected in much of the research in this tradition (for a comprehensive review, see W. R. Scott 1995). Although there are elements of rational choice, e.g., sometimes conformity is motivated by incentives (e.g., grants) or disincentives (e.g., penalties), more often conformity is less conscious, e.g., in the case of societal "taken for granteds," or based on motives that have little to do with furthering organizational ends, e.g., in the case of acting "morally" correct. Institutionalists can even envision organizational actors resisting changes that could further the interest of the organization on technical grounds, because they violate these "common understandings that are seldom explicitly articulated" (Zucker 1983:5). In other cases, conditions exogenous to the organization change and the organization is either left better or worse off than before. In its later (i.e., cognitive) versions (e.g., DiMaggio and Powell 1991; W. R. Scott 1995) there is not much room for agency or individual discretion as institutional forces would swamp any independent managerial initiatives [for a critique, see DiMaggio (1988) and Hirsch (1997)].

## B. Adaptation Models

In contrast to selection theory, adaptation theory argues that organizations can and will restructure themselves and their task environment to ensure their survival and achieve their goals. That is, senior management can and will formulate general strategies and implement specific tactics that will reduce costs, ensure the ample flow of resources, and protect the good name or legitimacy of the organization. If one wants to explain differences in organizational behavior, one looks to the strategic initiatives of managers. Adaptation models are clearly descendants of the rationalist tradition in organizational theory.

Chandler defined strategy as "the determination of the basic long-range goals and objectives of an enterprise, and the adoption of courses of action and allocation of resources necessary for carrying out these goals" (1962:13). Although commonly accepted in management circles, the merits of the strategy perspective have been debated in the academic literature. Scott (1992:287) cautions that one must be careful not to confuse actions with intentions. He cites Mintzberg's (1987; see also Pennings 1985) distinction between "intended" strategy (i.e., plans), "emergent" strategy (i.e., unplanned patterns of behavior) and "realized" strategy (i.e., actual behavior whether planned or unplanned). Pennings (1985:2–3) added that often strategy is nothing more than the after-the-fact social construction that firms use to rationalize their actions. These are important distinctions. Firms can have a strategy even though they did not intend to—thus decoupling rational calculation from strategy. Furthermore, we need not know the rationale or mind-set of decision-makers nor even who made the decision or the chaos surrounding the making of the decision in order to study the effects of strategy on organizational change.

Another curiosity of this literature is that often it makes assumptions that senior management is rational and a faithful servant of organizational goals. Yet research has shown that management will act irrationally in the face of threats [e.g., Staw, Sandelands, and Dutton's (1981) threat-rigidity response], is often uninformed and must rely on unreliable organizational "givens" (Simon 1957; March and Simon 1958), and will use organizational resources to serve their own utility instead of their principals' (Jensen and Meckling 1976). That senior management does not always act rationally or in good faith complicates the discussion considerably.

At the risk of oversimplifying, we posit that strategic management has three basic choices (see Table 1.1).[3] First, they can position themselves either for growth or for consolidation. The latter includes scaling back on their initiatives, harvesting the fruits of their labor, and even shrinking a bit. Second, management can target its energies either internally or externally. It can do something about its own organization or try to do something about its environment. And, third, management can focus its efforts on improving and marketing its products and services (managerial tactics), or it can do something about its institutional or political situation.

The third set of options deserves further comment. Oftentimes when discussing strategy, academics and practitioners only think of those so-called managerial tactics. However, they might think about strategy more broadly. Borrowing from stakeholder theory (Evan and Freeman 1988; Freeman 1984), we suggest that organizations should be sensitive not

*Table 1.1.* Typology of Organizational Strategies and Tactics

| Strategy: | Growth | | Consolidation |
|---|---|---|---|
| Tactics: | Managerial | Political | Retrenchment |
| **Arena:** | | | |
| Internal | •Institute a planning process<br>•Tighten financial controls<br>•Eliminate waste and duplication of effort<br>•Reorganize executive/administrative offices<br>•Implement product quality controls | •Institute affirmative action programs, diversity training<br>•Acquire external referents of prestige<br>•Make audits, tax forms, annual reports available to public | •Do not replace staff who leave<br>•Freeze salaries and benefits<br>•Postpone capital improvements |
| External | •Do market research<br>•Advertise<br>•Acquire competitors<br>•Acquisitions<br>•Expand geographically<br>•Undercut competitors on price<br>•Strategic alliances, joint ventures | •Lobby legislatures, create PACs<br>•Do image marketing<br>•Make charitable contributions<br>•Seek endorsements | •Divest businesses<br>•Eliminate program areas<br>•Merge with another organization<br>•Liquidate assets |

only to suppliers, customers, competitors, and the investment community, but to public opinion, regulators, accrediting bodies, professional associations, and legislatures. These actors are important because they set the rules, regulations, norms, and expectations that constitute organizations' institutional environment. In formulating organizational strategies, managers should be as interested in gaining control over elements in their institutional environment as in their various markets. In fact, for some organizations the rules, norms, and taken-for-granteds are more salient to the long-term survival of the organization, for resources are contingent upon their being seen as legitimate. To be sure, the day-to-day "business" of these organizations is to ensure that there is a match between their structures and processes and what institutional gatekeepers expect.

*Managerial Tactics.* There are numerous managerial tactics that administrators can employ to be more competitive in product, capital, and labor markets. In Table 1.1 we identify two general types—one that attempts to change conditions inside the organization, and one that attempts to cope with conditions in the environment. Examples of the former include making the organization more efficient, instituting tighter controls, eliminating redundancy, and ensuring quality. All these tactics seek to strengthen the technical core of the organizations and have a long history in management theory. Alternatively, organizations can employ external tactics. For example, they can market their goods and services more aggressively, do more research, compete on price, acquire competitors, or co-opt threats in their environment. Market penetration, product development, predatory pricing, and advertising are standard business practices. Reducing transaction costs is also an important goal of managerial tactics. Tactics like vertical integration, strategic alliances, joint research and development, or relational contracting give organizations direct control over problematic inputs and opportunistic distributors (Williamson 1975, 1981; Barney and Ouchi 1986). In sum, the basic idea underlying managerial tactics is that the organization benefits by garnering more sales, while reducing its production, labor, and transaction costs.

*Political Tactics.* There are many different tactics to co-opt or placate elements in one's institutional environment. In a pioneering article, Oliver (1991) argued that organizations have the capacity and will to resist, decouple, conceal, buffer, challenge, attack, or manipulate those who make regulative or normative demands upon them. We label efforts to adapt to or change these rules, norms, and taken-for-granteds political (Bigelow, Stone, and Arndt 1996) or legitimation (Bielefeld 1992a) tactics. In Table 1.1 we again distinguish between internal and external tactics. On the one hand, organizations will put programs and policies into place that further societal goals (e.g., affirmative action plans, drug rehab programs for employees, parental leave), institute and enforce a code of ethics, acquire referents of prestige, or revamp services to reflect institutional priorities. On the other hand, organizations can try to manipulate institutional gatekeepers. Suchman (1995) described tactics to gain and maintain organizations' pragmatic, moral, and cognitive legitimacy in the larger environment. To gain legitimacy organizations need either to conform or to create or select domains or audiences that would appreciate what they do, or to create new definitions of reality through public relations, advertising, or collective/political action (see also Fombrun 1996). Alternatively, organizations should get some institutional gatekeeper to validate the organization, e.g., become affiliated with a respected federated donor (Singh, House, and Tucker 1986; Singh, Tucker, and House 1986; Singh, House, and Tucker 1986), be listed in community directories

(Singh et al. 1991), secure research grants from well-reputed agencies (Perrow 1961), obtain endowments and/or endorsements from prominent politicians (Pfeffer and Salancik 1978), recruit prominent people to the board of directors (Zald 1969; Handy 1995), recruit elite volunteers (Galaskiewicz 1985a), or receive governmental funding (Baum and Oliver 1996; Galaskiewicz 1985a). To maintain legitimacy, organizations need to scan the environment for changes in audience reactions and to foresee emerging challenges, "protect accomplishments," and stockpile goodwill and support among elites and publics. Finally, to repair legitimacy firms should offer normalizing accounts when things go wrong, restructure, and never act hastily.

*Retrenchment Tactics.* Adaptation theory argues that organizations will sometimes pare their operations so as to become "leaner and meaner" and thus more capable of adjusting to change in their technical environment (Whetten 1980). This point is illustrated in the case of the medium-size organization. As noted by Hannan and Freeman (1977), organizations seldom compete across size categories—large organizations competing against small organizations—however, one often finds medium-size organizations competing against both. Medium-size organizations are thus caught in the middle. By strategically downsizing, organizations drop into a lighter weight class, which means that they now compete against only smaller organizations. Consolidation, therefore, is not necessarily a bad thing and may give organizations a competitive advantage. Whetten (1980), however, cautions that more often than not consolidation takes place under hostile conditions. If organizations are in unstable or shrinking markets, consolidation is a signal that they are losing ground and having a difficult time surviving. Thus consolidation, as an overall organizational strategy, must be implemented with care and interpreted cautiously.

Organizations retrench operations in a number of different ways. Internal tactics include furloughing staff, not filling staff vacancies, reducing the work week for paid staff, freezing salaries and benefits, defunding programs, cutting back on training, or postponing capital improvements. Examples of external tactics are divesting businesses, merging with other organizations, or liquidating assets (Roller 1996).

## C. Synthesis and Extension

While selection and adaptation theories operate at very different levels of analysis—the population and organization—and appear irreconcilable, there are ways to bridge the gap between the two. But how? In our opinion, the answer is to be found in the niche.

First, niche theory reminds us that not every organization competes against every other organization. Rather competition is segmented and takes place within niches. Structurally equivalent sets of organizations compete for capital, labor, sales, technology, etc. Their fates then are determined by the crowding or concentration within that niche and niche legitimacy, not by structural conditions in the environment as a whole. Thus for most organizations competition takes place in a very limited arena. Second, competition within niches is not unfettered or a free-for-all, but rather is subject to institutional influences, e.g., rules and regulations, social norms, and "taken-for-granteds." To the extent these are violated, organizations face censure and possibly expulsion. To the extent these are honored, organizations come to enjoy legitimacy and are allowed to "play the game." This bundle of institutional effects that sets limits on organizational behavior we call an institutional framework (W. R. Scott 1995:43; see also DiMaggio and Powell 1991; Friedland and Alford 1991).

Some examples of these institutional frameworks may help. Niches are often highly regulated. In some niches providers need to be licensed by the state (e.g., lawyers, doctors, barbers). In others, organizations are expected to have equal opportunity and affirmative action plans (e.g., organizations receiving government grants or contracts). In some niches organizations are prohibited from distributing residual earnings to owners or shareholders (e.g., nonprofit organizations); in others managerial authority is challenged if managers do not maximize shareholder value. Norms are also operative within niches. In some niches it is appropriate to be self-interested and instrumentally rational (e.g., securities markets), while in others it is more appropriate to be public spirited and respectful of norms of formal equality and democracy (e.g., when competing for grants or arguing a position before the city council). In some niches service providers are expected to put the needs of the client ahead of their own needs (e.g., doctors and teachers), while in others service providers are to express little or no interest in the customer (e.g., checkout clerks in supermarkets). Niches also differ in terms of cognitive scripts. What may seem natural in higher education, e.g., open sharing of research results, would be unheard of in industry where management worries about leaking proprietary information.

Third, and more importantly, niche theory gives us a way to understand why some organizations rely more on managerial tactics while others rely more on political tactics. Scott (1998:138) reminds us that different criteria govern resource allocation within different environments (we would say niches). In product markets, winners and losers are determined by "the characteristics of the outputs produced by organizational production systems. Products or services are produced that can be assessed in terms of the relative cost or quality, giving rise to outcome controls. These are the controls that we tend to associate with technical rationality" (ibid.). Organizations that participate under these controls we call utilitarian organizations (Albert and Whetten 1985). "By contrast, institutional environments emphasize the extent to which the organization is conforming to the norms of formal rationality, the extent to which the appropriate processes are being carried out and suitable structures are in place. The use of these procedural and structural controls is intended to garner legitimacy and to guarantee accountability. In these environments it is more difficult to assess outcomes independently of knowledge of the processes that produced them (Scott 1998:138)." Organizations that operate under these controls we label normative organizations (Albert and Whetten ibid).

Scott (ibid.) goes on to argue that in some environments (again, we would say niches) outcome controls are very powerful and process controls are weak, whereas other organizations face more stringent process controls and weaker outcome controls. Still other organizations confront both strong outcome and process controls; and some organizations exist in niches in which they are subject to only weak controls of each type. General manufacturing and entertainment (e.g., movies, professional sports, etc.) would be examples of the first. Their survival chances are dependent on the quality of their products and services, and how cheaply they can sell them. Institutional mandates are minimal and have few material consequences for those who deviate. Schools, churches, research institutes, and mental health clinics would exemplify the second. Their funding and survival chances are dependent upon how well they conform to the external institutional environment. Outputs are not considered valid indicators of their value, and thus they are seldom taken into account. Airlines, banks, and general hospitals would epitomize the third, and amateur athletic teams and block clubs the fourth. The former's inputs and survival depend on both institutional conformity and output quality; while the latter operates under weak mandates and has few measurable outputs.

Clearly, conditions vary across niches, and depending upon which controls are most salient, i.e., have resources attached to them, organizations will select different tactics. We predict that organizations that are in niches where they are rewarded for their outputs should become more efficient, devise long-term strategic plans, market their goods and services more aggressively, advertise more, etc. In other words, they should utilize more managerial tactics over time as they strive to compete in this arena. Organizations that are in niches where they are rewarded for their processes and the appropriateness of their structures should lobby more frequently, employ public relations, engage in public information efforts, conform to affirmative action and EEO regulations in hiring, etc. In other words, they should utilize more political tactics over time as they strive to compete in that arena. If organizations find themselves in niches were they are subject to both sets of controls, they will likely use both managerial and political tactics.

We recognize that in making these predictions it seems as if competition for scarce resources has come to replace institutional processes as the driving force in organizational fields. Indeed if organizational rewards are tightly coupled to procedural or processual conformity, then conformity is nothing more than a tactic to get one's piece of the pie. Yet we believe that institutional frameworks—the rules, norms, and taken-for-granteds—exist and motivate behavior independent of material rewards. This is what makes institutional theory attractive. Certain practices come to be institutionalized within niches that have no impact on resource acquisition, i.e., ways of doing things become ritualized and take on mythlike features. For example, organizations in niches under strong output controls may employ the latest management fad, simply because they believe that it is the correct thing to do and not because they expect that it will enhance performance. That is why we say that organizations' tactics will be driven by the desire to maximize inputs, yet at the same time organizations will abide by institutional rules, norms, and taken-for-granteds, even if there is nothing tangible to gain or lose. In other words, resource-based models may explain a great deal of variation in organizational behavior, but they will not be able to explain it all.

In sum, organizational change is going to be affected as much by structural conditions in their niches (e.g., the degree of crowding, concentration, legitimation), as by the rules, norms, and taken-for-granteds, as by the tactics they pursue to procure resources. Even if niche conditions are favorable in terms of competition, organizations may fail if they ignore institutional expectations. Even if organizations comply with the expectations of institutional gatekeepers, they can be "done in" by structural conditions within their various niches. Furthermore, if resources are allocated on the basis of strong process controls and organizations are not willing to employ the right political tactics, or resources are allocated on the basis of strong output controls and organization are not willing to employ state of the art managerial tactics, again they will fail. Thus organizations must be savvy to changing conditions in both their technical and institutional environment as well as be ready to adopt the latest tactical innovations.

## D. Structural Embeddedness Models

Structural embeddedness theory argues that strategy formulation and implementation are not as frictionless as adaptation theory would suggest. Senior management is not always free to act rationally or intentionally in light of environmental contingencies but rather is embedded within structural contexts internal and external to the organization that constrain and influence their choices and actions (Baum and Dutton 1996). Although now fashionable, this is basically a restatement of an important point that Chandler (1962) made years ago. Unless the structure of role relationships, decision-making, and control processes all changed as well, the organization that changed its strategy was doomed to failure. Miles and Snow (1978) extended Chandler's work, arguing that organizations can be typed depending upon their general orientation to their environment and that each type will have its own particular configuration of technology, structure, and process that is consistent with its strategy. The four types are the familiar Defender, Reactor, Analyzer, and Prospector. The important point is that strategy and structure must go hand in hand, and that unless structures change along with strategies, the former will likely fail.

We argue that formal and informal structures affect the likelihood that organizations will embrace different tactics and successfully implement their strategies. In this section we focus on the organization's size and age, the way power and authority are distributed within the organization, and organizations' social network ties to others.

*Size and age.* While senior management may want to implement change they are often constrained by the structure of the organization in which it is embedded. In fact, structural factors may exert pressure on organizations to move in directions that are orthogonal to the strategic concerns outlined above. No matter how "rational" it may be to adapt to environmental contingencies in certain ways, senior management is unable to because of structural constraints.

No structural variable has received as much attention as organizational size. The hypothesis that differentiation and integration increase with size has roots back to Durkheim and Spencer. The application of this general hypothesis to organizations was Blau's (1972) work on the growth of bureaucratic organizations (for a review of this literature, see Scott 1992). The problem was to manage an increasingly large and heterogeneous work force. Breaking down tasks so that they could be easily taught and learned, instituting written rules that applied universally within the organization, instituting a meritocracy, standardizing procedures, and creating an administrative cadre to coordinate different parts of the organization were all attempts to "rationally" solve problems of motivation and coordination.

Once the organization solved the problem of control, it found itself heavily bureaucratized and burdened with procedures, rules, and routines which made it increasingly difficult to change even though the efficiencies first realized start to turn into costs (Hannan and Freeman's (1984) structural inertia thesis). One would think that larger organizations would have more resources (or slack) and thus would be better able to change, e.g., they can acquire competitors, vertically integrate, spend more on new product development, have more generous employee benefits, and engage in more community outreach and political activity. Yet layers of bureaucracy, rules, and routines encumber organizational decision-making, and management has a difficult time reacting to changing environmental conditions. Still the research on how size affects change is inconclusive (Barnett and Carroll 1995).

Age is another structural constraint on strategic action. Stinchcombe's (1965) classic article on the liability of newness tried to explain why younger organizations were more likely to fail than older organizations. Stinchcombe argued that organizations just starting out often lacked the expertise, trust among members, a stock of faithful customers and suppliers, legitimacy, and slack that enabled more mature organizations to absorb environmental shocks. We would add that opportunities for certain strategic initiatives may present themselves to managers in newer organizations, but these organizations do not have the capacity to take advantage of the situation. Newer organizations just do not have the intellectual, social, or financial capital to seize and exploit opportunities.

It is important to keep in mind that size and age are two distinct factors that influence organizational change. Organizations that age do not always grow and become heavily bureaucratized (e.g., mom and pop grocery stores); and organizations that are younger are not always smaller and less bureaucratized (e.g., corporate spin-offs). Furthermore, the dynamics underlying the effects of size on organizational change are different than those underlying the effects of age on change. The former are wrapped up with rules, regulations, and structural inertia; the latter with knowledge and social capital. While it is tempting to think of organizations as having a "life cycle" where they age, get big, and then shrink and die, this is not the history of most organizations and, if taken seriously, can lead analysts astray.

***Decision-making Structures and Power Relations.*** Another set of structural factors that constrain managers' abilities to implement strategies is the distribution of power and authority within the organization. This argument is based on the premise that organizations are best conceived as political bargaining systems within which interest groups, work groups, and coalitions vie for power (Bacharach and Lawler 1980; Mintzberg 1983). Each group or coalition has different authoritative and allocative resources at its disposal. Recent work has also highlighted the importance of interest groups external to the organization that seek to change its behavior and practices (Davis and Thompson 1994). Organizational goals and policies are not determined by some rational calculation of what would be truest to the organization's mission or most efficient, but rather means and ends are chosen that further the interests of warring coalitions within the organization and factions outside the organization.

By distinguishing between authoritative (power based on the "imperatively coordinated" static, stable hierarchy of offices) and allocative resources (power based on the informal exchange of valued resources among organizational actors), this literature gives us two ways to explain how organizations can change. On the one hand, according to Bacharach and Lawler (1980:42), "informal influence processes enhance the discretion of organizational members, and more discretion, in turn, increases the organization's capacity to adapt internally and externally." We would add that the exercise of informal power is a function of how concentrated or dispersed formal power is. In this framework organizational change is a function of counter elites being able to organize opposition to the status quo, build coalitions, and strike bargains, all in an effort to impose their agenda on the organization, and not unimportantly, propel themselves into leadership roles. However, the chances of counter elite success will be directly affected by how much formal power they have. If an interest group is 'out of the loop,' they will have little chance at success. On the other hand, it is important to remember that while organizations may owe their adaptability (and thus survival) to informal influence patterns, decentralized structures can make it more difficult for senior management to carry out change agendas. To the extent that interest groups—other than the top management team—have informal or formal power, they can stymie and sabotage change initiatives from above.

*Social Networks.*   Organizations are embedded in a wide variety of networks that both constrain their actions and provide them with opportunities to achieve their goals (Granovetter 1985). Organizations do not function in a vacuum devoid of ties to others, but rather are linked to other organizations and individuals through a myriad of social relationships: friendships between salespersons and purchasing agents, common club memberships among executives, trade association memberships, interlocking directorates, informal exchanges of resources and information, ties to politicians through PAC contributions, and ties to local elites, to name but a few.[4] Social networks are different than other types of organizational resources. They are not uniformly available nor easily tradeable, thus giving those who have them significant and long lasting advantages over those who do not (Oliver 1996).

One way that social networks can facilitate strategy implementation is that they can empower organizations by increasing their capacity to leverage favors. At the most elementary level social networks enable organizations to win an account, secure a loan, or receive a donation, because others trust their people. Because there is a *social* relationship between ego and alter, alter can trust that ego will not behave opportunistically. Alter can also count on ego to repay the favor someday. There is a sense of mutual obligation in the dyad which is the reason why alter will grant the favor. In all likelihood this explains the consistently strong correlation between network centrality and measures of organizational power (see Mizruchi and Galaskiewicz 1994 for a detailed review of the literature). Those who have extensive network ties have more opportunity to grant and cash in on favors.

Another way that networks can affect strategy implementation is that they can give organizations access to others. Oliver (1996:177) argues that having "connections to 'friends in high places,' having 'good contacts,' as well as resource acquisition based on 'who you know' create differential advantages among firms in their ability to access and exploit opportunities." Those in one's social networks can be used to gain access to others that one is not directly tied to. Since resources are not randomly distributed across social space, but tend to be concentrated in subpopulations, market segments, government agencies, foundations, and corporations, organizations need information on these "pockets" of resources and a way to tap into key players in these arenas. One's network connections supposedly can make the introductions. For example, Galaskiewicz and Rauschenbach (1988) found that nonprofit arts organizations increased their corporate contributions, the more corporate executives were on their boards. They argued that nonprofits used these executives to gain access to company foundations and contributions committees.

A third advantage of social networks is that they can give an organization credibility. For us actors have credibility, if others have an opinion or evaluation of their merits, integrity, or value. The tie-in between credibility, status, and reputation is clear. Some actors are thought highly of, others are despised, and still others are ignored. To get something done often requires that there is someone willing to testify on the organization's behalf, to be a reference. Who has a more authoritative opinion than someone who has dealt with the organization in the past? Networks are full of gossips who freely give their opinions of others to others.

A fourth way that networks can affect strategy formulation is that they can facilitate learning. Research has focused on the role that social networks play in facilitating the flow of information within and across organizational boundaries (e.g., Powell and Brantley 1992). This can have enormous consequences for organizational change. In the words of Powell, Koput, and Smith-Doerr (1996:119), "a network serves as a locus of innovation because it provides timely access to knowledge and resources that are otherwise unavailable, while also testing internal expertise and learning capabilities." By enhancing the diffusion of information and the availability of resources, networks create the possibility for further innovation by bringing together different operating assumptions and new combinations of information (Powell and Brantley 1992). The downside is that secrets and new technology can 'leak' out of the organization into the hands of competitors. Also the dissemination of inaccurate information can be catastrophic for network participants. Thus 'networking' is risky business, and it is important that learning takes place through *social* networks, i.e., relationships characterized by trust, integrity, and a commitment to "community."

Social networks among organization can empower organizations and give them a strategic advantage, but this means that considerable effort must be exercised to replenish and maintain them. Networks are different than other organizational assets, because one never knows when they will come in handy. Thus it is hard to rationalize a budget line item devoted to "networking" or for accountants to valuate an organization's "social capital" on the balance sheet. Yet maintaining and building networks can absorb a considerable amount of time and energy, and often it means that company representatives have to do a lot of favors and engage in a lot of chit-chat that does not seem to have an immediate pay-off for their organizations. As a result, much of what goes on, especially at the boundaries of the organization, may seem superfluous or even wasteful to stakeholders and line managers as well.

### E.   Toward an Integrated Theory of Organizational Change

Clearly no one theory is complete in and of itself. The selection model is too deterministic. It is an "over-socialized" view of organizations in that it ignores agency and the fact that managers do have some control over their own organization and the directions that it takes (Granovetter 1985). Organizations are mini-sovereign states—or in Coleman's (1974) terminology, corporate actors—with enormous discretion and power over participants. This is especially true in the United States where the state has delegated responsibility for many public projects to the private sector (Jepperson and Meyer 1991). In contrast, the adaptation model puts too much emphasis on the initiatives of managers. The perspective is "under-socialized," meaning that it ignores the contexts in which organizations are embedded and that managers are often not free to choose among alternative courses of action. The embeddedness perspective also has its shortcomings. In addition to ignoring environmental variation/selection and strategic initiatives, it is not really a theory of change. That is, structural factors alone cannot explain why an organization changes. Rather they typically modify the effects of environmental conditions on tactical choice and the effects of tactics on organizational outcomes.[5]

Before we begin to outline our theory of change we need to make clear our underlying assumptions: resource procurement is the key factor driving organizational change, yet this impulse is tempered by the needs to be legitimate and to control costs. In selection theories, both efficiency (in ecological theory) and legitimacy (in institutional theory) are important in explaining survival. In adaptation theories, political tactics are used to enhance legitimacy, while managerial tactics are used to achieve efficiencies. Yet in all our theories there is a heavy emphasis on procuring resources or inputs from other actors in the environment, whether it be customers, investors, donors, government agencies, or grant makers. Organizations cannot seem to survive without these inputs, and thus, we assume, their procurement drives most organizational decision-making and behavior.

To make resource acquisition central to our theory is controversial. There is a literature on "alternative" organizations, which place their ideology, morality, and identity above resource needs and defy institutional pressures to conform (Rothschild-Whitt 1979). Examples include feminist organizations (Bordt 1997), grass-roots organizations (Smith 1997), cooperatives, social movement organizations, and sects/cults. Our position also relegates program effectiveness, mission, or even outputs (e.g., clients served, patients cured, students graduated; for an extended discussion of this problem, see Herman and Renz 1997) to a lesser role. This also implies that board, staff, and administrators all have the same goals: to optimize organizational inputs. Social constructionists would object that often those in organizations have little idea what their goals are until they reach them. Political theorists would argue that this ignores goal conflicts and that players within organizations are only out to further their own personal agendas. Furthermore, sociologists often pride themselves on *not* finding any organizational utility in how organizations behave. Yet we argue that the fate of organizations depends upon their access to resources, and understanding how they access resources can go a long way in helping us to understand organizational behavior.

To help us integrate the various perspectives on organizational change, we offer Figure 1.1. Although many of the effects identified in the model will be discussed more thoroughly and tested empirically in later chapters, our purpose for presenting the model here is to get the reader to

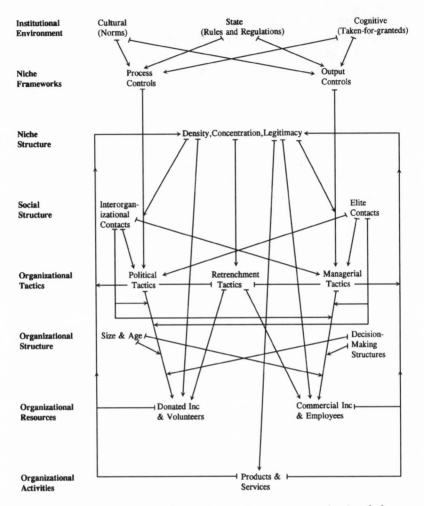

*Figure 1.1.* Schema showing factors impinging upon organizational change.

think holistically about the problem of organizational change and to show that selection, adaptation, and embeddedness perspectives on change can be incorporated into a single action framework.

*Selection Effects.* The most impermeable exogenous factors affecting organizations are institutional. It is very difficult for organizations to change rules and regulations, cultural norms, and cognition, although not impossible. Certainly some organizations are specifically dedicated to changing the institutional order, but most are not. Through coercive, normative, and mimetic processes, societal priorities, social obligations, and taken-for-granted assumptions eventually find their way into the ecological environment of organizations. Within ecological fields we argued that one can identify niches. Niches are made up of structurally equivalent sets of actors whose membership in the niche is based on their active competition for the same scarce resources (Burt and Talmud 1993). Within ecological niches the institutional environment is given operational meaning in institutional frameworks. Competition for resources in different niches is governed by different legal rules, constrained by different norms, and shaped by different "taken-for-granteds." Organizations come to enjoy legitimacy and oftentimes material support, if they conform to the frameworks and "play by the rules." Earlier we drew the distinction between niches where resource allocation was governed by strong output controls (the price and quality of goods and services produced) and niches where resource allocation was governed by strong process controls (conformity to appropriate procedures, processes, and standards).

Structural conditions within niches are also important for organizations. Niches can be densely or sparsely populated, resources can be highly concentrated or dispersed, and incumbents can have high or low status. Each of these factors affects competition for resources within the niche. For instance, the levels of competition and legitimacy may affect growth and decline in resources, just as the ecologists found that they affected organizational foundings and deaths. In niches where competition is intense and/or legitimacy low, organizations should lose donated income, volunteers, commercial income, and employees over time.

*Adaptation.* Within the ecological field, organizational decision-makers initiate action. We are particularly concerned with action that relates to resource procurement. Whether they are operating in niches with strong process controls or output controls, organizations do what they can to procure the resources they need. Adaptation theory argues that in niches where output controls are strong, organizations increase their resources by making operations more efficient, improving product quality, making their products and services more accessible to customers, making sure customers pay their bills on time, and monitoring their workers' behaviors. Managerial tactics aim either to reduce production and transaction costs, increase output, or expand the customer base. Organizations that increase their use of managerial tactics should increase their commercial income and employees over time. In niches with strong process controls organizations enhance their inputs by making themselves more public regarding, responsive to community needs, trustworthy. They do this by accruing referents of prestige, opening their books to the public, adopting a code of ethics, being model corporate citizens, and changing priorities to reflect those of funders. In return foundations, corporations, and individuals will give them grants and donations, government agencies will give them contracts and grants, and volunteers will want to come and work for them.

Structural conditions within an ecological niche should also influence the choice of tactics. As conditions within the niche become more competitive or the niche lacks legitimacy, the pressure to "do something" increases. On the one hand, an organization can try harder to outcompete its neighbors. On the other hand, organizations can flee their niche. That is, competition and/or the low status of the niche could motivate organizations to migrate. Operationally, this means that organizations would try to develop new products and services, become smaller (retrench operations), switch funding arenas (e.g., from donations to sales), or switch their labor inputs (e.g., replace employees with volunteers).[6]

*Embeddedness Effects.* The choice of tactics will also be directly influenced by an organization's social network ties. Networks are highly fluid, follow the personal interests of managers and staff, and are more particularistic. There is no overarching structure to a social network, and the effects on behavior are much more local in nature. In explaining the choice of tactics, we would expect that organizations would be influenced by trusted others in the community and those with whom they have contact. Through their interorganizational and social network ties, organizations learn what others, whom they know and trust, have done, and then do it themselves. We also expect that organizations will mimic those they perceived as successful (DiMaggio and Powell 1983). This is especially tempting under conditions of extreme uncertainty. It is cheap and easy to rationalize to boards of directors and stakeholders outside the organization. Contacts with local elites can also affect the choice of tactics, as elites encourage administrators and managers to become, for example, more businesslike or political.

Formal structures, latent power structures, and social networks should also moderate the effect of tactics on organizational change. As Chandler (1962) demonstrated, existing structures and processes can get in the way of strategy implementation or they can facilitate it. Once the strategy has been decided on, the next task is to reposition the organization so as to achieve this end. The problem, of course, is that there are a number of constraints under which top management operates. First, the size and age of an organization can affect how quickly and effectively strategies are implemented. The former often is correlated with bureaucratization, the latter with competencies. Strategy implementation (i.e., translating tactics into outcomes) should be easier and quicker the smaller and the older the organization. Second, managers can carry out their prerogatives only if they have enough formal authority and informal influence to carry out their plans in the face of competing coalitions (Child 1972). Thus we expect that strategy implementation should be easier and quicker the more centralized the power structures. And, third, social networks are also important. Informal ties to other organizations and to high-status actors can empower an organization and enable it to translate tactics into outcomes. Thus although adaptation theorists want us to believe that managers are rational and adaptive to changing environmental contingencies, our discussion suggests that the likelihood of successful implementation will be moderated by formal and informal structures within and outside the organization in which organizations are embedded.

Finally, we expect that as organizations change, the structure of their niche will change as well. If organizations get larger, if they increase their dependency on earned or donated income, if they come to rely more on volunteers than employees, if they change their clientele or members, if they change their activities or products all in response to their current niche conditions and/or their structural context, they effectively migrate to a new niche. This will subject them to a different set of constraints and expose them to a new set of competitors. It also changes the composition of the old and new niche, e.g., their old niche becomes less dense while the density of their new niche increases. In turn, this will affect the organization's subsequent choice of tactics and activities/products, which will again change the organization's niche. Thus although the model is generally linear in form, it does allow for feedback loops.

## PUBLIC CHARITIES

We conclude this first chapter by addressing the question, Can our theory of organizational change be applied to nonprofit organizations? We make certain assumptions about what drives organizations, and it is not immediately clear that these assumptions are appropriate for all types of organizations. We will argue that nonprofits operating in niches with strong process controls are under considerable pressure to demonstrate their conformity to rules, norms, and taken-for-granteds, but are under little pressure to be efficient. In contrast, nonprofits operating in niches with strong output controls are under pressure to cut costs and economize operations, but legitimacy is not as critical to their survival. However, we present evidence that both types of nonprofits strive to maximize revenues and labor inputs.

## A. Nonprofits and Organizational Niches

In this section we make the argument that nonprofit organizations are not a homogeneous lot and operate in very different niches.[7] In a nonprofit organization, no one owns the right to share in any profit or surplus, and the organization is exempt from taxes on corporate income (Weisbrod 1988:14). The nondistribution constraint does not prohibit nonprofits from earning a "profit"; rather it prohibits individuals (or corporate actors) from laying claim to any surplus (or net income) or any revenues realized from the sale of organizational assets. There are no owners or shareholders and thus no lawful opportunity for personal financial gain beyond ordinary wages. All residual earnings must either be retained by the nonprofit corporation or given to other nonprofits (Simon 1987; Hansmann 1980).[8] What it comes down to is that there are not that many differences across sectors after you get past the nondistribution constraint and the exemption from corporate income taxes. Nonprofits, like for-profits, can operate to serve private as well as public interests; they can sell related and unrelated products and services to customers as well as receive donations and grants from donors; they can produce easy-to-evaluate ordinary goods as well as trust-type or collective goods; and they can utilize employees as well as volunteers. In other words, there are few institutional barriers to keep nonprofits from behaving like their for-profit brethren. As we shall see, the United States and state and local governments offer incentives to nonprofits to behave differently (see Weisbrod 1998), but simply having nonprofit status does not, for the most part, prevent nonprofits from acting like business firms.

*Charities and Clubs.*  Nonprofit organizations fall into two general categories: *charitable organizations* and *clubs* or *mutual benefit organizations*. Charitable organizations can be further divided into public charities and private foundations. The former provide services; the latter provide funding, usually drawing on the assets of an estate or contributions from a business corporation. It is assumed that charitable organizations provide certain types of services and that they benefit the public at-large (i.e., people outside the organization; Weisbrod 1988:9).[9] Smith (1993) called them "public benefit organizations." Among public charities we find art museums, schools, hospitals, community organizations, social service agencies, and churches.[10] Clubs differ from charitable organizations in that they provide benefits primarily to people who belong to the organization (Weisbrod 1988:9). Smith (1993) called them "mutual benefit organizations." Examples of clubs or mutual benefit organizations include unions, business leagues, cooperatives, professional associations, advocacy groups (e.g., AARP), country clubs, and fraternal groups (e.g., Elks, VFW). Both charitable organizations and clubs are bound by the nondistribution constraint and are exempt from federal corporate income tax.[11]

The federal, state, and local governments all recognize the special role of charitable organizations and grant them special privileges. Because they are public benefit organizations, individual and corporate donors can deduct contributions of cash or property to these organizations from their gross earnings for income tax purposes. Contributions are also deductible for estate and gift tax purposes (Simon 1987).[12] Many, but not all, public charities also qualify for reduced postal rates and free public service advertising on radio and TV. In many states public charities receive exemptions from property tax, sales tax as well as state corporate income taxes (Simon 1987).[13] For the rest of this chapter we focus our attention exclusively on public charities.

*Commercial-Type and Donative-Type Charities.* Public charities differ dramatically in terms of their funding patterns, outputs, and labor inputs (see Table 1.2). A common distinction is between *commercial-type charities* and *donative-type charities* (Hansmann 1980). The former provides goods and services directly to a consumer who is required to pay some fee or dues for the output; the latter receive their revenues from donors or third parties who give with the intent that the nonprofit generates some public good or provides free or reduced-cost goods and services to others. Individuals, businesses, other nonprofits, and government agencies are sometimes consumers of public charity outputs and sometimes donors to public charity causes. Examples of commercial charities include colleges that charge tuition to students, theaters that sell tickets to their performances, and little leagues that require parents to pay a participation fee. Donative charities would include relief organizations such as the Red Cross or CARE, food shelves, and public television.

One of the theoretically important differences between the two types of transactions is that donative-type charities enjoy greater information advantages over buyers than commercial-type charities. In contrast to a commercial-nonprofit that sells its goods and services directly to a buyer/consumer, the donative nonprofit peddles its wares to a buyer/donor who is often unaware of the results of its gift. The donor, or third party buyer, gives her money to the nonprofit provider, which in turn promises to provide certain goods or services to some client group or to generate some public good. Yet unlike buyer/consumers, it is often difficult for donors to know the quality of nonprofit output (Tassie, Murray, Cutt, and Bragg 1996) or if her contribution actually increased the quantity or quality of the public goods produced (Hansmann 1987:30). Thus, if the service provider fails to deliver, it is much more difficult for buyer/donors to discipline providers (i.e., cease to donate funds) than buyer/consumers.

Table 1.2. Typology of Public Charities

| | Commercial Charities | | Donative Charities | |
|---|---|---|---|---|
| | *Employee* | *Volunteer* | *Employee* | *Volunteer* |
| Ordinary goods and services | Arts organizations, colleges, zoos | Swim leagues, Little League baseball | CARE, Salvation Army | Foodshelves, travelers' aide |
| Trust-type goods and services | Nursing homes, day care centers, drug rehab | Boy/Girl Scouts | Red Cross, orphanages | Special Olympics, Big Brothers/Sisters |
| Public or collective goods | XXXXX | XXXXX | Public TV, scientific research | Community crime watch, social justice |

*Ordinary Goods, Trust-Type Goods, and Collective Goods.*   We also distinguish between *ordinary goods producers, trust-type nonprofits,* and *collective-type nonprofits.* Ordinary goods producers are public charities whose output is separable (or divisible) and relatively easy to evaluate in terms of quality, e.g., a food shelf, a performing arts organization, or travelers' aide. Trust-type nonprofits also provide separable goods but their outputs are much more difficult for the consumer to evaluate in terms of quality, e.g., day care centers, drug rehabilitation centers, and orphanages are potential examples. Collective-type nonprofits provide collective or public goods that produce widely shared benefits. The important feature of collective goods, of course, is that they are nondivisible. That is, once produced, it is difficult if not impossible to prevent those who did not contribute to their provision from enjoying their benefits. Examples include scientific research and community crime watch programs.

Trust goods and services have more information problems for buyers than ordinary goods and services. Hansmann (1980) argued that under some conditions consumers are particularly disadvantaged vis-à-vis service providers regarding information on quality and quantity of the service or product they consume. Even though they directly consume the product or service themselves, consumers often do not have the information to evaluate the quality of the product intelligently. If the service provider fails to deliver top quality goods, it is less likely that ill-informed consumers will be able to discipline providers than fully informed consumers.

The provider has information advantages over the buyer with respect to collective goods as well. Here we have the familiar argument that buyers will be reluctant to contribute to these ventures unless they expect to realize disproportionate benefits in the final analysis (Olson 1965). If the buyer is large or expects to reap huge benefits, he may be willing to carry others who choose to free-ride. Olson refers to the exploitation of the large by the small. However, if the donor doubts that his returns will outweigh his investments, he will feel like he is being "suckered" if he contributes. Public goods providers, of course, are always suspected of inflating their promises to donors and downplaying the benefits going to free-riders. Since the actual benefit of any collective good is almost impossible to measure beforehand or in the short term, the prospective donor can only trust in the promises of the provider.

*Employee and Voluntary Organizations.*   Finally, we can distinguish between charities that are *employee organizations* and *voluntary associations* (Smith 1993, 1995; Knoke 1990). The former are characterized by paid staff whose livelihood depends upon employment by the organization. The latter are staffed by volunteers who donate their time and labor to the organization. There is no assumption that the former are better trained or have more education or training than the latter, and employees appear to be highly committed to organizational goals (Onyx and Maclean 1996). Also it does not appear that volunteers are more religiously, politically, or socially ideological (or idealistic) than nonvolunteers.[14] In many organizations, volunteers work side by side with paid staff—sometimes harmoniously, sometimes not (see, for example, Hall 1990).

DiMaggio and Anheier (1990:142) argue that during the Progressive era many nonprofits came to be dominated by paid professional staffs. They brought with them a service ethos, autonomy from market values, and a belief that expertise should be used on behalf of the common good. Many were university trained. They also note how these professionals institutionalized certain patterns: governance systems with considerable professional participation and revenue systems that empowered professionals who had ties to outside funding sources (especially government). Because of their "new class" social and political views many nonprofits became bastions of liberalism, modernism (a belief in science and rational problem solving), and credentialism.

In contrast, J. Scott (1995) describes communitarian types of voluntary associations as highly cooperative, value rich, in search of the common good, and with an emphasis on governance, mission, participation, coproduction, networking, and community building. Messer (1994) showed that in Alcoholics Anonymous there is a strong emphasis on shared emotional experiences, group consciousness, egalitarianism, and group autonomy/self-reliance (see also Bloomfield 1994 for a similar description of AA). Smith (1997) paints a similar picture of grass-roots associations, where there is an emphasis on social support, mutual help, self-expression, happiness, and activism among members. Lohmann's (1992) description of the "commons" has given us some of the richest images of life in a voluntary association: free participation, common or shared purpose, common or shared holdings/resources, mutuality or friendship, and a concern for fairness/justice.[15] For many identity, shared experiences, shared values, and activism are attractive alternatives to science, credentialism, relativism, and treatment.

The relationship between labor and employee nonprofits parallels that of buyers and commercial nonprofits, and the relationship between volunteers and voluntary nonprofits that of donors and charity nonprofits. Terms of a labor contract are relatively easy to spell out, and both the worker and the employee are able to calculate the utility they each derive. Indeed, it is marginal utility that sets the wage and terms of the employee contract. Information problems are minimal. With volunteers everything is up for grabs. Clearly the organization is getting something for nothing, but without a wage that one could use as a rough indicator of labor's value, neither party—and especially the volunteer—has a clue as to the latter's worth. Thus the transaction between labor and provider is fraught with uncertainty, and is plagued by the lingering doubts that either the volunteer is being exploited by the organization or is really a liability instead of an asset.[16]

*Discussion.* Our point is that public charities differ radically among themselves and function in very different niches. In the upper left part of Table 1.2 we have a prototype of the utilitarian organization subject to strong output controls. It relies on fees for services, has employees, and provides ordinary (easy to evaluate) separable goods. In the lower right part of the table we have a prototype of the normative organization subject to strong process controls. It relies on donations, has volunteers, and provides either collective goods or hard-to-evaluate trust goods.[17] Relating back to our earlier discussion, we speculate that the former should be preoccupied with economizing on costs and achieving efficiencies; while the latter needs to ensure that it is perceived as legitimate by institutional gatekeepers for its continued access to resources. More importantly, not all nonprofits are the same, and nonprofit behavior should be very different as we move across the cells in Table 1.2. Thus the different theories that talk about behavior in niches with different control systems should be applicable across a sample of nonprofits, since charities are scattered across all the cells of the table.

## B. Do Charities Maximize Inputs?

The discussion of nonprofit niches suggests that not all nonprofits are equally driven to establish their legitimacy or achieve efficiencies, but are nonprofits and particularly charities driven to maximize inputs? Given that public charities are unable to distribute residual earnings to owners and are obligated to provide public service, they may be less resource-driven than for-profits or clubs.

Institutional economists have argued that the nondistribution constraint removes one of the most important incentives from organizational decision-making: claims to residual earnings or profits. Weisbrod argues:

> The conventional argument is that it (the nondistribution constraint) reduces the incentive for efficiency because the manager of a nonprofit organization may not lawfully share in any profit or surplus generated by his or her managerial skills (Alchian and Demsetz 1972). What is less recognized is that the nondistribution constraint has additional effects—it also reduces the incentive to engage in activities that, while privately profitable, are socially inefficient. A legally nonprofit organization has little incentive, for example, to pollute the air or water with waste products in the pursuit of

organization profit. Similarly, a nonprofit organization has little incentive to skimp on quality of output or otherwise take advantage of poorly informed consumers.

The nondistribution constraint on nonprofits can also affect the manner of distribution of outputs—that is, to whom outputs go. A profit maximizer has the incentive to sell its goods and services to the highest bidders because that is the route to maximum returns to stockholders and managers. A nonprofit organization, by contrast, with no stockholders but with managers facing the nondistribution constraint, has no financial incentive to provide its output to the highest bidders. (1998:72)

The "bottom line" for Weisbrod (1988, 1998) is that charities will be bonoficers not profit maximizers. They lack an important incentive to reduce costs and maximize revenues and thus are free to pursue other ends. Baum and Oliver echo these sentiments, arguing that nonprofits will be "more oriented toward community responsiveness, noncompetitive behavior, cooperative activities, social image, and the fulfillment of social needs" (1996:1388).

Yet critics of the sector claim that many charitable organizations provide a narrow range of benefits (i.e., they are really clubs-in-disguise), many are as materially motivated as for-profits, and the nondistribution constraint does little to deter "socially inefficient" behavior among public charities (i.e., they are really for-profits in-disguise). The first critique questions whether or not public charities distribute benefits broadly enough and beyond the borders of the organization's membership or immediate circles to meet their public service obligations (e.g., Wolpert 1993a; selections in Clotfelter 1992). That is, public charities behave more like mutual benefit organizations than charitable organizations (for examples, see O'Neill 1994).[18] DiMaggio and Anheier (1990:141) remind us that status group identities—and especially upper-class identities—were the stimulus for many of the nonprofits that today are among the most prestigious public benefit organizations (e.g., universities and arts organizations), and many continue to serve primarily upper-/upper-middle-class constituents (Ostrower 1996). We have also seen that charities will engage in political advocacy on behalf of some group they serve (e.g., the poor, people with AIDS); think tanks, political philanthropies (e.g., Newt Gingrich's Progress and Freedom Foundation), and "educational" nonprofits often verge on propagandizing (Kahn 1996); and we have already noted how churches often minister only to their own congregations.

There is also growing evidence that very little of the sector's activities are redistributive. Steinberg and Gray (1993:304) pointed to efforts at the local government level to rescind tax exempt status of hospitals based on hospitals' lack of effort to provide charity care.[19] Wolpert (1993a, 1996) found that there was very little redistribution of nonprofit revenues across city / suburban boundaries. He estimated that 85–90% of donations are raised and spent locally. This is consistent with research done by Bielefeld, Murdoch, and Waddell (1997), which showed that nonprofits were mostly influenced by the demographics of the neighborhoods closest to them. Wolpert also found that the bulk of nonprofit outputs are in the nature of amenity, not redistributive goods (1993a). In his volume on the benefits of nonprofit activity, Clotfelter (1992) showed that only a small number of nonprofits serve the poor as a primary clientele. In sum, many public charities may not be so public-regarding, but rather serve very limited numbers in the population if not only people immediately affiliated with—or in close proximity to—the organization. This would not be such a big concern except that providing public benefits—which includes but is not restricted to helping the poor—is crucial in rationalizing the tax privileges surrounding the public charity.

The second critique charges that many public charities and their leaders have a strong interest in accruing material resources.[20] Economic research has found that nonprofit organizations are not simple profit maximizers, but not all are bonoficers. To quote from Steinberg:

> One finds an abundance of suggested objective functions in the literature, such as maximizing budget (Tullock 1966; Niskanen 1971), maximizing quality and quantity in proportions specified by the manager (Newhouse 1970; Hansmann 1981), maximizing use of preferred inputs (doctors, high-technology and prestigious medical procedures, or handicapped employees; see Lee 1971; Clarkson 1972; Pauley and Redisch 1973; Feigenbaum 1987), maximizing a combination of commercial and charitable or public benefit outputs (James 1983; Schiff and Weisbrod 1991; Eckel and Steinberg 1993), maximizing 'profits' (Preston 1988), or social welfare (see Holtman 1983). (1993:17)

On top of this, Steinberg (1993) cautions that functions can change depending on conditions in the organization's funding environment, personnel, the relative power of patrons, and the level of competition (see also Bush 1992).

Organizational research has found that many nonprofits seem to be heavily driven by resource enhancement, i.e., they maximize income and labor inputs. For example, Chang and Tuckman (1990) found that larger nonprofits tend to have large accumulated surpluses at the end of the year.[21] The literature is also replete with studies that show how the desire for resources—rather than public service—was crucial in explaining resource allocation within the United Way (Pfeffer and Leong 1977; Provan, Beyer, and Kruytbosch 1980), budgeting in colleges and universities (Pfeffer and Salancik 1974), funding of human service agencies (Levine and White 1961), the choice of board members of cultural organizations

(Galaskiewicz and Rauschenbach 1988), and the goals and activities of nonprofits, e.g., the National Foundation for Infantile Paralysis, which became the March of Dimes (Sills 1957). More recently, Kraatz and Zajac (1996) found that the strategies and changes within liberal arts colleges between 1971 and 1986 directly mirrored changes in their market conditions and defied institutional pressures. However, in their study of day care centers, Baum and Oliver (1996) found that nonprofits were more likely to cooperate than compete, and to invest in external social legitimacy than for-profits, supporting the position that the two sectors have different underlying logics.

A third concern is whether the nondistribution constraint is effective in discouraging opportunistic behavior among nonprofits. If Weisbrod is correct, nonprofits will behave with more integrity than for-profits, because they do not have an incentive to chisel. The research, however, is mixed. On the one hand, Steinberg and Gray reviewed research on differences between for-profit and nonprofit hospitals and concluded that "nonprofits had either similar or lower expenses than did for-profits, and all showed that the costs to third-party payers were substantially higher in for-profit hospitals than in nonprofits" (1993:306). They also reported that more "unnecessary" services were provided in for-profit than in nonprofit hospitals and "more ominously, various forms of fraudulent behavior have apparently been a modus operantis of several hospital companies in the mental health, substance abuse treatment, and physical rehabilitation fields" (ibid.:307). They also found that "all studies that have compared for-profit and nonprofit hospitals have found that for-profits extracted higher levels of revenues" (ibid.).

On the other hand, Clarke and Estes (1992) found that there were few differences between for-profit and nonprofit home health agencies they studied in terms of the socioeconomic status of clients served, services provided, and staff. Weisbrod (1988) found significant positive differences in staffing between nonprofit nursing homes and facilities for the mentally handicapped and proprietary firms. He also found significant positive differences in outputs between church-affiliated nonprofits and proprietary firms (e.g., treatment, facilities, customer satisfaction), but he found no differences in outputs between non-church-affiliated nonprofits and proprietary firms. Krashinsky (1998) found no major differences in the quality of care between for-profit and nonprofit day care centers, and Mauser (1998) found that only a minority of parents considered auspice when choosing day care centers for their children, although quality among nonprofits tended to be higher.

In summary, there is little disagreement that public charities have a strong institutional incentive to provide socially desirable outputs—for otherwise they could lose tax deductible contributions and some tax privileges—and a strong disincentive to economize, skimp on output, or chisel uninformed consumers—because of the nondistribution constraint. Yet the research we just reviewed and other findings (see DiMaggio and Anheier 1990; Ferris and Grady 1989) strongly suggest that charitable organizations, their directors, leaders, and staff are as materially motivated as their brethren in the for-profit sector. Clearly most public charities are neither pure profit maximizers, nor pure bonoficers. However, it is probably safe to assume that most seek to maximize income in order to better carry out their mission and make life more pleasant for employees and volunteers who work for the organization.

## DISCUSSION

While the last part of our discussion may depress or even outrage some of our readers, it is consistent with our general thesis. An important argument of this monograph is that institutional categories such as "for-profit," "nonprofit," or "public charity" are not that important in explaining how organizations behave with respect to resource procurement. We believe that there is enough evidence to justify the claim that nonprofits are as interested in amassing caches of resources as for-profits. This is not to say that all nonprofits behave the same as all for-profits. There will be differences, but they will not be attributable to the legal status of organizations or different levels of interest in acquiring resources.

The crux of our thesis is that organizations' fates are influenced by their niche position, their choice of tactics, and formal and informal social structures. Some organizations procure resources through consumer and labor markets and their activities are subject to strong output controls. Other organizations procure resources through donations and volunteering and their activities are subject to strong process controls. Some believe that nonprofits are more heavily dependent upon the latter, while for-profits are more dependent upon the former, but we beg to differ. Going back to Table 1.2, many nonprofits are as enmeshed in market arenas as for-profits, and these organizations find that it is more important to be efficient and businesslike than to embrace public service goals and adopt symbols of trustworthiness (Bielefeld 1992b).[22] To repeat, in explaining organizational behavior, the distinction between for-profits and nonprofits may not be as important as the degree to which organizations are dependent upon different niches for their inputs and conditions within these niches.

We are now prepared to argue that the theory we outlined in the first part of this chapter is applicable to the study of nonprofit behavior and change. That is, the theory we outlined should be generalizable to both for-profits and nonprofits. For utilitarian nonprofits that are heavily dependent upon markets for their inputs, adaptation theory would hypothesize that they will do what is necessary to procure resources in that arena, i.e., utilize managerial tactics; for normative nonprofits that are more heavily dependent upon grants economies for their inputs, adaptation would expect that they will do what is necessary to enhance resources in that arena, i.e., utilize political tactics. Furthermore, we see no problem in directly adapting selection theories to the nonprofit organization. Competition for donated revenues and volunteers (measured in terms of density or resource concentration) can be just as stiff as competition for fees and paid employees—although, of course, the competition takes on a very different character. Niche legitimacy—both constitutive and sociopolitical—should also affect the likelihood of growth or decline regardless of whether organizations succor earned income, employees, donated income, or volunteers. Finally, embeddedness theories should hold up as well. Size, age, and decision-making structures should moderate the effect of managerial and political tactics on organizational outcomes, and both types of nonprofits are susceptible to social network influences.

Now armed with theory that should be able to explain change in a population of nonprofit public charities, we turn to the data. However, before we test to see how well the theories outlined in this chapter can account for change among public charities, we describe the research site in detail, our methodology, and provide some preliminary descriptive statistics on our case study.

## ACKNOWLEDGMENTS

We would like to thank Andy Van de Ven, Burton Weisbrod, and Mark Hager for a very thoughtful reading of this chapter and Evelyn Brody for her comments on an earlier draft. Their comments helped us to reorganize and refocus the chapter. Of course, any shortcomings are solely the responsibility of the authors.

## NOTES

1. For a complete review of the various theories of organizational change, see Barnett and Carroll (1995) and Van de Ven and Poole (1995). Absent from our review are life cycle (Kimberly and Miles 1980) and dialectical theories of change (Benson 1977).

2. Less attention has focused on why organizations do not change. In light of Hannan and Freeman's (1977, 1984, 1989) provocative discussions of organizational inertia, this is unfortunate.

3. The strategy literature is massive and covers both content and process. We can review only a fraction of what has been written in the field. For a review of this literature as it relates to nonprofits, see Roller (1996).

4. There are numerous literature reviews of this growing subfield of organizational studies. See, for example, Galaskiewicz (1985b), Nohria and Eccles (1992), Mizruchi and Galaskiewicz (1994), Powell and Smith-Doerr (1994), Knoke and Guilarte (1994), and Bielefeld, Scotch, and Thieleman (1995).

5. The exception is dialectical theory, which looks for contradictions in the structures of organizations for the source of change. See Benson (1977) for examples.

6. We do not expect that organizations will necessarily abandon their old ways completely; more than likely organizations will branch out in new directions that will have the beneficial effect of diffusing their risks without having to incur the liabilities of newness (for an extended discussion of this topic, see Hannan and Freeman 1989).

7. For an overview of the different kinds of nonprofits, their legal status, and their privileges, see Hansmann (1980), Simon (1987), and Bowen, Nygren, Turner, and Duffy (1994). We draw liberally from their discussions.

8. Steinberg and Gray (1993) tell us that now some form of profit sharing can occur under special circumstances. Nonetheless, the nondistribution constraint—and the exemption from corporate income taxes—is still regarded as the distinguishing feature of the not-for-profit form in the United States.

9. The Internal Revenue Service grants charitable status to an organization if it passes the inurement test and promises to conduct its activities primarily for one or more of the purposes listed in section 501(c)(3). The organization must demonstrate that it is organized and operated exclusively for religious, charitable, scientific, testing-for-public safety, literary, or educational purposes, or to foster national or international amateur sports competition, or for the prevention of cruelty to children or animals. It must also demonstrate that the organization serves (either directly or indirectly) a public rather than private interest.

10. Churches are a sticky problem. Although the IRS recognizes them as public charities, in many cases benefits accrue only to members (for a review of this debate, see O'Neill 1994). Different authors put them into different categories. In this book we will treat them as mutual benefit organizations following the lead of Smith (1993) even though they enjoy all the legal privileges of the public charity.

11. Public charities, private foundations, and churches are exempt under section 501(c)(3) of the Internal Revenue Service code. Many of the very interesting advocacy groups, labor unions, country clubs, chambers of commerce, and other mutual benefit organizations described above are exempt under section 501(c)(4)–(21). Nonprofits exempt under other parts of the IRS code include political parties, pension plans, and consumer and farmer cooperatives (see Simon 1987:69–72).

12. In the case of the charity or public benefit nonprofit, the rationale for subtracting donations from taxable income is straightforward. Simon reminds us that taxable income is "the sum of a taxpayer's (1) consumption and (2) wealth accumulation (increase in net worth) during a given tax reckoning period. An item

of revenue received by the taxpayer and then given away to charity during the same period does not increase the taxpayer's net worth [nor does it] constitute consumption" (which for tax purposes means the consumption of divisible, not public, goods; 1987:73–74). It then follows that dues paid to a club or mutual benefit nonprofit should not be tax deductible since the goods provided by a club are consumed by the individual and are not distributed widely. It also follows that if benefits produced by a public charity were not widely available or disperse but reserved for donors, then donations to these organizations should not be tax deductible as well.

13.    Although we will treat churches as clubs, as noted, the IRS regards them as charitable organizations. Thus churches are eligible for most of the privileges reserved for charitable organizations.

14.    Stebbins (1996) argues that volunteering now has become a form of serious leisure, i.e., an avenue to personal enrichment, self-actualization, self-expression, self-image, self-gratification, recreation, financial return, social opportunities, and group experiences. There is very little idealism here. Wuthnow (1991) suggested as much in his study of volunteerism, and studies by Sundeen (1992) and Cnaan, Kasternakis, and Wineburg (1993) have found mixed results when comparing the values and attitudes of volunteers and nonvolunteers (for a review of this literature, see also Smith 1994:251–52). Ideals, however, may be more important among teen volunteering than among adults (see Sundeen and Raskoff 1995).

15.    However, in his review of Lohmann's work Stanley (1993) adds that while there is a strong emphasis on equality/fairness/justice within these groups, these values do not necessarily apply to other groups in society.

16.    We are, of course, speaking of public charities that utilize volunteers, not clubs or mutual benefit organizations. The latter clearly appeal to the material interest of volunteers, since they will likely be the beneficiaries of the organization's initiatives and have a very good idea of the benefits their actions realize for themselves. This is also true in consumer-controlled nonprofits like day care cooperatives (see Ben-Ner and Van Hoomissen 1991) and self-help groups like AA.

17.    Note that two cells are empty. This is because a provider cannot charge fees for collective goods.

18.    In all fairness, we should remember that many clubs behave more like charities than mutual benefit organizations. For example, fraternal groups will often raise money for medical research or scholarships that benefit the community as a whole (for other examples, see O'Neill 1994 and Smith 1993).

19.    Steinberg and Gray (1993) also report that nonprofit hospitals charge third-party payers substantially less than for-profit hospitals. That prices are lower could be taken as a signal that more people have access to their goods and services.

20.    This complaint is often voiced in the mass media and nonfiction. For example, recent articles in the *Philadelphia Inquirer* (see Gaul and Borowski 1993) described the wealth of the sector, its assets, and the salaries of its top executives. Glaser's (1994) detailed account of the fall of United Way's former president, William Aramony, showed how nonprofit executives can come to abuse their power and privileges.

21.   Chang and Tuckman (1990:127) found that for tax year 1983, 86% of the larger public charities they studied were "profitable" and that the average surplus was $2.7 million. However, they caution that merely finding a surplus does not mean that nonprofit managers are feathering their own nest or that nonprofits are chiseling on the quality of their service. A surplus can be generated by effective grants management (see Gronbjerg 1993) and used to subsidize charitable services, grow or expand programs, hedge against funding uncertainty, or establish autonomy from the donors and the marketplace. We believe it is safe to conclude that organizations are simply stockpiling resources.

22.   One commentator suggested that once nonprofits compete for customers, they become almost hypercompetitive, i.e., they will radically slash prices to increase market share, even if it means that they cannot cover costs. This happens primarily because there are not shareholders who will keep nonprofit managers accountable (Hewitt quoted in Borger 1997).

# 2

# A Profile of the Twin Cities Public
# Charity Sector: 1980–1994

## With Mark Hager and Cheryl Jorgensen

This chapter provides an overview of economic, political, and social conditions and philanthropic and charitable activity in Minneapolis–St. Paul covering the period from 1980 to 1994. We describe the research methodology and the data used in this book. We conducted cross-sectional surveys of public charities in the Twin Cities and gathered data current for 1980, 1984, 1988, and 1992, as well as a panel study that followed the original (1980) sample of public charities, reinterviewing them and gathering information for 1984, 1988, 1992, and 1994. Finally, we present descriptive statistics on nonprofits' activities, employees, volunteers, expenditures, and revenues comparing changes in the Twin Cities' nonprofit community to changes that have been taking place nationally.

## THE TWIN CITIES OF MINNEAPOLIS–ST. PAUL

This book is a case study of a single metropolitan area—Minneapolis–St. Paul. Doing multiple surveys in a single community is still a case study—even if the surveys covered a fifteen-year period. A case certainly can inform residents, administrators, and local officials of changes in their community, but it is very difficult to generalize to the nation as a whole or even to other cities. Some argue that for a case to be "worth the while," it has to be interesting—an outlier, if you will, which lessens our ability to generalize even more. We believe that we can make the case that while the Twin Cities are certainly not as intriguing as New York, Tokyo, or London, what happened there is worthwhile studying—although we make no claim that it is representative of American metropolitan communities.

The Minneapolis–St. Paul metropolitan area has gained something of a reputation for its philanthropy, charitable organizations, quality of life, and civic-minded business community. As we noted in an earlier volume

Between 1976 and 1981 articles about the social responsibility of Minneapolis–St. Paul firms appeared in *Fortune* ("Minneapolis Fends Off the Urban Crisis," January 1976), the *Wall Street Journal* ("A Midwestern City Where Fine Arts Flourish," September 15, 1977), the *Chicago Tribune* ("A Club That Means Business," June 26, 1979), the *Boston Globe* ("Where the Arts Flourish: Minneapolis," May 4, 1980), the *New York Times* ("Minnesota a Model of Corporate Aid to Cities," July 27, 1981), and even the *Harvard Business Review* ("In Minnesota, Business Is Part of the Solution," July–August 1981). . . . The cities of Minneapolis and the state of Minnesota have shared the spotlight with their companies. In another *Wall Street Journal* ("A Northern City That Works: How Minneapolis Manages It," August 5, 1980), it was reported that Chicago is no longer the city that works, and that Minneapolis has taken its place. . . . In 1980 the *Chicago Tribune* ("Our Cities: Some Bests and Worsts," April 4, 1980) did an extensive analysis of the quality of life in 11 American cities. Minneapolis was cited as having the best municipal government, the best city planning office, the best civic leadership, the best downtown mall, and the best innovation in urban living (the downtown skyway system). In 1984 *Time* magazine printed a feature article ("Minnesota's Magic Touch," June 11, 1984) praising the partnership between government, business, labor, and educational leaders that has worked to develop new high-technology enterprises in the state of Minnesota. (Galaskiewicz 1985a:1)

In the next ten years the accolades continued, despite some less than complimentary coverage later on. The Twin Cities and Minnesota received the most positive coverage of institutional innovations that grew out of this "partnership" between political, nonprofit, and business leaders. Spurred by companies interested in containing health care costs, Minnesota became a leader in the area of managed care, and the Health Maintenance Organization movement (*Washington Post*, "Two Cities— HMO Lessons for All," December 5, 1989; *New York Times*, "Companies Make HMO Deals," October 1, 1991; *Washington Post*, "Some Employers Express Dissatisfaction with Twin Cities' Experiment," September 15, 1992; *Wall Street Journal*, "Strong Medicine: Employers' Attack on Health Costs Spurs Change in Minnesota," February 26, 1993; *New York Times*, "In a Stronghold for HMOs, One Possible Future Emerges," September 2, 1995). Again prompted by the business community (in coalition with the governor, Rudy Perpich) Minnesota was the first state to allow parents statewide to choose their own public schools, thus making districts, schools, and teachers compete with one another (*Fortune,* "Saving the Schools: How Business Can Help," November 7, 1988). In an effort to bring business management practices into the educational sector, Minneapolis was the first major school district to contract out the superintendent's responsibility to a private management firm and make its pay contingent on student performance (*Los Angeles Times,* "Private Firm to Run Schools in Minneapolis," November 5, 1993; *Wall Street Journal,* "Minneapolis Board Picks Consultant as Superintendent, Ties Pay to Goals," November 8, 1993; *New York Times,* "Schools in Minneapolis Try a Corporate Approach," December 1, 1993). In 1992 St. Paul began experimenting with the highly entrepreneurial charter school, which gives teachers considerable freedom but whose public funding depends upon student performance (*Detroit News and Free Press,* "Classroom Pioneers," November 21, 1993; *Washington Post,* "Embracing New Schools of Thought," December 5, 1995).

From 1989 through 1993 *Fortune Magazine* identified "The Best Cities for Business." The Twin Cities ranked number ten in 1989 on overall attractiveness (Kirkpatrick 1989). In 1990 they were ranked number two (behind Salt Lake City) as the best place to find quality workers (Sellers 1990:49). The Twin Cities did not rank among the top ten places in 1991 on "value" because of their high corporate and personal incomes taxes and high lease rates at that time (Kretchmar 1991). Nor did they rank in the top ten places in 1992 on global competitiveness because of their "insularity" (Saporito 1992:66). However, in 1993 they made it again into the top ten as one of the best places to find knowledge-workers (Labich 1993:50). Throughout the period the Twin Cities were cited for their quality of life, an educated work force, a strong work ethic, affordable housing, low crime rate, and companies deeply involved in their community.

The negative stories, focused on crime, appeared more recently. Back in 1989 the *Chicago Tribune* noticed escalating crime in Minneapolis ("It's a Crime, But This City Is Losing Its Small-Town Peaceful Image," February 23, 1989). In 1992 the *New York Times* carried two feature stories on the murder of police officer Jerry Haaf in south Minneapolis. With the alarming increase in murder rates in 1995 and 1996 stories on violent crime in Minneapolis were carried by the *Washington Post* ("Murderous Toll in an Unlikely City," November 25, 1995) and *New York Times* ("Nice City's Nasty Distinction: Murders Soar in Minneapolis," June 30, 1996). In fact, the crime rates of Minneapolis were not that extraordinary, but the tone of most of these articles was one of shock and surprise that Minneapolis had any crime at all. In true Minnesota form, the murder rates dropped dramatically in 1997 due in large part to a partnership between city, government, police, neighborhood groups, and business that bolstered community policing programs.

*Economic Conditions.*[1]   In most parts of the country, the 1970s, 1980s, and early 1990s were a period of stops and starts for the economy. The region's economy survived the recession of 1975 without much problem and prospered in the late 1970s. During the recession of 1981 the upper Midwest and Minnesota in particular did not do well, and its recovery after the recession was slow. In 1985 and 1986 the region was growing slower than the nation as a whole, and a lagging farm economy and problems in banking did not help. This was also the period when the computer industry was reorganizing and there were significant layoffs among Twin Cities–based high-technology firms. The area bounced back in 1987 and 1988, despite the stock market crash, with growth in agriculture and business services. This pattern of growth continued into the beginning of 1989 with job growth and drops in unemployment. However, layoffs by Control Data Corporation, Unisys Corporation, and Honeywell in 1989 signaled that not all was right. In 1990 the national economy was headed for another recession, and by the middle of 1991 economic growth in the upper Midwest slowed to near zero.

In the mid- to late 1980s the Twin Cities business community was preoccupied with takeovers, corporate losses, and corporate moves. There was the threatened hostile takeover of Dayton-Hudson Corporation by the Dart Group of Maryland (1987), the acquisitions of Pillsbury by Grand Metropolitan PLC of London (1988) and NWA (parent to Northwest Airlines) by Wings Holding Inc. of Los Angeles (1989), the departure of American Hoist and Derrick (1989), and significant losses at Control Data Corporation (1989), Northwest Bancorp (Norwest) (1987), First Bank System (1988), and Honeywell (1988). This followed ConAgra's earlier acquisition of Peavey (1982), Burlington-Northern's relocation to Seattle (1982), earlier losses at Honeywell (1986), Control Data Corporation (1985 1986), General Mills (1985), Economics Laboratory (Ecolabs) (1983), and the St. Paul Companies (1984), and attempted hostile takeovers of Control Data Corporation, Ecolabs, and Honeywell.[2]

The 1990s were much better. As of January 1997, all of the 30 Minnesota-based Fortune 500 industrials or service 500 listed in 1990 were still headquartered in Minnesota (*Fortune* 1990a, 1990b).[3] NWA, Soo Line Railroad, and Cray Research were acquired by out-of-town buyers in 1989, 1990, and 1996, respectively, but the headquarters of the business unit remained in the Twin Cities. In 1992 Control Data Corporation reorganized as Ceridian and in 1995 Northwestern National Life Insurance was renamed ReliaStar Financial Corporation, but both remained headquartered in the Twin Cities. In 1994, the last year that *Fortune* listed industrials and services separately, the number of Fortune 500/500 companies headquartered in Minnesota was 31 (*Fortune* 1994a, 1994b).[4] The *Wall Street Journal* ("After Years of Growth, Minneapolis Economy Enters a Risky Phase," April 10, 1995) noted that in the wake of the recession "Minneapolis / St. Paul has enjoyed steady, near-boom conditions for several years, playing the 1990s almost perfectly. The Twin Cities' gross product grew an average of about 4% a year in 1992–1994, personal income soared, and by late 1994 the jobless rate was below 3%. It's now 3% (in 1995)." The article goes on to cite the high demand for downtown office space, strong bank balance sheets, and lots of outside investments coming into the cities.[5] By 1996 Minneapolis had the largest number of companies on a per capita basis list on the NASDAQ—a stock exchange dominated by small- and mid-size firms—signaling that the region had become a hub of entrepreneurial activity as well (Tyson 1996).

One of the underlying reasons for the relative prosperity of the region, despite the reversals in the 1980s, was that the economic base was highly diversified. In addition to a strong farm economy, there was a solid manufacturing base (e.g., medical devices and electronics) and a number of thriving service industries (including tourism). In 1990 manufacturing accounted for only 25.4% of total earnings (91st in rank out of 281 SMSAs) and services accounted for 22.4% of total earnings (140th in rank) (U.S. Department of Commerce 1991). The *Washington Post* ("Upper Midwest Relies on a Diversified Base," January 27, 1991) noted that in addition to a diversified employment base, the Twin Cities had many high-technology firms and exporters of food products that helped to fortify the region from recessions.

*Political Conditions.*   Politically, the situation was always entertaining, but on the whole fairly stable.[6] In the 1976, 1980, 1984, 1988, 1992, and 1996 presidential elections Minnesota voted Democrat. This was partly because Walter Mondale ran as the Democratic vice-presidential candidate in 1980 and then as the presidential candidate in 1984. Two Republicans, both fiscal conservatives but social moderates, served in the Senate throughout the 1980s. David Durenberger served from 1978 to 1995 and Rudy Boschwitz served from 1978 to 1991. In the 1990s politics became more controversial. In 1990 Paul Wellstone, liberal Democrat, was elected to the Senate defeating Boschwitz. He again defeated Boschwitz in 1996. David Durenberger was censured by the Senate for improper billings and left the Senate in disgrace in 1995. He was replaced by a conservative Republican, Rod Grams, whose term expires in 2001.

Throughout the 1980s and 1990s the governor's office was occupied by moderate politicians who were probusiness and the state houses were dominated by the Democrats. Al Quie, a Republican from Dennison, was in office from 1979 to 1983. He was replaced in 1983 by a moderate Democrat from northern Minnesota, Rudy Perpich, who had strong ties to Twin Cities businesses. In 1990 Perpich lost to Arne Carlson, a moderate Republican who had been the state auditor and has been very probusiness during his administration. Carlson was reelected governor in 1994. From 1980 to 1996 the Democratic party held a significant majority in the Minnesota Senate and, except for three years (1979, 1985, and 1986), held a majority in the Minnesota House. Perhaps more importantly, between 1980 and 1996 Minnesota ranked between fifth and tenth nationwide in state government spending per capita, with expenditures increasing at an average annual rate of 7.9%.[7] There were about as many state employees in 1996 (72,674) as in 1980 (about 73,000) although the number did decrease to 61,000 in 1986 to rebound in the 1990s.[8] With one exception, throughout this period the mayors of Minneapolis and St. Paul have all been Democrats. In Minneapolis, Don Fraser, a former Democratic congressman, was mayor from 1980 to 1993. He was succeeded by the first black mayor of Minneapolis, Sharon Sayles-Belton, who was reelected in 1997. In St. Paul, George Latimer served as mayor from 1976 to 1989. He was succeeded by Charles Scheibel, who served to 1993. In 1994 Norm Coleman was elected as a Democrat but declared himself a Republican in 1996. He was reelected in 1997 as well.

*Social and Demographic Conditions.*   During the 1980s and 1990s the state and metropolitan area grew in size. Between 1980 and 1990 the state's population increased by 7.3% (from 4.1 million in 1980 to 4.4 million in 1990) and the Twin Cities metropolitan statistical area's (MSA) population increased by 15.3% (2.14 million in 1980 to 2.46 million in 1990) (U.S. Department of Commerce 1991). Looking at the 85 largest MSAs in 1990, except for Washington, D.C., Minneapolis–St. Paul experienced the greatest growth among northern and eastern cities (Wolpert 1993a:51–53). Between 1990 and 1995 the metro area continued to grow. The Metropolitan Council and the Minnesota State Demographer's Office reported a metro area population of 2.65 million in 1995.[9]

Twin Cities residents tended to be better off than those in other MSAs, but there were still pockets of poverty in the central cities. Out of 281 MSAs, it ranked 15th in personal income per capita ($19,371 in 1988), 21st in average annual pay ($24,372 in 1989), 19th in cost of living (1990), and 240th in unemployment (3.8% in 1989) (U.S. Department of Commerce 1991). However, the cities of Minneapolis and St. Paul are very different than their suburbs. Table 2.1 shows that in 1990 Minneapolis and St. Paul residents were more likely to be older, non-white, unemployed, and poorer than suburban residents, while families in the cities were more likely to be headed by a female (without a male present) and poorer than suburban families.[10] Minimal differences in educational attainment between city and suburb were to a large extent due to the fact that the University of Minnesota and other colleges and universities have campuses and faculty neighborhoods in both Minneapolis and St. Paul proper.

*Table 2.1.*   Demographic Characteristics of Minneapolis, St. Paul, and Suburbs, 1990

|  | Minneapolis | St. Paul | Suburbs |
|---|---|---|---|
| Population size[a] | 368,383 | 272,235 | 1,648,103 |
| Population under 18 years (%)[a] | 20.6 | 24.6 | 27.3 |
| Population over 65 years (%)[a] | 13.0 | 13.7 | 8.5 |
| Population nonwhite (%)[a] | 21.6 | 17.7 | 3.9 |
| Population below poverty line (%)[b] | 17.8 | 16.2 | 4.4 |
| Number of families (%)[b] | 78,461 | 63,260 | 446,432 |
| Families female headed (without male) (%)[b] | 25.2 | 22.5 | 11.0 |
| Families earning less than $10,000 a year (%)[b] | 13.4 | 11.4 | 3.4 |
| Families below poverty line (%)[b] | 14.1 | 12.4 | 3.4 |
| Persons 25 years and over[b] | 243,676 | 172,290 | 1,048,179 |
| Persons 25 years and over with bachelor's or graduate degree (%)[b] | 30.3 | 26.5 | 27.8 |
| Persons 16 years and older in civilian labor force[b] | 206,289 | 141,962 | 954,750 |
| Persons 16 years and older in civilian labor force unemployed (%)[b] | 6.7 | 6.0 | 3.9 |

[a] U.S. Department of Commerce (1992).
[b] U.S. Department of Commerce (1993).

*Generosity and the Charity Sector.*   The Twin Cities lived up to their reputation as a center for nonprofit activity and philanthropy. Hodgkinson and Weitzman (1996:234–35) presented data on the number of private foundations and public charities per capita for different states. In 1987 Minnesota ranked 10th (80th percentile); in 1995 it ranked 14th (72nd percentile). Wolpert (1993a:42–44) presented data on "generosity" for the largest 85 metropolitan areas circa 1989–1990.[11] Looking at United Way contributions per employee in 1989, the Twin Cities ranked 8th (91st percentile); for contributions per Jewish resident to the Jewish federation in 1990, the Twin Cities ranked 3rd (96th percentile); for gifts and grants to metro area nonprofits per capita in 1989, the Twin Cities ranked 20th (76th percentile); and for donations per capita to the American Kidney Foundation in 1990, the Twin Cities ranked 37th (56th percentile). He also presented data on 35 states. Looking at contributions per capita to the Diabetes campaign, Minnesota ranked 1st (97th percentile); for contributions per capita to the Heart campaign it ranked 10th (71st percentile); for contributions to Cancer campaigns it ranked 4th (88th percentile); for contributions to public TV it ranked 4th (88th percentile); for contributions to public radio it ranked 2nd (94th percentile); for contributions to Planned Parenthood it tied for 13th (62nd percentile); and for contributions to AIDS-related causes it ranked 6th (82nd percentile).

The February 22, 1994, issue of the *Chronicle of Philanthropy* ranked the 50 largest U.S. cities in terms of per capita contributions to ten charities and community foundations and per capita grants by independent foundations, community foundations, and corporate foundations. Overall, Minneapolis had the highest rankings.[12] It scored in the top five in per capita contributions to the United Way, the Jewish Federation, Disabled American Veterans, Habitat for Humanity, and the community foundation and in per capita grants by corporate foundations. However, data presented in the July 26, 1994, issue of the *Chronicle of Philanthropy* for states was less complimentary. Analyzing federal tax returns for 1992 where filers took deductions for charitable contributions (about 26% of all returns), Minnesota ranked 8th in per capita giving (84th percentile), but only 35th in contributions per itemized return (30th percentile) and 38th in contributions per return claiming charitable deductions (22nd percentile). In a subsequent analysis of filers for 1995, the July 24, 1997, issue of the *Chronicle of Philanthropy* reported that Minnesota ranked 41st in contributions per return claiming charitable deductions (18th percentile).[13]

Simply noting that there were more nonprofits per capita or that giving per capita was well above average does not describe the myriad of initiatives that emerged from the nonprofit sector. We already described innovations in health care and how Minnesota was the home to the HMO. As of this writing, all HMOs in Minnesota are not-for-profit. In the arts much national attention was showered on the Guthrie Theatre, the St. Paul Chamber Orchestra, Minnesota Public Radio, and the Walker Art Center for their creativity, exhibitions, productions, and innovative programming. In the area of economic development there have also been several innovations. In 1981 the McKnight Foundation set aside $17 million creating the Minneapolis–St. Paul Family Housing Fund. The purpose of the Fund was to get low- and moderate-income people into affordable housing during a recession and a period of high interest rates. This project, done in partnership with the cities of Minneapolis and St. Paul, stimulated over 100 development projects in the cities and gave families mortgages far below market rates, augmenting this with addition loans for the poorer families (*San Diego Union-Tribune*, "The Helping Hands Are Huge," August 15, 1984). The Northwest Area Foundation has been involved in a number of innovative projects from supporting economic development corporations that do microlending for women trying to start their own businesses (*Los Angeles Times*, "Women Changing Face of Philanthropy," April 25, 1985), to supporting community organizations that counsel and provide interest-free loans to delinquent homeowners to help prevent foreclosures (*Denver Post*, "Keeping Troubled Owners in Homes," April 18, 1995), to supporting research on the economic viability and environmental advantages of sustainable agriculture (*Chicago Tribune*,

"Sustainable Farms May Mean Less Profit, but Better End Result," December 10, 1994), to helping to support the first native-American reservation-based nonprofit development corporation to provide technical assistance and loans to fledgling businesses (*New York Times,* "Philanthropy and Grit Give Hope to Oglala Sioux," November 9, 1987). The list could go on and on, which of course shows that what has been done in the Twin Cities nonprofit community is much more impressive than simply the number of nonprofits or the degree to which people in the Twin Cities and Minnesota were more generous than others.

*Discussion.* In sum, the Twin Cities and the state of Minnesota have continued to remain a very attractive place to live, even though Minneapolis experienced an increase in violent crime in the early 1990s (which later subsided) and both cities had major pockets of poverty. At the institutional level there was a healthy tension but reasonable co-existence between business and Democratic politics. On the one hand, many public sector initiatives had business backing and even reflected business values, e.g., introducing competition and performance-based pay into education. On the other hand, many businesses invested considerable amounts of money and executive time in the community, and the fact that so many firms voluntarily stayed in Minnesota over this 15-year period showed a certain tolerance and respect for the state's relatively high personal and corporate income taxes and active public sector.

In light of all these data, can we now explain why the nonprofit community thrived? While we cannot test why the Twin Cities and Minnesota were more "charitable" or had more nonprofits than other parts of the country, because we do not have comparable data on other states and cities, we can speculate. One explanation is that the area's economic prosperity helped to bolster philanthropic and nonprofit activity. This is consistent with Wolpert's (1993b:287) findings that metropolitan areas with increasing per capita incomes were more generous in their United Way contributions (per employee) than declining areas. Prosperity frees up private dollars that could be directed to philanthropic causes, which feeds the growth of new nonprofits and sustains the activities of the old. Furthermore, prospering firms also have large payrolls, and employee benefits such as health insurance and tuition subsidies feed/sustain nonprofit industries.

A second explanation is that a Democratic legislature, moderate governors, and hefty state expenditures accounted for the vitality of the sector. As Salamon (1987; Gronbjerg 1993) and others pointed out, a very large proportion of nonprofit income comes from government contracts and grants, especially in the areas of health and human services. Salamon noted that "the regions in which government relies most heavily on nonprofits to deliver publicly funded services (the Northeast and North Central regions) also turn out to have the highest number of nonprofit organizations and the largest nonprofit expenditures per capita. In contrast, the regions in which government makes the least use of nonprofits (the South) also has the least well-developed nonprofit expenditures" (1987:107). Using metropolitan areas as the units of analysis, Corbin (1995) found that local government expenditures on welfare had a significant positive influence on nonprofit sector employment and a significant negative influence on for-profit sector employment. Nonprofits are an example of "third party government," where the private sector carries out government mandates by delivering its services. Thus as public expenditures increase, so should revenues to nonprofit organizations.

Cultural regionalists offer a third explanation. Elazar (1972) characterized regions by their political cultures: moralistic, individualistic, and traditionalistic. As summarized by Schneider:

> East Anglian Puritans and their Yankee descendants established the moralistic or communitarian political culture initially in New England. Harboring strong convictions about the public interest rooted in a commitment to make of secular arrangements the same consensual commonwealth that defined their religiosity, the Puritans carried their moralistic communal politics into northern New York and Ohio, the Great Lakes area, and then the upper Mississippi Valley. Along the way, they were joined by Scandinavians and other northern Europeans whose religious orientation was analogous and served to reinforce the moralistic political culture. (1996:201)

Schneider goes on to argue that political cultures translate into civic cultures: "[I]n philanthropy, the decision to act draws fundamentally on the actor's understanding of what the individual's responsibilities in society are vis-à-vis those of the collective community (1996:203)." In the moralistic community, philanthropy and nonprofits are not seen as substitutes for government or the antidote against government, but rather as another way to fulfill civic duties, build cohesiveness, empower others, reduce inequities, and promote the commonweal in partnership with government. Histories of Minnesota, e.g., Blegen (1975), clearly point to a strong Yankee presence in the late 19th century, especially in the business communities of Minneapolis and St. Paul, and significant Lutheran immigration from Scandinavian countries. The combination may have had a long-term impact on the civic culture of the region as Schneider suggested.

Comparative research on these issues is scant, but Bielefeld and Corbin (1996) examined the political culture, wealth, and government spending in Minneapolis and Dallas to explain differences in nonprofit activity between the two cities and found support for Schneider's (1996) thesis. In

Minneapolis they found a more extensive nonprofit sector (in absolute numbers and size) and state and local government spending on human services was higher. Also they found that government provided more funding to nonprofit organizations in Minneapolis. Yet Dallas was larger, wealthier, and had a more vigorous economy than Minneapolis. Bielefeld and Corbin concluded that wealth, then, was not all important. Instead they argued that both government spending *and* nonprofit activity could be explained by the differences in the respective political cultures of the two cities—Minneapolis having a moralistic political culture and Dallas having a more traditional individualistic culture.

Obviously our research cannot settle this debate. However, it is important to remember as we proceed with our study that nonprofits within the Twin Cities were operating in a very favorable environment. It was richer than others in terms of philanthropy and government spending, and there was a civic culture—which included both Democrats and Republicans—that viewed philanthropy and nonprofits in a very positive light. Although our analysis will focus less on the larger context than perhaps it should, we are fully aware that the environment in which Twin Cities nonprofits lived out their existence was an exceptional one.

## DATA AND METHODOLOGY: CROSS-SECTIONAL SURVEYS AND THE PANEL STUDY

This book relied primarily on survey and interview data collected on four cross-sectional sample surveys of public charities in the Minneapolis–St. Paul metropolitan area current for 1980, 1984, 1988, and 1992 and one panel study that reinterviewed the 1980 sample to gather data for 1984, 1988, 1992, and 1994.

*Cross-Sectional Surveys.* Our goal was to compile a list of all non-religious public charities headquartered in the Minneapolis–St. Paul metropolitan region in 1980, 1984, 1988, and 1992. Government Publication 78, the *Cumulative List of Organizations* (U.S. Department of the Treasury 1979, 1983), was used to generate the first two sampling frames (1980 and 1984). This is an alphabetical listing of public charities (including some churches) and foundations that have 501(c)(3) status in the United States. The volumes we used were current for October 31, 1979, and October 31, 1983.[14] To develop our sampling frame for 1988 we obtained a tape copy of the Exempt Organizations/Business Master File from the IRS with the names of all 501(c)(3) organizations with a mailing address in Minnesota. This file is updated continuously by the IRS with the assumption that inactive organizations are eliminated from the file. The file we used was current for April 1989. To make our 1988 listing comparable to the 1984 sampling frame (which was current for October 31, 1983), we selected only organizations that had ruling dates prior to October 31, 1987.[15] For the 1992 survey we purchased a copy of the Business Master File from the National Center for Charitable Statistics. The file only contained 501(c)(3) organizations that had zip codes in the seven-county area. It was current for April 27, 1992. We then selected organizations that had ruling dates prior to October 31, 1991.

We used several criteria in developing our sampling frame. The first was geography. To identify those public charities headquartered in the Minneapolis–St. Paul metropolitan area in 1980, a research assistant went through the *Cumulative List* for 1979 by hand and selected all those organizations with mailing addresses in the five-county area (Anoka, Dakota, Hennepin, Ramsey, and Washington). Names of cities and towns in each county were used to assist in the coding. To develop our sampling frame for 1984, two research assistants went through the *Cumulative List* for 1983 independently and selected organizations with mailing addresses in the seven-county area (Carver and Scott were added to the initial five counties). To select organizations headquartered in the seven-county area for 1988, we did a computer run on the Business Master File, where we selected cases based on zip codes in the seven-county area. Since the NCCS had sent us only organizations in the seven-county area in 1992, no further editing of this file was necessary.

Next we selected on organization type. The files contained nonreligious public charities, some congregations, and foundations. We subsequently excluded private nonoperating foundations (which included corporate foundations) from our sampling frame. However, we retained community and operating foundations. The IRS coded private nonoperating foundations in both their published lists and the Business Master File, and these were not difficult to flag.

We also wanted to study only nonreligious public charities. Thus we wanted to exclude religious congregations (e.g., churches, ministries, missions) but to include organizations closely affiliated with a religion but that provided primarily a charitable service (e.g., a Methodist college or a Catholic hospital).[16] This was not straightforward. Some service providers, e.g., parochial schools, claim exemption as part of a parish or church and do not file separately and will be absent from our sampling frames; others, e.g., colleges, typically will (although not all religiously affiliated colleges do). More significantly, individual churches do not have to file for tax-exempt status with the IRS, and thus the IRS does not have a complete list of churches at its disposal. To illustrate, Bowen et al. (1994:10) found 56,320 churches in the Business Master File for 1991. This is out of an estimated 341,036 churches in the country circa 1991–1993 (National Council of the Churches of Christ in the U.S.A. 1995).

Purging the sampling frame of the congregations while keeping religiously affiliated service providers was not trivial. Using a list of identifiers (e.g., church, mission, synagogue, ministry, temple, Christian fellowship), research assistants went through the files and flagged organizations that appeared to be congregations. If they were unsure, they tried to contact the organization by phone and determine what the primary activity was. If worship or spiritual development was primary, the case was coded as a congregation and excluded; however, some congregations were missed and slipped into our study. When we discovered this, we regarded the case as "not applicable—religious" and did not enter its data into our files.

Next we decided to keep both "primary" and "supporting" nonprofits. The former provide direct services, e.g., a hospital or museum. The latter are organizations that operate solely for the benefit of and in conjunction with other public charities. As Bowen et al. (1994:10) noted, they are often fund-raising arms of the larger organizations being supported or are pass-through organizations. Sometimes they support private public charities; other times they support public entities, e.g., the University of Minnesota Foundation is a public charity that raises money for a state university. Bowen et al. (1994) decided to exclude these from their study, because it was very difficult to interpret their finances and activities. We decided to include them.[17] According to Bowen et al. (1994), only 5.2% of the non-church public charities in the 1991 Business Master File were supporting organizations.

Finally, we had to decide whether to include both "centrals/parents" and "subordinates/branches." To quote Bowen et al.:

> Some nonprofits have multiple branches that perform similar functions. . . . IRS regulations permit the entire family of organizations to obtain tax-exempt status as a group under a provision known as "group exemption." The branch organizations are called "subordinates" (or sometimes affiliates), and the central organization is known as the "parent." (1994:11)

The problem with these organizations was that sometimes centrals choose a group option; sometimes subordinates receive their own ruling. If subordinates choose to have their own ruling, they are listed in the Business Master File with a special code; however, they are not listed in the *Cumulative List*. Thus for the 1979 and 1983 sampling frames we excluded subordinates de facto. For the 1987 and 1991 sampling frames we had to remove subordinates from our files.[18] The treatment of subordinates is not trivial. Bowen et al. (1994:7) estimated that 23.7% of nonreligious public charities were subordinates in 1991. In 1987 we found that 25.3% of all

Twin Cities area nonreligious public charities were subordinates. In 1992 we found 30.0% of the nonreligious public charities to be subordinates.

After excluding organizations located outside the Twin Cities metro area, private nonoperating foundations, strictly religious organizations, and subordinates (in 1987 and 1992), the sampling frames for each year were 1601 in 1979, 1951 in 1983, 2735 in 1987 and 2834 in 1991.[19] Figure 2.1 plots the number of charitable organizations (less foundations) by year for the Twin Cities and nationally. (The raw data are in Table 2.2.) We learn that the growth in the number of Twin Cities public charities was a little different than increases in public charities nationally.[20] In the Twin Cities there was modest growth between 1979 and 1983 and then a marked increase in public charities between 1983 and 1987 followed by a more modest increase between 1987 and 1991.[21] Nationally, the increase in the number of charities was more linear. Nonetheless, both nationally and locally the increase was considerable over the 12-year period. Nationally, the number of nonfoundation charities increased by 71.8%; locally, the number of nonfoundation charities increased by 77.0%.[22]

Before we drew our first three samples, we stratified our sampling frames by functional area (e.g., cultural, education, health and welfare, environmental, civic, mass media, recreational, legal, housing/urban development, miscellaneous, and unidentified).[23] Organizations in the pop-

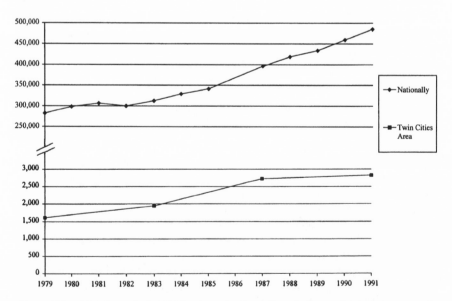

*Figure 2.1.* Number of charitable organizations (less independent and corporate foundations).

*Table 2.2.* Number of Tax-Exempt Charitable Organizations (All 501(c)(3) Organizations), Independent Private Foundations, and Corporate Foundations, 1977–1994

|  | Charitable Organizations (Nationally)[a] | Independent & Corporate Foundations (Nationally)[b] | Charitable Organizations – Independent & Corporate Foundations (Nationally) | Charitable Organizations – Independent & Corporate Foundations – Churches – Subordinates (Twin Cities Area) |
|---|---|---|---|---|
| 1979 | 304,315 | 21,839 (estimate) | 282,476 | 1,601 |
| 1980 | 319,842 | 21,407 (estimate) | 298,435 | |
| 1981 | 327,758 | 21,263 | 306,495 | |
| 1982 | 322,826 | 22,728 | 300,098 | |
| 1983 | 335,757 | 23,349 | 312,408 | 1,951 |
| 1984 | 352,884 | 23,709 | 329,175 | |
| 1985 | 366,071 | 24,712 | 341,359 | |
| 1986 | 393,051 | Not available | — | |
| 1987 | 422,103 | 26,389 | 395,714 | 2,735 |
| 1988 | 447,525 | 28,860 | 418,665 | |
| 1989 | 464,138 | 30,256 | 433,882 | |
| 1990 | 489,882 | 30,461 | 459,421 | |
| 1991 | 516,554 | 31,251 | 485,303 | 2,834 |
| 1992 | 546,100 | 33,501 | 512,599 | |
| 1993 | 575,690 | 35,180 | 540,510 | |
| 1994 | 599,745 | 36,270 | 563,475 | |

[a] *Source:* Department of the Treasury, Internal Revenue Service. Various editions. *Annual Report*. Washington, D.C.: U.S. Government Printing Office.
[b] *Source:* Renz, Qureshi, and Mandler (1996:25, Table 24).

ulation were assigned to a specific category based upon their name and information about them found in community directories. In 1987 we also relied on the activity code that was assigned to each case in the Business Master File. Any organization that could not be categorized was placed in the "unidentified" category, and research assistants tried to call them for more information. In 1980 and 1984 we alphabetized organizations within each stratum, randomly selected one of the first five in each stratum, and then selected every fifth organization within that stratum going down the alphabetized list. In 1988 we again alphabetized within strata but then drew a one-in-eight (12.5%) random stratified sample.[24] In 1991 we proceeded differently. Instead of a stratified sample, organizations were listed alphabetically by name. A one-in-eight (12.5%) random sample was then taken of this list. The sample sizes were 326 in 1979, 387 in 1983, 329 in 1987, and 355 in 1991 (see Table 2.3). The original sample upon which we built the panel analysis later on is listed in Appendix A.

*Table 2.3.*  Status of 1980, 1984, 1988, and 1992 Cross-Section Organizations
(Percentages in Parentheses)

|  | 1980 | 1984 | 1988 | 1992 |
|---|---|---|---|---|
| Completed questionnaires | 229 (70.2) | 266 (68.7) | 230 (69.9) | 252 (71.0) |
| Unable to locate | 42 (12.9) | 58 (15.0) | 24 (7.3) | 24 (6.8) |
| Known to be defunct | 18 (5.5) | 33 (8.5) | 22 (6.7) | 37 (10.4) |
| Trust | 22 (6.7) | 11 (2.8) | 7 (2.1) | 12 (3.4) |
| Not applicable (church, moved out of area, for-profit, etc.) | 0 (0.0) | 4 (1.0) | 7 (2.1) | 10 (2.8) |
| Refusal/questionnaire never returned | 15 (4.6) | 15 (3.9) | 39 (11.8) | 20 (5.6) |
| Total | 326 (99.9) | 387 (99.9) | 329 (99.9) | 355 (100.0) |

Having identified the organizations in the sample each year, the task of
interviewing them began. In 1980–1982, face-to-face interviews were conducted with either the president, executive director, or the top administrator of the organization. Mail surveys and phone interviews were used
to gather data in 1984–1986 and 1988–1990. In 1993–1995, almost all of the
data were collected by phone.[25] Table 2.3 shows that we obtained data
from 229 organizations in 1980–1981 (70.2% response rate), 266 in 1984–
1985 (68.7%), 230 in 1988–1989 (69.9%) and 252 in 1994–1995 (71.0%).
Most of the organizations not surveyed either could not be located or a
contact person could not be found. This was the fate of 42 (12.9%) organizations in 1980–1981, 58 (15.0%) organizations in 1984, 24 (7.3%) organizations in 1988–1989, and 24 (6.8%) organizations in 1992–1993.[26] The
remainder of those not contacted were known by informants to be defunct or paper organizations (trusts). Strictly religious organizations, organizations that moved out of the area, for-profits, and government
agencies were excluded as well. In three of the four surveys, only a small
number of organizations refused to participate: 15 (4.6%) in 1980, 15
(3.9%) in 1984, 39 (11.8%) in 1988, and 20 (5.6%) in 1992.

In each of the four time periods, survey questions focused on three
different areas. One set of questions asked about the type of work that the
organization engaged in (health, educational, cultural, etc.). Another set
of questions gathered information on the numbers of employees and
volunteers who did the work of the organization, as well as the number of
people served. Finally, we asked organization representatives to provide
detailed financial information, including their income sources and their
total expenditures.

*Panel Study.*  Of the original 229 nonprofits interviewed in late 1980,
1981, and 1982, we reinterviewed 201 in late 1984 and 1985 and 174 in late

1988, 1989, and 1990. In late 1994 and 1995 we returned to the field and interviewed 162 organizations. By the end of our study period—the summer of 1996—156 organizations were still in our panel. Thus we had panel data for five points in time: 1980 (229 organizations), 1984 (201 organizations), 1988 (174 organizations), 1992 (162 organizations), and 1994 (156 organizations). This resulted in an attrition rate of 31.9% with 73 organizations exiting our panel.

Figure 2.2 provides an overview of those organizations that exited our panel. An organization "closed or disbanded" when a knowledgeable informant (usually the former top administrator or a former board member) verified that two conditions had been met: no program or board activity had occurred since January 1 of the targeted year, e.g., January 1, 1984, and none was expected in the following year, e.g., 1985 (Hager, Galaskiewicz, Bielefeld, and Pins 1996:982). Informants felt comfortable with these criteria and all felt that our definition of death (or closure) corresponded to their definition, i.e., organizations we believed to be dead were also believed to be dead by our informants.

The definition of mortality will have consequences for any analysis such as ours. The definition can range from legal dissolution to a change that is significant enough to justify the claim that a "different" organiza-

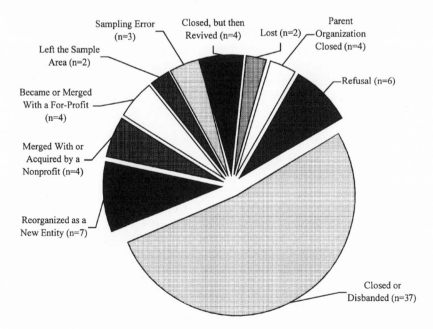

*Figure 2.2.* Representation of the distribution of exits from the panel ($N$ = 73).

tion has emerged and displaced its predecessor (Wilson 1985). Definitional considerations need to be sensitive to the fact that nonprofits are community resources. The cessation of activity, then, represents a "loss" to the community, irrespective of whether it was occasioned by the organization relinquishing its IRS status, moving out of the area, or becoming dormant for some period of time. The situation is somewhat more ambiguous when a conversion to for-profit status is involved. While the legal change is clear, the "new" organization may or may not operate essentially the same as it did while it was a nonprofit. One might suspect that the existence of new ownership rights would lead to operational differences, but this is an empirical question. The same kinds of considerations are relevant for mergers or acquisitions. These can be very complex phenomena, whose study in the nonprofit sector is just beginning (Singer and Yankey 1991; Wernet and Jones 1992). From the legal standpoint, again, things are relatively clear; an organization ceases to exist. From the community standpoint, however, even though ownership rights are not an issue, the same resources either may or may not exist in their previous (or any) form.

Figure 2.2 shows that about half (37) that fell out of the study did so due to outright closure. Six left because of refusal. Seven nonprofits reorganized into new entities, most often into churches or government agencies. Four merged with or were acquired by other NPOs. Another four became or merged with for-profit organizations. Two organizations relocated to other areas, and another three were found to have never actually been based in Minneapolis–St. Paul.[27] Four organizations ceased operations to the extent that we were convinced that they should be dropped from the sample, but they revived later. Four more organizations closed due to the closure of a parent organization. The fate of two nonprofits is unknown because they disappeared without a trace between waves of data collection.

## PUBLIC CHARITY ACTIVITIES

In 1980, 1984, 1988, and 1992, respondents from the cross-sectional surveys were asked to rank-order eight activities in terms of how important they were to the mission of the organization. The eight categories were health and welfare, educational, legal, recreational, cultural, scientific, housing and urban development, and other.[28] Looking only at the activity area(s) that received a ranking of 1 from each organization in each year, we can make some inferences about the number of Twin Cities public charities that provided different services. For comparative purposes we included the number of public charities by activity area for the nation as a whole as estimated by the peak association Independent Sector. Our results are summarized in Table 2.4

Overall we do not see much change over the 12-year period, and generally the percentages for the Twin Cities match up closely to those reported by the Independent Sector. There was a slight decline in the percentage of health and welfare organizations from 1980 to 1988, but then an increase in 1992. The percentage of cultural organizations went up a little from 1980 to 1988, but then declined in 1992. The percentages of scientific and legal organizations stayed about the same.[29] The percentage of educational organizations also stayed about the same, but there was a larger percentage of educational organizations in the Twin Cities than in the nation as a whole. One reason is that in our surveys many public interest groups, e.g., environmental, public affairs, foreign affairs, and

*Table 2.4.* Distribution (%) of **Nonreligious** Public Charities in the Twin Cities and Nationally

| | Minneapolis–St. Paul (Self-Attributions) | | | | National (NTEE Categories)[a] | |
|---|---|---|---|---|---|---|
| | *1980* | *1984* | *1988* | *1992* | *1987[b]* | *1989[b]* |
| Health & Welfare | 38.9 | 33.8 | 26.5 | 32.1 | 34.1 | 32.6 |
| Education | 31.4 | 30.5 | 33.5 | 31.0 | 22.8 | 22.6 |
| Culture | 11.8 | 14.7 | 18.7 | 14.3 | 14.7 | 14.4 |
| Recreation | 6.6 | 12.0 | 11.7 | 13.1 | 7.3 | 6.9 |
| Housing & Urban Development | 6.1 | 4.5 | 4.8 | 9.9 | 8.7 | 9.4 |
| Scientific | 4.4 | 2.6 | 2.2 | 2.4 | 2.2 | 2.3 |
| Legal | 2.6 | 3.4 | 4.8 | 2.4 | 2.0 | 2.0 |
| Other | 5.2 | 8.6 | 10.9 | 5.6 | 8.2 | 9.8 |
| Environmental | — | — | — | — | (1.8) | (2.0) |
| Animal Related | — | — | — | — | (1.6) | (2.9) |
| Public Safety | — | — | — | — | (1.4) | (1.6) |
| Foreign Affairs | — | — | — | — | (0.8) | (1.0) |
| Public Affairs | — | — | — | — | (2.6) | (2.3) |
| No Activities | 2.6 | 0.0 | .4 | 0.0 | (0.0) | (0.0) |
| Total | 109.6[c] | 110.1 | 113.5 | 110.8 | 100 | 100 |

[a] To make the NTEE categories comparable to ours we collapsed accordingly: Arts, culture, humanities = Culture; Education = Education; Health-general/Mental health/Disease, disorder related/Employment/Food,agriculture/Youth development/Human services = Health/Welfare; Medical research/Science/Social science = Scientific; Crime, legal related/Civil rights = Legal; Housing, shelter/Community improvement = Housing, Urban Development; Recreation, sports = Recreation; Environment/Animal related/Public safety/International, foreign affairs/Public affairs = Other. We also recomputed the NTEE's denominator. From the total number of 501(c)(3) organizations we subtracted Unknown, unclassified, Mutual/membership benefit, Religion related, and Philanthropy, voluntarism organizations. The latter category included private nonoperating foundations.
[b] *Source:* Hodgkinson, Weitzman, Toppe, and Noga (1992:196, Table 5.3).
[c] Totals are greater than 100%, because respondents were free to identify more than one activity area as primary.

even animal-related groups, checked education as their primary area when they saw no other option. The Independent Sector has separate categories for these organizations and we list them in the table as "other." It is also important to remember that our educational category included private educational institutions, libraries, alumni groups, and student service providers, as well as public information providers and social movement organizations.

There was also a slight increase in the percentage of housing and urban development organizations between 1988 (4.8%) and 1992 (9.9%). This category included housing rehabilitation, senior citizen housing, shelters, neighborhood block clubs, and rural and community development corporations. The NTEE also included service clubs and community funds and federated giving programs under community improvement. We classified service clubs as other and community funds on the basis of what area, e.g., health, education, or social services, they benefited. The number of housing and urban development organizations, however, was small. The 1992 figures for the Twin Cities were comparable to national figures, which were around 8 or 9% in the late 1980s. This slight increase possibly was due to the partnership in production of services between the nonprofit and the public sector.

The only significant increase was in the percentage of recreational organizations, and the percentage of recreational organizations in the Twin Cities was larger than the percentage nationally. The percentage of recreational groups among Twin Cities public charities almost doubled between 1980 (6.6%) and 1992 (13.1%). This category includes sports camps, sports clubs, physical-fitness programs, street fairs, and festivals. This finding reminds us of Bowen et al.'s (1994) analysis of the founding dates of public charities listed in the IRS Business Master File for 1991, where they found recreation and leisure organizations to be the fastest growing activity group throughout the 1980s. They attributed this increase to the growing popularity of physical-fitness programs and sports-training activities. We suspect that large cohorts of Baby Boomer children may also have contributed to this increase.

Finally, there was little change in the percentage of organizations in the Other category. Typically, the organizations found in the Other category consisted of community crime prevention programs, service groups, civic organizations, and environmental groups.

## PUBLIC CHARITY EMPLOYEES AND VOLUNTEERS

Next we turn to the number of full-time and part-time employees and volunteers affiliated with the public charities in our four sample surveys and the panel.[30] These data were also taken from the mail and phone surveys for the cross-sectional and the face-to-face interviews for the panel organizations. In some years we asked for two years of information. In these cases we averaged across the two years.

Table 2.5 presents frequency distributions for both cross-sectional and panel organizations based on the number of part-time employees, full-time employees, and volunteers affiliated with the organization in 1980, 1984, 1988, 1992, and 1994. Looking first at the cross section we find that the percentage of nonprofits with *no* full-time employees increased slightly from 46.5% in 1980 to 54.4% in 1992, but the percentage of organizations with over 100 full-time employees has remained about the same (around 4%) since 1984. We find a similar pattern of stability for part-time employees. The percentage of nonprofits with no part-time employees remained around 42% from 1980 to 1992, and the percentage of organizations with more than 100 part-time employees has remained steady as well. Among the panel organizations the pattern is different. The percentage of organizations without full-time employees decreased from 46.5% in 1980 to 35.3% in 1994, and the percentage with 100 or more full-time employees increased from 7.5% in 1980 to 10.9% in 1994. From Hager et al. (1996) we learned that smaller and younger organizations were the most likely to drop out of our panel (these results will be reviewed in more detail in Chapter 3). Thus the figures for the panel can be partially explained simply by the changing composition of the panel.

The situation for volunteers was different. The percentage of organizations in our cross-sectional surveys with no volunteers decreased dramatically from 1980 to 1984 and remained at about 21% through 1992. At the same time, the percentage of organizations with over 100 volunteers increased from 1980 to 1984 and remained at about 21% through 1992. The situation for panel organizations was a little different. Between 1980 and 1984 there was a marked decrease in the percentage of panel organizations that had no volunteers and an increase in the percentage of those which had 100 or more. The panel, however, continued to become more dependent upon volunteers. Between 1984 and 1994 the percentage of panel organizations with 100 or more volunteers increased from 21.4 to 34.6%.

## PUBLIC CHARITY EXPENDITURES AND REVENUES

Finally, we turn to revenues and expenditures. The funding of nonprofits was very complicated, and there were several different sources of income. Some were in the form of gifts with no restrictions; others were very specific commercial transactions; others had all kinds of stipulations attached, e.g., contracts. Most but not all income was tax exempt, e.g.,

Table 2.5. Frequency Distribution (Percentage in Parentheses) of Full-Time, Part-Time, and Volunteers for the Cross-Section and Panel Organizations

| | Cross-Section Organizations | | | | Panel Organizations | | | |
|---|---|---|---|---|---|---|---|---|
| | 1980 | 1984 | 1988 | 1992 | 1984 | 1988 | 1992 | 1994 |
| Full-Time Employees | | | | | | | | |
| None | 106 (46.5) | 122 (46.2) | 119 (52.2) | 137 (54.4) | 84 (41.8) | 66 (37.9) | 60 (37.0) | 55 (35.3) |
| 1–10 | 78 (34.2) | 88 (33.3) | 71 (31.1) | 67 (26.6) | 68 (33.8) | 57 (32.8) | 47 (29.0) | 46 (29.5) |
| 11–100 | 27 (11.8) | 43 (16.3) | 30 (13.2) | 37 (14.7) | 36 (17.9) | 35 (20.1) | 39 (24.1) | 38 (24.4) |
| Over 100 | 17 (7.5) | 11 (4.2) | 8 (3.5) | 11 (4.4) | 13 (6.5) | 16 (9.2) | 16 (9.9) | 17 (10.9) |
| Missing | 1 | 2 | 2 | 0 | 0 | 0 | 0 | 0 |
| Total | 229 | 266 | 230 | 252 | 201 | 174 | 162 | 156 |
| Part-Time Employees | | | | | | | | |
| None | 96 (41.9) | 108 (41.1) | 102 (44.7) | 105 (41.7) | 80 (39.8) | 49 (28.2) | 59 (36.4) | 55 (35.3) |
| 1–10 | 98 (42.8) | 117 (44.5) | 96 (42.1) | 107 (42.5) | 91 (45.3) | 86 (49.4) | 62 (38.3) | 61 (39.1) |
| 11–100 | 28 (12.2) | 34 (12.9) | 27 (11.8) | 28 (11.1) | 25 (12.4) | 32 (18.4) | 31 (19.1) | 31 (19.9) |
| Over 100 | 7 (3.1) | 4 (1.5) | 3 (1.3) | 12 (4.8) | 5 (2.5) | 7 (4.0) | 10 (6.2) | 9 (5.8) |
| Missing | 0 | 3 | 2 | 0 | 0 | 0 | 0 | 0 |
| Total | 229 | 266 | 230 | 252 | 201 | 174 | 162 | 156 |
| Volunteers | | | | | | | | |
| None | 89 (39.2) | 60 (22.8) | 47 (20.6) | 54 (21.6) | 38 (18.9) | 26 (14.9) | 30 (18.5) | 29 (18.6) |
| 1–10 | 32 (14.1) | 48 (18.3) | 52 (22.8) | 44 (17.6) | 48 (23.9) | 31 (17.8) | 24 (14.8) | 22 (14.1) |
| 11–100 | 76 (33.5) | 99 (37.6) | 83 (36.4) | 96 (38.4) | 72 (35.8) | 70 (40.2) | 54 (33.3) | 51 (32.7) |
| Over 100 | 30 (13.2) | 56 (21.3) | 46 (20.2) | 56 (22.4) | 43 (21.4) | 47 (27.0) | 54 (33.3) | 54 (34.6) |
| Missing | 2 | 3 | 2 | 2 | 0 | 0 | 0 | 0 |
| Total | 229 | 266 | 230 | 252 | 201 | 174 | 162 | 156 |

unrelated business income is taxable. There has been a great deal of research recently on nonprofit funding streams and the problems associated with managing them. For example, see Gronbjerg (1991a, 1991b, 1993), Kingma (1993), and Chang and Tuckman (1991), who described the characteristics of each type of funding and caution against analyzing them as if they were distinct and unrelated to one another.

We identified 17 revenue sources in 1980, and we tried to use these same revenue sources throughout the study. The original 17 were foundation grants, corporate (and corporate foundation) or business grants and gifts, individual grants and gifts, bequest/trusts, grants from federated fund-raising organizations (e.g., the United Way), net income from special benefit events, income from trusts, grants and contracts from federal agencies, grants and contracts from state agencies, grants and contracts from county agencies, grants and contracts from city or municipal agencies, membership dues, interest/rents/royalties, net income (loss) from the sale of assets, net income from the sale of unrelated services, program service revenue, and income from miscellaneous sources. In later years we asked about contributions from churches and nonprofits and contracts with other nonprofits. Before we present data from both the cross-sectional and panel studies, we should discuss each of these sources in detail.

*Private/Donated Income.* Under private/donated income we included individual and business gifts and grants, grants from foundations and federated donors, income from trusts and bequests, net income from special benefits events, and dues. Grants from foundations and federated donors were relatively straightforward in both the cross-sectional and panel surveys. Sometimes organizations folded these data in with individual gifts/donations and corporate/business gifts/donations, but most of the time respondents could easily estimate the separate revenue streams. Business gifts/grants were also unproblematic. Our only concern was that some nonprofits may have included revenues from sponsorships in this category. It could be argued that sponsorship dollars should be folded in with sales of unrelated services, but we suspect that nonprofits seldom did this. Individual gifts/grants and income from bequests/trusts also presented no problem. At first, we were unsure what to do with dues. However, when we examined our data we decided to count dues as private/donated income, since many of the largest dues organizations, e.g., public radio and television, were using "membership" as a marketing gimmick to solicit donations from listeners. Net income from special benefit events was more problematic. We asked for the net figure, because we wanted to know what money would be available for exempt purposes. Thus this underestimated total revenues. Also we know that this line item included revenues both from individuals and businesses that were folded together. Hopefully respondents did not double-count these revenues when they gave us their figures.

*Governmental Income.* We counted grants and contracts from federal, state, county, and city governments as governmental income. As most students of the sector now recognize, it is very difficult to get estimates of where government monies come from. As reported by Gronbjerg (1991a:168), funds can originate at different levels of government; they can be passed through the system as intergovernmental transfers to other levels before they are granted to nonprofits; funds from one level of government can be "mixed" with funds from another level of government before being disbursed; or funds can go from governments to nonprofits, which then pass them on to other nonprofits. Thus it is very difficult to determine just where the funds originated. Our solution to the problem was simply to ask respondents to assign the dollars to whatever level of government "signed the check." Although this was clear enough for almost all respondents, it meant that many funds that we recorded as county or state could ultimately have come from the federal government.

Another problem is that there are several forms of payment. Government agencies can make outright grants to nonprofits with little or no accountability or timetable specified, or government agencies can fund nonprofits through contracts-for-service. In this situation the agency has very specific expectations of the nonprofit, and often payment is not made until the service has been provided (Gronbjerg 1993). A third kind of payment is the reimbursement or third-party payment. This is similar to the contract-for-service, but the individual (or her parent or doctor) decides which service provider to use and as long as that service provider is approved by the funder, the consumer is free to make her own choice of provider. A thesis could be written on each of these three types of funding streams, but for our purposes we coded government grants and contracts as income from government sources and government reimbursements and third-party payments as program service revenue. Respondents were given instructions to this effect, and we had very little difficulty explaining to them what we meant.[31]

*Commercial Income.* Under commercial income we included program service revenues (e.g., individual fees-for-service, private third-party payments, and reimbursements from government entitlement programs) and net income from the sale of unrelated services. As noted earlier, one complication was that nonprofits had folded government contracts into their program service revenue in preparing their IRS Form 990 and often did not have this figure readily available. On a case-by-case basis we had to make sure that respondents broke government contracts out from program service revenues.

We also had problems with net gain/loss from the sale of unrelated services. This item was problematic, because it often related to income that could be regarded as unrelated business income and thus subject to taxation. It is called unrelated income, because it results from the sale of some good or service that was unrelated to the tax-exempt purpose of the organization. Thus there were incentives for nonprofits to underreport it, fold it into gross program service revenues, or simply put it under "miscellaneous." In practical terms, it referred to museum store sales, revenues from travel services, and possibly income from corporate or business promotions such as a cause-related marketing campaign.

We had considerable missing data on this item, since usually respondents could only provide gross figures. Because losing this item meant losing a case, we decided to estimate net figures where we were able. For the cross section we used information from cases in a given year where we had figures for both gross and net income. We computed the ratios of net to gross, took the average ratio, and multiplied this by gross income for the cases where we had gross but not net to estimate a value of net income. For the panel we pursued a different strategy. We examined an organization's income statements for the period before or after, and if it reported both gross and net for either year, we computed the ratio of net to gross and then multiplied that ratio by gross for the year we were missing net.[32]

*Other Income.* In this category we included income from interest/rents/royalties and net gain/loss on the sale of assets. We also included most miscellaneous income. Sometimes, though, we moved items recorded as miscellaneous by our respondents to other lines. For example, in a couple of cases respondents listed fees from conferences they hosted as "other." However, they were clearly program service revenue and we coded as such. In the earlier studies respondents put donations from churches and nonprofits and contracts with other nonprofits with miscellaneous income. In later surveys we included three additional line items for income from these sources, but in the analyses presented here, they were still coded as "other," although clearly gifts from nonprofits and churches were donated income and contract revenue could be coded as either donated (parallel to how we handled government contracts) or earned income.

In 1980 we asked for revenue and expenditures data for fiscal 1977–1978 (or calendar year 1978), 1978–1979 (or calendar year 1979), and 1979–1980 (or calendar year 1980). In the 1984 cross section we asked for 1982–1983 (or calendar year 1983) and 1983–1984 (or calendar year 1984).

In the 1984 panel we asked for fiscal 1979–1980 (or calendar year 1980), fiscal 1982–1983 (or calendar year 1983), and fiscal 1983–1984 (or calendar year 1984). In the 1988 cross section we asked for fiscal 1986–1987 (or calendar year 1988) and fiscal 1987–1988 (or calendar year 1988). In the 1988 panel we asked for fiscal 1983–1984 (or calendar year 1984), fiscal 1986–1987 (or calendar year 1987), and fiscal 1987–1988 (or calendar year 1988). In the 1992 cross-sectional survey, we asked for fiscal 1991–1992 (or calendar year 1992) and fiscal 1992–1993 (or calendar year 1993). Finally, in the 1992 and 1994 panel interviews we asked for fiscal 1991–1992 (or calendar year 1992), fiscal 1992–1993 (or calendar year 1993), and fiscal 1993–1994 (or calendar year 1994).

Because of missing data problems, we decided to average over two-year periods, using, when necessary, one year's data when we had information on only one year. We pursued this strategy for both cross-sectional and panel organizations. For example, for the 1980 organizations we averaged expenditures for fiscal 1978–1979 (or calendar year 1979) and fiscal 1979–1980 (or calendar year 1980). If respondents failed to provide data for one year, we used data for the other.

If a panel organization failed to provide us with data for either of the adjacent years, we faced a serious problem. Since expenditures and income from various streams will be important variables in our panel analysis, organizations missing data on one income item for one year will drop out of the panel study. This called for an innovative approach to the missing data problem. Our approach was to write out each income item and total operating expenditures for each panel organization for each of the five periods of the panel (1979–1980, 1983–1984, 1987–1988, 1991–1992, and 1993–1994). To derive an estimate of income from a funding stream or expenditures for a year where we had missing data, we estimated a regression equation using the data from years for which we had the information. We set $X$ equal to the year (e.g., 1980, 1988, 1992, 1994) and $Y$ equal to the dollar amount from a given income stream in the respective years (e.g., individual contributions in 1980, 1988, 1992, and 1994). We then regressed $Y$ (e.g., individual contributions) on $X$ (e.g., year) and derived an estimate of the regression coefficient $b$ and the slope $a$. To estimate the income or expenditure item for the missing year we substituted the year for which we had missing data (in this example 1984) into our equation and hand-calculated the expected value of $Y$ (e.g., the expected value of individual contributions in 1984). As long as we had two data points, this strategy was used. If we had less than two data points, the item remained as missing. This reduced missing data considerably. Table 2.6 summarizes the percentage of missing data for income and expenditure variables before and after adjustment using estimates from the regression analyses.

Table 2.6. Percentage of Missing Data for Income and Expenditure Variables in the Panel Study Before and After Adjustment

| Expenditures and Funding Streams: | 1979–1980 % Missing | | 1983–1984 % Missing | | 1987–1988 % Missing | | 1991–1992 % Missing | | 1993–1994 % Missing | |
|---|---|---|---|---|---|---|---|---|---|---|
| | Unadj. | Adj. | Unadj. | Adj. | Unadj. | Adj. | Unadj. | Adj. | Unadj. | Adj. |
| Operating Expenditures | 3.1 | 1.3 | 3.0 | 0.0 | 2.9 | 0.0 | 0.6 | 0.0 | 0.6 | 0.0 |
| Individuals | 3.5 | 1.0 | 2.5 | 0.0 | 4.6 | 0.0 | 1.9 | 0.0 | 0.0 | 0.0 |
| Businesses | 3.1 | 1.0 | 2.0 | 0.0 | 4.6 | 0.0 | 1.9 | 0.0 | 0.6 | 0.0 |
| Foundations | 3.1 | 1.0 | 2.0 | 0.0 | 4.6 | 0.0 | 0.6 | 0.0 | 0.6 | 0.0 |
| Federated | 2.2 | 1.0 | 2.0 | 0.0 | 4.0 | 0.0 | 0.0 | 0.0 | 0.0 | 0.0 |
| Trusts/bequests | 2.6 | 1.0 | 2.0 | 0.0 | 4.6 | 0.0 | 0.0 | 0.0 | 0.0 | 0.0 |
| Benefit events (net income) | 2.2 | 1.0 | 2.0 | 0.5 | 2.9 | 0.6 | 5.6 | 0.0 | 0.0 | 0.0 |
| Dues | 2.2 | 1.0 | 2.0 | 0.0 | 3.4 | 0.0 | 0.6 | 0.0 | 0.6 | 0.0 |
| Federal government | 2.2 | 1.0 | 2.0 | 0.0 | 4.0 | 0.0 | 0.0 | 0.0 | 0.6 | 0.0 |
| State government | 2.2 | 1.0 | 2.0 | 0.0 | 4.0 | 0.0 | 0.0 | 0.0 | 0.0 | 0.0 |
| County government | 2.2 | 1.0 | 2.0 | 0.0 | 4.0 | 0.0 | 0.0 | 0.0 | 0.0 | 0.0 |
| City government | 2.2 | 1.0 | 2.0 | 0.0 | 3.4 | 0.0 | 0.0 | 0.0 | 0.0 | 0.0 |
| Program service | 3.9 | 1.0 | 2.0 | 0.0 | 3.4 | 0.0 | 1.9 | 1.2 | 0.6 | 0.0 |
| Unrelated service (net income) | 2.6 | 1.0 | 4.0 | 0.0 | 3.4 | 0.0 | 3.7 | 0.0 | 0.6 | 0.0 |
| Interest/rents/royalties | 2.6 | 1.0 | 2.5 | 0.0 | 4.0 | 0.0 | 1.2 | 0.0 | 0.6 | 0.0 |
| Sale of assets (net income) | 2.2 | 1.0 | 2.5 | 0.0 | 4.6 | 0.0 | 0.6 | 0.0 | 0.6 | 0.0 |
| Other | 2.6 | 1.0 | 2.0 | 0.0 | 4.6 | 0.0 | 2.5 | 0.0 | 1.3 | 0.0 |

*Expenditures.*    Average expenditures of public charities both in our cross sections and panel increased dramatically during our study period. Figure 2.3 plots expenditures in constant dollars for the panel, the four cross sections, and survivors. The latter included only those 156 organizations still in the panel in 1994. Between 1980 and 1992 average expenditures in our cross-sectional surveys increased by 70.5% in inflation-adjusted dollars. In the panel, average expenditures increased by 270% between 1980 and 1994 in inflation-adjusted dollars. Among survivors, expenditures increased by 175%. It is important to note, however, that the standard deviations increased as well. This tells us that the distribution of expenditures around the mean broadened considerably, thus making the average a less reliable indicator of what was happening in the sector as a whole. The reason why the averages for the panel and survivors rose more steeply than for the cross section was that the panel was constantly shedding smaller organizations due to attrition (see Hager et al. 1996) and these organizations were never included among the survivors.

Table 2.7 gives us another angle on expenditures. In all four cross-sectional surveys roughly the same percentage of organizations had total expenditures under $500,000 (between 76.7 and 84.1%), under $100,000

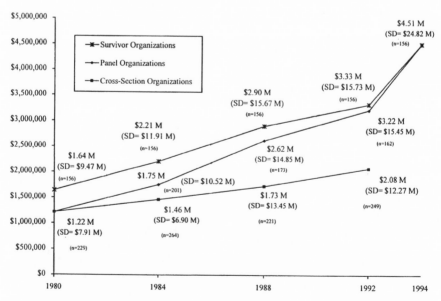

*Figure 2.3.*    Average expenditures for survivor, panel, and cross-sectional organizations, 1994 constant dollars.

*Table 2.7.*  Frequency Distribution (%) across Expenditure Categories for Cross-Sectional and Panel Organizations

| Expenditures | Cross-Section Organizations | | | |
|---|---|---|---|---|
| | *1980* | *1984* | *1988* | *1992* |
| $100,000 | 125 (55.3) | 147 (55.7) | 126 (57.0) | 133 (53.4) |
| $100,000–$499,999 | 65 (28.8) | 60 (22.7) | 55 (24.9) | 58 (23.3) |
| $500,000–$999,999 | 9 (4.0) | 18 (6.8) | 11 (5.0) | 19 (7.6) |
| $1,000,000–$9,999,999 | 22 (9.7) | 31 (11.7) | 24 (10.9) | 28 (11.2) |
| $10,000,000+ | 5 (2.2) | 8 (3.0) | 5 (2.3) | 11 (4.4) |
| Missing | 3 | 2 | 9 | 3 |
| Total | 229 | 266 | 230 | 252 |

| Expenditures | Panel Organizations | | | | |
|---|---|---|---|---|---|
| | *1980* | *1984* | *1988* | *1992* | *1994* |
| $100,000 | 125 (55.3) | 101 (50.2) | 73 (42.0) | 56 (34.6) | 53 (34.0) |
| $100,000–$499,999 | 65 (28.8) | 50 (24.9) | 51 (29.3) | 45 (27.8) | 36 (23.1) |
| $500,000–$999,999 | 9 (4.0) | 22 (10.9) | 15 (8.6) | 19 (11.7) | 24 (15.4) |
| $1,000,000–$9,999,999 | 22 (9.7) | 22 (10.9) | 26 (14.9) | 32 (19.8) | 31 (19.9) |
| $10,000,000+ | 5 (2.2) | 6 (3.0) | 9 (5.2) | 10 (6.2) | 12 (7.7) |
| Missing | 3 | 0 | 0 | 0 | 0 |
| Total | 229 | 201 | 174 | 162 | 156 |

(between 53.4 and 57.0%), between $1 million and $10 million (between 9.7 and 11.7%), and exceeding $10 million (between 2.2 and 4.0%).[33] How was it that average expenditures increased in our cross-sectional surveys, while the percentage distribution remained about the same? The answer is that resources in the sector became much more concentrated, and this relates back to the large standard deviations. Although the percentage of nonprofits in our cross sections with expenses exceeding $10 million had only increased from 2.2 to 4.4%, these organizations accounted for 63.0, 64.9, 79.6, and 76.8% of total expenditures in 1980, 1984, 1988, and 1992, respectively. Among the panel organizations, while the percentage of organizations with expenditures under $100,000 decreased, the percentage with expenditures over $10 million increased. But resources became more concentrated among panel organizations as well. Panel organizations with inflation-adjusted expenditures over $10 million accounted for 63.0, 66.2, 75.8, 75.4, and 81.5% of all expenditures in 1980, 1984, 1988, 1992, and 1994, respectively.

In sum, we have to be very careful when drawing generalizations about the size of public charities in the Twin Cities. Most of the attention recently has been on very large organizations and particularly hospitals. For example, *Corporate Report Minnesota*, a local business magazine, reported that in 1996, 16 Minnesota nonprofits had revenues over $100

million (Smith and Kratz 1996). We did find that, *on average*, public charities in 1992 were nearly 70% "richer" in constant dollars than their counterparts in 1980, but this was because wealthier organizations in 1992
were much wealthier than their counterparts in 1980, while the small and
median-size organization was about the same size in 1992 as in 1980. Thus
any broad gauge statements about the "typical" charity must be qualified,
as should any gross generalizations about the wealth of the sector as a
whole. Also we have to be sensitive to attrition in evaluating our panel
results. Again, it was younger and smaller organizations that tended to
leave the panel over time (Hager et al. 1996). Thus the increase in expenditures among the panel was greatly influenced by the fact that resource
poor organizations had left the panel.

  *Income Streams.*    Next we turn to the analysis of income streams. As
noted above, nonprofit organizations derived their income from a variety
of sources. We aggregated our income streams into four types to sim-
plify our analysis: private, government, commercial, and other income.
When respondents reported negative net income from special benefit
events, sale of assets, or sale of unrelated services, we coded the item
zero. This is because we only wanted to focus on revenues available to
the organization, not on losses or costs that the organization had to absorb. Our measure of total income was simply the sum of revenues from
all the above sources for a given year. All monetary figures were again
adjusted to 1994 dollars using the producer price index to facilitate meaningful comparisons across years. There are two very different sets of
numbers. First, there is the average income that organizations received
from each source. Second, we took the total amount of income from each
source and divided it by the total amount of income from all sources and
multiplied by 100. Both sets of statistics are presented in Table 2.8.[34] The
Independent Sector also analyzed the percentage of income from different sources for filers in 1987 and 1992 (Hodgkinson and Weitzman
1996:228, Figure 5.10).[35] These data are presented in Table 2.8 for comparative purposes.

  For both the Twin Cities cross sections and panel surveys as well as the
national sample, commercial income was the most important source of
income throughout the study period. We also found that the average
amount of commercial income increased dramatically over the period for
both cross-sectional and panel organizations. Among our cross-sectional
organizations we also found an increase in the percentage of funding that
came from commercial sources. The percentage of commercial income for
the cross section increased from 62.1% in 1980 to 65.6% in 1984, to 82.1%
in 1988. By 1992 commercial income was at 76.0% of total income. Among
the panel organizations, change was less dramatic with only a slight

Table 2.8. Average Income (Thousands of Dollars) and Percentage (in Parentheses) of Funding from Fees & Sales (Commercial Income), Government, Private Donors, and Other Sources (Listwise Deletion)

| | Cross-Sectional Organizations | | | | Organizations Nationally | |
|---|---|---|---|---|---|---|
| | 1980 (N = 227) | 1984 (N = 261)[a] | 1988 (N = 220) | 1992 (N = 247)[a] | 1987 | 1992 |
| Commercial income | $ 787.4 (62.1) | $ 954.5 (65.6) | $1,436.1 (82.1) | $1,610.9 (76.0) | (69.2) | (73.6) |
| Government income | 224.3 (17.7) | 207.0 (14.2) | 81.8 (4.7) | 176.8 (8.3) | (7.9) | (7.5) |
| Private/donated income | 156.0 (12.3) | 219.1 (15.1) | 184.6 (10.6) | 256.6 (12.1) | (11.6) | (10.2) |
| Other income | 100.3 (7.9) | 73.9 (5.1) | 46.8 (2.7) | 74.9 (3.5) | (11.3) | (8.7) |
| Total | $1,268.0 (100.0) | $1,454.5 (100.0) | $1,749.3 (100.0) | $2,119.3 (100.0) | (100) | (100) |

| | Panel Organizations | | | | | Organizations Nationally | |
|---|---|---|---|---|---|---|---|
| | 1980 (N = 227) | 1984 (N = 200) | 1988 (N = 173) | 1992 (N = 160) | 1994 (N = 156) | 1987 | 1992 |
| Commercial income | $ 787.4 (62.1) | $1,030.1 (59.1) | $1,744.8 (62.1) | $2,731.4 (64.6) | $3,628.0 (68.0) | (69.2) | (73.6) |
| Government income | 224.3 (17.7) | 328.7 (18.8) | 476.6 (17.0) | 687.4 (16.3) | 659.7 (12.4) | (7.9) | (7.5) |
| Private/donated income | 156.0 (12.3) | 240.0 (13.8) | 392.8 (14.0) | 439.4 (10.4) | 554.2 (10.4) | (11.6) | (10.2) |
| Other income | 100.4 (7.9) | 145.4 (8.3) | 194.9 (6.9) | 368.2 (8.7) | 492.8 (9.2) | (11.3) | (8.7) |
| Total | $1,268.1 (100.0) | $1,744.2 (100.0) | $2,809.1 (100.0) | $4,226.4 (100.0) | $5,334.7 (100.0) | (100) | (100) |

[a] Excludes United Way and community foundation.

increase toward the end of the study period: 62.1% in 1980, 59.1% in 1984, 62.1% in 1988, 64.6% in 1992, and 68.0% in 1994. Independent Sector found among its filers that commercial income increased slightly as a percentage of total revenue from 69.2 to 73.6% between 1987 and 1992.

The average amount of government revenues decreased among our cross-sectional organizations but increased among the panel organizations. However, among both the overall percentage of income from government sources decreased over time. In 1980, government dollars constituted 17.7% of the income of the organizations in our cross-sectional sample, in 1984 they were at 14.2%, and in 1988 they dipped to only 4.7% of total income. By 1992 they were back at 8.3%. Among the panel, government grants and contracts accounted for 17.7, 18.8, 17.0, 16.3, and 12.4% of total income in 1980, 1984, 1988, 1992, and 1994. Independent Sector found that among filers, government grants stayed about the same, 7.9 to 7.5% as a percentage of total revenue between 1987 and 1992. The smaller percentage of government funding in the national sample was probably due to the fact that we included both government grants and contract revenue among our government revenues, while the Independent Sector only included government grants.

The inflation-adjusted average income from donations fluctuated among the cross-sectional organizations, and increased among the panel organizations. However, the percentage of donated income was relatively constant over time for both cross-sectional and panel organizations. In the cross section donated income comprised 12.3% of income in 1980. By 1984, it was 15.1%. By 1988 the percentage of donated dollars dropped to 10.6% and increased slightly by 1992 (12.1% of income). There was comparable stability among the panel organizations. Contributed income as a percentage of total income was 12.3, 13.8, 14.0, 10.4, and 10.4% of total incomes across the five time periods. Studying filers, the Independent Sector also found stability: private contributions were 11.6 and 10.2% of total revenues in 1987 and 1992.

Finally, we see that among the cross-sectional average revenues from other sources stayed about the same while among the panel average revenues from other sources increased. Among both samples the percentage of revenues from other sources was relatively stable. Among the cross-sectional organizations the percentage of income from other sources in 1980, 1984, 1988, and 1992 was comparable (fluctuations between 2.7 and 7.9%). Among panel organizations there was even less change, fluctuations between 6.9 and 9.2% of total income. The Independent Sector found that revenue from other sources decreased slightly, from 11.3 to 8.7% between 1987 and 1994 (Hodgkinson and Weitzman 1996:228).

## DISCUSSION

Unfortunately, there are very powerful caricatures of the charitable sector that are not entirely accurate. On the one hand, the sector is depicted as swimming in cash and corruption. Recent articles in the *Philadelphia Inquirer* (see Gaul and Borowski 1993) described the wealth of the sector, its assets, and the salaries of its top executives. Glaser's (1994) detailed account of the fall of United Way's former president, William Aramony, showed how nonprofit executives can come to abuse their power and privileges. One comes away with the image that there are many more "for-profits in disguise" than truly public benefit organizations. On the other hand, we read stories in the press about nonprofits going out of business or being in desperate straits because of a lack of funding. Government cutbacks are often cited as the culprit. We also read heroic accounts of nonprofit staffers and volunteers helping out the poor and needy.

Which caricature is correct? Are nonprofits "rolling in dough" and becoming for-profits in disguise or is the sector being strangled to death and on the brink of extinction? This chapter hoped to examine the sector in the Minneapolis–St. Paul metropolitan area. If nothing else, we showed how diverse the charitable sector is. We found that some organizations had enormous economic power, while many had only shoestring budgets. Some had numerous employees and charged fees for their services comparable to for-profit firms, while others were run exclusively by volunteers and depended solely on donations. Some were engaged in more traditional nonprofit activities, e.g., health, social services, education, while a growing segment of the sector is into recreational activities. We relied heavily on quantitative indicators, but we were well aware that these cannot tell us how effective these organizations were, whether or not nonprofits bilked their donors, or what these organizations and their activities meant to those being helped, volunteers, and nonprofit staffs and boards.

Furthermore, we found that not much changed in the basic structure of the charity sector. Roughly the same percentage of organizations provided health/welfare, educational, legal, scientific, housing and urban development, and cultural services. The only significant increase was in the area of recreational services. We did find that, on average, cross-sectional and panel organizations had considerably more revenues and expenditures in 1992 and 1994 than in 1980. This mirrors findings of other studies of nonprofits in the 1980s and 1990s that document growth among public charities (e.g., Gibelman and Demone 1990; Stevens 1994; Hodgkinson and Weitzman 1996).[36] But much of the increase in the Twin Cities was due to growth among the very largest organizations. Looking at the cross-sectional organizations, we found that roughly the same percentage (about 55%) had expenditures under $100,000 in 1980, 1984, 1988, and 1992 and about the same percentage (about 86%) had expenditures under $1 million over the same period. Among the panel the percentage with expenditures under $100,000 and under $1 million shrank, but this was because smaller organizations were more likely to leave the panel than larger organizations (Hager et al. 1996). This led us to conclude that the growth was really among the larger organizations: the rich got richer. As noted in the text, one consequence of all this was that resources in the sector became more concentrated in the hands of a smaller percentage of very large organizations. This, however, is not unusual and high concentration ratios have been reported in other cities (Salamon, Altschuler, and Myllyluoma 1990:6; Salamon 1997a:30).

The question of whether public charities in the Twin Cities were becoming more businesslike—and less communal or charitable—was not as easy to answer. Similar to nonprofits in other cities, e.g., Baltimore (Salamon, Altschuler, and Myllyluoma 1990:5; Salamon 1997a:47), Twin Cities charities were most dependent upon commercial income for their revenue throughout the study period.[37] Looking at trends over time, among cross-sectional organizations a greater percentage of revenues came from fees and program service income in 1992 than in 1980; however, among panel organizations there was little change over time. There was no significant change in the percentage of revenues from donations and/or grants for either cross-sectional or panel organizations. Finally, we found among the cross-sectional organizations a greater dependency on volunteers in 1992 than in 1980 and less dependency upon employees. Among the panel organizations, we found a greater percentage with more than 100 volunteers, a smaller percentage with no volunteers, but also a greater percentage with employees. Overall, we think it is safe to conclude that the sector was not overrun by "for-profits in disguise" and that the normative or communal organization was as well represented in the sector in 1994 as in 1980.

The Twin Cities nonprofit sector faced many challenges throughout the 1980s and 1990s, but our analysis suggests that, while there were some casualties, the sector weathered the events of the decades very well and has not changed as much as some have imagined. Needless to say, we cannot predict the future, and authors at the national level (e.g., Salamon 1997b) and at the local level (McCormack 1996; Pratt and Sullivan 1995) have warned the charitable sector that government cutbacks in spending will be significant over the next several years and the devolution of responsibilities to the state level will result in a "shakeout" of the sector. Our data did confirm that the government sector has become less important for nonprofits in the Twin Cities. Average income from government sources stayed about the same for cross-sectional organizations, increased among panel organizations, but government revenue as a percentage of total income decreased significantly among cross-sectional organizations and slightly among our panel.

Nonprofits are called on to plan, develop results-oriented budgets, build coalitions and lobby, and become more "businesslike" in their management practices. Is this their ticket to success? While we do not pretend to predict the future, we do have a great deal of data on past nonprofit behavior. In the following chapters we will use these data to try and explain how and why Twin Cities nonprofits changed. Perhaps those who worry about the next 15 years can learn something from studying what public charities did in the last 15 years and the effects this had on their condition.

## ACKNOWLEDGMENTS

We would like to thank Murray Weitzman, Loren Renz, and David Ward for their advice and counsel on different sections of this chapter. Any shortcomings are, of course, the responsibility of the authors.

## NOTES

1. This brief description of recent economic conditions was distilled from various publications of the Federal Reserve Bank of Minneapolis including the *Quarterly Review* (1977 to 1984), *District Economic Conditions* (1985 to 1991), and *Summary of Commentary on Current Economic Conditions* (1990 to 1996).

2. By 1989 there were 26 Fortune 500/50 publicly held firms and mutual insurance companies headquartered in the Twin Cities, but only 13 of these were on the Fortune lists in 1979. The 13 newcomers were all local firms that grew into the Fortune 500/50 lists, went public, or were spinoffs of other local firms. No new major firms moved into the area between 1979 and 1989.

3. We did not include IDS Life as a local firm, since it was owned by American Express Company in New York.

4. Again, IDS Life was not counted as a local firm.

5. The article cautioned that a labor shortage, vacant retail space, and over-aggressive lending on the part of local banks could spell trouble for the future. However, as of the end of 1997, no serious economic problems appeared on the horizon.

6. Unless noted otherwise, all the data for this section were taken from various issues of the *Minnesota Legislative Manual*, published by the Minnesota Secretary of State's Office.

7.  Spending per capita on education increased at an average annual rate of 6.1%, while public welfare expenditures per capita rose an average of 8.5% and hospital and health expenditures per capita rose an average of 6.1% each year.

8.  The data on state expenditures and employees were taken from various issues of the *Statistical Abstract of the United States* published by the U.S. Bureau of the Census, 1981 through 1996.

9.  The figure for the 1995 MSA population was not published. It was computed for us by Cathy Johnson of the Metropolitan Council and James Hibbs of the State Demographer's Office, September 27, 1996.

10.  The Twin Cities MSA generally includes seven counties: Anoka, Carver, Dakota, Hennepin, Ramsey, Scott, and Washington. Minneapolis is entirely contained in Hennepin County and St. Paul is located in Ramsey County. To derive the numbers for the suburbs we subtracted the Minneapolis numbers from Hennepin County and the St. Paul numbers from Ramsey County and then added together the numbers for the seven counties.

11.  The actual number of cases differs depending upon the measures examined. Thus we present both the rank and percentile.

12.  St. Paul was neither ranked nor was it mentioned in the article, leading us to conclude that the numbers presented were only for Minneapolis.

13.  The authors cautioned that the figures on tax-deductible contributions included contributions to churches. This was illustrated by the fact that Utah ranked number one in per capita donations and contributions per itemized return.

14.  We used the 1979 and 1983 volumes instead of the 1980 and 1984 volumes, because we wanted to get into the field in 1980 and 1984 and did not want to wait until the end of that year to develop our sampling frame. The problem with the *Cumulative List* was that it is published only once a year and thus contained organizations that were already defunct.

15.  The problem with this strategy was that some organizations could have died between October 31, 1987, and April 1989 and been eliminated by the IRS by the time we received the tape in April 1989. Thus we probably undercounted the population for October 31, 1987. However, none of the organizations that died between October 31, 1987, and April 1989 would have been around to be interviewed by the time we went into the field in 1989.

16.  The reason for excluding exclusively religious organizations was a substantive judgment. As noted in Chapter 1, we regarded churches, ministries, synagogues, and other religious groups more as mutual benefit nonprofits than as public benefit nonprofits. In this study we only wanted to focus on the latter. On the other hand, many organizations affiliated with religious denominations provide valuable public benefits and were included in our study.

17.  In this study we decided on the following ground rules. If the primary nonprofit was listed by the IRS as a separate 501(c)(3) or the primary organization was a public institution, we coded the characteristics of the supporting nonprofit. Thus even if they reported no employees, although employed staff from the primary organization did the work of the organization, we coded the number of employees as zero. If the primary nonprofit was not listed separately as a 501(c)(3), we asked respondents about the parent and combined data on both the primary and supporting nonprofit and used the combined figures in our analysis.

Another problem was that a supporting organization reports all the gifts it received as revenue (as well as interest income and other sources of revenues), however, many will immediately turn around and pass this through to the primary organization. Some of these organizations list these flow-through dollars as part of the operating expenditures; others do not. In the case of the latter this gives them significant "profits" for that year (revenues-operating expenditures). In our interviews we not only found out what organization(s) they supported, but how much they passed on to the organization(s) in a given year. We added these sums to their operating expenditures, although technically they were not funds spent on "operations." This creates a weird anomaly in some cases: huge cash flows, no activities, no service population, and no employees. It also means that some dollars in the sector are double-counted (Bowen et al. 1994:11), i.e., as income to the supporting organization and then again as income to the primary organization.

Finally, following the lead of the National Taxonomy of Exempt Entities, we assigned the activity codes of the primary organization to the supporting organization. Thus the University of Minnesota Foundation would be regarded as an educational organization.

18.   We subsequently went back to the 1987 Business Master File and wrote out the cases that were subordinates and intermediates (and that we had excluded from our 1987 sampling frame) and compared this list to the *Cumulative List,* which was current for October 31, 1987. As we expected, none of them were there. To purge the 1991 subordinates, we took our population of public charities (sans independent and corporate foundations and congregations) and checked this against the *Cumulative List* current for October 31, 1991. Organizations that were not in the printed copy were subsequently jettisoned from the sampling frame on the grounds that they *probably* were subordinate or intermediate organizations. Visual inspection of the cases excluded confirmed this presumption.

19.   Although we do not have the total number of 501(c)(3) organizations in the Twin Cities area for the earlier years, we do have these for the latter. The 1987 sampling frame constituted 53.3% of all charitable organizations (non-religious public charities, congregations, subordinates, intermediaries, private non-operating foundations) identified in the Twin Cities area in 1987; the 1991 sampling frame constituted 54.5% of all charitable organizations identified in the Twin Cities area in 1991.

20.   To derive the total number of independent and corporate foundations from the Foundation Center table, we subtracted the number of grant-making operating foundations from their total of private foundations for the years 1981 through 1994. For 1979 and 1980 we estimated the number of grant-making operating foundations by taking the ratio of grant-making operating foundations in 1981 and multiplying this by total private foundations in 1979 and 1980. These estimates were then subtracted from total private foundations for these two years to derive our figures in Table 2.2.

21.   This pattern could also be explained by how we compiled our sampling frames. In 1979 and 1983 we relied on the printed *Cumulative List of Organizations;* in 1987 and 1991 we relied on computer tapes. The smaller number of organizations in the earlier years could be due to clerical oversights in identifying Twin Cities area nonprofits by visual inspection of mailing addresses.

22.   To put this into perspective we should remember that in 1992 charitable organizations (public charities and foundations) represented only 2.2% of all organizations in the United States, which paled in comparison to business organizations at 93.8% (Hodgkinson and Weitzman 1996:37). However, the number of charitable organizations grew at an annual rate of 4.7% between 1977 and 1992, far outpacing business organizations, which grew at an annual rate of only 3.0% during that same period (Hodgkinson and Weitzman 1996:26).

23.   We did not stratify by size (e.g., operating expenditures), because this information was not available to us for the organizations in 1979 and 1983. On the Business Master Files for 1987 and 1992 there were asset and income estimates for some organizations. Because these data were incomplete, we did not use them for sampling purposes.

Unfortunately, the National Taxonomy of Exempt Entities was not available to us in 1980. Their categories and guidelines for coding would have been very useful to us.

24.   The reason for changing the sampling percentage was simply because the sampling frame increased from 1601 in 1979, to 1951 in 1983, to 2735 in 1987 and budgetary constraints made it impossible for us to survey a 20% sample.

25.   It may strike the careful reader as odd that each time it took close to three years to collect the survey data. As we will see, many of these organizations were quite small and some were obscure. Many did not have listed phone numbers, and research assistants had to spend days locating a contact person for the organization. Finding organizations (in the case of smaller nonprofits) and getting the right person with the right information (in the case of larger nonprofits), not refusals, were the big problems. Unfortunately, we did not keep records of the number of callbacks for each organization, but it was significant. Only about 20–30% of the mail surveys that we sent were returned and usable. The rest of the data had to be gotten from new mailings and personal phone calls. In 1993–1995 we tried to secure the organization's IRS Form 990 from the Minnesota State's Attorney Office before contacting the organization. This greatly aided the interviewer in getting the right information from a respondent. At no point did we just use the data on Form 990. In all cases we verified the numbers with the organization.

26.   The lower rates for the more recent years could be due to our use of the Business Master Files in 1987 and 1991, which supposedly included only active charities, or it could be due to organizational learning, i.e., knowing where to find the more obscure organizations.

27.   One organization, based in New York City, filed its paperwork to maintain its nonprofit status in the home state of its president. The organization fell into our sample because the president in the late 1970s happened to live in our sampling area. However, his successor lived in another state. Consequently, the paperwork for the organization moved with the new president and the organization no longer existed as a Minnesota nonprofit. The other organization was a Minnesota nonprofit, but never began operations sufficiently to the point where its organizers considered it as a founding. They referred to the enterprise as "a waste of the fee for filing for nonprofit status." The third case was a school, but it did not

have exemption under 501(c)(3). Although none of the organizations "survived" until 1984, we considered all three to be part of the original sample for 1980, thus keeping our $N$ at 229.

28. The reader might notice that the activities used to stratify the sampling frames in 1980, 1984, and 1988 were different than those listed here. We made this unfortunate mistake back in 1980 and decided to live with it for the rest of the study. Unfortunately, we also lumped health and social services together to create a combined health and welfare category. The experiences of these subsectors during the 1980s and 1900s were very different as noted by Hodgkinson and Weitzman (1996:8–10).

Respondents were also offered the option Organizational Development. Organizations that checked this option were subsequently given an activity code that best reflected their mission statement. Many organizations that checked this category were supporting organizations and, being faithful to our decision-rule (see note 17), were given the same activity code as their primary organization.

29. Those organizations falling into the legal category were advocacy groups, civil rights organizations, and organizations providing legal counseling services to groups or individuals. We should also note that we put crime prevention groups and correctional facilities in our "Other" category, while the Independent Sector categorized these as "Crime, legal related." Thus these categories are not directly comparable.

30. Tallying the number of employees and volunteers in a given year was more difficult than we expected, and we wish that we could say that we were consistent throughout the study. In some of the surveys/interviews we asked respondents to give us their best estimate of full- and part-time employees for some day or month, e.g., December 31. Other times we asked them to "average" over the 12-month period. In gathering data on volunteers we were more consistent with one exception. In the first three cross sections and in all panel studies we asked for the unduplicated number of people who volunteered in a given year. We asked respondents not to include board members in their count of volunteers, even though few directors are paid. In the 1992 cross-sectional survey we did not ask them to exclude board members in their tally nor did we ask them for the number of board members. To adjust the 1992 figures, we took the mode of board members in the 1988 cross-sectional survey (mode = 5) and subtracted this from the number of volunteers reported in 1992 by each organization.

31. We used IRS Form 990 extensively in the 1992 cross-sectional survey and panel studies to help "jar" respondents' memories, and this was very effective. However, because the 990 asks that government contracts be folded into program service revenue, we asked respondents to break program service revenues down: private payments (including private insurance company payments), government reimbursements (or entitlements like Medicaid and Medicare), and government contracts. We then added the latter to government grants so as to make the 1992 data comparable to other years. This exercise also gave respondents a chance to verify the numbers on the 990s. In light of the research by Froelich and Knoepfle (1996), verification seemed to be an important step in the process.

32. We employed similar decision rules when we were missing net gain/loss

from sale of assets and special benefit events, but the incidence of missing net figures for these two items was minimal.

There were two special cases where we decided to handle this problem differently. In the panel we had two large local colleges. In some years gross income from the sale of unrelated services (e.g., auxiliary services such as book store sales, rents from dorms) was folded in with program service revenue (tuition); other years figures for gross and net incomes were given; in still other years we were given only gross unrelated and program service revenues. We checked the IRS 990s for both schools, and gross sales from auxiliary services were folded in with tuition, which in these cases makes sense. Thus for only these two cases for all panel years we added gross income from unrelated sales to program service revenue and treated it all as program service revenue.

33.   Looking at nonreligious public charities that filed usable 990 tax returns in 1992, the Independent Sector found slightly more large organizations. Over 70% of the public charities had total expenses under $500,000 and 41% had expenses under $100,000 (Hodgkinson and Weitzman 1996:221). Approximately 15% had total expenses between $1 million and $10 million, and only 3.5% had total expenses exceeding $10 million (ibid.). The reason that Independent Sector found more large organizations is that organizations with annual revenues of less than $25,000 and religious congregations were not required to file a return. Thus their sample underrepresented small organizations. Of the 493,984 public charities identified by the IRS in 1992, only 164,968 filed forms with usable financial data (ibid.:233).

34.   The initial results for the cross section were quite startling, as there were dramatic fluctuations in donated income. We subsequently discovered that a United Way and community foundation were in the 1984 and 1992 surveys, but not in the 1980 or 1988 surveys. In all subsequent analysis, these organizations were eliminated from our cross-sectional analyses.

35.   In their study, private donations included gifts and grants from individuals, corporations, foundations, bequests, and federated donors (e.g., United Way) but not dues and assessments. Government funds included only grants from various levels of government, while we coded government grants *and* contracts as government income. Their commercial revenue included fees for related services, and government contracts and reimbursements (e.g., Medicaid and Medicare payments). We included private fees and government reimbursements but not government contracts under commercial revenue. In the Independent Sector study, other income included dues and assessments, interest, dividends, net rents, other investment income, net income from the sale of assets, net income from fund raising events, and net income from the sale of unrelated services. We included dues and assessments under private/donated income.

36.   Stevens's (1994:8) research is especially useful since she studied Minnesota nonprofits between 1988 and 1994. The only downward movement was between 1990 and 1992, the height of the recession. She also points out that nonprofits in the $500,000 to $1,000,000 category experienced the least volatility during the seven-year period of their study.

37.   Two studies were done on income patterns of Minnesota nonprofit orga-

nizations. Using IRS Form 990 data for 1993, Pratt and Sullivan (1995:10) also found that public charities were most dependent upon commercial revenue for income (39.4%) and then charitable contributions (27.3%). In contrast, Stevens's (1994:6) sample was most dependent upon government grants and contracts. One reason for the disparities was that our study and Pratt and Sullivan (1995) included hospitals in the samples, while Stevens (1994) excluded hospitals a priori.

# 3

# Growth and Decline among Nonprofit Organizations

With Mark Hager, Yoshito Ishio, and Joel Pins

This chapter addresses the question, Why did some public charity organizations grow while others shrank during the course of our study? We examine change in two types of resources or organizational inputs: revenues and labor. Revenues are further broken down into private donations, commercial income, government grants and contracts, and miscellaneous income; labor is broken down into employees and volunteers.

We first turn to selection theory for explanation. Building on the work of the ecologists and institutional theorists in sociology, we look at characteristics of organizations' niches and organizations' overlapping niche affiliations. We hypothesize a nonmonotonic relationships (in the shape of an inverted U) between niche density and growth. We also expect that growth is greater in more concentrated niches. Furthermore, organizations in niches enjoying more sociopolitical legitimacy should grow more. We also hypothesize that specialists will grow more than generalists, controlling for niche conditions.

Second, we focus on tactics. We hypothesize that managerial tactics will enhance commercial income and lead to the hiring of more employees, while political and managerial tactics will enhance donated income and attract volunteers. Third, we test if the effects of tactics on growth are conditional upon organizations' size, age, decision-making structure, and network ties to other organizations and local elites. An organization's structure should therefore modify the effect of tactics on outcomes. This last set of analyses tests the proposition that strategy implementation is embedded in and thus influenced by formal and informal social structures.

## ORGANIZATIONAL GROWTH AND DECLINE

Although the meaning of growth and decline may seem obvious enough, there is often a great deal of confusion surrounding these concepts. Cameron, Kim, and Whetten (1987; see also Cameron, Sutton, and Whetten 1988) caution that growth and decline are not the same as certainty and uncertainty: both can engender uncertainty; decline is not the same as retrenchment but can be both the cause and consequence of retrenchment; both growth and decline can introduce discontinuities (or turbulence) into organizational life: thus researchers should not equate growth with placidity and decline with turbulence; and, especially in nonprofits, decline is not the same as ineffectiveness and growth does not mean effectiveness. In their study of colleges and universities Cameron Kim, and Whetten (1987) operationalized growth/decline in terms of enrollments and revenues as well as respondent's perceptions of these changes. Other indicators can be used to measure growth/decline as well, including change in assets, stock prices, number of employees or volunteers, number of customers/clients, debt/equity, profits, and sales (see D'Aveni 1989; Weitzel and Jonsson 1989). Alternatively, analysts could look at the number and types of product lines or activities, divisions or subsidiaries, and work sites.

It is also important to recognize that organizational growth and decline mean different things in different environmental contexts. For example, Whetten (1980) distinguished between stagnation and cutback. Organizations that are in stable or growing markets will pare their operations so as to become "leaner and meaner" and thus more capable of adjusting to changes in their technical and institutional environment. "Paring down" is a strategy to enable one to better exploit opportunities as they present themselves. In contrast, if organizations are in unstable or shrinking markets, paring operations is a signal that the organization is losing ground and having a difficult time competing against its peers. Both organizations may "shrink" by 5 or 10%, but the meaning of the shrinkage is very different (see also Greenhalgh 1983; Cameron and Zammuto 1983; Weitzel and Jonsson 1989). Changes in the resource environment or tactics may result in organizational growth or decline, but other factors can explain why an organization grows or shrinks as well, e.g., internal political conflict, mismanagement, outdated technology, or expiring product life cycles (Levine 1978; Bibeault 1982; Kotler 1980; Tushman, Newman, and Romanelli 1986).

### A.  Selection, Growth and Decline

Selection theory has contributed greatly to our understanding of organizational change. Ecological theory sensitized us to the role of competition and constitutive legitimacy, and institutional theory has focused on the role that sociopolitical legitimation plays. As noted in Chapter 1, ecologists have documented a strong relationship between population density and organizational births and deaths (Carroll 1984; Singh and Lumsden 1990). Accelerating birth rates and shrinking death rates accompany increases in population density. This is due to certain organizational forms taking on constitutive legitimacy. At some point, though, birth rates begin to decline and death rates increase as the population reaches its carrying capacity and competition begins to "thin" the population. In measuring population size, ecologists typically use numbers of organizations that have a certain form or produce a certain product.

Ecologists as well as industrial economists have also looked at resource concentration. Patterns of concentration affect industry profits (Burt 1993) as well as birth and death rates (Carroll 1985; Swaminathan 1995; Barnett and Carroll 1987). Market share is one popular measure, e.g., the percentage of total sales in an industry accounted for by the two or four largest producers (e.g., Burt 1983). Others have used Gini coefficients (Carroll 1985), while one could also compute the percentage of organizations that account for a certain percentage of sales, e.g., 75 or 90%, in an industry.

Institutionalists have focused on sociopolitical legitimacy (see Baum and Powell 1995; Hannan and Carroll 1995b). Sociopolitical legitimacy refers to organizations being rewarded for behavioral conformity to—or punished for violation of—some law, norm, or standard by authorities, publics, or institutional gatekeepers. Rewards might be in the form of grants or contracts or simply social recognition. Punishments range from fines to penalties or ostracism. In this monograph we test for both constitutive as well as sociopolitical legitimacy effects. The former will be assessed using the strategy of the ecologists (e.g., testing for nonmonotonic effects of density); the latter will be operationalized by measuring organizations' reputation among local elite populations.

Instead of focusing on populations of organizations, we focus on niches. Niches are an attractive alternative to populations, because incumbents are identified relationally rather than on the basis of shared organizational traits. Niches are locations in multidimensional space defined by the distribution of resources in the environment (McPherson 1983; see also Baum and Singh 1994a; Baum and Oliver 1996; Hannan and Freeman 1989). Niches are the sites where organizations compete for technology, labor inputs, customers, grants, capital, etc. Thus organizations are in the same niche if they are structurally equivalent to one another vis-à-vis valued resources (see Burt and Talmud 1993). The niche space (see Figure 3.1) provides a way to visualize the distribution of organizations in an ecological field (McPherson 1983). In our example of community based nonprofit organizations, environmental niches (the "blocks" within Figure 3.1) can be defined in terms of financial inputs (e.g., commercial income, public

EXPENDITURES

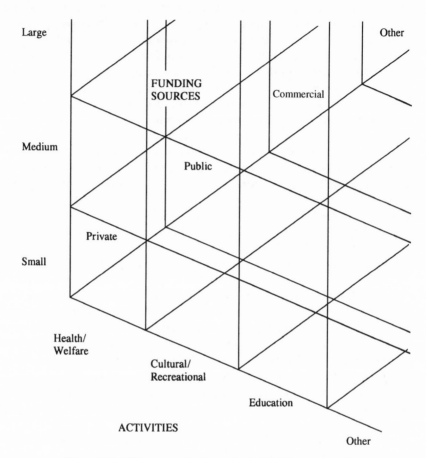

*Figure 3.1.*   Diagram of a hypothetical niche space.

grants/contracts, private donations, or other income), outputs (activities/products/services), and capacity (e.g., expenditure).[1]

Variables measured at the population level can also be measured at the niche level. For example, if there are many organizations that produce and distribute the same product, draw on the same revenue streams, and have similar capabilities, then the niche is "dense" (e.g., Baum and Singh 1994a). If there are few organizations producing the same product, drawing on the same revenue sources, or having similar capabilities, the niche could be characterized as "sparse." Similarly one could measure the level of resource concentration (or inequality) within a niche and niche legitimacy by either looking at the niche as a whole or organizations within the niche.

The niche perspective also enables us to study organizations' "micro-niches" and thus to identify generalist and specialist organizations. We define the microniche from the perspective of the organization. It is the area in the niche space where the organization "feeds" (McPherson 1983). An organization may procure all its resources within one niche i.e., it receives only donations and provides only educational services, but more likely it draws on several, crossing niche boundaries. If it procures its resources from a single niche, then we say it is a specialist. If it competes for resources in several niches, we call it a generalist.

*Hypotheses.* How does this all relate to organizational growth and decline? Taking our cue from the ecologists and institutional theory, we offer simple hypotheses about the relationship between niche characteristics and the growth and decline of revenues and labor. First, we expect a nonmonotonic relationship between niche density and growth and decline in resources. In niches that are sparsely settled, organizations should shrink; in moderately populated niches, organizations should grow; and in densely populated niches, organizations should shrink once again. On the other hand, organizations in more concentrated niches should grow, while those in niches where resources are more evenly distributed should shrink. Niche legitimacy should also have an effect on growth and decline. Organizations in niches with greater sociopolitical legitimacy should grow in size, while those in niches with less legitimacy should shrink. Finally, specialists will outcompete generalists, with the former growing over time while the latter shrink.

The reasoning behind these hypotheses is straightforward. The first hypothesis is the familiar density dependence argument. Growth is negative in sparsely settled niches, since the small numbers of organizations signal that the niche is not yet legitimate nor, perhaps, organized. Thus even though it is relatively easy for organizations to differentiate themselves from one another, the lack of constitutive legitimacy keeps donors, volunteers, customers, employees as well as entrepreneurs away. In niches that have more organizations, constitutive legitimacy is less a problem and customers, employees, donors, and volunteers feel comfortable with organizations in the niche, resulting in significant growth. However, in densely populated niches, it becomes more difficult for organizations to differentiate themselves from one another. In niches with strong output controls, where organizations compete for customers, companies gain a competitive advantage by lowering their prices. Competitors follow suit, and revenues to the organization drop. In niches with strong process controls, where organizations compete for donors and volunteers, the situation is somewhat different, but the result is the same. Organizations seldom ask donors and volunteers for less, because the assumption is that the organization is already operating at cost. Instead they target their solicitations at fewer prospective donors and volunteers. However, with fewer donors and volunteers, revenues and labor decline. Thus whether dependent upon sales and employees or donations and volunteers, high levels of competition should lead to organizational inputs shrinking over time. To summarize,

> H1:   *Organizations in more dense niches are likely to increase commercial income, donated income, employees, and volunteers, up to a point, after which they are likely to lose commercial income, donations/grants, employees, and volunteers over time.*

Levels of resource concentration within niches should also affect growth and decline. Taking our cues from the industrial economics literature, we expect that as niches become more concentrated, growth should be greater. The argument is that in niches where concentration is low organizations are competing for customers or donors on an even footing. This suggests that efforts to differentiate oneself on the basis of quality and price are more intense and revenues will be lower. In contrast, in niches where resources are more concentrated, dominant organizations can collude on price or overhead costs and increase their revenues. Smaller organizations at the edge of the niche can benefit from their initiatives as they free-ride on the strategy of dominant players. In the end, both large and small players benefit.

> H2:   *Organizations in more concentrated niches are likely to increase commercial income, donated income, employees, and volunteers over time.*

The sociopolitical legitimacy attached to a niche should also have an independent effect on organizational growth and decline. In effect, organizations in niches that enjoy high sociopolitical legitimacy are able to take advantage of the high status of their niche mates. Customers and donors are willing to pay higher fees or make bigger donations and employees and volunteers are willing to accept less compensation, because of the reputed higher quality of the services produced in the niche, the social benefits produced by actors in the niche, or the desire to be identified with a highly legitimate niche. Thus even if competition is stiff, organizations in high-status niches should increase both their revenues and labor inputs. In sum,

> H3:   *Organizations in niches with greater sociopolitical legitimacy are likely to increase commercial income, donated income, employees, and volunteers over time.*

Finally, specialists should grow more than generalists. Generalists are organizations whose activities span a broad range of niches. They have many different products and draw resources from many different sources. Specialists are organizations whose activities are confined to one or two niches. They produce few products and are dependent on one or two types of sources for their inputs. We are familiar with the ecologists' hypothesis that specialists should outcompete generalists in stable environments (Hannan and Freeman 1977, 1989). The reason is twofold. First, specialists should have a deeper knowledge and understanding of the products, technology, and markets in which they do business. This should give them a competitive edge over generalists, who need to keep up on developments in a range of businesses and markets. Second, as specialists compete against generalists, the latter have considerably more "baggage" to carry. Because they are fighting battles on several fronts, generalists cannot bring all their resources to bear on any single confrontation. Furthermore, the capacities they carry to do battle in other niches can become costs or overhead in the struggle against "leaner and meaner" specialists. The only time when generalists will outcompete specialists is when there is a coarse grain change that virtually destroys a niche and, of course, all specialists in that niche (Hannan and Freeman 1977). In sum,

H4: *Organizations that are specialists are likely to increase commercial income, donated income, employees, and volunteers over time, while organizations that are generalists should lose resources over time.*

## B. Adaptation, Growth, and Decline

Adaptation theory argues that organizational success is the result of managers choosing strategies and tactics that will do their organization the most good. Yet this is not always easy to do. From contingency theory we learn that there is no one best way to structure an organization, but rather the structure of an organization must "fit" conditions in the environment (Lawrence and Lorsch 1967). Core technologies and productive capabilities must be protected, uncertainty kept to a minimum, and resource flows ensured. But there is no one best means to achieve these ends. We extend this logic to the formulation and implementation of organizational strategy and tactics. It is all contingent on the context, i.e., different strategies and tactics work better in different situations. In our earlier discussion we distinguished between managerial tactics, which are useful to extract resources from niches that are governed by output controls, political tactics, which are useful to extract resources from niches that are governed by process controls, and retrenchment tactics, which enables one to shrink and drop one into a "lighter" weight class.

In Chapter 1 we drew the distinction between niches governed by strong output controls and niches governed by strong process controls (Scott 1998:138–39). We argued that both are part of the technical environment and described different criteria that are used to allocate resources within niches. In the first, the quality and price of divisible outputs produced by an organization are paramount. Resources—usually in the form of sales—go to those who are able to produce better products at a lower cost. We usually think of a market for some good or service as an example of a niche governed by strong output controls, and we labeled organizations within these niches utilitarian (Albert and Whetten 1985). Niches characterized by strong process controls allocate resources based on the appropriateness of organizational procedures, routines, and structures. Resources—usually in the form of grants or donations—go to those whose practices conform to the rules, norms, and taken-for- granteds stipulated by institutional gatekeepers. We usually think of grants economies as an example of niches governed by process controls. We labeled organizations in these niches normative (ibid.).

The unique feature of the adaptive approach is that it argues that organizations can do something to make themselves more competitive in both types of niches. That is, the structural characteristics of the niche alone, e.g., its density, will not determine an organization's fate. It can engage in long-term planning, retool its technical core, implement control systems, rationalize its accounting systems, and reduce production and transaction costs. That is, it can implement managerial tactics to make itself more competitive in niches with strong output controls. It can also accrue external referents of prestige, publicize its good works, showcase its effort to conform to normative standards, and adopt processes and structure that are in sync with dominant forms in the larger institutional environment. That is, it can implement political or legitimation tactics to make itself more competitive in niches with strong process controls (see Oliver 1991; Suchman 1995).

*Hypotheses.* If adaptation theory is correct, the use of different tactics should lead to different types of growth. For example, managerial tactics should lead to an increase in commercial income and employees. Internal managerial tactics (see Table 1.1) should enable firms to deliver more high-quality goods and services more effectively. External managerial tactics should open up new markets for the organization's products and services. Thus, even if niche competition is intense or legitimacy low, organizations will come out ahead, if they have a better product that they can deliver to more customers on time and without complications and without outside interference. Thus,

H5:   *Organizations that employ more managerial tactics are likely to increase commercial income and employees over time.*

In contrast, political tactics should lead to an increase in donated income and volunteers. Internal political tactics should help to align the organization's structures and process with normative expectations by putting into place programs, practices, and procedures mandated (or expected) by institutional stakeholders. External political tactics should help to align public opinion, laws, and policies with the interests of the organization. Growth is the result of stakeholders rewarding organizations with gifts, grants, contracts, and favors for their conformity, public service, and (apparent) trustworthiness. Thus even if competition is intense and legitimacy is low, organizations that utilize political tactics are in a position to differentiate themselves from others, make their case to institutional gatekeepers, curry favor with donors and volunteers, and grow in size. Thus,

H6:   *Organizations that employ more political tactics are likely to increase donated income and volunteers over time.*

DiMaggio and Powell (1983) made the interesting argument that institutional gatekeepers are often as interested in how well organizations are able to accrue the trappings of managerialism as they are in serving the public interest. Instead of tactics being simply a set of tools or techniques to better compete in different niches, they become symbolic representations. Planning, implementing quality and financial controls, being concerned with the bottom line and measuring performance, and acting in a "businesslike" manner are important signals to prospective donors and volunteers that organizations are accountable and reliable. Indeed this is another way to ensure prospective donors and volunteers that the organization is worthy of their confidence. Although embracing modern managerial practices may not actually improve the quality of services (e.g., in a collective goods type organization) and may even hinder operations and add costs, the interest of gatekeepers in nonprofits demonstrating their commitment to the business model justifies the implementation of these tactics. If DiMaggio and Powell were correct, then we would expect the following hypothesis to be true as well:

H7:   *Organizations that employ more managerial tactics are likely to increase donated income and volunteers over time.*

Finally, if organizations decide to consolidate, retrenchment is an important tactic. Downsizing or retrenchment are purposeful efforts to eliminate programs and/or staff in order to reduce the organization's scale of operations. Why would an organization do this? As noted earlier, Whetten (1980) argued that downsizing can make an organization "leaner and meaner" and thus better able to compete for resources. We interpret this as meaning that retrenchment enables an organization to drop into a lighter weight class, which means that it now competes against smaller organizations. This is an especially attractive tactic for medium-size organizations, which often find themselves competing against large organizations as well as other medium-size organizations (Hannan and Freeman 1977). Retrenchment, therefore, is not necessarily a bad thing and may give the organization a competitive advantage. Nonetheless, we expect that organizations that pursue retrenchment tactics over time will indeed have fewer inputs, regardless of their size.

H8:    *Organizations that employ more retrenchment tactics are likely to lose commercial income, donated income, employees, and volunteers over time.*

## C.  Structural Embeddedness, Growth, and Decline

The structural embeddedness argument stipulates that strategy implementation is not frictionless but rather faces a host of obstacles (Baum and Dutton 1996). Simply because senior management says something is going to happen does not mean that it does. As we argued in Chapter 1, senior management is not always free to act rationally or intentionally but rather is embedded within structural contexts, internal and external to the organization, that constrain its choices and affect the likelihood of tactics having the intended effect. We focus on organization's size, age, decision-making structures, and network ties to others outside the organization and the implementation of managerial and political tactics. In general, we argue that formal and informal structures will modify the effects that tactics have on growth and decline.

*Hypotheses.*   In Chapter 1 we said that organizational size and age would be important in facilitating and/or stymieing strategy implementation. The effect of organizational size is straightforward, if one accepts the assumption that large organizations are more bureaucratized. The procedures, rules, and routines endemic to a bureaucracy make it unlikely that it would be able to change or that change strategies could be successful. There just would not be the room to maneuver. In contrast, small organizations are more likely to implement successfully change tactics, because they are still held together by interpersonal networks and personal loyalties and are more flexible. They are not burdened by rules, routines, and systems of accountability. Paradoxically, the ecologists see this as one of the great liabilities of smaller organizations (Hannan and Freeman 1989). In sum,

H9:   *The effects of managerial tactics on increases in commercial income and employees and political tactics on increases in donated income and volunteers will be stronger, the smaller the organization.*

Age effects on strategy implementation are more ambiguous. On the one hand, one could assume that age is also correlated with bureaucratization; and it, like size, should have a dampening effect on strategy implementation. On the other hand, age could be correlated with competencies. In this scenario, older organizations have the know-how to implement tactics, while younger organizations flounder because they do not have the skills or competencies to make the right decisions. Having years of accumulated knowledge could make an organization less prone to change or make it more difficult to change, but having experience and know-how also mean that an organization's efforts to change the organization would be more successful. We hypothesize that age will facilitate strategy implementation, controlling for organizational size. To summarize,

H10:   *The effects of managerial tactics on increases in commercial income and employees and political tactics on increases in donated income and volunteers will be stronger, the older the organization.*

We also argued in Chapter 1 that senior management can more easily implement tactics if it has the power to do so. If power is too broadly distributed, different interest groups in the organization can stymie the implementation of tactics initiated from above and push their own agenda. While recognizing that power is both allocative and distributive, we focus on the formal distribution of authority within an organization. That is, we want to know who has the right to make binding decisions on the group. To the extent that this power resides in the hands of a single functionary, e.g., the board, the decision-making structure of the organization is highly centralized. If this power is more broadly distributed, e.g., among staff, administrators, even volunteers, decision-making is more decentralized. If only one group is "in charge," others will have little chance at stopping initiatives from above and the dominant coalition should be more successful at pushing its agendas and implementing tactics. This line of argument suggests the following hypothesis:

H11:   *The effects of managerial tactics on increases in commercial income and employees and political tactics on increases in donated income and volunteers will be stronger, the more centralized decision-making authority.*

We argued earlier that social network ties are important for strategy implementation, because they can provide organizations with favors, access, and references. All of this hinges on the trust that grows out of ongoing social relationships. Because partners trust the organization, they are willing to extend the latter favors. They know that the organization will honor the norm of reciprocity and will pay back in the future. Because partners trust the organization they are willing to give the organization access to others. They know that the organization will not embarrass them or do them harm and thus are willing to introduce the organization to others with whom they have contacts. This is what we commonly call networking. Because partners trust the organization, they are willing to give testimony on behalf of the organization. That is, they are willing to vouch for the character of the organization to others. They become an organization's reference. Favors, access, and references are intangible assets that are difficult to buy in the marketplace—although not impossible—but that naturally emanate from social relationships. The importance of social network ties to our discussion is that being able to ask for favors, having access to third parties, and having someone to vouch for your character can facilitate the implementation of tactics aimed at legitimating the organization.

Our research focuses on two types of network ties: First, we examine interorganizational ties among the panel of organizations. We look at which organizations exchanged resources with one another and how many ties each organization had to other nonprofits in the panel. Second, we examine ties between the panel of organizations and local community elites. We obtained information from local elites on which nonprofits in our panel they personally gave assistance to (e.g., as a donor, volunteer, consultant, or board member), which ones they or their families used personally, and which ones they believed provided essential services or had achieved extraordinary accomplishments.

The argument is that organizations that had ties to many other organizations, or had more ties to, and better reputations among, members of the local community elite, were able to realize greater returns on their efforts to align their procedures, structures, and activities with institutional rules, norms, and taken-for-granteds. Network partners should extend them favors, give them access to their contacts, and testify on their behalf, which is crucial in building reputations. Although an organization can try to demonstrate its credibility to prospective donors and volunteers without such contacts, this will be more effective if others help "grease the skids," make the introductions, and open up otherwise inaccessible social circles. More specifically,

H12: *The effects of political tactics on increases in donated income and volunteers will be stronger, the greater the number of network ties to other organizations.*

H13: *The effects of political tactics on increases in donated income and volunteers will be stronger, the greater the number of network ties to the local community elite and the more the elite values the organization.*

## DATA, METHODS, AND VARIABLES

In this chapter we used data from the 1980, 1984, and 1988 cross-sectional surveys and the 1984, 1988, 1992, and 1994 panel studies (see Chapter 2 for descriptions of these data). Thus we begin with 229 panel organizations in 1980 and analyze 201 in 1984, 174 nonprofits in 1988, 162 in 1992, and 156 in 1994. We should remind the reader that all the panel data were gathered in face-to-face interviews with the chief executive or operating officer. When the top-ranking officer of the organization did not have the needed data, we secured the data from others in the organization.

*Size.* The first task was to operationalize organizational size for the panel. One measure was annual operating expenditures. We averaged total expenditures across 1979 and 1980. These data were converted into 1994 dollars using the producer price index, and we computed the natural log. We obtained information on organizations' total full- and part-time employees and volunteers for 1980, 1984, 1988, 1992, and 1994. We subsequently added full- and part-time employees together. Since these variables were highly skewed, we computed their natural logs as well.[2]

We also obtained data on organizations' revenue. As in Chapter 2, we distinguished between *commercial-type revenues* and *donative-type revenues.* The former came directly from consumers, who were required to pay some fee in exchange for some good or service; the latter came from private donors or third parties, who gave with the intent that the nonprofit generated some public good or provided valued goods and services to others for free or at reduced cost. Commercial-type revenues included program service revenues and net earnings from the sale of unrelated services. Donative revenues came from grantmakers and donors. In the private sector we had individual donations, dues, corporate gifts and grants, foundation grants, trusts and bequests, net income from special fund-raising events, and grants from federated fund drives (e.g., United Way). A third type of revenue was *government revenue,* which came in the form or grants and contracts from federal, state, county, and local government. There were also *miscellaneous revenues.* This included interest/ rents/royalties, net income from the sale of assets, donations from churches and other nonprofits, and miscellaneous income. Data on these four revenue streams were converted into 1994 dollars and averaged over 1979–1980, 1983–1984, 1987–1988, 1991–1992, and 1993–1994. We computed the natural logs of commercial- and donative-type revenues; we created a dummy variable for government revenues, where a 1 indicated that it received public funding in a given year and a 0 otherwise. We did this because the distributions of all these variables were highly skewed.

We used the data on the different revenue streams, employees, and volunteers to construct two aggregate measures of organizational inputs. To measure commercial activity we combined the log of commercial income with log of total employees; to identify donative activity we combined the logs of donative income and total volunteers. Before we computed our constructs using principal components analysis, we pooled our data from 1980, 1984, 1988, 1992, and 1994.[3] The factor loadings for the commercial income/employees construct were .807 (the eigenvalue was equal to 1.30 and the construct explained 65.1% of the variance). The factor loadings for the donative income/volunteers constructs were .879 (the eigenvalue equaled 1.55 and the construct explained 77.3% of the variance). The factor scores for the commercial income/employees construct were skewed to the right; the factor scores for the donative income/volunteers construct were approximately normal with a slight tendency toward positive skewness. We then disaggregated the data by year. The zero-order correlations between the commercial income/ employee factor scores and the donative income/volunteers scores were .274, .350, .410, .337, and .415 in 1980, 1984, 1988, 1992, and 1994, respectively. See Table 3.1 for the relevant descriptive statistics of all the size measures.

*Age.* The age of the organization was computed simply by subtracting the year of founding from 1980. Since this variable was highly skewed to the right, we computed its natural log as well.

*Activities/Services.* Each year of the panel we handed our respondents a list of eight service areas: health/welfare, educational, legal, cultural, recreational, scientific, housing/urban development, and other. We asked them to rank-order them in terms of their organization's priorities. They could tie ranks if they wished. In this chapter we focus only on service areas that received a ranking of one; however, many organiza-

*Table 3.1.* Variable Descriptions and Descriptive Statistics (All Income and Expenditure Data Converted to 1994 Dollars)

| Variable Descriptions | Mean | SD | N |
|---|---|---|---|
| Log of total operating expenditures averaged over 1979 and 1980 | 10.9 | 2.99 | 226 |
| Factor scores from a principal components analysis combining log of commercial income and total employees, 1979–1980 | −.148 | .931 | 227 |
| Factor scores from a principal components analysis combining log of commercial income and total employees, 1983–1984 | −.131 | .965 | 201 |
| Factor scores from a principal components analysis combining log of commercial income and total employees, 1987–1988 | .044 | 1.00 | 174 |
| Factor scores from a principal components analysis combining log of commercial income and total employees, 1991–1992 | .095 | 1.01 | 160 |
| Factor scores from a principal components analysis combining log of commercial income and total employees, 1993–1994 | .239 | 1.07 | 155 |
| Factor scores from a principal components analysis combining log of donated income and volunteers, 1979–1980 | −.435 | .956 | 227 |
| Factor scores from a principal components analysis combining log of donated income and volunteers, 1983–1984 | −.061 | .933 | 200 |
| Factor scores from a principal components analysis combining log of donated income and volunteers, 1987–1988 | .206 | .911 | 173 |
| Factor scores from a principal components analysis combining log of donated income and volunteers, 1991–1992 | .201 | 1.03 | 162 |
| Factor scores from a principal components analysis combining log of donated income and volunteers, 1993–1994 | .276 | 1.00 | 156 |
| Support from government grants and contracts, 1979–1980 (dichotomous) | .427 | .496 | 227 |
| Support from government grants and contracts, 1983–1984 (dichotomous) | .473 | .500 | 201 |
| Support from government grants and contracts, 1987–1988 (dichotomous) | .483 | .501 | 174 |
| Log of organizational age, 1980 | 2.19 | 1.00 | 228 |
| Log of organizational age, 1984 | 2.68 | .716 | 201 |
| Log of organizational age, 1988 | 3.01 | .602 | 174 |
| Health or welfare primary activity, 1980 (dichotomous) | .389 | .489 | 229 |
| Health or welfare primary activity, 1984 (dichotomous) | .348 | .478 | 201 |

*(continued)*

*Table 3.1.* Continued

| Variable Descriptions | Mean | SD | N |
|---|---|---|---|
| Health or welfare primary activity, 1988 (dichotomous) | .414 | .494 | 174 |
| Health or welfare primary activity, 1992 (dichotomous) | .401 | .492 | 162 |
| Education primary activity, 1980 (dichotomous) | .314 | .465 | 229 |
| Education primary activity, 1984 (dichotomous) | .313 | .465 | 201 |
| Education primary activity, 1988 (dichotomous) | .299 | .459 | 174 |
| Education primary activity, 1992 (dichotomous) | .358 | .481 | 162 |
| Recreational or cultural primary activity, 1980 (dichotomous) | .183 | .388 | 229 |
| Recreational or cultural primary activity, 1984 (dichotomous) | .214 | .411 | 201 |
| Recreational or cultural primary activity, 1988 (dichotomous) | .201 | .402 | 174 |
| Recreational or cultural primary activity, 1992 (dichotomous) | .185 | .390 | 162 |
| Other primary activity, 1980 (dichotomous) | .175 | .381 | 229 |
| Other primary activity, 1984 (dichotomous) | .174 | .380 | 201 |
| Other primary activity, 1988 (dichotomous) | .195 | .398 | 174 |
| Other primary activity, 1992 (dichotomous) | .179 | .385 | 162 |
| Herfandahl index score measuring degree of funding and activity diversification based on investments in four funding streams and four activity areas, 1980 | .291 | .233 | 217 |
| Herfandahl index score measuring degree of funding and activity diversification based on investments in four funding streams and four activity areas, 1984 | .309 | .238 | 195 |
| Herfandahl index score measuring degree of funding and activity diversification based on investments in four funding streams and four activity areas, 1988 | .333 | .250 | 171 |
| Number of retrenchment tactics employed between 1980 and 1984 | 1.32 | 1.89 | 201 |
| Number of retrenchment tactics employed between 1984 and 1988 | 1.29 | 1.85 | 174 |
| Number of retrenchment tactics employed between 1988 and 1992 | .776 | 1.37 | 161 |
| Number of retrenchment tactics employed between 1988 and 1994 | 1.35 | 1.83 | 155 |
| Number of political tactics employed between 1980 and 1984 | 2.83 | 2.20 | 201 |
| Number of political tactics employed between 1984 and 1988 | 3.11 | 2.24 | 174 |
| Number of political tactics employed between 1988 and 1992 | 2.80 | 2.22 | 157 |

*(continued)*

*Table 3.1.* Continued

| Variable Descriptions | Mean | SD | N |
|---|---|---|---|
| Number of political tactics employed between 1988 and 1994 | 3.78 | 2.37 | 151 |
| Number of managerial tactics employed between 1980 and 1984 | 5.63 | 3.59 | 201 |
| Number of managerial tactics employed between 1984 and 1988 | 5.64 | 3.68 | 173 |
| Number of managerial tactics employed between 1988 and 1992 | 4.57 | 3.37 | 160 |
| Number of managerial tactics employed between 1988 and 1994 | 6.81 | 3.48 | 154 |
| Log of the degree centrality scores based on position in resource and information exchange networks, 1984 | 1.21 | .942 | 198 |
| Log of the degree centrality scores based on position in resource and information exchange networks, 1988 | 1.12 | .864 | 171 |
| Factor scores from a principal components analysis combining number of community elites supporting the organization (ln), using the services of the organization (ln), and thinking the organization provides essential services and/or has achieved extraordinary accomplishments (ln), 1980 | .000 | 1.00 | 229 |
| Factor scores from a principal components analysis combining number of community elites supporting the organization (ln), using the services of the organization (ln), and thinking the organization provides essential services and/or has achieved extraordinary accomplishments (ln), 1988 | .000 | 1.00 | 174 |
| Decentralization of decision-making index, 1988 | 1.30 | .974 | 172 |
| Niche density score, 1980 | .810 | 1.13 | 216 |
| Niche density score, 1984 | .936 | 2.05 | 195 |
| Niche density score, 1988 | .997 | 1.91 | 171 |
| Niche concentration score, 1980 | .690 | .149 | 216 |
| Niche concentration score, 1984 | .696 | .116 | 195 |
| Niche concentration score, 1988 | .696 | .113 | 171 |
| Log niche legitimacy score, 1980 | 1.75 | .640 | 216 |
| Log niche legitimacy score, 1988 | 1.37 | .641 | 171 |

tions indicated that two and sometimes three areas were "most important." Because there were relatively few organizations in some of the service areas, we collapsed across categories. Cultural and recreational organizations were folded together as were scientific, legal, housing/ urban development, and other. The rationale for the first was that recreational and cultural products are typically in the nature of private goods, which consumers can easily understand and evaluate. The latter were

lumped together because they were mostly collective goods with no immediate consumer or individual beneficiary.[4] The proportions of panel
respondents identifying different activity areas as primary are found in
Table 3.1.

*Specialism/Generalism.* With the data on revenues and activities we
computed a measure of specialism/generalism (or diversification). Our
goal was to measure the extent to which organizations were dependent
upon one or several funding sources and invested in one or several activity areas. We felt that a measure based on the Herfandahl index would be
most appropriate. We used the proportion of funding from the four main
funding sources (commercial, donative, government, and miscellaneous)
for each year. We also used the proportion of organization effort invested
in the four primary activity areas (health/welfare, education, cul-
ture/recreation, other) for each year.[5] More formally,

$$G_i = 1 - \Sigma_{jk}((r_{ij}a_{ik})^2) \tag{1}$$

where $G_i$ was the measure of generalism or diversification for panel organization $i$, $r_{ij}$ was the proportion of total revenues from each of four
sources ($j = 1, 4$) for actor $i$, and $a_{ik}$ was the proportion of total effort
devoted to each of four activities ($k = 1, 4$) by actor $i$. The maximum value
of $G$ is 1 and the minimum approaches zero. The descriptive statistics for
each year are in Table 3.1.[6]

*Tactics.* To measure organizational tactics we compiled a list of 36
possible internal and external tactics and, in 1984 and 1988, asked administrators to check off the tactics that their organization pursued during the
previous four years. In 1994 we asked them to check off the tactics pursued first between 1988 and 1992 and then between 1992 and 1994. Based
on the substantive content of the items, we created three additive indexes
for 1980–1984, 1984–1988, 1988–1992, and 1988–1994.[7] Retrenchment tactics included: reduced service delivery staff, reduced administrative or
support staff, reduced staff training, reduced staff benefits, instituted sal-
ary freezes, reduced work week for paid staff, left unfilled staff vacancies,
reduced service levels to those served, and eliminated specific services
or programs. Political tactics included: approached a new funder type
for money, used the board more for fundraising, tried to make services
look more relevant to the priorities of specific funders, engaged in lobbying efforts on our own, adapted services to priorities of local funders,
sought endorsements from prominent people, sought endowments
from prominent people, gave cash contributions to other nonprofits, gave help (noncash) free of charge to other nonprofits, and contributed (cash or noncash) to community causes. Managerial tactics included: started management program to increase efficiency, increased

staff workload, reorganized executive or administrative staff, engaged in long-range (over 2 years) planning, developed a long-range funding strategy, set up a profit-making venture or subsidiary, became more businesslike, tightened eligibility requirements for services, increased or instituted service fees, made greater efforts to collect fees due, changed the way services were provided, upgraded staff and equipment, assessed community needs, and carried out market studies.[8]

To ensure the reliability of these indexes we computed Cronbach's $\alpha$ for each measure. The $\alpha$s for the retrenchment index for 1980–1984, 1984–1988, 1988–1992, and 1988–1994 were .779, .752, .713, and .762; the $\alpha$s for the political items were .694, .685, .700, and .701; and the $\alpha$s for the managerial items were .823, .836, .809, and 806, respectively. We examined items within each construct to see if we could improve the internal reliability. We subsequently eliminated one item from the political index—"gave cash contributions to other nonprofits"—which increased the $\alpha$s to .707, .703, .704, and .715, respectively. However, the correlations among the retrenchment, political, and managerial constructs were high: .435, 474, and .708 for 1980–1984; .256, .408, and .608 for 1984–1988; .403, .495, and .684 for 1988–1992; and .434, .410, and .704 for 1988–1994. The high correlations between the political and managerial indexes (between .608 and .708) tell us that we need to be aware of possible multicollinearity when they are included in the same models.

We subsequently did an exploratory factor analysis on these 33 items. For the 1980–1984, 1984–1988, 1988–1992, and 1988–1994 items we derived only two factor solutions. Given the high correlations among our indexes, this was not surprising. For 1980–1984, after rotation, all the retrenchment items and one managerial tactic loaded highly on one factor and all the other managerial and political items loaded highly on the second. For the 1984–1988 items, after rotation, all the retrenchment items and two management tactics loaded high on one factor, and all the other managerial and political items loaded high on the second. For 1988–1992, after rotation, all the retrenchment items loaded highly on one factor along with three managerial tactics and two political tactics. All the rest of the managerial and political items loaded highly on the second factor. For 1988–1994, after rotation, all the retrenchment items loaded highly on one factor, and all the managerial and political items loaded highly on the second.[9]

*Network Position.*    We computed two measures of organizations' network position. The first was based on organizations' centrality in a resource and information exchange network. In 1984 and 1988 we asked respondents to check off the panel organizations that they recognized, and then we asked them to indicate to and from which nonprofits they gave and received information about community affairs, information about technical matters, and various resources (e.g., personnel, facilities, etc.). With the responses to this question, we constructed two symmetric arrays, one for 1984 and one for 1988. In these arrays a 1 indicated that respondent $i$ said that it either gave to or received from nonprofit $j$ information on community affairs, technical affairs, or resources. We counted a tie between organization $i$ and $j$ if either noted a flow of resources in either direction. On average, organizations in 1984 and 1988 cited (or were cited by) 4.19 and 3.42 other organizations (SD = 5.19; SD = 4.22); 198 of the 201 panel survivors in 1984 provided us with data; 171 of the 174 organizations in 1988 had data for this item. This variable was skewed to the right (skewness = 1.93; skewness = 2.83)—with 25.8 and 26.3% of the organizations having no ties at all in 1984 and 1988, respectively. We subsequently computed the natural log of actors' degree centrality scores for each year. The descriptive statistics for these items are in Table 3.1 as well.[10]

A second measure of network position was based on local elite's association with and opinions about the panel organizations. We surveyed a sample of 90 prominent citizens in the metropolitan area in 1981 and a new sample of 108 elites in 1989. The selection of the 1981 sample was described in Galaskiewicz (1985a:Appendix B); the procedures followed in 1989 were exactly the same.[11] During the course of both the 1981 and 1989 interviews we handed respondents our lists of panel nonprofits and asked them to indicate which organizations they or their family members had used in the last couple of years. We then asked them to identify the panel organizations to which they donated funds or served as a volunteer, consultant, or board member. For each organization we tallied the number of respondents that said that they (or their families) had used the organization in the past couple of years and the number of respondents who said that they had supported (in any way) the organization in the past couple of years. The distributions of these variables were highly skewed with 72.9 and 63.3% of the panel nonprofits in 1981 and 59.8 and 64.4% in 1989 having no elites consume their services or support their operations with volunteer time or donations. We subsequently computed the natural logs of all four variables.

In the course of the interviews with the elite we also asked about their opinions of the nonprofits in the panel and our cross-sectional survey and used these data as our measures of sociopolitical legitimacy.[12] In 1981 we handed them a list of the 229 not-for-profits that were in our sample. They went through the list and were asked to check off those nonprofits that they recognized. Then of those they recognized, they were asked to circle those they thought were providing essential services to the community; and then of those they recognized, they were asked to underline those they thought had achieved outstanding accomplishments in their respective fields. In 1989 we asked the same questions but proceeded a little differently. Instead of handing them the complete list, we handed them an 80.0% random sample of panel nonprofits that survived the eight-year period. In 1981 and 1989 we computed the percentage of respondents that said that the nonprofit was either essential or had achieved outstanding accomplishments. These scores were highly skewed to the right, and we computed their natural logs.

To arrive at a summary measure of elite-nonprofit linkages for 1981 and 1989, we did a principal components analysis that included the number of elite respondents supporting the organization (ln), the number of elite respondents using the organization personally (ln), and the percentage of respondents saying the organization either provided essential services or had achieved extraordinary accomplishments (ln). The loadings of these three variables were .931, .878, and .896 in 1981 and .916, .914, and .915 in 1989. Factor scores were subsequently assigned to each case. It is important to remember, however, that both sets of factor scores were still highly skewed to the right (skewness equaled 1.99 in 1981 and 1.61 in 1989).[13]

*Decision-Making Structures.* Next we turn to our measures of decision-making power. In our interviews with the top administrative officers in 1988, we asked: "Hypothetically speaking, who would have the final formal authority to make the following decision?"[14] Then we listed six potential decision-makers, $i$ [the board, chief administrative officer, program director(s), professional staff, clients, and volunteers], and cross-tabulated these with seven decisions, $j$ (revise mission statement, enter a new service area, approach new funder for contributions, launch a capital campaign, borrow money, dismiss/replace board members, and dismiss/replace professional staff). Respondents then checked as many "cells" as they felt appropriate. If the organization had no professionals, volunteers, or clients we assigned a missing value to the respective rows of the table. If the organization never considered a decision, the column was left blank.

Our index measures the degree to which decision-making power was concentrated in the hands of a few or dispersed among many actors. For each organization we scanned the decisions that they would consider (on average, respondents considered 4.9 decisions in 1988) and noted how many different actors had "final authority" across the decisions. We then divided this tally by the number of actors who could have decision-making authority (not every organization had clients or volunteers, for example) and multiplied by 100. Thus our measure is the percentage of possible decision-makers who have final authority over organizational decisions. The variable ranges in value from 16% (one out of six possible decision-makers) to 100%. It was positively skewed (.917) with a median of 33.3%.

At this point it may be informative to examine this variable more closely. In Figure 3.2 we present a chart where the horizontal axis is the percentage of possible decision-makers who have final authority over decisions (recoded to match the distribution as closely as possible), and the vertical axis is the percentage of all actors who were involved in the decision who were board members, chief administrative officers, program directors, professional staff, clients, and volunteers. Data were for 1988. Where fewer actors made key decisions, i.e., decision-making is centralized, the *board* dominated. Where more actors made key decisions, i.e., decision-making was decentralized, actors such as the chief administrative officer, program director, and professional staff came to share power with the board.

*Niche Space and Variables.*    The computation of the niche variables was more involved, and we describe our methods in detail in Appendix B. Our goal was to derive measures that would give us an estimate of the amount of crowding in an organization's niche, the degree of resource

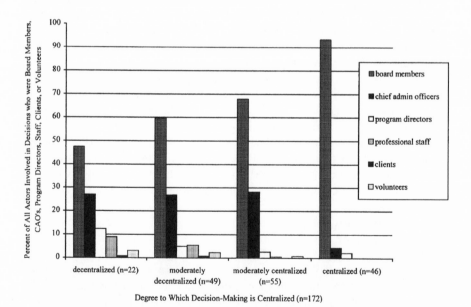

*Figure 3.2.*    Participation of board members, CAOs, program directors, professional staff, clients, and volunteers in decision-making by the degree to which decision-making is centralized within the organization.

concentration, and the legitimacy of organizations in the niche. Once the niche spaces were constructed for 1980, 1984, 1988, and 1992 using the cross-sectional data, we assigned weighted niche density, concentration, and status scores to each nonprofit in our panel for each of these years, which took into account their type of income, size, and services / activities in that year. The scores for niche legitimacy were highly skewed, so we computed their natural logs. The descriptive statistics for these three variables for 1980, 1984, and 1988 are in Table 3.1.[15]

## MODELS OF GROWTH AND DECLINE

The models that we estimated were straightforward and have been used before in studies of organizational growth and decline (e.g., Freeman and Hannan 1975). The model takes the following form:

$$Y_t = \beta_0 + \beta_1 Y_{t-n} + \Sigma_i \beta_i X_{i,t} + \Sigma_j \beta_j W_{j,t-n} + \epsilon_t \qquad (2)$$

where $Y_t$ is a measure of organizational size at time $t$, $Y_{t-n}$ is the same variable measured $n$ years earlier, $X_{i,t}$ are exogenous variables measured between $t - n$ and $t$, and $W_{j,t-n}$ are exogenous variables measured $n$ years earlier as well. Equation 2 is attractive because it gives us a dynamic representation of the growth and decline process.[16] The unstandardized regression coefficient $b_i$ shows the extent to which a unit change in $X_{i,t}$ or $W_{j,t-n}$ results in a change in $Y_t$ net of the initial value of $Y$ measured at $t - n$. We will analyze four time periods: 1980 to 1984, 1984 to 1988, 1988 to 1992, and 1988 to 1994.[17]

One can use ordinary least squares (OLS) to estimate (2) if the normal assumptions are not violated. For example, error terms (or disturbances) must be uncorrelated with regressors; otherwise parameter estimates are biased. This is often a problem when analysts include lagged dependent variables as regressors, because the disturbances associated with $Y_t$ may be correlated with the disturbances associated with $Y_{t-n}$ (Markus 1979:50). If so, then the error terms in (2) will be correlated with the regressor, $Y_{t-n}$. We had hoped that autocorrelation would not be a serious problem, because our observations were spaced several years apart. Markus (ibid.) points out that autocorrelation is more of a problem if observations are over a shorter time period. Furthermore, we suspected that the causal structure explaining $Y$ varied over time, even though our hypotheses were ahistorical.

We checked for autocorrelation using the methods suggested by Breusch (1978) and Godfrey (1978), and modified by Greene (1997:597).[18] We reported these diagnostics in the tables. We considered several options to correct for autocorrelation. Because of the small number of cases in each period, we did not estimate a fixed-effects model. We did estimate instrumental variables using two-stage least squares (2SLS) as suggested by Markus (1979:52) for the periods where we found evidence of autocorrelation.[19] However, we discovered that the regressors in the substantive equation were highly correlated with the instrumental variables. Thus we present both the OLS results with the raw scores for the lagged dependent variable and the 2SLS results with the instrumental variable.

We focus our discussion on the OLS results, but we must be cautious. Since the autocorrelation in our models was negative, we know that the OLS estimates of $\beta_1$ were biased downward and the estimates of the other parameters upward in these equations (ibid.:51). Also the standard errors associated with each coefficient are often too small. This can lead to incorrect inferences and false attributions of statistical significance. Again, though, the seriousness of these problems depended on the extent of autocorrelation in our models, which, as we shall see, was not great.

A second assumption of OLS is that error variances must be constant across observations. This can be a problem where the units of observation differ greatly in size, which is often the case when studying a sample of organizations (Freeman and Hannan 1975; Baum and Mezias 1993). One way to check for heteroskedasticity is to compute the squared values of the disturbances, regress them on the independent variables in the equation, and test to see if $N * R^2$ is statistically significant (White 1980). The product is asymptotically distributed as chi-squared with $P - 1$ degrees of freedom, where $P$ is the number of regressors in the regression, not including the constant (Greene 1997:550). Where heteroskedasticity was a problem, we used the correction outlined by White (1980), which adjusts the covariance matrix and corrects the standard errors. The advantage of this method is that no assumptions need to be made about the form of the heteroskedasticity (Greene 1997:547; Fox 1991:52).

Finally, with a panel design, there is the potential for sample selection bias. Stromsdorfer and Farkas (1980), Berk (1983), Winship and Mare (1992), and Stolzenberg and Relles (1997) discuss the problem, and Heckman (1976, 1979) and Goldberger (1981) provide more technical treatments. In this research we used the Heckman solution despite its shortcomings.[20] In sum, it is necessary to estimate both selection and substantive equations. Equation (2) was our substantive model, and Equation (3) was our selection model:

$$S_t = \beta_0 + \Sigma_j \beta_j V_{j,80} + \mu_t \tag{3}$$

$S_t$ is a binary variable indicating an organization's survival status (e.g., whether or not it survived the 1984 panel) and $V_{j,80}$ is a set of predictor variables measured in 1980 that hopefully are related to $S_t$. If the error terms $e_t$ and $m_t$ in Equations (2) and (3) are correlated, then it is advisable to treat Equation (3) as a probit model, save the predicted values, compute the inverse Mills ratio (the hazard rate), and estimate the following substantive equation:

$$Y_t = \beta_0 + \beta_1 Y_{t-n} + \beta\lambda + \Sigma_i\beta_i X_{i,t} + \Sigma_j\beta_j W_{j,t-n} + \epsilon_t \qquad (4)$$

where $Y_t$, $Y_{t-n}$, $X_{i,t}$, and $W_{j,t-n}$ are defined as before and $\lambda$ is the inverse Mills ratio or "hazard rate" variable.

The results for the selection model are easy to summarize. Fortunately, there is an extensive literature on organizational closure that we can draw on. For extended discussions of survival and death among organizations in this panel, see Bielefeld (1994) and Hager, Galaskiewicz, Bielefeld, and Pins (1996). To summarize briefly, we hypothesized that the likelihood of nonprofit survival in our panel was directly related to organizational size (natural log of 1980 operating expenditures) and age (natural log of organizational age in 1980) (Stinchcombe 1965). We did four probit analyses, where organizations were coded 1 if they survived until 1984, 1988, 1992, and 1994, respectively, and 0 otherwise.[21]

The four probit models did reasonably well. The $\chi^2$ statistics were 13.5 ($p = .001$), 19.8 ($p = .000$), 24.4 ($p = .000$), and 24.8 ($p = .000$). As attrition increased, the percentage of correct predictions decreased, as expected. In the four periods, we were able to predict the fate of 88.0, 77.8, 74.7, and 72.9% of the cases. The analyses showed that between 1980 and 1984, organizations that had more expenditures in 1980 ($p < .001$) were more likely to survive, but age had no effect on survival. Between 1980 and 1988, 1980 and 1992, and 1980 and 1994, organizations that had more expenditures in 1980 or were older in 1980 were more likely to survive. All of the latter effects were significant at the .05-level or lower. In this and the following chapters we estimated sample selection models that included both log of expenditures (1980) and log of age (1980).[22]

## TESTING FOR NICHE AND TACTICS EFFECTS: HYPOTHESES 1 THROUGH 8

Let us now summarize Hypotheses 1 through 8. We expected that increases and decreases in revenues and labor would be a function of niche conditions (Hypotheses 1, 2, 3, and 4), the use of managerial and political tactics (Hypotheses 5, 6, and 7), and the use of retrenchment tactics (Hypothesis 8). Two sets of equations will be estimated: one with commercial income and employees as the dependent variable, and one with donated income and volunteers as the dependent variable. For each we will estimate four equations: growth and decline between 1980 and 1984, 1984 and 1988, 1988 and 1992, and 1988 and 1994. The general model for hypotheses 1 through 8 is:

$$Y_t = \beta_0 + \beta_1 Y_{t-n} + \Sigma_i \beta_i X_{i,t} + \Sigma_j \beta_j W_{j,t-n} + \Sigma_k \beta_k Z_{k,t-n} + \beta\lambda + \epsilon_t \ (5)$$

where $Y$ refers to the size of the organization (commercial income and employees, donated income and volunteers); $X_i$ were the tactics variables (managerial, political, retrenchment) measured between $t - n$ and $t$; $W_j$ were the niche variables (density, concentration, legitimacy) measured at $t - n$; $Z_k$ were the control variables (activities, public funding) measured at $t - n$;[23] and $\lambda$ was the sample selection term. We first estimated these models using OLS and then corrected for heteroskedasticity where necessary using the methods suggested by White (1980). If the test statistic for heteroskedasticity was significant at the .10-level, this was noted in the tables and the corrected results were presented. We then tested for autocorrelation where we could. If this was problem, we reestimated the equation using 2SLS. Both OLS and 2SLS results are presented in Table 3.2. Autocorrelation was not a problem in Table 3.3. To avoid models with collinear terms we first estimated all models with density and its square included—to measure the ecologists' density dependence effect—and then dropped the squared term if it was not significant and reestimated the equation. In only one case was the squared term significant at the .10-level (predicting change in commercial income and employees between 1988 and 1994). For those models where the density squared was not significant, we included only the density variable in the equation.[24]

Multicollinearity was a problem in three of the eight models. The low tolerance scores of the niche concentration ($T = .327$ in column 1 of Table 3.2 and $T = .324$ in column 1 in Table 3.3) and niche legitimation variables ($T = .348$ in column 1 of Table 3.2 and $T = .351$ in column 1 in Table 3.3) for the period from 1980 to 1984 were due to the strong correlations between these variables ($r = .539$) and with niche density in 1980. In columns 4a and 4b in Table 3.2, multicollinearity was due to the inclusion of both niche density and its square. Multicollinearity in models that include squared terms is not an uncommon problem. In the two models where heteroskedasticity was a problem (see columns 2 and 4 in Table 3.3), we applied the White correction and presented the corrected results. Autocorrelation was a problem in three models (see columns 2a, 3a, and 4a in Table 3.2), being prevalent in the analyses of commercial income and employees. In all three cases there was negative autocorrelation. The reader is warned to interpret OLS coefficients cautiously in these models, since the coefficients associated with lagged variables are biased downwards while the rest of the coefficients are biased upwards. We also present 2SLS results for these models, but warn that the tolerance scores associated

*Table 3.2.* OLS and 2SLS with Commercial Income and Employees as Dependent Variable, Unstandardized Regression Coefficients and Standard Errors in Parentheses

| | Dependent Variable: Commercial Income & Employees$_t$ | | | | | | |
|---|---|---|---|---|---|---|---|
| Independent Variables | (1) 1980–1984 OLS$^a$ b (SE) | (2a) 1984–1988 OLS$^a$ b (SE) | (2b) 2SLS$^a$ b (SE) | (3a) 1988–1992 OLS$^a$ b (SE) | (3b) 2SLS$^a$ b (SE) | (4a) 1988–1994 OLS$^b$ b (SE) | (4b) 2SLS$^b$ b (SE) |
| Commercial Inc & Empl$_{t-n}$ | .684(.053)*** | .712(.049)*** | .956(.075)*** | .744(.054)*** | .947(.072)*** | .780(.051)*** | .983(.068)*** |
| Donated Inc & Vols$_{t-n}$ | -.008(.045) | .027(.042) | .046(.047) | .087(.054) | .074(.057) | .072(.050) | .062(.054) |
| Gov't Grants & Contracts$_{t-n}$ | .397(.093)*** | .201(.089)* | .066(.099) | .182(.097)# | .071(.106) | .327(.091)*** | .219(.098)* |
| Niche Density$_{t-n}$ | -.085(.038)* | -.002(.017) | .006(.019) | .016(.024) | .001(.025) | .072(.041)# | .092(.043)* |
| Niche Density$_{t-n}$ $^2$ | | | | | | -.018(.011)# | -.028(.012)* |
| Niche Concentration$_{t-n}$ | .756(.428)# | .766(.379)* | .286(.437) | -.359(.469) | -.650(.495) | -.360(.442) | -.469(.465) |
| Niche Legitimacy$_{t-n}$ | .113(.092) | | | -.243(.082)** | .197(.087)* | .190(.079)* | .143(.084)# |
| Generalist vs. Specialist$_{t-n}$ | -.339(.182)# | -.470(.167)*** | -.612(.185)*** | -.227(.191) | -.263(.201) | -.652(.188)*** | -.793(.201)*** |
| No. of Managerial Tactics$_t$ | .030(.012)* | .049(.012)*** | .036(.014)* | -.020(.015) | .006(.016) | .038(.013)** | .026(.014)# |
| No. of Retrench Tactics$_t$ | -.048(.023)* | .006(.019) | .002(.021) | -.022(.031) | -.038(.033) | -.015(.022) | -.023(.023) |
| Health/Welfare$_{t-n}$ | .087(.096) | .052(.098) | .052(.107) | .039(.098) | .014(.103) | .003(.096) | .011(.101) |
| Education$_{t-n}$ | .037(.105) | .197(.091)* | .225(.099)* | -.044(.102) | -.081(.107) | -.031(.098) | -.044(.103) |
| Culture/Recreation$_{t-n}$ | .109(.113) | -.069(.104) | -.057(.115) | -.044(.119) | -.005(.125) | -.139(.111) | -.097(.118) |
| λ | -.189(.451) | .112(.245)*** | .549(.334) | .041(.238) | .265(.253) | -.231(.218) | .013(.227) |
| Constant | -.956(.242)** | -.774(.277)** | -.401(.324) | -.187(.333) | .149(.356) | .373(.310) | .346(.335) |
| R$^2$ | .741*** | .823*** | .791*** | .796*** | .764*** | .853*** | .829*** |
| Adj. R$^2$ | .723 | .810 | .775 | .777 | .743 | .838 | .812 |
| N | 196 | 172 | 167 | 159 | 158 | 151 | 151 |
| White test statistic for heteroskedasticity | 12.1 (df=13) | 16.7 (df=12) | — | 7.03 (df=13) | — | 10.2 (df=14) | — |
| Modified Breusch-Godfrey test statistic for autocorrelation | — | 3.57*** | — | 2.26** | — | 1.81* | — |

*** $p < .001$; ** $p < .01$; * $p < .05$; # $p < .10$.
$^a$ Regressors were lagged four years ($n = 4$).    $^b$ Regressors were lagged six years ($n = 6$).

Table 3.3. OLS with Donated Income and Volunteers as Dependent Variable, Unstandardized Regression Coefficients and Standard Errors in Parentheses

| | Dependent Variables: Donated Income & Employees $_t$ | | | |
|---|---|---|---|---|
| Independent Variables | (1) 1980–1984[a] b (SE) | (2) 1984–1988[a,b] b (SE) | (3) 1988–1992[a] b (SE) | (4) 1988–1994[b,c] b (SE) |
| Commercial Inc & Empl $_{t-n}$ | .037(.064) | .017(.051) | −.034(.062) | .035(.057) |
| Donated Inc & Vols $_{t-n}$ | .630(.055)*** | .683(.055)*** | .865(.062)*** | .830(.069)*** |
| Gov't Grants & Contracts $_{t-n}$ | .084(.111) | .062(.122) | .059(.111) | .035(.121) |
| Niche Density $_{t-n}$ | −.016(.045) | −.018(.021) | −.046(.027)# | −.037(.024) |
| Niche Concentration $_{t-n}$ | .557(.513) | −.260(.462) | .496(.544) | −.034(.470) |
| Niche Legitimacy $_{t-n}$ | .017(.110) | | −.129(.095) | −.040(.089) |
| Generalist vs. Specialist $_{t-n}$ | −.020(.217) | −.130(.197) | −.074(.220) | −.099(.237) |
| No. of Managerial Tactics $_t$ | .034(.018)# | .041(.017)* | .046(.019)* | .003(.021) |
| No. of Political Tactics $_t$ | .058(.029)* | .026(.021) | .036(.027) | .077(.028)** |
| No. of Retrench Tactics $_t$ | −.032(.028) | −.038(.017)* | −.031(.036) | −.009(.025) |
| Health/Welfare $_{t-n}$ | .030(.114) | −.016(.130) | −.196(.113)# | −.215(.122)# |
| Education $_{t-n}$ | .008(.128) | −.069(.111) | −.395(.118)*** | −.343(.138)* |
| Culture/Recreation $_{t-n}$ | −.006(.137) | .064(.110) | −.094(.138) | −.063(.125) |
| λ | −.479(.542) | −.418(.341) | −.273(.283) | −.039(.233) |
| Constant | −.520(.292)# | .287(.342) | −.121(.387) | .085(.353) |
| $R^2$ | .608*** | .701*** | .730*** | .733*** |
| Adj. $R^2$ | .577 | .677 | .705 | .707 |
| N | 195 | 172 | 161 | 155 |
| White test statistic for heteroskedasticity | 20.7 (df=14) | 19.9 (df=13)# | 19.0 (df=14) | 21.2 (df=14)# |
| Modified Breusch-Godfrey test statistic for autocorrelation | — | .491 | .121. | 088 |

*** $p < .001$; ** $p < .01$; * $p < .05$; # $p < .10$.

[a] Regressors were lagged four years (n = 4).

[b] Standard errors corrected for heteroskedasticity using White (1980).

[c] Regressors were lagged six years (n = 6).

with the instrumental variables were .272, 367, and .335 in models 2b, 3b, and 4b in Table 3.2.

*Size Effects.* Looking first at the size effects across the two tables, we see that in each analysis size at a previous time was a key predictor of size at a later time ($p < .001$). More interestingly, commercial income and employees at $t - 4$ and $t - 6$ had little effect on the growth in donated income and volunteers; and private donations and volunteers at $t - 4$ and $t - 6$ had little effect on the growth in commercial income and employees. In separate analyses we added a change score variable, $U_t - U_{t-n}$, to the OLS models in Tables 3.2 and 3.3, where $U$ was donated income and volunteers for the models in Table 3.2 and commercial income and employees for the models in Table 3.3 and $n$ equaled 4 or 6. In none of the eight equations we estimated were the change score variables significant at the .20-level. Thus it appears that these two resource streams grew and shrank independent of one another as well.

*Niche Effects.* As noted earlier, we first tested to see if there was a nonmonotonic relationship between niche density and growth/decline. Only once did we find a significant effect. In explaining change in commercial income and employees between 1988 and 1994, density had a positive effect ($p < .10$ in OLS and $p < .05$ in 2SLS) and its square a negative effect ($p < .10$ in OLS and $p < .05$ in 2SLS). Niche density had a significant stand-alone effect on growth and decline twice. Organizations in more dense niches in 1980 lost commercial income and employees between 1980 and 1984 ($p < .05$), and organizations in more dense niches in 1988 lost donated income and volunteers between 1988 and 1992 ($p < .10$).

Organizations in more concentrated niches in 1980 increased their commercial income and employees between 1980 and 1984 ($p < .10$), and organizations in more concentrated niches in 1984 increased their commercial income and employees between 1984 and 1988 ($p < .05$ in OLS and NS in 2SLS). Organizations in more legitimate niches in 1988 increased their commercial income/employees between 1988 and 1992 ($p < .01$ in OLS and $p < .05$ in 2SLS), and organizations in more legitimate niches in 1988 increased their commercial income and employees between 1988 and 1994 ($p < .05$ in OLS and $p < .10$ in 2SLS).[25] Neither niche concentration nor legitimacy had a statistically significant effect on changes in donated income and volunteers in any period.

These results, however, must be qualified, because of the high correlation between niche concentration and legitimacy in 1980. When we remove legitimacy from the equations explaining change between 1980 and 1984, the effect of concentration got stronger in the model predicting change in commercial income and employees ($b = 1.10$; $p = .001$) but was still not significant in predicting change in donated income and volunteers. When we remove concentration from the same models, the effect of legitimacy got stronger in the model predicting change in commercial income and employees ($b = .219; p = .002$), but it again had no significant effect on changes in donations and volunteers.[26]

We also see that specialist organizations increased their commercial income and employees over time, while generalists lost commercial income and employees. This effect was significant at the .10-level in explaining change between 1980 and 1984, the .01-level (OLS) and .001-level (2SLS) between 1984 and 1988, and the .001-level (both OLS and 2SLS) between 1988 and 1994. This variable had little effect on changes in commercial and employees between 1988 and 1992 or on changes in donated income and volunteers in any of the periods.

*Tactics.* With two exceptions, managerial tactics had a positive effect on growth in commercial income/employees and growth in donated income/volunteers. Organizations that utilized more managerial tactics increased their commercial income and employees between 1980 and 1984 ($p < .05$), 1984 and 1988 ($p < .001$ OLS; $p < .05$ 2SLS), and between 1988 and 1994 ($p < .01$ OLS; $p < .10$ 2SLS); and they increased their donated income and volunteers between 1980 and 1984 ($p < .10$), 1984 and 1988 ($p < .05$), and between 1988 and 1992 ($p < .05$). The effects of managerial tactics on growth in commercial income and employees between 1988 and 1992 and on growth in donated income and volunteers between 1988 and 1994 were not statistically significant.

Political tactics led to increases in donated income and volunteers between 1980 and 1984 ($p < .05$) and between 1988 and 1994 ($p < .01$), but their effects on changes in donations and volunteers between 1984 and 1988 and between 1988 and 1992 were not statistically significant at the .10-level. However, multicollinearity was again a concern. Throughout the years, political and managerial tactics were correlated between .608 and .708. When we eliminate political tactics from the model predicting changes in donated income and volunteers between 1988 and 1994, the effect of managerial tactics was much stronger ($b = .032; p = .052$). When we remove managerial tactics from all four models predicting change in donated income and volunteers, the effect of political tactics increased significantly: $b = .090$ ($p = .000$) in 1984; $b = .047$ ($p = .016$) in 1988; $b = .067$ ($p = .006$) in 1992; and $b = .079$ ($p = .000$) in 1994.

Finally, retrenchment tactics resulted in organizations losing commercial income and employees between 1980 and 1984 ($p < .05$), but they had no statistically significant effect on changes in commercial income and employees between 1984 and 1988, 1988 and 1992, or 1988 and 1994. Retrenchment tactics led to a decrease in donated income and volunteers between 1984 and 1988 ($p < .05$), but they had no statistically significant effect on changes in donated income and volunteers in the other periods.

*Control Variables.* We see that health and welfare organizations lost donated income and volunteers between 1988 and 1992 ($p < .10$) and between 1988 and 1994 ($p < .10$). Educational organizations also lost donated income and volunteers between 1988 and 1992 ($p < .001$) and between 1988 and 1994 ($p < .05$). However, educational organizations also experienced an increase in commercial income and employees between 1984 and 1988 ($p < .05$ in both OLS and 2SLS). Cultural and recreational organizations experienced no significant change in commercial income / employees or donated income / volunteers in any of the periods. In contrast, organizations that had government funds at $t - n$ increased their commercial income and employees between $t - n$ and $t$. This effect was significant at the .001-level in 1984, the .05-level in 1988 (NS in 2SLS), the .10-level in 1992 (NS in 2SLS), and the .001-level in 1994 ($p < .05$ in 2SLS). Organizations that had government funding at $t - n$ did not increase their donated income or volunteers significantly in any period.

## TESTING FOR EMBEDDEDNESS EFFECTS: HYPOTHESES 9–13

The last set of analyses tested the embeddedness hypotheses. All involved testing for significant interaction effects. To review briefly, Hypotheses 9 and 10 suggested that managerial tactics and political tactics would be implemented more successfully in smaller and older organizations. Hypothesis 11 stated that tactics would be implemented more successfully in more centralized organizations. Hypothesis 12 argued that political tactics would be implemented more successfully by organizations that had more interorganizational relations, and Hypothesis 13 argued that political tactics would be implemented more successfully by organizations that had more direct ties to and better reputations among local community elites. All of these hypotheses argued that the return on an organization's investment in different tactics would be contingent upon its formal and informal structural circumstances. To test these models we improvised on Equation (5), adding an interaction term to equations, which included statistically significant effects (at the .10-level) as identified in Tables 3.2 and 3.3. All variables were centered before we computed the product terms, and this ensured that multicollinearity was minimal in the models we tested. We tested for heteroskedasticity using the same methods as before. Where heteroskedasticity was a problem we again applied the White (1980) correction. We also did a preliminary analysis in which we included a dummy for the five cases where we substituted the mean for missing data on the political variables for 1988–1992. Again, in none of the analyses was the dummy significant at the .10-level, and the tolerance scores for the dummy were all above .950.

The OLS results are simple to summarize without a table. There were ten interactions that we tested where commercial income and employees was the dependent variable, managerial tactics (at $t$) was the independent variable, and age (ln), commercial income and employees at $t - n$ (our size measure), and decision-making structure (measured for 1998 only) were the moderating variables. We found only one significant interaction effect. The age $\times$ managerial tactics product term was significant in predicting growth in commercial income and employees between 1980 and 1984. The coefficient was positive ($b = .019$) and significant at the .10-level ($p = .082$). Interpreting the simple slope results, we conclude that among middle-aged and older organizations, the use of managerial tactics between 1980 and 1984 resulted in greater growth, while among younger organizations the effect of managerial tactics on growth in commercial income and employees between 1980 and 1984 was much weaker. Although this supports our hypotheses, none of the other nine interaction terms were statistically significant at the .10-level.

There were also ten interactions that we tested where donated income and volunteers was the dependent variable, political tactics (at $t$) was the independent variable, and age (ln), donated income and volunteers at $t - n$ (our size measure), and decision-making structure (measured for 1998 only) were the moderating variables. We found only two significant interaction effects. The size $\times$ political tactics product term was significant in the model predicting growth in donated income and volunteers between 1988 and 1992 and between 1988 and 1994. The coefficients were negative ($b = -.047$; $b = -.041$) and significant at the .05- and .01-levels, respectively. We also found that the coefficients associated with political tactics were statistically significant ($p < .05$ for 1988–1992 and $p < .001$ for 1988–1994). Thus, in both periods, among medium-size and smaller organizations, the use of political tactics resulted in greater growth, while among larger organizations the effect of political tactics on growth was significantly less. While these two results supported our hypotheses, we should remember that eight other tests produced no significant interaction effects.

Hypotheses 12 and 13 argued that the relationship between the use of political tactics and donated income/volunteer would be greater, the more network ties an organization had. Our network variables included the log of the degree centrality scores for the resource and information exchange network and a construct measuring the extent to which organizations served, were supported by, and were thought well of by a sample of community elites.[27] The results are again easy to summarize. After centering our variables, computing the product terms, and correcting for heteroskedasticity, we discovered that one of the eight interactions was significant at the .10-level. The product term where we multiplied the number of political tactics used between 1988 and 1994 by the elite contact and reputation scores for 1988 and predicted growth in donated income and volunteers between 1988 and 1994 was negative ($b = -.031$) and significant ($p = .022$). To gain some insight into this unexpected result, we computed the simple slopes of the elite contact and reputation measure setting the number of political tactics one standard deviation above and below its mean. The results were informative but not as we expected. In the case where firms utilized many political tactics, the effect of elite contacts and reputation on growth in donated income and volunteers was minimal ($b = -.009; p = .801$); however, where organizations utilized fewer political tactics, the effect of elite contacts and reputation on growth was positive and significant at the .05-level ($b = .122; p = .049$).

Finally we examined more closely the effects of our network variables on growth and decline in donated income and volunteers. In several preliminary analyses we observed that the network variables had an independent effect on the growth in donated income and volunteers. We summarize these OLS results in Table 3.4. Again, we included variables that were significant in Table 3.3 and made the appropriate corrections for heteroskedasticity, which was a continuing problem throughout this analysis. Although not significant at the .10-level, organizations more central in interorganizational networks in 1984 increased their donated income and volunteers between 1980 and 1984 ($p = .133$). Between 1984 and 1988 organizational centrality had a statistically significant independent effect on growth in donated income and volunteers ($p < .10$). Furthermore, organizations with more elite contacts and a better reputation among the elite in 1980 increased their donated income between 1980 and 1984 ($p < .10$) and between 1984 and 1988 ($p < .05$). Elite network contacts and reputation had no independent effect on growth or decline in donated income and volunteers between 1988 and 1992 or between 1988 and 1994.

## DISCUSSION

How well did our theories do in explaining the growth and decline of nonprofits? Well, it depends upon the theory. Some did better than others. The good news for ecological theory was that niche conditions were often

Table 3.4. OLS with Donated Income and Volunteers as Dependent Variable, Unstandardized Regression Coefficients and Standard Errors in Parentheses

| Independent Variables | Dependent Variables: Donated Income & Volunteers $_t$ | | | | | | | |
|---|---|---|---|---|---|---|---|---|
| | (1) 1980–1984[a,b] | (2) | (3) 1984–1988[a,b] | (4) | (5) 1988–1992[a,b] | (6) | (7) 1988–1994[b,c] | (8) |
| | b(SE) | b(SE) | b(SE) | b(SE) | b(SE) | b(SE) | b(SE) | b(SE) |
| Donated Inc & Vols$_{t-n}$ | .630(.052)*** | .601(.055)*** | .661(.056)*** | .650(.058)*** | .838(.075)*** | .860(.069)*** | .817(.076)*** | .838(.064)*** |
| No. of Managerial Tactics$_t$ | .032(.017)# | .040(.017)* | .045(.014)** | .052(.013)*** | .042(.015)** | .047(.016)** | | |
| No. of Political Tactics$_t$ | .033(.029) | .044(.027)# | −.039(.017)* | −.032(.016)* | | | .073(.021)*** | .076(.021)*** |
| No. of Retrench Tactics$_t$ | | | | | | | | |
| Niche Density$_{t-n}$ | | | | | −.033(.023) | −.033(.023) | | |
| Interorganizational Network Centrality$_{t-n}$[d] | .091(.061) | | .089(.051)# | | .043(.069) | | .052(.069) | |
| Elite Network Contacts and Reputation$_{t-n}$[e] | | .077(.039)# | | .086(.040)* | | −.011(.039) | | .012(.040) |
| Health/Welfare$_{t-n}$ | | | | | −.189(.104)# | −.193(.097)* | −.217(.104)* | −.210(.097)* |
| Education$_{t-n}$ | | | | | −.356(.112)** | −.375(.100)*** | −.321(.125)** | −.335(.119)*** |
| λ | −.651(.348)# | −.523(.315)# | −.413(.327) | −.335(.312) | −.139(.251) | −.150(.247) | .005(.218) | .012(.220) |
| Constant | .283(.077)*** | .244(.073)*** | .380(.122)** | .335(.116)** | .237(.144)# | .243(.145)# | .217(.141) | .211(.143) |
| R² | .603*** | .605*** | .689*** | .691*** | .711*** | .721*** | .719*** | .730*** |
| Adj. R² | .593 | .594 | .680 | .682 | .697 | .708 | .707 | .719 |
| N | 197 | 200 | 172 | 173 | 158 | 161 | 153 | 156 |
| White test statistic for heteroskedasticity | 11.9 (df=5)* | 11.8 (df=5) | 13.5 (df=5) | 16.1 (df=5)** | 14.5 (df=7)* | 13.2 (df=7)# | 10.8 (df=6)# | 11.9 (df=6)# |

*** $p < .001$; ** $p < .01$; * $p < .05$; # $p < .10$.

a Regressors were lagged four years ($n = 4$).

b Standard errors corrected for heteroskedasticity using White (1980).

c Regressors were lagged six years ($n = 6$).

d For 1980–1984 and 1984–1988, used Interorganizational Centrality, 1984; for 1988–1992 and 1988–1994, used Interorganizational Centrality, 1988.

e For 1980–1984 and 1984–1988, used Elite Network Contacts and Reputation, 1980; for 1988–1992 and 1988–1994, used Elite Network Contacts and Reputation, 1988.

(although not always) important in explaining growth and decline in commercial income and employees, independent of the tactics used by organizations, their size, and their activities; the bad news was that they had almost no effect on changes in donated income and volunteers.

The effects of density on growth and decline were evident in only three of the eight OLS models.[28] Density had negative effects on growth in earned income and employees between 1980 and 1984 and growth in donated income and volunteers between 1988 and 1992. This latter effect, however, disappeared once we controlled for the network variables (see Table 3.4). Density had a nonmonotonic effect on changes in earned income and employees between 1988 and 1994 in the shape of an inverted U, but this was the only evidence of density dependence in the eight models. The weak showing of density was disappointing especially since we spent considerable effort operationalizing niche density and found a number of intuitively reasonable patterns when describing the niche space of our organizations and how the space changed over time (see Appendix B).

Concentration and legitimacy performed much better in the OLS models. Organizations in niches that were marked by high levels of resource concentration increased their commercial income and employees between 1980 and 1984 and between 1984 and 1988, however, concentration had little effect on changes between 1988 and 1992 or between 1988 and 1994. Organizations in niches occupied by highly legitimate actors were likely to increase their commercial income and employees between 1988 and 1992 and between 1988 and 1994 (we did not measure legitimacy in 1984 and thus its effect on growth between 1984 and 1988). Furthermore, specialists increased their commercial revenue and employees between 1980 and 1984, 1984 and 1988, and 1988 and 1994. However, none of these variables had a significant effect on changes in donated income and volunteers.

That niche variables could explain changes in commercial income and employees but not donated income and volunteers suggests that while the underlying dynamics in market economies is competition, this may not be the case in grants economies. The number of competitors, the degree to which resources were concentrated or dispersed, or even the legitimacy of actors in the niche had little effect on who gained or lost donated income and volunteers. Frankly, this surprised us given that ecologists have found strong density dependency effects in samples of nonprofits. Perhaps the nonprofits they studied were primarily dependent upon commercial income/employees instead of donated income/volunteers. Nonetheless, our findings suggest that when studying grants economics, reserachers might think twice before assuming that competition is a key element in allocating resources.

The news for adaptation theory was very good. With two notable exceptions (growth in earned income and employees between 1988 and 1992 and growth in donated income and volunteers between 1988 and 1994), efforts to make oneself more efficient, rational, and to reach out to customers paid off with an increase in commercial income and employees and donated income and volunteers. These effects were independent of niche conditions and organizational size and activities. In contrast, organizations that chose not to employ these tactics lost revenues and personnel.

The reasons why managerial tactics resulted in growth in earned income and employees seem clear enough, but why did managerial tactics affect growth in donated income/volunteers? Earlier we said that this was due to coercive isomorphism, i.e., donors and volunteers required donees to make themselves look more businesslike before making grants or donating their labor to the organization. However, it is possible that rationalizing operations helps an organization to solicit, follow up, pursue, and nail down contributions and volunteers more effectively. That is, becoming more businesslike may make an organization better able to achieve its goals—whatever those goals may be. This alternative explanation of the effects we found is as valid as that offered by institutional theory and is worthy of further investigation. Thus, while our analysis shows that the use of managerial tactics positively affected donations and volunteers, we still are not sure why.

While managerial tactics nudged out political tactics in head to head competition, it is probably safe to argue that the use of political tactics—in all periods—also led to an increase in donated revenues and volunteers. Political tactics had a direct effect on growth between 1980 and 1984 and between 1988 and 1994; for medium-size and smaller organizations, political tactics had a positive effect on growth between 1988 and 1992; and in all four periods political tactics were collinear with managerial tactics and had a significant impact on growth once managerial tactics were removed from the equation.

The only bad news for adaptation theory had to do with retrenchment. Retrenchment tactics only explained changes in commercial income and employees between 1980 and 1984 and donated income and volunteers between 1984 and 1988. We had expected that organizations that cut programs, pay, and staff would have fewer revenues, employees, and volunteers over time. This happened to a certain extent, but not as much as we had expected. Clearly, retrenchment did not seem to be another kind of signal to stakeholders that the organization was responsible. If it was, then retrenchment tactics would have been positively related to growth—which, of course, they were not. Still, that cutting staff and programs did not trigger a downward spiral raises an interesting prospect: that a certain amount of retrenchment is simply business as usual among many nonprofits and does not precede decline.

Finally, we had mostly bad news for structural embeddedness theory. Except for a few exceptional cases, the efficacy of managerial and political tactics was unaffected by the size or age of the organization, its decision-making structure, network ties to other organizations, or network ties to and reputations among local elites. We thought that formal and informal structural conditions would modify the effect of tactics on growth and decline. We were especially surprised by the fact that extensive network ties to other organizations or to local elites did not result in greater returns on organizations' political tactics. Thus we had to conclude that larger as well as smaller, older as well as younger, participatory as well as autocratic, and "networked" as well as isolated organizations were able to implement political and managerial tactics just as well or poorly.

The only good news for embeddedness theory was that in some periods ties to other organizations and local elites had a direct effect on growth and decline. Having ties to and a good reputation among elites had a direct, independent effect on growth in donations and volunteers between 1980 and 1984 and between 1984 and 1988. Elite contact also resulted in growth in donations and volunteers between 1988 and 1994, if organizations used fewer political tactics. However, elite contacts had little effect on growth between 1988 and 1992. That network contacts to and reputation among elites had such an important direct effect on donations and volunteers prompted us to see if it had a similar effect on growth in commercial income and employees. After selecting the regressors in our four OLS models that predicted growth in commercial income and employees between $t - n$ and $t$ (see Table 3.2), we added our elite contact/reputation score and reestimated our models using OLS. In none of the four periods was the latter statistically significant at the .10-level. Thus this social capital variable only seemed to be important for procuring donations and volunteers. Finally, interorganization network centrality had a statistically significant effect on donations and volunteers between 1984 and 1988, but not during the other periods.

What is our explanation of these network and reputational effects? One could argue that organizations in the center of networks can shape the environment so as to make themselves more legitimate. Through their networks they can broadcast to the community who they are. Network ties, especially with elites, can also be a kind of market signal that the organization is trustworthy, credible, and of good character—and thus worthy of donations and volunteers. In that case, our network effect should be interpreted as a sociopolitical legitimacy effect. Indeed our measure is reminiscent of Baum and Oliver's (1996) relational density measure and Singh et al.'s (1991) indicators of organizations' sociopolitical legitimacy. Alternatively, donors may like the fact that nonprofits are collaborating with one another (Bigelow et al. 1996) or serving elite populations. Clearly these arguments are developed from an adaptation perspective, and each is worthy of further investigation.

Yet the selection perspective may also help us to understand these findings. Just as organizations are situated in a resource niche that affects their growth and decline, organizations may also be situated in a *social* niche that exercises an equally powerful selection effect. Certain organizations receive donations and volunteers simply because they are in the center of networks. They do not have to do anything in particular and the donations and help just keep coming in. Indeed, we used fund transfers, sharing personnel and facilities, as well as information exchange to operationalize linkages among organizations and between our sample and the elite. Thus those who have relationships to funding sources and free labor get more donations and free labor over time. Resource inputs are routinized, habitual, and built on the ongoing relationships that the organization has with others in its environment. Those who have, get; those who have not, get not.

In this chapter we attempted to test our model of organizational growth and decline as outlined in Figure 1.1. Some hypotheses were supported, others were not. In the next chapter we use our model to explain why organizations increased or cut back on their use of managerial, political, and retrenchment tactics. Again we will draw on extant theory and test causal hypotheses using Figure 1.1 to guide our inquiry.

## NOTES

1.  Niche position can also be defined in terms of labor inputs (employees vs. volunteers), characteristics of clients (Baum and Oliver 1996), geography (Baum and Oliver 1996), or characteristics of members (McPherson 1983).

2.  Clients/patients/students could be viewed as resources as well, the raw material, if you will. However, organizations count the number of people served in different ways (e.g., some use duplicated counts while other use unduplicated counts), and some have no way of (or interest in) counting the number of people served (e.g., collective-goods-producing or public education organizations). Also it is not clear that clients/patients/students are comparable. Is a college student who attends class three days a week for nine months equivalent to a patient who stays overnight for some tests? Thus we decided not to use people served as an indicator of size.

3.  The reason for pooling across the years before doing the principal components was to ensure that we had a comparable metric across the different time periods. Since factor scores are standardized they are based on a standard deviation. If separate constructs were estimated for each year, the scores across years would not be comparable. Since we are trying to explain change over time, it is

important that size measures are scaled similarly. For a further discussion of these issues see Kim and Ferree (1981).

4.   Among legal organizations were legal aid organizations, which did have immediate beneficiaries; however, this category also included social justice organizations and some community crime watch programs, which produced more collectivelike goods and services.

5.   Our proportions were based only on the number of activities cited by the organization as "primary." Thus if the organization said that only education was most important, 100% of its effort was devoted to education and 0% was allocated to the other three areas. If it said education and culture/recreation, then 50% of its effort was devoted to education, 50% to culture/recreation, and 0% to the other two areas. Unfortunately, we did not have the amounts budgeted for each activity area.

6.   There were considerable missing data for this item: 12, 6, and 3 cases in 1980, 1984, and 1988, respectively. To check if missing data were random, we correlated dummies for missing data for each year with log expenditures, log age, and activities (health/welfare, culture/recreational, education, and other). We discovered that in each year, smaller organizations were more likely to have missing data (−.426, −.330, and −.382 respectively), and in 1980 organizations that were health/welfare organizations were more likely to provide us with data (−.173). Otherwise the correlations were typically between −.10 and .10. Although 12 may seem like a large number of cases to lose in 1980, 7 of these cases did not survive to 1984 and thus only 5 cases were actually lost in our analysis of change scores.

7.   For the period from 1988 to 1994 we took the union of tactics used between 1988 and 1992 and between 1992 and 1994.

8.   There were three additional items: made more use of volunteers, made more use of part-time staff, and started new programs and services. We did not use these three, since many of our analyses will attempt to explain growth in volunteers, paid staff, and starting up new programs and services.

9.   There were no missing data for the data we collected for 1980–1984, and there was only one case with missing data for managerial tactics for 1984–1988. For 1988–1992 and 1988–1994 there were more problems. One case had missing data for all the items, one case had missing data for political and managerial tactics, and three cases were missing data on only the political items. Where there were missing data for a tactics variable, we used mean substitution. To check to see if the five cases with missing data on political tactics for 1988–1992 and 1988–1994 were different than the rest of the panel, we created a dummy variable and correlated it with log expenditures, log organizational age, and whether or not it provided health/welfare, cultural/recreational, educational, or other services in 1992. The correlations ranged between −.059 and .054.

10.   This measure of network centrality was flawed but we are not sure how we could have corrected for the shortcoming. The correct way of sampling network ties is to have a true random sample of nodes, which are then asked to identify the linkages among themselves (Frank 1978). This enables one to estimate such measures as degree centrality and network density. If we would have asked the network questions of our sample in 1980, this condition would have been met.

Alternatively, we could have asked respondents to describe ties to the new samples of nonprofits in 1984 and 1988. However, we did not. Instead we asked the questions only of survivors in 1984 and 1988.

11.   To develop our population we scanned Marquis's *Who's Who in America, 1980–81* (1980) and *Who's Who in America, 1988–89* (1988) for names of people who lived in the Twin Cities seven-county area. In 1980 we found 820 names; in 1988 we found 952 names. We felt the need to augment this list, because individuals have the option of not being listed in *Who's Who* and Marquis's criteria for inclusion are not clearly defined. Thus we went to two positional leaders in different sectors of the community (business, education, health, culture, law, government/politics, sports, and religion), handed them a list of *Who's Who* names for their sector, and asked them to add the names of any other prominent people in their sector. All the names mentioned by our informants were added to our population. If someone was identified as being in two sectors, s/he was randomly assigned to one or the other sector. This gave us a grand total of 1242 names in 1980 and 1299 names in 1988. We drew a 7% stratified systematic sample in 1980 and an 8% stratified systematic sample in 1988. Of the 90 people drawn in 1980, we interviewed 80 for a response rate of 88.9%; of the 108 people drawn in 1988, we interviewed 93 for a response rate of 86.1%. Only 36.7% of the sample in 1981 and 31.9% in 1989 were owners or managers of business enterprises. The rest were educators, lawyers, scientists, health care workers, artists, performers, government officials, sports celebrities, clergy, and a wide range of miscellaneous professionals.

12.   It is important to remember that in 1981, the panel and the cross-section organizations were the same and thus elite respondents were evaluating both simultaneously. We then used the same data to create niche legitimacy (see Appendix B) as well as individual organizational legitimacy scores. In 1989 the elite evaluated two sets of organizations: cross-section and panel organizations. The data on the cross-section were used to create niche legitimacy scores, and the data on the panel were used to create individual organizational legitimacy scores.

13.   Although the data were collected in 1981 and 1989, for the sake of exposition we hereafter refer to elite network contacts and reputation in 1980 and 1988.

14.   These items were not asked for 1980 or 1984.

15.   Although we created and analyzed two niche spaces in Appendix B—one based on income sources, size, and activities and the other based on labor inputs, size, and activities—we analyze niche variables for only the first. The amount of missing data associated with the second was too large to make these measures useful.

Still there were considerable missing data for the niche variables based on income, size, and activities: 13 cases in 1980, 6 cases in 1984, and 3 in 1988. However, in 1984 and 1988 these cases overlapped completely with those missing data on our generalism (diversification) measure, and in 1980 there was complete overlap except for one additional case missing data on the niche variables. The reader should remember that organizations missing data on these items were smaller, and also that many left the panel within four years. For example, of the 13 cases missing data on the niche variables in 1980, only 5 survived until 1984, and thus only these 5 cases were lost in our analysis of growth and decline between 1980 and 1984.

16. Coleman (1968) showed that Equation (8) is a solution to the following differential equation:

$$dY/dt = b_0 + b_1 Y + b_2 X$$

This equation states that the rate of change is a function of the size of the organization, $Y$, and some other factors, $X$. In practice, however, researchers have estimated Equation (2), interpreted the unstandardized regression coefficients, and have not transformed parameter estimates from the ordinary least squares solution into the estimates of the differential equation (Freeman and Hannan 1975; see also Hannan and Young 1977).

I would like to thank Chris Winship for pointing out the possible problems with the model we chose and the advantages of alternative approaches.

17. Instead of pooling our data across observations, we decided to examine the change in income and personnel over discrete time periods. We estimated separate equations for each period to be sensitive to the historical context. Our discussion thus far has assumed that the processes we describe are *ahistorical*, yet this period— 1980 to 1994—was quite tumultuous in the history of nonprofit organizations. We felt uneasy pooling our data and assuming that effects were stationary over time (for a discussion of these issues, see Hannan and Young 1977).

18. We regressed $e_t$ on $e_{t-n}$ and the set of explanatory variables ($X$s, $W$s and lagged $Y$) in the original equation and tested the joint significance of the coefficients on the residuals with the standard $F$-test. There were only four sets of disturbances to correlate: $e_{84}$, $e_{88}$, $e_{92}$, and $e_{94}$, since we were not able to estimate models where $Y_{80}$ was the dependent variable.

19. In the 2SLS the instrument for $Y_{t-n}$ was estimated as a function of all the regressors in the substantive model (measured two time periods earlier) predicting the lagged independent variable plus all the regressors in the substantive model.

20. The Heckman approach has come under considerable scrutiny recently, and Winship and Mare (1992) and Stolzenberg and Relles (1997) proposed several diagnostics to ensure that Heckman's correction for sample selection bias does not do more harm than good. To respond to their concerns we examined the tolerance scores in each of our regressions to ensure that lambda was not too strongly correlated with other regressors and examined the correlation between the error terms in the selection and substantive models. Throughout this monograph neither collinearity involving lambda nor unusually high correlations among the error terms were a problem. The error terms in our sample selection models were not normally distributed, but this is not unusual for probit models. We also note the percentage of cases that were censored for each year in each of our selection models. As we might expect, attrition is more of a problem in the later years of the panel, where we lose nearly 30% of the original sample and our model is less able to predict the percentage of survivors and departures than in earlier periods.

21. It is important to remember that departure did not always mean closure or death. See Chapter 2 for a description of the various ways organizations left the panel.

22.   All models were estimated using LIMDEP, Version 5. This software program estimates both a selection model and a substantive model, which includes the inverse Mills ratio in the latter. It also adjusts the standard errors in the substantive model accordingly. When we needed to correct for heteroskedasticity, we wrote out the inverse Mills ratio and included it simply as another regressor in an OLS that used the White (1980) correction.

23.   When we analyzed growth in commercial income/employees, we included the organization's donated income and volunteers at $t - n$ as a control. When we analyzed growth in donated income/volunteers, we included earned income and employees at $t - n$ as a control.

24.   Because we used mean substitution in 1988–1992 and 1988–1994 for political tactics, we did a preliminary analysis of the 1992 and 1994 data where we included a dummy for the five cases where we substituted the mean for missing data. In analyzing total income/personnel and donated income/volunteers, the dummy was not significant at the .10-level, and the tolerance scores for the dummy never dropped below .950 indicating that the dummy was not correlated with the other regressors. In the following tables we present results without the dummy in the equation.

25.   We added to the models for 1988–1992 and for 1988–1994 the percentage of local elites in 1988 that thought the organization was providing essential services or had outstanding accomplishments (ln). The effect was not significant at the .10-level, and the effect of niche legitimacy remained significant at the .01-level. This suggests that it was a niche legitimacy and not an organizational legitimacy effect that explained growth and decline.

26.   We added to the model the percentage of the elite in 1980 that thought the organization was providing essential services or had achieved extraordinary accomplishments (ln). Again we found that the individual reputational measure was not significant, while the niche level variable remained significant at the .01-level.

27.   It would be ideal if we had interorganizational network data for 1980 and elite contact data for 1984. However, we did not have the foresight to collect the former nor the resources to collect the latter. Thus we computed our respective product terms for 1980 and 1984 using the 1980 elite contact and reputation construct and the 1984 organizational centrality scores, respectively. This was not a problem in 1988, since we had both interorganizational centrality and elite contact and reputation scores for that year.

28.   We will summarize results from the OLS analysis, although the reader should keep in mind the 2SLS results as well. Also we regard effects at the .10-level to be statistically significant.

# 4

## Environmental and Embeddedness Effects on Organizational Tactics

Strategic management models often assume that the organization's choice of tactics or products is the "rational" response to a set of environmental contingencies (Pfeffer and Salancik 1978). They are based on a careful cost-benefit analysis and are in concert with more broadly defined organizational strategies and goals—whether they be profits, conquest, or the elimination of hunger in developing countries. More specifically, adaptation theory would argue that choices are resource driven and aim to improve the organization's material or resource position and thus enable it to better achieve its goals. Organizational and/or noneconomic factors are simply assumed to be unimportant or as something that get in the way.

This model has not gone unchallenged. As noted earlier, Pennings (1985) argued that often organizations discover why they selected the tactics they used only after the fact. That is, in the process of rationalizing or defending their tactics to others, they discover the "strategy" behind their actions. Others embrace what sometimes is called a "garbage-can" model of decision-making (Cohen, March, and Olsen 1972). A wide range of tactics is out there for the taking, and the final choice of tactics is almost by chance as managers grope for solutions to problems they do not fully understand. As Scott observed: "Which solutions get attached to which problems is largely determined . . . by what participants with what goals happened to be on the scene, by when the solutions or the problems entered, and so on" (1992:298). Tactics are not the product of strategic planning and research and are often not instrumentally rational. Tactics emerge out of a situation that is developing, changing, and in flux. Managers act first and then figure out what they did later. Rather than being well-oiled rational machines, organizations and decision-making processes are better characterized as organized anarchies (Cohen et al. 1972).

A third approach falls somewhere between the previous two and focuses attention on how the choice of tactics is structurally embedded

(Baum and Dutton 1996). That is, the social network ties that the organization and its members have to others will also affect the choice of tactics. Organizational decision-makers work under conditions of bounded rationality and thus are susceptible to social influences. As noted by DiMaggio and Powell (1983) and others, decision-makers learn from those who are in their social networks. Social networks are conducive to learning because actors trust, share norms with, and feel a sense of mutual obligation to one another. What executives learn, however, is not always best for the organization, and learning can devolve into rote imitation. Thus while social learning may explain why organizations pursue the tactics they do, it does not necessarily lead to goal attainment.

A fourth approach is really an antitheory of strategy formulation. Ecologists argue that there are costs to change and that while organizations will initially chose certain tactics, they will be reluctant to change tactics over time. Radically changing tactics resets the organization's clock and makes it vulnerable to the liabilities of newness (Hannan and Freeman 1989). Even under threatening conditions, "smart" organizations will reaffirm their commitments and stay the course. Selective forces are powerful enough; moving into areas where competencies are questionable can only make the organization more vulnerable.

## ORGANIZATIONAL TACTICS AND ACTIVITIES

We look at three types of tactics—political, managerial, and retrenchment tactics—and attempt to explain why organizations increased or decreased their use of each over time. We also wanted to see if and why organizations changed their activities. We draw on resource dependency, ecological, and embeddedness theories to understand these types of organizational change.

### A.  Resource Dependency and Tactical Choice

Resource dependency theory would argue that the use of specific tactics will depend upon where an organization gets its resources. In Chapter 1 (see Figure 1.1) we made the distinction between organizations that were heavily dependent upon niches that had strong output controls and those dependent upon niches with strong process controls. We argued that the former typically was characterized by the sale of products and services to customers and paid labor. Thus organizations in these niches needed to be concerned with realizing efficiencies, quality control, ensuring customer satisfaction, and the like. The latter was characterized by donated income and grants and volunteer labor. Here organizations needed to be more concerned with legitimation, image, the views of opinion makers in the larger environment, conformity to rules, and donor preferences. Indeed a major part of our argument in Chapter 1 was that the key difference among organizations was not that they were for-profit or nonprofit, but that they drew their resources from different niches, and this is what explained their different behaviors. We labeled the former utilitarian organizations and the latter normative organizations, but their identity was tied to their niche and not to their form per se.

Resource dependency theory would argue that an organization's dependencies upon one or the other arena is correlated with its choice of organizational tactics. For example, managers dependent upon niches with strong output controls (i.e., heavily dependent upon sales of services to customers and employees) are likely to increase their use of managerial tactics. They need to pay attention to their customers, redesign work to cut unnecessary costs, and coordinate and control workers and technical activities (Scott 1987:127). The focus will be on rationalizing operations so as to deliver services more effectively. Thus,

H1:    *Organizations that are more dependent on commercial income and employees are likely to increase their use of managerial tactics over time.*

In contrast, managers heavily dependent upon niches with strong process controls (i.e., heavily dependent upon gifts and grants and volunteers) are likely to pursue more political and managerial tactics. They need to ensure the legality of their organizations' actions, influence public policy through lobbying and PAC contributions, protect their image in the larger society by acting in a socially responsible way, conform to local customs and folkways, state statutes and regulations, and be sensitive to donor / grantmaker preferences. The focus is on co-opting old and pursuing new donors and grantmakers and volunteers by ensuring that the organization is perceived as the servant of the public interest and trustworthy. They also need to demonstrate their managerial expertise (DiMaggio and Powell 1983). They need to show that they can act in a businesslike fashion, rationalize their operations, and engage in strategic planning to institutional gatekeepers, who then will view them as reliable and accountable.

H2a:    *Organizations that are more dependent upon donated income and volunteers are likely to increase their use of political tactics over time.*

H2b:    *Organizations that are more dependent upon donated income and volunteers are likely to increase their use of managerial tactics over time.*

In sum, organizations will do what they need to do in order to secure resources in their respective niches. If nonprofit organizations are heavily dependent upon dues, fees, the sale of unrelated services, and paid employees, then they will utilize more managerial tactics and act more like utilitarian organizations. If nonprofits are heavily dependent upon contributions, gifts, and grants, then they will utilize more political and managerial tactics and act both like normative and utilitarian organizations. This perspective argues that tactical choice—and thus organizational style—is directly related to where the organization procures its resources and the type of resources it is looking for.

Complications arise, however, when conditions in an organization's niche are highly competitive. For example, in niches where competition for resources is more intense, resource dependency theory would hypothesize that organizations would shift gears and try to find a new, less competitive niche (e.g., Baum and Singh 1996). Adaptation theory assumes that organizations are rational and that they will pursue a course of action that yields the greatest material benefits to the organization. If staying in one's resource niche would result in a net loss to the organization, it should pursue new initiatives and find a new niche.

Operationally, how could we measure and test this? In Chapter 3 we introduced the concept of the niche space, which we used to make predictions about organizations' growth and decline. The niche space was created by surveying a sample of nonprofit organizations; gathering data on their funding sources, labor inputs, activities, and size; and using these data to identify organizations' resource niches. We then measured the density of each niche and the degree to which resources were dispersed or concentrated. In this chapter we will look to see what organizations did when situated in either a dense (or crowded) niche or a niche where resources were dispersed. Both conditions were indicators of within-niche competition.

We can also use the niche space to identify alternative tactics that organizations can pursue. We have already shown that managerial tactics gave organizations capacities to compete more effectively for customers and employees and that political and managerial tactics gave organizations capacities to compete for private donations and volunteers. We can extend this line of thinking by arguing that organizations that were in highly competitive niches will try to enter new niches by using tactics that tap into new and different resource streams. Furthermore, building on the concept of the niche space, we can envision organizations changing niches by changing their activities or downsizing (i.e., finding a niche where there are smaller organizations). The latter is accomplished by retrenchment. Since one's competitive arena is defined as much by an organization's activities and size as where it gets its resources, an organization can change its position in the niche space by changing any of these factors.

In light of the preceding discussion resource dependency theory would predict that organizations located in denser and/or less concentrated niches will "flee" their niche. They will do this by either pursuing funding tactics that access new funding/labor imputs, changing their products and services (activities), or downsizing. To summarize:

H3: *In more competitive niches, organizations that are more dependent on commercial income and employees are likely to increase their use of political tactics over time.*

H4: *Organizations that reside in more competitive niches are more likely to change their products and services over time.*

H5: *Organizations that reside in more competitive niches are likely to increase their use of retrenchment tactics over time.*

## B. Selection and Tactical Choice

Ecologists have also paid considerable attention to competition and its effects on organizations, but their approach is different than what we found in the strategic management literature. Ecologists have long recognized that organizations pursue different strategies, e.g., some are generalists while others are specialists, and that some strategies work better than others (Hannan and Freeman 1977). What is different about ecological thinking is that it hypothesizes that certain strategies will be *selected* by the environment over others. For example, Hannan and Freeman hypothesized that in fine-grained environments, specialists will outcompete generalists, but in coarse-grained environments generalists will outcompete specialists. Another interesting difference is that ecologists hypothesize that organizations increase their chances of failure if they try to change their strategies or tactics (Hannan and Freeman 1984, 1989; see also Barnett and Carroll 1995). Change effectively resets the organization's clock and makes it vulnerable to the liabilities of newness (Hannan and Freeman 1984, 1989). Routines are disrupted, relationships to suppliers and customers are undermined, new technologies need to be learned (Barnett and Carroll 1995), and, in general, the firm becomes much less reliable and accountable. Peters and Waterman's (1982) famous prescription, "Stick to the knitting," echoes this sentiment, and examples of where firms have gone too far astray liter the gossip columns of business magazines.

As one might expect, the inertia argument has come under considerable attack, and even ecologists have conceded that organizations will diversify into related product lines without risking too much—as long as they do not change their mission, forms of authority, basic technology, or marketing strategy (Hannan and Freeman 1989). For example, Delacroix and Swaminathan (1991) showed that wineries that moved into adjacent product lines lowered their failure rates. Baum and Singh (1996) found that smaller and older day care centers that expanded their niche (ages served) in response to competition improved their survival chances. Also Haveman (1992) found that savings and loans that went into related businesses reduced their failure rates and enhanced performance.

Yet it is difficult to decide a priori just how far is OK and how far is too far. Among for-profits, one could look within two-digit SICs and predict that movement across four-digit SICs (but within two-digit codes) would be reasonable. One could expect that charitable organizations—which are bound by IRS guidelines—will not go into product lines that would jeopardize their charitable status—as well as their reputation. Thus a church might open an elementary school but not a gas station; a hospital would offer outpatient drug rehabilitation counseling but would not acquire a manufacturer of breakfast cereals; or a community crime watch program would home-deliver hot lunches to the elderly but would not sell cosmetics door-to-door. Yet knowing how far is too far is still a problem.

The intriguing question is, What do organizations do when embedded in a highly competitive niche? As noted earlier, adaptation theory anticipates flight. In contrast, ecologists expect them to stay and fight it out. They certainly do not expect that organizations will flee their niche by changing tactics, activities, or size. If anything, organizations should compete harder, increasing their efforts to extract resources from their current funding sources and/or labor inputs. This can be summarized in the following hypotheses:

H6:  *In more competitive niches, organizations that are more dependent on commercial income and employees are likely to increase their use of managerial tactics over time.*

H7a:  *In more competitive niches, organizations that are more dependent on donated income and volunteers are likely to increase their use of political tactics over time.*

H7b:  *In more competitive niches, organizations that are more dependent on donated income and volunteers are likely to increase their use of managerial tactics over time.*

## C.  Social Embeddedness and Tactical Choice

Earlier we argued that networks can affect strategy formulation, because they can facilitate learning. According to Powell et al. (1996) social networks can facilitate the transfer of knowledge and information across organizational borders. This, in turn, provides an opportunity for innovation and new strategies by bringing together different operating assumptions and new combinations of information (Powell and Brantley 1992). The downside is that networks can disseminate inaccurate information and competitors can steal one's ideas. Thus it is important that learning take place through *social* networks, i.e., relationships characterized by trust, integrity, and a commitment to community.

Once the tie-in between organizational learning and social networks has been made, there is a plethora of research on network diffusion that organizational theory can draw on to explain organizational change or the adoption of new ideas by organizations. For example, there have been a number of network studies of social influence among organizational actors. Most researchers have argued that social learning takes place through direct contacts among actors in a network (Galaskiewicz 1985b; Galaskiewicz and Wasserman 1989). People exchange information in conversations. "Early" adopters describe their experience with some innovation, idea, technology, etc., to a friend or acquaintance, and the latter decides to adopt if the experience was positive. The more that an organization is exposed to trusted others doing certain things, the more confidence it will have to try out the innovation itself. In an interorganizational field, organizations might be influenced by those with whom they exchange resources or by managers and staff whom they know personally. In either case, top management can observe directly the efficacy (or inefficacy) of different innovations before they decide to adapt themselves.

Alternatively, organizations may selectively imitate practices that have been used by some subset of other organizations. Haunschild and Miner (1997) call this trait-based imitation. DiMaggio and Powell argued that "[o]rganizations tend to model themselves after similar organizations in their field that they perceive to be more legitimate or successful" (1983:152). That the organization was successful legitimatizes the practices that it employed. By doing what higher-status organizations did organizations may even increase their own status (Haunschild and Miner 1997). DiMaggio and Powell further argued that the greater the environmental uncertainty, the more likely actors will model themselves after those they perceive to be successful. Uncertainty is held to be "a powerful force that encourages imitation" (1983:151). Indeed, imitation is an inexpensive alternative to costly research, evaluation, and planning. It is not critical that what's mimicked actually is rational from the point of view of the organization, its goals, or its funding. In fact, the appeal of DiMaggio and Powell's thesis is that these mimetic effects are independent of the resource needs of the organization and what may or may not be actually good for the organization. They are due more to cognitive crises and the need to do something reasonable in the face of uncertainty.[1]

In the spirit of testing these ideas, we offer three hypotheses. We argue that managers and organizations adopt tactics that are used by those whom they know and trust. We assume that organizations would know and trust those with whom they have directly worked in the past. We also assume that they know and trust folks in other organizations who are friends or acquaintances of senior management. Finally, we expect that under conditions of uncertainty, organizations will mimic those organizations that managers believe have been particularly successful. In sum,

> H8:   *Organizations are likely to increase their use of political and/or managerial tactics if they had direct resource exchanges with other organizations that used political and/or managerial tactics extensively in the past.*

> H9:   *Organizations are likely to increase their use of political and/or managerial tactics if managers knew personally other managers who used political and/or managerial tactics extensively in the past.*

> H10:   *Under conditions of uncertainty, organizations are likely to increase their use of political and/or managerial tactics if managers perceived other organizations as successful that used political and/or managerial tactics extensively in the past.*

All three of these hypotheses are based on the assumption that organizational change through social learning is prompted by visibility and that social learning takes place in an embedded network of relations. Some of these networks are cognitive (who strategic management thinks is successful), some are resource based (the organization has exchanged resources with the organization), and some are highly personal (who strategic management knows personally). But regardless of the basis, organizational change results from learning about what others in the organizational field are doing and then following suit.

Again borrowing from DiMaggio and Powell (1983), we also expect that organizations' involvement with the local community elite will result in the greater use of managerial tactics. We argue that local community elites are institutional gatekeepers that strive to push the bureaucratic or rational form across the nonprofit organizational field. Rather than representing class interests, we propose that elites within communities today represent "rationality agendas." Case studies that described what happened when business leaders assumed power in nonprofit organizations support our claim (Hall 1990). If indeed elites are committed to the managerial model, we suspect that elites may press organizations to embrace and increase managerial tactics. Drawing on DiMaggio and Powell's (1983) discussion of coercive isomorphism, we argue that in exchange for their services to and / or patronage of the organization, community elites will expect that the organization becomes more rational or businesslike—whether or not it is dependent upon earned income and employees for its resources. Thus we hypothesize:

H11: *Organizations are likely to increase their use of managerial tactics if more members of the community elite personally used or supported their organization with donations, volunteer help, board memberships, and consulting services.*

A number of other factors may influence the choice of tactics or products. Clearly organizational size may be important. On the one hand, larger organizations can do more things, e.g., add new products/services, go after new markets, simply because of their size and slack resources (Thompson 1967). On the other hand, Hannan and Freeman (1984) argued that size is correlated with structural inertia, which would discourage organizational change. Also we need to control for products and services. Styles may differ depending upon whether nonprofits are cultural/recreational, health/welfare, or educational organizations. However, at this point we have no predictions as to how these styles might affect the choice of tactics.

## DATA, METHODS, AND VARIABLES

To test these hypotheses we used data from the panel study of nonprofits up through 1992. Our goal was to see if we could explain changes in products/services and the number of political, managerial, and retrenchment tactics used between 1984 and 1988 and between 1988 and 1992. The reader should remember that we tallied the number of tactics used between 1980 and 1984, 1984 and 1988, and 1988 and 1992. Many of the variables that we analyze in this chapter have been described in Chapter 3 and Appendix B, e.g., political tactics (1984, 1988, 1992), managerial tactics (1984, 1988, 1992), retrenchment tactics (1984, 1988, 1992), activities (or industry) (1984, 1988, 1992), dependency upon commercial income and employees (1984, 1988), dependency upon contributions/gift/grants and volunteers (1984, 1988), dependency upon government grants and contracts (1984, 1988), niche density (1984, 1988), niche concentration of resources (1984, 1988), and elite support of the organization (1980, 1988).[2] We also include in our equations the lambda computed from the sample selection model described in Chapter 3 in order to control for sample selection bias.[3] What we add that is new in this chapter are a number of network variables and a measure of environmental uncertainty. These will be used in combination with our tactics variables to test hypotheses on network embeddedness effects.

*Uncertainty.* Environmental uncertainty is a key concept in theories dealing with relations between organizations and their environments (Dill 1958; Duncan 1972; Thompson 1967; Lawrence and Lorsch 1967; Downey and Ireland 1979; Downey, Hellriegel, and Slocum 1975) and is generally held to pose potentially serious problems for organizational administration and action (Daft 1989:52). Researchers have identified a number of characteristics of organizational environments that can contribute to uncertainty. These include the number of environmental elements that must be considered, their instability, their unpredictability, the lack of coordination among them, and the lack of data about them (Pfeffer and Salancik 1978).

An organization's environment is perceived to be uncertain when an individual feels that s/he is lacking information about some important aspect of it. A number of dimensions, or types, of perceived environmental uncertainty have been identified (Milliken 1987). One important dimension is the degree of uncertainty about the current or future state of the environment. This would include such things as the probability and nature of general environmental changes, how specific components of the environment may be changing, or how the parts of the environment are interrelated. This analysis focuses on nonprofit financial environments and will use the lack of knowledge of important factors relevant to funding as a measure of "state uncertainty."

During the 1984 and 1988 interviews, respondents were asked a series of questions designed to measure their uncertainty about the income stream from the organization's major funder type (for more details, see Bielefeld 1992a). Respondents were handed a list of eleven funder types and asked to identify the funder type that provided them with the largest amount of income for fiscal years 1984 and 1988. These questions did not refer to income from a single funder, but from a type of funder. This means that those who reported that foundations were their major funder type, for example, were basing this on their total income from all of their foundation funders, however many that might have been. The funder types included on the list and the percentage of nonprofits citing them as their major source of income in 1984 and 1988 are shown in Table 4.1.

Respondents were then asked questions about the funder type that they were most dependent upon for funds. In 1984 the questions pertained to 1984 or the period between 1980 and 1984. In 1988 the questions pertained to 1988 and the period between 1984 and 1988. This analysis will use respondent reports about the adequacy of information about their major funder type (0 = no uncertainty; 1 = uncertainty) and the certainty of

*Table 4.1.* Organizations' Major Funding Sources for 1984 and 1988

| Major Funding Source | 1984 | | 1988 | |
|---|---|---|---|---|
| | *Frequency* | *Percent* | *Frequency* | *Percent* |
| Private / community foundations | 31 | 7.0 | 8 | 4.7 |
| Individual gifts | 20 | 10.8 | 20 | 11.8 |
| Federated givers | 5 | 2.7 | 7 | 4.1 |
| Corporations / corporate foundations | 6 | 3.2 | 11 | 6.5 |
| Federal government | 9 | 4.8 | 9 | 5.3 |
| State government | 9 | 4.8 | 9 | 5.3 |
| County government | 18 | 9.7 | 13 | 7.6 |
| City / metropolitan government | 7 | 3.8 | 8 | 4.7 |
| Members | 29 | 15.6 | 29 | 17.1 |
| Patients / clients / etc. | 60 | 32.4 | 41 | 24.1 |
| Other | 10 | 5.4 | 15 | 8.8 |
| Total | 186 | 100.0 | 170 | 100.0 |

income next year from them (0 = no uncertainty; 1 = uncertainty). Finally, an uncertainty index for each year was computed by summing the responses. The distributions of index values are shown in Table 4.2. The descriptive statistics for the uncertainty scores are in Table 4.3.

*Network Variables.* As noted in Chapter 3, in 1984 and 1988, panel respondents were handed a list of all the nonprofits in the panel. They were then asked a series of questions about the nonprofits on the list. Their responses were used to measure an organization's resource ties to, personal ties to, and perceptions of the success of the other organizations in the panel. After asking respondents to check off the organizations that they recognized, we asked them to indicate to and from which nonprofits they gave and received information about community affairs, information about technical matters, and various resources (e.g., personnel, facilities, etc.). We next asked them to identify the organizations where they knew

*Table 4.2.* Distribution of Uncertainty Index for 1984 and 1988

| Index Value | 1984 | | 1988 | |
|---|---|---|---|---|
| | *Frequency* | *Percent* | *Frequency* | *Percent* |
| 0 | 98 | 52.7 | 83 | 49.1 |
| 1 | 54 | 29.0 | 59 | 34.9 |
| 2 | 34 | 18.3 | 27 | 16.0 |
| Total | 186 | 100.0 | 169 | 100.0 |

*Table 4.3.*   Variable Descriptions and Descriptive Statistics

| Variable Descriptions | Mean | SD | N |
|---|---|---|---|
| Uncertainty index, 1984 | .656 | .771 | 186 |
| Uncertainty index, 1988 | .669 | .738 | 169 |
| Number of managerial tactics utilized by organizations that exchanged resources or information with the focal organization, 1984 | 34.2 | 44.0 | 198 |
| Number of managerial tactics utilized by organizations that had exchanged resources or information with the focal organization, 1988 | 26.0 | 34.4 | 171 |
| Number of managerial tactics utilized by organizations where senior managers in the focal organization knew someone personally, 1984 | 57.3 | 58.7 | 196 |
| Number of managerial tactics utilized by organizations where senior managers in the focal organization knew someone personally, 1988 | 52.3 | 48.7 | 173 |
| Number of managerial tactics utilized by organizations that senior managers perceived to be successful organizations, 1984 | 63.9 | 57.0 | 196 |
| Number of managerial tactics utilized by organizations that senior managers perceived to be successful organizations, 1988 | 66.8 | 44.9 | 172 |
| Number of political tactics utilized by organizations that had exchanged resources or information with the focal organization, 1984 | 17.8 | 22.6 | 198 |
| Number of political tactics utilized by organizations that had exchanged resources or information with the focal organization, 1988 | 13.9 | 18.6 | 171 |
| Number of political tactics utilized by organizations where senior managers in the focal organization knew someone personally, 1984 | 30.0 | 30.6 | 196 |
| Number of political tactics utilized by organizations where senior managers in the focal organization knew someone personally, 1988 | 29.3 | 27.5 | 173 |
| Number of political tactics utilized by organizations that senior managers perceived to be successful organizations, 1984 | 33.8 | 28.5 | 196 |
| Number of political tactics utilized by organizations that senior managers perceived to be successful organizations, 1988 | 38.1 | 25.9 | 172 |

someone personally. Then they were asked to identify the other nonprof its that they felt had "adapted particularly well since 1980 to government retrenchment or the recession." In the final question, they were asked to indicate which nonprofits "seemed particularly well thought of by corporations or foundations."

With the responses to these questions, we constructed three arrays, *P*, *R*, and *S*, for each year. In the "personally know someone" array *P*, a 1 indicated that respondent *i* said that s/he knew personally someone in organization *j*. Because of the nature of this question, the network data were asymmetric. Diagonals were set to zero. On average, in 1984 and 1988 organizations cited 7.42 and 6.74 other organizations where they knew someone personally (SD = 7.58; SD = 6.27). In 1984, 196 of the 201 panel survivors provided us with data; in 1988, 173 panel survivors gave us the information. In the resource exchange array *R*, a 1 indicated that respondent *i* said that they either gave or received information on community affairs, technical affairs, or resources to (and/or from) nonprofit *j*. We counted a tie between organization *i* and *j* if either noted a flow of resources in either direction. Thus these data arrays were symmetric. Diagonals were again set to zero. On average, in 1984 and 1988 organizations cited (or were cited by) 4.19 and 3.42 other organizations that they exchanged resources with (SD = 5.19; SD = 4.22). In 1984, 198 of the 201 panel survivors provided us with data; in 1988, 171 organizations gave us the data. In the perceived successful array *S*, a 1 indicated that respondent *i* said s/he thought nonprofit *j* either adapted well to government cutbacks or the recession *or* was particularly well thought of by corporations or foundations. The asymmetric nature of these items was also retained. Again, diagonals were set to zero. On average, in 1984 and 1988 organizations cited 7.80 and 8.04 other organizations that they felt were successful (SD = 7.32; SD = 5.59). This time 196 and 172 organizations responded in 1980 and 1988.[4]

*Social Influence and Mimicry Effects.* Since the hypotheses said that we expected organizations to adopt the tactics of those where there was a personal connection, those they thought were successful organizations, or those which they had exchanged resources with in the past, we needed to create six multiplicative terms for each period. We did this by multiplying two vectors (each containing the number of tactics of a given type *k* used by each organization) by each of the three arrays *P*, *S*, and *R*, thus producing the six new vectors for each year. More formally,

$$PY_{ik} = \Sigma_j(p_{ij} * y_{jk}),  \tag{1}$$

$$SY_{ik} = \Sigma_j(s_{ij} * y_{jk}),  \tag{2}$$

$$RY_{ik} = \Sigma_j(r_{ij} * y_{jk}),  \tag{3}$$

where $y_{jk}$ was the number of tactics *k* used by actor *j* between 1980 and 1984 (or between 1984 and 1988), $p_{ij}$ was whether or not the respondent in organization *i* knew someone personally in organization *j* in 1984 (or

1988), $s_{ij}$ was whether respondent $i$ thought organization $j$ was a successful organization in 1984 (or 1988), $r_{ij}$ was whether organization $i$ gave or received resources or information to or from organization $j$ in 1984 (or 1988), and $PY_{ik}$, $SY_{ik}$, and $RY_{ik}$ were the total number of tactics $k$ used by actor $i$'s various network contacts in 1984 (or 1988). The descriptive statistics for the network product terms are in Table 4.3.

## TESTING FOR RESOURCE DEPENDENCY AND NICHE EFFECTS: HYPOTHESES 1–7

The models and procedures we employed in this chapter are similar to those used in Chapter 3 to explain growth and decline of resources. For the regression analyses we estimated a sample selection model and then included the inverse Mills ratio in our substantive equations. Next we tested for multicollinearity by examining the tolerance score associated with each regressor. We then tested for heteroskedasticity using the methods suggested by White (1980). We also tested, where possible, for autocorrelation using the method outlined by Breusch (1978) and Godfrey (1978) and modified by Greene (1997). Unless noted in the text, neither multicollinearity, heteroskedasticity, nor autocorrelation was a problem in the models we tested. We also estimated our models using Poisson regression and present the results along with the OLS findings. This is because our additive indexes, measuring organizational tactics, are count data.

Hypotheses 1, 2a, and 2b stated that organizations that are more heavily dependent upon commercial income and employees will increase their use of managerial tactics over time, while organizations more dependent upon grants, donations, and volunteers will increase their use of political and managerial tactics over time. Hypothesis 3 stated that in more competitive niches, organizations that are more dependent upon commercial income and employees will increase their political tactics. Hypothesis 4 stated that organizations in competitive niches were more likely to change their products and services over time, and Hypothesis 5 stated that organizations in competitive niches will increase their use of retrenchment tactics. Finally, Hypotheses 6, 7a, and 7b stated that in more competitive niches, organizations that are more dependent upon commercial income and employees will increase their managerial tactics, and that organizations that are more dependent upon donated income and volunteers will increase their political and managerial tactics. Hypotheses 6, 7a, and 7b differ from Hypotheses 1, 2a, and 2b in that they argue that niche competition will tighten the coupling of resource dependencies to tactics.

With a few minor changes, the OLS equation to test Hypotheses 1, 2a, 2b, and 5 is basically the same used in Chapter 3:

$$Y_t = \beta_0 + \beta_1 Y_{t-n} + \Sigma_i \beta_i X_{i,t-n} + \Sigma_j \beta_j W_{j,t-n} + \Sigma_k \beta_k Z_{k,t-n} + \beta\lambda + \epsilon_t \ (4)$$

where $Y_t$ now refers to the number of tactics used by the organization between $t - 4$ and $t$ and $Y_{t-n}$ is the number of tactics used between $t - 8$ and $t - 4$ (political, managerial, retrenchment);[5] $X_i$ are the size variables (commercial income and employees, donated income and volunteers); $W_j$ are the niche variables (density, concentration); $Z_k$ are the control variables (activities, presence of government funding); and $\lambda$ is the sample selection term. We estimated six models: three for the period from 1984 to 1988 and three for the period from 1988-1992. None of the OLS models had to be corrected for heteroskedasticity, and the three models where we could apply the modified Breusch-Godfrey test showed no signs of autocorrelation. Multicollinearity was a slight problem in all the equations. This was because both the number of political tactics and the number of managerial tactics were on the right-hand side together. The tolerance scores for managerial tactics varied between .387 and .392 and the tolerance scores for political tactics varied between .384 and .560 across the six different models.

In columns one and two, three and four, and five and six of Table 4.4 we present separate analyses for each tactic. We should note that in 1988 the correlations between managerial, political, and retrenchment tactics were .608, .408, and .256. In 1992 the correlations were .684, .495, and .404. Thus it was somewhat surprising that the variables explaining the change in tactics across years were different.

There was qualified support for Hypothesis 1 (see Table 4.4, models 1a, 1b, 2a, 2b). Commercial income and employees in 1984 predicted increases in the number of managerial tactics used between 1980–1984 and 1984–1988 ($p < .01$ in OLS and $p < .10$ in Poisson). Furthermore, this variable had little effect on the change in the number of political tactics used between 1980–1984 and 1984–1988. In 1988 commercial income and employees were again predictive of increases in the number of managerial tactics used between 1984–1988 and 1988–1992 ($p < .01$ in both OLS and Poisson); however, this variable had a positive effect on the use of political tactics as well ($p < .01$ in OLS and $p < .05$ in Poisson). There was also qualified support for Hypotheses 2a and 2b (Table 4.4, models 3a, 3b, 4a, and 4b). Donated income and volunteers in 1984 predicted increases in the number of political tactics used between 1980–1984 and 1984–1988 ($p < .01$ in both OLS and Poisson), but this variable was unrelated to changes in the number of managerial tactics used between 1980–1984 and 1984–1988. In 1988 the amount of donated income and volunteers was predictive of increases in both political ($p < .001$ in both OLS and Pois-

Table 4.4. OLS and Poisson Regression with Number of Managerial, Political, and Retrenchment Tactics as Dependent Variables

| | Dependent Variable: No. of Managerial Tactics$_t$ | | | |
|---|---|---|---|---|
| | (1a) 1984–1988 OLS b (SE) | (1b) Poisson b (SE) | (2a) 1988–1992 OLS b (SE) | (2b) Poisson b (SE) |
| Independent Variables | | | | |
| Commercial Inc & Empl$_{t-4}$ | .696(.296)* | .098(.050)# | .986(.326)** | .184(.060)** |
| Donated Inc & Vols$_{t-4}$ | .181(.258) | .003(.044) | .782(.314)* | .157(.059)** |
| Gov't Grants & Contracts $_{t-4}$ | 2.32(.538)*** | .441(.095)*** | .089(.542) | .054(.093) |
| Health/Welfare$_{t-4}$ | −1.72(.562)** | −.321(.100)** | −.169(.557) | .011(.101) |
| Culture/Recreation$_{t-4}$ | −1.75(.587)** | −.348(.104)*** | .192(.654) | .085(.117) |
| Education$_{t-4}$ | −.692(.542) | −.118(.093) | −.247(.550) | −.061(.099) |
| No. of Managerial Tactics$_{t-4}$ | .321(.083)*** | .065(.014)*** | .178(.092)# | .049(.016)** |
| No. of Political Tactics$_{t-4}$ | −.225(.137)# | −.036(.022) | .088(.125) | .013(.022) |
| No. of Retrench Tactics$_{t-4}$ | .020(.124) | .001(.018) | −.006(.139) | .002(.022) |
| Niche Density$_{t-4}$ | −.248(.105)* | −.038(.017)* | .021(.127) | .009(.025) |
| Niche Concentration$_{t-4}$ | 7.39(2.24)*** | 1.57(.409)*** | −2.65(2.33) | −.809(.421)# |
| λ | −1.78(1.56) | −.237(.277) | −.927(1.37) | −.119(.253) |
| Constant | 5.23(.846)*** | 1.45(.147)*** | 3.44(.930)*** | 1.05(.174)*** |
| R² | .539*** | | .391*** | |
| Adj. R² | .504 | | .341 | |
| N | 171 | | 158 | |
| Log likelihood | | −408.7 | | −385.6 |
| White test statistic for heteroskedasticity | 6.68 (df=12) | | 11.6 (df=12) | |
| Modified Breusch-Godfrey test statistic for autocorrelation | — | | .000 | |

*** p < .001; ** p < .01; * p < .05; # p < .10.

140

Table 4.4 (Continued)

|  | Dependent Variable: No. of Political Tactics$_t$ | | | |
|---|---|---|---|---|
|  | (3a) 1984–1988 OLS b (SE) | (3b) Poisson b (SE) | (4a) 1988–1992 OLS b (SE) | (4b) Poisson b (SE) |
| Independent Variables |  |  |  |  |
| Commercial Inc & Empl$_{t-4}$ | .199(.206) | .029(.068) | .680(.229)** | .185(.076)* |
| Donated Inc & Vols$_{t-4}$ | .595(.181)** | .197(.064)** | .794(.220)*** | .286(.078)*** |
| Gov't Grants & Contracts$_{t-4}$ | .927(.377)* | .333(.130)* | .449(.381) | .203(.122)# |
| Health/Welfare$_{t-4}$ | -1.25(.398)** | -.403(.134)** | .041(.389) | .035(.129) |
| Culture/Recreation$_{t-4}$ | -.514(.414) | -.172(.133) | -.438(.460) | -.132(.156) |
| Education$_{t-4}$ | -.613(.380) | -.189(.123) | .083(.385) | .044(.128) |
| No. of Managerial Tactics$_{t-4}$ | .019(.058) | .015(.019) | -.050(.064) | -.010(.021) |
| No. of Political Tactics$_{t-4}$ | .131(.096) | .033(.030) | .089(.088) | .023(.028) |
| No. of Retrench Tactics$_{t-4}$ | .147(.085)# | .034(.024) | -.049(.097) | -.006(.030) |
| Niche Density$_{t-4}$ | -.074(.074) | -.010(.024) | .066(.090) | .029(.031) |
| Niche Concentration$_{t-4}$ | 2.70(1.57)# | .991(.546)# | .244(1.63) | -.103(.552) |
| λ | .503(1.05) | .225(.358) | -.628(.955) | -.120(.320) |
| Constant | 2.56(.582)*** | .809(.193)*** | 2.66(.655)*** | .777(.224)*** |
| R² | .390*** |  | .322*** |  |
| Adj. R² | .344 |  | .265 |  |
| N | 172 |  | 155 |  |
| Log likelihood |  | -333.7 |  | -304.7 |
| White test statistic for heteroskedasticity | 14.9 (df=12) |  | 11.2 (df=12) |  |
| Modified Breusch-Godfrey test statistic for autocorrelation | — |  | .036 |  |

*** $p < .001$; ** $p < .01$; * $p < .05$; # $p < .10$.

141

Table 4.4 (Continued)

| Independent Variables | Dependent Variable: No. of Retrench Tactics$_t$ | | | |
| --- | --- | --- | --- | --- |
| | (5a) 1984–1988 OLS b (SE) | (5b) Poisson b (SE) | (6a) 1988–1992 OLS b (SE) | (6b) Poisson b (SE) |
| Commercial Inc & Empl$_{t-4}$ | .152(.181) | .188(.103)# | .338(.146)* | .343(.159)* |
| Donated Inc & Vols$_{t-4}$ | −.270(.159)# | −.236(.090)** | .213(.140) | .247(.161) |
| Gov't Grants & Contracts$_{t-4}$ | .976(.332)* | .737(.208)*** | −.416(.243)# | −.294(.230) |
| Health/Welfare$_{t-4}$ | .165(.350) | .075(.201) | .145(.249) | .432(.266) |
| Culture/Recreation$_{t-4}$ | .014(.364) | −.136(.230) | .415(.293) | .619(.296)* |
| Education$_{t-4}$ | −.092(.334) | −.056(.190) | .001(.246) | .087(.257) |
| No. of Managerial Tactics$_{t-4}$ | .010(.051)# | .088(.031)** | −.001(.041) | .035(.041) |
| No. of Political Tactics$_{t-4}$ | −.097(.085) | −.066(.047) | .050(.056) | .070(.054) |
| No. of Retrench Tactics$_{t-4}$ | .293(.075)*** | .137(.033)*** | .255(.062)*** | .200(.047)*** |
| Niche Density$_{t-4}$ | −.068(.065) | −.059(.034)# | .024(.057) | .030(.064) |
| Niche Concentration$_{t-4}$ | 1.10(1.39) | .833(.856) | −1.58(1.04) | −2.70(1.05)* |
| λ | .388(.920) | .524(.544) | −.231(.606) | −.217(.680) |
| Constant | .126(.512) | −1.04(.330)** | .379(.415) | −1.48(.453)** |
| R² | .277*** | | .271*** | |
| Adj. R² | .223 | | .217 | |
| N | 172 | | 159 | |
| Log likelihood | | −254.94 | | −178.8 |
| White test statistic for heteroskedasticity | 18.3 (df=12) | | 13.9 (df=12) | |
| Modified Breusch-Godfrey test statistic for autocorrelation | — | | .243 | |

*** p < .001; ** p < .01; * p < .05; # p < .10.

142

son) and managerial ($p < .05$ in OLS and $p < .01$ in Poisson) tactics between 1984–1988 and 1988–1992. Thus between 1980–1984 and 1984–1988 dependencies upon commercial income / employees and increases in the use of managerial tactics were tightly coupled and dependencies upon donated income / volunteers and increases in the use of political tactics were tightly coupled; the two pairings of resource streams and tactics were independent of one another. Between 1984–1988 and 1988–1992, things were different: big organizations—whether commercial or donative—increased both their managerial and political tactics.[6]

Other variables affected changes in the number of managerial and political tactics as well. Organizations with government funding in 1984 increased their use of managerial tactics between 1980–1984 and 1984–1988 ($p < .001$ in both OLS and Poisson) but not between 1984–1988 and 1988–1992. Government-funded organizations increased their political tactics between 1980–1984 and 1984–1988 as well ($p < .05$ in both OLS and Poisson) and to the lesser extent between 1984–1988 and 1988–1992 (NS in OLS and $p < .10$ in Poisson). Health / welfare organizations in 1984 pursued fewer managerial ($p < .01$ in both OLS and Poisson) and political ($p < .01$ in both OLS and Poisson) tactics in the period 1984–1988 than in the period 1980–1984—but saw no change between 1984–1988 and 1988–1992. Cultural and recreational organizations pursued fewer managerial tactics in 1984–1988 than in 1980–1984 ($p < .01$ in OLS and $p < .001$ in Poisson). Organizations in more dense niches in 1984 employed *fewer* managerial tactics in 1984–1988 than in 1980–1984 ($p < .05$ in both OLS and Poisson). Organizations in niches where resources were less concentrated in 1984 employed *fewer* managerial ($p < .001$ in both OLS and Poisson) and political tactics ($p < .10$ in both OLS and Poisson) in 1984–1988 than 1980–1984. We had not hypothesized a direct effect of niche competition on changes in tactics and were surprised that competition—at least in 1984—resulted in organizations cutting back on their use of managerial and political tactics—rather than moving aggressively forward. Finally, we found only one niche effect between 1984–1988 and 1988–1992. In the Poisson regression, organizations in less concentrated niches in 1988 pursued more managerial tactics in 1988–1992 than in 1984–1988 ($p < .10$).

There was little support for Hypothesis 5 (Table 4.4, models 5a, 5b, 6a, 6b). In our Poisson regressions we found that organizations in less concentrated niches in 1988 increased their retrenchment tactics between 1984–1988 and 1988–1992 ($p < .05$); and organizations in less dense niches in 1984 increased their retrenchment tactics between 1980–1984 and 1984–1988 ($p < .10$). None of the niche variables had a significant effect on changes in retrenchment tactics in our OLS analysis. Organizations with government funding in 1984 increased their use of retrenchment tactics between 1980–1984 and 1984–1988 ($p < .05$ in OLS and $p <$ .001 in Poisson), but publicly funded organizations reduced their retrenchment tactics between 1984–1988 and 1988–1992 ($p < .10$ in OLS and NS in Poisson). Organizations with more donated income and volunteers reduced the number of retrenchment tactics used between 1980–1984 and 1984–1988 ($p < .10$ in OLS and $p < .01$ in Poisson) but not between 1984–1988 and 1988–1992. The only consistent finding was that organizations with more commercial income and employees in 1984 and 1988 increased their use of retrenchment tactics between 1980–1984 and 1984–1988 (NS in OLS and $p < .10$ in Poisson) and between 1984–1988 and 1988–1992 ($p < .05$ in both OLS and Poisson), respectively. Dependency upon commercial activities seemed to encourage the use of retrenchment tactics.

Hypotheses 3, 6, 7a, and 7b speculated further on what organizations would do if situated in a highly competitive niche. Again, niche competition was measured in two ways: the density/sparseness of the niches in which an organization was embedded (based on adjusted residuals), and the level of resource concentration in these same niches. Hypothesis 3 speculated that organizations within highly competitive niches would respond aggressively and switch resource arenas; Hypotheses 6, 7a, and 7b said that organizations in highly competitive niches would intensify their efforts within their current arenas. These hypotheses entailed testing multiplicative interaction effects where each measure of niche competition is multiplied by variables measuring the extent to which organizations are dependent upon commercial income and employees or donated income and volunteers. To test Hypotheses 3 and 7a we estimated the following OLS equation:

$$Y_t = \beta_0 + \beta_1 Y_{t-n} + \Sigma_i \beta_i X_{i,t-n} + \Sigma_j \beta_j W_{j,t-n} + \beta_6 (W_1 * X_1) - \beta_7 (W_2 * X_1) + \beta_8 (W_1 * X_2) - \beta_9 (W_2 * X_2) + \Sigma_k \beta_k Z_{k,t-n} + \beta \lambda + \epsilon_t \quad (5)$$

where $Y_t$ now refers to the political tactics used by the organization between $t$ and $t - 4$ and $Y_{t-n}$ is the number of political tactics used between $t - 8$ and $t - 4$; $W_1$ and $W_2$ are the two niche variables (density, concentration); $X_1$ and $X_2$ are the resource variables (commercial income and employees, donated income and volunteers, respectively); $Z_k$ are the control variables (activities, presence of government funding); and $\lambda$ is the sample selection term. The coefficients associated with the interaction terms were key to testing these hypotheses. Hypothesis 3 would be supported if the estimate of $\beta_6$ was positive and $\beta_7$ negative.[7] This would mean that in more competitive niches organizations that had more commercial income and employees increased their political tactics—thus thrusting them into a new funding arena. Hypothesis 7a would be supported if the estimate of $\beta_8$ was positive and $\beta_9$ was negative. That is, in more competitive niches organizations with more donated income and volunteers increased their political tactics over time.

Hypotheses 6 and 7b were tested by substituting managerial tactics for political tactics ($Y_t$, $Y_{t-n}$). Testing the significance of the parameter estimates of the regression coefficients associated with each of the four interaction terms would be key to testing Hypotheses 6 and 7b as well. This time, if the estimate of $\beta_6$ was positive and $\beta_7$ was negative, Hypothesis 6 would be supported. That is, in more competitive niches, organizations that had more commercial income and employees increased their managerial tactics over time. Hypothesis 7b would be supported if the estimate of $\beta_8$ was positive and $\beta_9$ was negative. That is, in more competitive niches, organizations with more donated income and volunteers increased their managerial tactics over time. Empirical support for Hypothesis 3 would support adaption theory, while support for Hypotheses 6, 7a, and 7b would support ecological theory and the inertia hypothesis.

All of the regressors listed in Table 4.4 were included on the right-hand side of each equation we estimated, including, of course, the number of managerial and political tactics used between $t - 8$ and $t - 4$. The niche variables and the income/personnel variables were already centered, so we were able to minimize correlations between the product terms and the other regressors in the model. We again checked for heteroskedasticity, but in none of the 16 models was it a problem. We estimated models using both OLS and Poisson regression. As we shall see, the results were very different.

The results are in Table 4.5. To save space we only present the coefficients associated with the product terms, their standard errors in parentheses, and indicate if the effect was statistically significant. In none of the 16 OLS models that we estimated did we find an interaction term significant at the .10-level. However, we did find a number of significant interaction effects in the Poisson regressions.

Because these findings are complicated, let us address them in terms of the four hypotheses that we are testing. Adaptation theory would argue that as conditions within niches become more competitive (i.e., more dense or less concentrated) organizations should switch funding arenas (H3). Thus the effects in cells (3, 2) and (3, 4) should be significant and positive, and the effects in cells (4, 2) and (4, 4) should be significant and negative. None of these four effects were statistically significant in either our OLS or Poisson regression. Clearly there was little support for adaptation theory.

Selection theory argues that as conditions with niches become more competitive organizations should "gird their loins" and do more of what they know best so as to compete more effectively (H6, H7a, H7b). Thus the effects in cells (1, 1), (1, 2), (1, 3), (1, 4), (3, 1), and (3, 3) should be

Table 4.5.  Interaction Effects from OLS and Poisson Regressions with Managerial and Political Tactics as the Dependent Variables

| | Dependent Variables | | | | | | | |
|---|---|---|---|---|---|---|---|---|
| | No. of Managerial Tactics$_{84-88}$ | | No. of Political Tactics$_{84-88}$ | | No. of Managerial Tactics$_{88-92}$ | | No. of Political Tactics$_{88-92}$ | |
| | (1a) OLS b (SE) | (1b) Poisson b (SE) | (2a) OLS b (SE) | (2b) Poisson b (SE) | (3a) OLS b (SE) | (3b) Poisson b (SE) | (4a) OLS b (SE) | (4b) Poisson b (SE) |
| Niche Density$_{t-4}$ * DonatedInc&Vols$_{t-4}$ | .021(.108) | .007(.018) | -.003(.076) | .006(.026) | -.154(.112) | -.042(.019)* | -.106(.078) | -.054(.024)* |
| Niche Concent$_{t-4}$ * DonatedInc&Vols$_{t-4}$ | -2.04(1.80) | -.585(.314)# | .301(1.27) | -.144(.448) | .563(2.16) | -.071(.382) | -1.37(1.51) | -.880(.504)# |
| Niche Density$_{t-4}$ * CommercialInc&Emp$_{t-4}$ | .015(.121) | .006(.019) | -.045(.085) | .000(.026) | -.144(.115) | -.033(.020)# | .033(.081) | .001(.024) |
| Niche Concent$_{t-4}$ * CommercialInc&Emp$_{t-4}$ | -1.46(1.56) | -.807(.353)* | -.550(1.36) | -.345(.460) | -2.63(1.92) | -.656(.337)# | -.671(1.36) | -.462(.435) |

*** $p < .001$; ** $p < .01$; * $p < .05$; # $p < .10$.

146

significant and positive, and the effects in cells (2, 1), (2, 2), (2, 3), (2, 4), (4, 1), and (4, 3) should be significant and negative. Poisson regression effects in seven of the twelve cells were significant. However, the signs in cells (1, 3), (1, 4), and (3, 3) were negative, while we hypothesized a positive effect; but the signs in cells (2, 1) (2, 4), (4, 1), and (4, 3) were negative, as we expected.

One way to make more sense of these findings is to rethink what we mean by density. As noted in Chapters 1 and 3, crowding could mean either competition or constitutive legitimacy. If we interpret density as the latter, then sparsely settled niches are more, not less hostile environments. With this interpretation in mind, we now have organizations that were heavily dependent upon donations and volunteers and in less legitimate (i.e., sparsely settled) niches in 1988, increasing their managerial tactics between 1984–1988 and 1988–1992 [cell (1, 3)]; organizations heavily dependent upon donations and volunteers and in less legitimate (i.e., sparsely settled) niches in 1988, increasing their political tactics [cell (1, 4)], and organizations heavily dependent upon commercial income and employees [cell (3, 3)] and in less legitimate niches in 1988, increasing their managerial tactics. If this reinterpretation of the density effect is acceptable, inertia theory has more support although the results are equivocal.

Finally, Hypothesis 4 stated that organizations that resided in more competitive niches were more likely to change their products and services. To test this hypothesis, we estimated a series of logit models. The dependent variables were whether or not the organization provided some service at $t$ (i.e., cited health/welfare, education, culture/recreation, or other as its top priority). It was coded 1 if yes and 0 if no. The independent variables were whether or not the organization provided the same service at $t - 4$ (coded 1 if yes and 0 if no) and the niche variables at $t - 4$ (coded 1 if niche scores were above the median and 0 if below). We estimated 16 logit models testing if there was a significant interaction effect of activities at $t - 4$, niche conditions at $t - 4$, and activities at $t$. For each year we had four activity scores and two niche measures (niche density and concentration). The analyses were done for the periods from 1984 to 1988 and 1988 to 1992. Our hypothesis was that the likelihood of engaging in an activity at $t - 4$ and the same activity at $t$ was contingent upon niche conditions at $t - 4$, i.e., whether the niche was dense or resources were dispersed or concentrated. We hypothesized that those organizations in more competitive (i.e., dense or less concentrated) niches at $t - 4$ were more likely to abandon activities by $t$ that they provided at $t - 4$ or to provide activities at $t$ that they did not provide at $t - 4$. The models that we estimated took on the general form:

$$\text{logit}_{i,j} = u_0 + u_{1(i)} + u_{2(j)} + u_{12(ij)} \tag{6}$$

where the $u$ were logit coefficients, $u_1$ corresponded to one of the four activities at $t - 4$, $u_2$ corresponded to one of our two measures of niche competition at $t - 4$, and $u_{12}$ corresponded to the interaction between activity and niche conditions at $t - 4$ (see Fienberg 1977:79). The application of the logit model to panel data was suggested by Goodman (1973) and is discussed in Fienberg (1977) and Markus (1979).

Table 4.6 presents the results for Equation (6). Note there was no correction for sample selection. To derive the logit coefficients ($u$) and test if the interaction effects were significant, we estimated the saturated model. We added 0.5 to all the cells before computation, because of zeros in the contingency table. The standard errors were computed using the formula described in Goodman (1972). The constant in Table 4.6 is the average log odds ratio of providing a given activity or not. A negative coefficient indicates that fewer than half of the organizations provided that service at $t$. Thus because 41% of the organizations cited health / welfare activities in 1988, the effect was negative but not statistically significant. In contrast, because a smaller percentage of organizations cited cultural / recreational, educational, or other activities, the effects were negative and oftentimes significant. The rest of the coefficients should be interpreted as deviations from this mean log odds ratio. The trickiest to interpret are the coefficients associated with the interaction terms. With the coding scheme we used, a positive interaction effect indicated that the log odds ratio of changing activities increased if the organization was in a more dense or more concentrated niche. A negative coefficient indicated that the log odds ratio of changing activities decreased if the organization was in a more dense or more concentrated niche.

The results show that organizations tended to cite the same activity at $t$ that they cited at $t - 4$. All effect parameters associated with the activity scores at $t - 4$ were statistically significant at the .01-level. In contrast, none of the niche variables were statistically significant at the .10-level. We found that some of the interaction effects were significant. As hypothesized, organizations that were in less concentrated (i.e., more competitive) niches in 1984 tended either to abandon educational activities or to move into this area by 1988 ($p < .10$). However, contrary to our expectations, cultural organizations that were in niches where resources were less concentrated (i.e., more competitive) in 1988 were more likely to replicate their activities than organizations in more concentrated (i.e., less competitive) niches ($p < .10$). While the first supported our hypothesis, the latter did not. Nevertheless, these were the only two significant interaction effects among the 16 that we tested. Thus is it safe to conclude that niche conditions did not lead organizations to either abandon products and

Table 4.6. Logit Analysis with Four Activities as the Dependent Variable

| | Dependent Variables | | | | | | | |
| --- | --- | --- | --- | --- | --- | --- | --- | --- |
| | Health & Welfare₈₈ | | Culture & Recreation₈₈ | | Education₈₈ | | Other₈₈ | |
| Independent Variables | u(SE) | u(SE) | u(SE) | u(SE) | u(SE) | u(SE) | u(SE) | u(SE) |
| Health & Welfare₈₄ | .863(.111)** | .848(.109)** | | | | | | |
| Culture & Recreation₈₄ | | | 1.35(.226)** | 1.16(.151)** | | | | |
| Education₈₄ | | | | | .684(.101)** | .671(.104)** | | |
| Other₈₄ | | | | | | | .713(.123)** | .788(.211)** |
| Niche Density₈₄ | −.038(.111) | | −.358(.226) | | −.001(.101) | | −.171(.123) | |
| Activity * Niche Density₈₄ | −.140(.111) | | .195(.226) | | .022(.101) | | −.056(.123) | |
| Niche Concentration₈₄ | | −.086(.109) | | −.010(.151) | | .074(.104) | | −.142(.211) |
| Activity * Niche Concentration₈₄ | | .132(.109) | | .021(.151) | | .189(.104)# | | .133(.211) |
| Constant | −.013(.111) | −.033(.109) | −.327(.226) | −.488(.151)** | −.267(.101)** | −.303(.104)** | −.384(.123)** | −.258(.211) |

| | Dependent Variables | | | | | | | |
| --- | --- | --- | --- | --- | --- | --- | --- | --- |
| | Health & Welfare₉₂ | | Culture & Recreation₉₂ | | Education₉₂ | | Other₉₂ | |
| Independent Variables | u(SE) | u(SE) | u(SE) | u(SE) | u(SE) | u(SE) | u(SE) | u(SE) |
| Health & Welfare₈₈ | 1.06(.129)** | 1.04(.127)** | | | | | | |
| Culture & Recreation₈₈ | | | 1.13(.160)** | 1.25(.216)** | | | | |
| Education₈₈ | | | | | .696(.106)** | .715(.108)** | | |
| Other₈₈ | | | | | | | .903(.135)** | .810(.141)** |
| Niche Density₈₈ | .107(.129) | | .206(.160) | | −.157(.106) | | .051(.135) | |
| Activity * Niche Density₈₈ | −.056(.129) | | .030(.160) | | .013(.106) | | −.016(.135) | |
| Niche Concentration₈₈ | | −.023(.127) | | −.158(.216) | | −.068(.108) | | .201(.141) |
| Activity * Niche Concentration₈₈ | | .041(.127) | | −.392(.216)# | | −.160(.107) | | −.178(.141) |
| Constant | −.153(.129) | −.169(.127) | −.526(.160)** | −.610(.216)** | −.061(.106) | −.073(.108) | −.471(.135)** | −.557(.141)** |

** $p < .01$; * $p < .05$; # $p < .10$.

149

services that they provided in the past or to add new products and services.

## TESTING FOR EMBEDDEDNESS EFFECTS: HYPOTHESES 8–11

The final set of analyses in this chapter tested the hypothesis that tactics are tied as much to, if not more than, social or network influences as to organizations' structural positions. The analysis to follow posits that a nonprofit's tactics at $t$ are a function of the tactics of others in its networks at $t - 4$ (H8, H9), the joint effect of funding uncertainty and the tactics used by successful others at $t - 4$ (H10), and the extent to which local elites used or supported the organization (H11). The model to test the social influence effects is a version of a generalized "network effects" model, as presented by Marsden and Friedkin (1993:138, equation 11):

$$Y_t = \beta_0 + \beta_1 Y_{t-n} + \beta_2 PY_{t-n} + \beta_3 SY_{t-n} + \beta_4 RY_{t-n} + \beta_5 U_{t-n}$$
$$+ \beta_6 (U_{t-n} * SY_{t-n}) + \beta_7 E_{t-n} + \Sigma_i \beta_i X_{i,t-n} + \Sigma_j \beta_j W_{j,t-n} + \Sigma_k \beta_k Z_{k,t-n}$$
$$+ \beta\lambda + \epsilon_t \tag{7}$$

To be more explicit, $Y_t$ and $Y_{t-n}$ are vectors containing the number of tactics of a particular type that each organization used between $t - 4$ and $t$ and between $t - 8$ and $t - 4$. As there were two tactics—managerial and political—there are two sets of vectors. Array $P$ was a binary asymmetric matrix denoting if the interviewee in organization $i$ knew personally someone in organization $j$; array $S$ was a binary asymmetric matrix denoting if the interviewee in organization $i$ thought organization $j$ was particularly successful; and array $R$ was a binary symmetric array denoting whether organization $i$ had sent or received resources or information from organizations $j$. $U$ is the degree to which the interviewee in the organization felt uncertain about her or his major funding stream,[8] and $E$ is the extent that the elite used or supported the organization. The other terms are the same as defined in Equation (4).

The analysis was performed separately for managerial and political tactics. The dependent variable was the number of tactics of a given type that the organization utilized between 1984 and 1988 and between 1988 and 1992, the same dependent variables as in our earlier analyses. To make our analysis more parsimonious, we identified all the variables that had significant effects in Table 4.4 and included only these in each set of regressions. Because the social influence variables were skewed positively, we computed the logs of $PY$, $SY$, and $RY$. We centered $SY$ as well as the uncertainty scores before computing our interaction term, $U * SY$.

Our assumption was that a positive, significant interaction shows that the effect of mimicry was greater the more uncertain managers were about their funding sources.

The usual tests for heteroskedasticity and, where appropriate, autocorrelation were performed. As shown in Tables 4.7 and 4.8, neither was a problem in any of the equations. We also computed tolerance scores for each regressor in the four analyses. In only one set of analysis—explaining changes in managerial tactics between 1980–1984 and 1984–1988—was multicollinearity a problem. Here managerial and political tactics had tolerance scores of .371 and .373, respectively. Since we used mean substitution for missing uncertainty scores in 1984 and 1988 (see note 8), we included a dummy variable where a 1 indicated that mean substitution was necessary and 0 otherwise. In none of the equations was the dummy significantly related to change in the number of managerial or political tactics at the .10-level, and thus we excluded the dummy in our final analyses.

The OLS and Poisson regression results are presented in Tables 4.7 and 4.8. Looking first at changes in the number of managerial tactics (see Table 4.7), we see that organizations increased their managerial tactics between 1980–1984 and 1984–1988, if organizations that they exchanged resources or information with utilized more managerial tactics between 1980–1984 ($p < .05$ in OLS and Poisson). The other social influence variable had little effect on changes in the number of managerial tactics in the OLS or Poisson regression. Unexpectedly, in the Poisson regression elite network contacts in 1980 led to a decrease in managerial tactics between 1980–1984 and 1984–1988 ($p < .10$; NS in OLS). Neither uncertainty in the funding environment, the mimicry variable, nor the interaction between uncertainty and the mimicry variable was statistically significant. Finally, all the variables that were significant predictors of change in the number of managerial tactics discussed earlier were still significant with the exception of commercial income and employees, which was not significant at the .10 level in the Poisson regression.

We also see that organizations increased their number of managerial tactics between 1984–1988 and 1988–1992 if organizations where they knew someone personally utilized more managerial tactics between 1984 and 1988 ($p < .05$ in OLS and $p < .01$ in Poisson). The other social influence variable had little effect on changes in managerial tactics, but elite network contacts now had a positive effect on change in the number of managerial tactics ($p < .10$ in the OLS and NS in Poisson). According to the OLS results, the more elites associated with the organization, the greater the increase in managerial tactics. Neither uncertainty in the funding environment nor the interaction between uncertainty and the mimicry variable was statistically significant. In the OLS results the use of manage-

*Table 4.7.* OLS and Poisson Regression with Number of Managerial Tactics as Dependent Variable

| | Dependent Variable: No. of Managerial Tactics$_t$ | | | |
|---|---|---|---|---|
| | (1a) 1984–1988 | (1b) | (2a) 1988–1992 | (2b) |
| Independent Variables | OLS b (SE) | Poisson b (SE) | OLS b (SE) | Poisson b (SE) |
| Commercial Inc & Empl$_{t-4}$ | .632(.297)* | .084(.052) | .698(.307)* | .139(.057)* |
| Donated Inc & Vols$_{t-4}$ | | | .674(.340)# | .117(.067)# |
| Gov't Grants & Contracts$_{t-4}$ | 2.31(.532)*** | .442(.096)*** | | |
| Health/Welfare$_{t-4}$ | −1.49(.468)** | −.303(.084)*** | | |
| Culture/Recreation$_{t-4}$ | −1.19(.526)* | −.237(.095)* | | |
| No. of Managerial Tactics$_{t-4}$ | .307(.086)*** | .061(.015)*** | .122(.086) | .032(.016)* |
| No. of Political Tactics$_{t-4}$ | −.294(.139)* | −.052(.023)* | | |
| Niche Density$_{t-4}$ | −.287(.109)** | −.043(.017)* | | |
| Niche Concentration$_{t-4}$ | 8.04(2.13)*** | 1.65(.396)*** | | |
| Elite Network Contacts$^a_{t-4}$ | −.300(.227) | −.064(.035)# | .433(.242)# | .032(.040) |
| Funding Uncertainty$_{t-4}$ | −.077(.282) | −.031(.051) | −.027(.292) | .014(.055) |
| No. Managerial Tactics of Exchange Partners$_{t-4}$ | .338(.161)* | .068(.031)* | .074(.184) | .016(.035) |
| No. Managerial Tactics of Personal Ties$_{t-4}$ | −.136(.164) | −.026(.030) | .363(.176)* | .124(.040)** |
| No. Managerial Tactics of Successful Others$_{t-4}$ | .177(.142) | .049(.037) | .204(.168) | .068(.039)# |
| Uncertainty * Managerial Tactics of Successful Others$_{t-4}$ | .228(.189) | .045(.036) | −.158(.199) | −.042(.042) |
| λ | −2.35(1.57) | −.352(.277) | −.912(1.30) | −.134(.246) |
| Constant | 5.59(.846)*** | 1.53(.143)*** | 4.00(.785)*** | 1.22(.150)*** |
| $R^2$ | .547*** | | .428*** | |
| Adj. $R^2$ | .503 | | .388 | |
| N | 168 | 168 | 154 | 154 |
| Log likelihood | | −398.5 | | −366.2 |
| White test statistic for heteroskedasticity | 7.18 (df=15) | | 14.3 (df=10) | |
| Modified Breusch-Godfrey test statistic for autocorrelation | — | | .007 | |

*** $p < .001$; ** $p < .01$; * $p < .05$; # $p < .10$.

*Table 4.8.* OLS and Poisson Regression with Number of Political Tactics as Dependent Variable

| Independent Variables | (3a) 1984–1988 OLS b (SE) | (3b) Poisson b (SE) | (4a) 1988–1992 OLS b (SE) | (4b) Poisson b (SE) |
|---|---|---|---|---|
| | *Dependent Variable: No. of Political Tactics$_t$* | | | |
| Commercial Inc & Empl $_{t-4}$ | | | .505(.191)** | .167(.067)* |
| Donated Inc & Vols $_{t-4}$ | .560(.185)** | .215(.070)** | .412(.240)# | .143(.086)# |
| Gov't Grants & Contracts$_{t-4}$ | .866(.346)* | .320(.122)** | | |
| Health/Welfare$_{t-4}$ | −.916(.304)** | −.352(.109)** | | |
| No. of Political Tactics$_{t-4}$ | .156(.085)# | .045(.028) | .023(.078) | .014(.026) |
| No. of Retrench Tactics $_{t-4}$ | .102(.082) | .020(.024) | | |
| Niche Concentration$_{t-4}$ | 2.48(1.32)# | 1.01(.479)* | | |
| Elite Network Contacts$_{t-4}$ | −.090(.150) | −.081(.045)# | .385(.170)* | .056(.050) |
| Funding Uncertainty$_{t-4}$ | .441(.196)* | .150(.065)* | −.167(.207) | −.049(.073) |
| No. Political Tactics of Exchange Partners$_{t-4}$ | .218(.128)# | .077(.046)# | .074(.153) | .021(.053) |
| No. Political Tactics of Personal Ties$_{t-4}$ | −.014(.132) | −.004(.047) | .335(.141)* | .171(.056)** |
| No. Political Tactics of Successful Others$_{t-4}$ | −.066(.111) | −.021(.039) | .073(.134) | .049(.054) |
| Uncertainty * Political Tactics of Successful Others$_{t-4}$ | .080(.148) | .008(.050) | .009(.160) | .021(.064) |
| λ | −.329(.986) | −.052(.348) | −.275(.906) | −.056(.312) |
| Constant | 2.54(.495)*** | .858(.172)*** | 2.64(.496)*** | .822(.172)*** |
| $R^2$ | .413*** | | .384*** | |
| Adj. $R^2$ | .364 | | .341 | |
| N | 169 | 169 | 152 | 152 |
| Log likelihood | | −322.9 | | −290.7 |
| White test statistic for heteroskedasticity | 13.6 (df=13) | | 12.6 (df=10) | |
| Modified Breusch-Godfrey test statistic for autocorrelation | — | | .036 | |

*** $p < .001$; ** $p < .01$; * $p < .05$; # $p < .10$.
a For the period from 1984 to 1988, used Elite Network Contacts, 1980; for the period from 1988 to 1992, used Elite Network Contacts, 1988.

153

rial tactics by successful others had little effect on the change in managerial tactics, but in the Poisson results it did ($p < .10$). Finally, except for the lagged dependent variable in the OLS results, all the variables that were significant predictors of change in managerial tactics discussed earlier were significant in these analyses as well.

The results for political tactics mirrored those for managerial tactics with one difference. Organizations increased their number of political tactics between 1980–1984 and 1984–1988 if organizations with which they exchanged resources or information utilized more political tactics between 1980 and 1984 ($p < .10$ in both OLS and Poisson). The other social influence variables had little effect on changes in political tactics, and elite network contacts had a negative effect on political tactics in the Poisson results ($p < .10$; NS in OLS). Uncertainty in the funding environment, however, had a positive effect on the change in the number of political tactics ($p < .05$ in both OLS and Poisson), but neither the mimicry variable nor the interaction between uncertainty and the mimicry variable was statistically significant. With the exception of the number of retrenchment tactics used in 1984 and the lagged dependent variable in the Poisson results, all the variables that were significant predictors of change in political tactics discussed earlier were still significant in these analyses.

Finally, organizations increased their number of political tactics between 1984–1988 and 1988–1992 if organizations where they knew someone personally utilized more political tactics between 1984 and 1988 ($p < .05$ in OLS and $p < .01$ in Poisson). The other social influence variable had little effect on changes in the number of political tactics, but elite network contacts again had a positive effect on change in political tactics in the OLS results ($p < .05$; NS in Poisson). Neither uncertainty in the funding environment, the mimicry variable, nor the interaction between uncertainty and the mimicry variable was statistically significant. Finally, except for the lagged dependent variable, all the variables that were significant predictors of change in political tactics discussed earlier were significant in these analyses as well.

Strictly speaking, we found limited support for Hypotheses 8 and 9 and no support for 10. In each period, and in analyzing each tactic, we found a positive direct effect of a social influence variable on changes in the number of tactics used. Thus there appeared to be some support for the argument that the choice of tactics was influenced by organizations in one's networks—independent of one's resource dependencies. However, only in one isolated analysis did organizations appear to mimic others that they felt were very successful, but this was an exception. We found no evidence that mimicry effects were contingent upon the degree of perceived uncertainty. There was qualified support for Hypothesis 11. In the OLS results there was a significant positive effect of elite network contacts on increases in both the number of managerial and political tactics between 1984–1988 and 1988–1992 (elite network contacts had little effect on tactic change between 1980–1984 and 1984–1988). However, in the Poisson results elite ties had little effect on changes in either tactic between 1984–1988 and 1988–1992 and a negative effect on changes in managerial and political tactics between 1980–1984 and 1984–1988.

## DISCUSSION

Which of our theories better explains changes in the number of tactics and organizational activities? We forewarned the reader in the first chapter that not all our hypotheses were going to be confirmed and that the reader should look at our analyses as a contest among competing theories. It is time once again to sort out the winners and losers.

Resource dependency and adaptation theory gets mixed grades. In general the theory argued that organizations are adaptive creatures. Organizations will do whatever it takes to maintain or increase revenues and personnel. In support of the theory, we found that organizations more dependent upon commercial income and employees in 1984 and 1988 increased their use of managerial tactics between 1980–1984 and 1984–1988, and between 1984–1988 and 1988–1992, respectively. We also found that organizations more dependent upon private donations and volunteers in 1984 and 1988 increased their use of political tactics between 1980–1984 and 1984–1988 and between 1984–1988 and 1988–1992. Furthermore, organizations more dependent upon donations and volunteers increased their use of managerial tactics between 1984–1988 and 1988–1992. Organizations did what they had to do to compete effectively against others that were going after the same resources. The result was that organizations that relied on commercial income and paid employees—a pattern characteristic of utilitarian organizations—came to look and behave more like businesses over time. In contrast, organizations that relied on donated income and volunteer work—a pattern characteristic of normative organizations—came to look and behave more like traditional charities and business organizations over time. This harkens back to a point we made in Chapter 1. Nonprofits' behavior is closely linked to where they obtain their resources. Over time, organizations extracting similar kinds of resources from their environment take on a certain style or character.

There were, though, some findings that resource dependency theory could not explain. For example, organizations with more donated income and volunteers in 1984 did not increase their managerial tactics between

1980–1984 and 1984–1988, and organizations with more commercial income and employees increased their political tactics between 1984–1988 and 1988–1992. The first finding may simply be due to a lag in organizational learning. In Chapter 3 we found that organizations that used more managerial tactics increased their donated income and volunteers throughout the study period. Perhaps nonprofit managers only came to realize this in the latter part of the decade, and those reliant on donated income and volunteers utilized both managerial and political tactics thereafter.

Explaining why organizations dependent upon commercial income and employees in 1988 increased their use of political tactics between 1984–1988 and 1988–1992 is more challenging. It could be that political tactics as well as managerial tactics led to an increase in commercial income and employees. We reran the analysis in Chapter 3 (see Table 3.5), adding political tactics to the equation predicting growth in commercial income and employees between 1980 and 1984, 1984 and 1988, 1988 and 1992, and 1988 and 1994. Political tactics only had a positive effect on growth in commercial income/employees between 1980 and 1984 ($p <$ .05) and no effects in any other period.[9]

Our findings lead us to question whether the distinctions between niches with strong output controls and niches with strong process controls (and between utilitarian and normative organizations) are as useful as we had first thought. As noted in Chapter 3, resource streams were independent of each other, but different tactics were not neatly coupled to different resource streams. Political and managerial tactics could increase commercial income and employees, donated income and volunteers. Whether one was dependent on earned income and employees or donated income and volunteers, organizations increased their use of managerial and political tactics between 1984–1988 and 1988–1992. To succeed in niches with strong output controls as well as in niches with strong process controls, you have to be managerial—and it is probably good to be political as well.

Support for ecological theory was also mixed. Ecologists argue that organizations may change in response to environmental conditions, but the "smart" organizations keep change to a minimum. Our test of ecological theory was to see what organizations did in more or less competitive niche environments: Did they stay the course or change? If the theory is correct, we would expect them to stay the course. If they did anything, they would intensify their efforts to extract resources from established funding sources when faced with greater competition.

We found little evidence that niche conditions prompted organizations to change niche position. Organizations that were dependent upon commercial income and employees did not increase their political tactics (and pursue donated income and volunteers), if their niche was more or less dense or more or less concentrated. From our Poisson regressions, we learned that if their niche was sparsely populated or resources were less concentrated, organizations that were dependent upon commercial income and employees increased their managerial tactics and organizations that were dependent upon donated income and volunteers increased their political and managerial tactics. Thus it seems that hostile environments led organizations to compete harder within their domain rather than to flee their niche and find a new home.[10]

Niche conditions did have some effect on the use of retrenchment tactics. The Poisson regressions showed that organizations in more sparsely settled niches in 1984 increased their retrenchment efforts between 1980–1984 and 1984–1988, and organizations in less concentrated niches in 1988 increased their use of retrenchment tactics between 1984–1988 and 1988–1992. There were no significant effects in the OLS results. Thus there is some evidence that hostile niche conditions drove organizations to downsize their operations.

There was, however, one interesting result regarding retrenchment that we had not anticipated. In both Poisson regressions (and one OLS regression) we found that organizations more reliant on commercial income and employees increased their retrenchment tactics between 1980–1984 and 1984–1988 and between 1984–1988 and 1988–1992. The relevance of these findings becomes clear, if we look back to Table 3.2. Here we learned that the use of retrenchment tactics led to a drop-off in commercial income and employees between 1980 and 1984, but in the other three periods had no statistically significant effect on changes in commercial income and employees. Thus while one might expect that implementing retrenchment tactics might cut into the capacities of organizations and start a downward spiral, instead we find commercial nonprofits routinely cutting staff, benefits, and programs without hurting their growth potential. In other words, among these kinds of organizations, retrenchment may be "business as usual": as you add new things, you eliminate some of the old.

We also found that in both periods organizations were very reluctant to change their products or services—even when facing a highly competitive environment. In fact, we found a case where organizations in more competitive niches, were actually *less* likely to change their products and services than their counterparts in less competitive niches.

We had sketched out two scenarios. Facing competitive environments organizations could respond either by escalating commitments to the tactics employed in the past or by changing their niche position. The results described above suggest the former, although we acknowledge the shortcomings of our tests. Under unfavorable conditions, organizations seemed to increase their efforts to extract resources from familiar sources; there was little evidence that they turned to new funding sources; and they did not change their mix of products and services. However, they did tend to scale back (i.e. downsize) their operations.

Either we chose the wrong tactics, our measures of competition were flawed, or organizations in less concentrated and less organized niches were really reluctant to change. Perhaps organizations realized intuitively what ecologists have long argued. Change resets an organization's clock and subjects it to the liabilities of newness. Change not only moves an organization into uncharted waters, it also jeopardizes its reliability and accountability by disrupting organizational routines (Hannan and Freeman 1989). Especially in disorganized or highly competitive situations, it seems best to simply ride out the storm or try a little harder at what one already knows. Do our findings support the inertia argument? A qualified yes.

Finally, we tested hypotheses derived from social network or embeddedness theory. Here again we had mixed results. Studying both tactics, we found that between 1984 and 1988 organizations seemed to be influenced by other organizations with which they had exchanged resources and information. If network partners utilized more managerial and/or political tactics in the past, an organization would increase its use of the same tactics over time." Between 1988 and 1992 organizations seemed to be influenced by organizations where the top managers knew someone personally. Again, if network partners utilized more managerial and/or political tactics in the past, an organization would increase its use of the same tactics over time.[11] However, in only one Poisson regression (explaining change in managerial tactics between 1984–1988 and 1988–1992) did we find that organizations mimicked organizations that they thought were successful, and in none of our analyses did we find that mimicry was contingent upon the level of uncertainty in organization's funding environment. This suggests that contagion in our sample was due more to direct observation and learning than to imitative processes. Finally, in our OLS analysis, organizations increased their use of both managerial and political tactics between 1984–1988 and 1988–1992 (but not between 1984 and 1988), if more members of the community elite used their services or supported their efforts with time and money. However, in our Poisson regressions more elite contacts led to organizations reducing their managerial and political tactics between 1980–1984 and 1984–1988.

The effects of elite network contacts on tactical choice are noteworthy. First, we were surprised that elite network contacts had a positive effect on both managerial and political tactics between 1988 and 1992. We had only expected an effect on managerial tactics. A simple explanation is that the two were highly correlated in all periods and if some variable affected one, it would affect the other. Alternatively, the elite may just push non-profits to do more. Organizations may learn managerial techniques from elites, but they may also learn about the importance of legitimation.

Explaining the period effects is more challenging. However, recall that in Chapter 3 we discovered that elite network contacts and reputation had a positive effect on growth in donations/volunteers between 1980 and 1984, between 1984 and 1988, and between 1988 and 1994 if the organization employed fewer political tactics. In conjunction with our findings here, one inference is that the elite's role in nonprofit organizations may have changed over time. In the earlier period the elite was a market signal that nonprofits used to show funders that they were credible, account-able, and worthy of support. Ties to the elite were rewarded with more donations and volunteers. In turn, it was the elite's job to monitor the organization. The negative effects that we found in the Poisson regres-sions suggest that earlier in the study period, nonprofits may have felt they could shed both political and managerial tactics if they had strong ties to the local elite. In the 1990s things changed. Instead of being a market signal and watchdog for the rest of the donor community, elites became more like extension agents, spreading the gospel of strategic man-agement. Their presence was important if the organization did not em-ploy political tactics, but was no longer important if it did. Rather elites were there to teach nonprofit boards and managers how to behave proac-tively— both in a managerial and political way. Obviously, more research needs to be done to see if this interpretation is correct, but our results are consistent with this story.

Finally, there were several findings that we did not anticipate and that our theories cannot explain. For example, we found that organizations more dependent upon government funding increased their use of mana-gerial, political, and retrenchment tactics between 1980–1984 and 1984–1988. Between 1984–1988 and 1988–1992, publicly funded organizations continued to increase their political tactics (according to our Poisson re-sults) but cut back on their use of retrenchment tactics. Also, health/welfare organizations cut back on their use of managerial and political tactics between 1980–1984 and 1984–1988 and cultural/recreational orga-nizations cut back on their use of managerial tactics between 1980–1984 and 1984–1988. However, neither type of organization increased or de-creased managerial or political tactics between the periods 1984–1988 and 1988–1992. Also, organizations that were more uncertain about their funding sources increased their political tactics between 1980–1984 and 1984–1988.

One way to make sense of the findings on government-funded organizations and health/welfare and cultural/recreational organizations is to put them into the context of the periods studied. As is well known, 1984 marked the end of President Ronald Reagan's first term in office and culminated four years of highly publicized cutbacks in federal government funding for the not-for-profit sector (Palmer and Sawhill 1982). Because of this, health/welfare and cultural/recreational organizations —whether or not they were receiving government funding—may have been alarmed. In response, these organizations hunkered down, pared operations a little, and tried to ride out the storm. When the threat passed by 1988, they no longer felt the need to cut back any more on their tactics.

However, organizations that were receiving government funds truly panicked. If there ever was niche flight, this was it! When faced with stiff competition or a mild threat, organizations may pursue a more conservative course of action and ride out the storm, but when they perceive a dramatic, coarse-grained change in their environment, organizations may panic and run. Remember, in Chapter 3 we found government-funded organizations increasing their commercial income throughout the study period. We obviously need to know more about why organizations with government funding behaved so aggressively, but we suspect that they faced a classic case of "punctuated equilibrium" in the mid-1980s and innovated accordingly (Tushman and Romanelli 1985).

But why did organizations that experienced more uncertainty increase their political tactics between 1980–1984 and 1984–1988? On the one hand, being unsure in a very uncertain environment may prompt organizations to take action. However, this does not explain why organizations did not increase their managerial tactics as well. On the other hand, all else being equal, nonprofit executives may believe that when conditions are unstable or in flux, a nonprofit organization can never have too much legitimacy. Earlier we referred to "garbage can" models of decision-making. It is possible that "becoming more legitimate" is an example of a garbage can tactic for nonprofits. It is there for the taking when folks are unsure about what to do next, just as "becoming more efficient" is what for-profits do when they cannot figure out any other way to solve their problems. Because we controlled for the organizations' material conditions, we are confident that these effects are due to decision-makers' bounded rationality. However, without psychometric data or extended fieldwork it is impossible to know for sure.

In this chapter we wanted to test theories that could explain why organizations changed their tactics over time. Again, we used the model outlined in Figure 1.1. We were partially successful. In the next chapter we see what effects changes in size and the use of different tactics had on other aspects of organizational life. In other words, we are looking for externalities of change. There is less theory to guide us in this inquiry, and so our discussion and analysis will be more exploratory in nature.

## NOTES

1. While these arguments are compelling and often cited (see, for example, Oliver 1991), direct evidence of the existence or extent of modeling behavior is scarce. Much of the research in the institutional perspective has been limited to the documentation of the diffusion of structural forms in the tradition started by Tolbert and Zucker (1983). These works, however, have not directly considered mimicry or uncertainty and have not included the modeling of tactics (for exceptions, see Fligstein 1985; Galaskiewicz and Wasserman 1989; Haunschild and Miner 1997).

2. In the previous chapter we used a construct based on elite support, use, and evaluations of the nonprofits in the panel. In this chapter we focus only on elite support and use of the organization. We computed the logs of the numbers of different members of the elite supporting the organization with donations, volunteer time, board service, or consulting and using the organization for personal reasons. These two variables were then combined in a principal components analysis. The loadings for each were .932 in 1980 and .937 in 1988.

3. The sample selection model for 1988 and 1992 included the log of organizational expenditures (1980) and the log of organizational age (1980). Detailed discussion of these models was presented in Chapter 3.

4. It is important to note that in 1984 and 1988 only 11.7 and 9.2% of our respondents had *no* informal ties to other organizations and only 13.8 and 8.7% of our respondents cited no other organization as successful. In contrast, 25.8 and 26.3% of our respondents said that they had no resource or information exchanges with other organizations in 1984 and 1988.

5. Since the tactics variables were on the left-hand side of our equations, we did not use mean substitution for the 1992 items as we did in Chapter 3. This resulted in some additional missing cases. The reader needs to remember that the dependent variable was the count of tactics used between 1984 and 1988 and between 1988 and 1982. Thus the lagged variable was the count of cases between 1980 and 1984 and between 1984 and 1988, respectively.

6. The reader should still note that in the period from 1984–1988 to 1988–1992, in explaining change in managerial tactics, the coefficients associated with commercial income and employees were larger than those associated with donated income and volunteers. Also in explaining change in political tactics, the coefficients associated with donated income and volunteers were larger than those associated with fees and employees. Thus there was still some differentiation in tactics and resources streams, although not as great as in the earlier period.

7. The reader should remember that low levels of concentration indicate high levels of competition.

8. As noted in Table 4.3, there were considerable missing data for the uncertainty scores in 1984 and 1988. To remedy this we computed the mean of the uncertainty scores for these years and substituted them for the missing data.

9.  The effect of managerial tactics remained statistically significant between 1984 and 1988 ($p < .001$) and between 1988 and 1994 ($p < .05$) but was no longer significant predicting growth in commericial income and employees between 1980 and 1984—no doubt due to the high correlation between the two tactics variables. The other significant effects in the 1980 to 1984 model remained significant at the .05-level after political tactics were included.

10.  One could argue that our test of the flight hypothesis is flawed, because we found that political tactics resulted in increased commercial income and employees between 1980 and 1984. We agree and encourage others to devise more rigorous tests of this thesis.

11.  We were not concerned that between 1984 and 1988 social influence was through networks of resource / information exchange and between 1988 and 1992 it took place via networks of personal acquaintanceship. In 1984 and 1988 the correlations between the number of managerial tactics used by one's cooperative contacts and one's personal acquaintances were .503 and .537, respectively. In 1984 and 1988 the correlations between the number of political tactics used by one's cooperative contacts and one's personal acquaintances were .488 and .497, respectively. Thus the effects are somewhat equivalent.

# 5

## Growth, Decline, Tactics and the Organizational Milieux

### With Sarah Allen Welter

Most organizational theorists as well as most working people would agree that it is always better to be associated with an organization that is "growing" than to be with an organization "in decline." Growth is good; it is a sign of goal attainment (Starbuck 1965), organizational fitness (Thompson 1967), effectiveness (Yuchtman and Seashore 1967). You are with a "winner." Decline is bad; it is the sign of failure; the organization is a "loser." This attitude may be peculiar to American culture, where there is a heavy emphasis on progress, change, and expansion. But it seems so commonsensical that salaries and wages would go up as revenues increase, job security would be ensured as firms expand into new markets, and people would have more meaningful work lives as organizations adopt the newest and most innovative technologies. It also seems commonsensical that decline results in all sorts of negative outcomes. Not only do people lose their jobs, wages and salaries decline, but life in general—within the organization—becomes unbearable. In his review of the literature Whetten concluded that "conflict, secrecy, rigidity, centralization, formalization, scapegoating, and conservatism increase (with a decline in resources), and morale, innovativeness, participation, leader influence and long term planning decrease" (1987:344–45; see also Levine 1978; Starbuck, Greve, and Hedberg 1977; Cameron, Whetten, and Kim 1987; Cameron, Kim, and Whetten 1987; D'Aveni 1989). Yet, is this really true?

This chapter examines these issues in depth and raises some questions. First, do growth and decline have the predicted effects on the organizational milieux? Are growing organizations really less secretive, less rigid, more decentralized, less formalized, less nasty, less rule bound than organizations in decline? Do growing organizations have better morale, are

163

they more innovative, is participation higher, and are there fewer disagreements and conflicts? Second, is it growth or decline that results in
these outcomes or is it the environmental context and tactics that organizational leaders employ as the organization grows or shrinks? As noted in
Chapter 3, growth and decline can mean different things to different
organizations. In that chapter we argued that environmental conditions
are key. In noncompetitive, sparsely populated niches, a little decline
might be a good strategy to reposition the organization for future growth.
In contrast, in competitive, crowded niches, decline may be a signal that
the organization has failed with no chance of recovery. How an organization responds to growth and decline can also be important—especially in
light of its history. In particular we will examine the use of retrenchment,
political, and managerial tactics in light of the organization's past pattern
of dependencies and evaluate the extent to which the organizational milieux is influenced more by the tactics that the top management team
employs than growth or decline per se.

## THE CONSEQUENCES OF CHANGE

In contrast to the previous chapters, which tried to explain organizational change using the extant organizational theories, this chapter examines the consequences of change—in particular, the consequences of
growth and decline and changing tactics. Most of the theories that we
have discussed have not addressed these questions, although a few have,
e.g., organizational ecology. However, organizational researchers have
studied these issues in depth for a number of years. Thus there is plenty
of research—but not much theory—to guide our inquiry. The literature
we review is eclectic. We focus on patterns of decision-making, reports of
alienation, organizational cultures that support creativity and innovation,
disagreements, and conflicts with employees. One might characterize
these as "quality of life" variables, but a difficulty is that all are affected
by different factors and are both individual (feelings and behaviors) and
organizational-level phenomena. While we try to explain changes in these
variables, our goal is not to develop and test theories of organizational
conflict, culture, or anomie, but rather to see if the changes we have
studied thus far affected these outcomes. We found that sometimes they
did, and sometimes they did not. For these reasons, we see this chapter
more as exploratory and applied than as an exercise in theory testing.

### A.   The Dynamics of Growth and Decline

Researchers think they know what happens when organizations grow.
As size increases, differentiation and formalization increase, and central-

ization and administrative intensity decrease (Ford 1980:590). The need to control ever more heterogeneous elements within the organization brings about the bureaucratization of the organization. Tasks need to be broken down into ever smaller parts so that the task is easier to teach and easier to learn. Rules need to be written that apply to all since direct supervision of workers and tasks becomes difficult. Decisions are delegated to those who have the knowledge, and when managers no longer do the work of the organization, workers are given more decision-making authority. Allegedly concerns over predictability, control, and efficiency drive the structural changes we see as organizations grow.

Research that has observed organizational decline, however, has not found that organizations readily dismantle the structures that arise during periods of growth. Studying the administrative component during periods of growth and decline has been a favorite exercise. Freeman and Hannan (1975) found that the number of administrative personnel decreased at a slower rate in declining school districts than it increased in growing districts. Akers and Campbell (1970) showed that the administrative component actually increased in some occupational associations that experienced decline (see Ford 1980:591). In his review of the literature McKinley (1992) concluded that it is erroneous to assume that the causal arrow can be reversed when organizations experience decline. For example, there is little evidence that management eases up on its control over workers as the organization gets smaller. There is no symmetry between growth and decline.

While efficiency and control seem to be paramount in periods of growth, it appears that other more "mundane" processes are activated when organizations experience decline. Whetten (1987) argued that during a downward spiral there is a complex interplay between ecological, political, and psychological processes. Arguments and conflicts erupt as organized and vocal special interest groups come to the fore to defend their turf and squabble over the use of ever scarcer resources. Morale subsequently deteriorates as a "mean mood" spreads over the organization. People become more selfish and antisocial and have less commitment to the organization's goals and mission. The top management team responds defensively (i.e., the threat-rigidity response of Staw et al. 1981), centralizes control (Singh 1986:567), discourages risk taking and creativity, which in turn reduces participation, centralizes information processing (D'Aveni 1989:581), and increases the likelihood that organizational members will scapegoat the leadership (see also Greenhalgh 1983:246). At the same time, fears and rumors about what management plans to do spread throughout the organizations (Greenhalgh 1982).

Irrational forces are unleashed at all levels within the organization. At the macro level, interest group politics takes hold (Ford 1980:594). Players who have a vested interest in either their jobs, power, or programs organize outside the legal structures and engage in informal strategies to protect their power and their interests. Bargaining among different interest groups rather than rational planning to achieve organizational goals governs decision-making. A crisis might also prompt a change in leadership as a new coalition seizes the opportunity to discredit its rivals and put itself and its agenda into power (Ocasio 1994). However, as the ecologists warn, putting into place a new agenda is always risky, because it turns back the organization's clock and can make the organization vulnerable to the liabilities of newness at a time when it needs to solve a crisis.

At a more micro level, individuals no longer have as many incentives to participate in the organization and thus withdraw. It is not that they *become* selfish; rather they can realize their interests better in contexts outside the organization (Ford 1980:592). Also at the micro level, managers find themselves in a defensive posture and consequently reaffirm their commitment to policy measures already in place. The idea that something seemed "rational" in the past leads managers to believe that it will be rational under changing conditions. Also changing anything would only be admitting that they had done something wrong or made mistakes, thus calling into question their reputations and even jeopardizing their legitimacy (Ford 1980:593).

A number of studies have shown that decline has a negative effect on organizational behavior. Cameron, Whetten, and Kim (1987) found that decline led to scapegoating, less innovation, greater turnover, and conflict. Cameron, Kim, and Whetten (1987) found decline related to scapegoating, low morale, lost leader credibility, conflict, and less innovation. In their review of the literature Ashforth and Lee (1990) argue that in the face of decline people overconform to rules and are less likely to innovate. Greenhalgh (1983:259) found that selfish (or antisocial) behavior was more frequent in the wake of decline, and D'Aunno and Sutton (1992) found that decline was associated with more competition among members and more rigid adherence to routines.

This leads us to our first hypothesis.

H1:   *Organizations that experience a decline in resources are more likely to have disagreements while making decisions, conflict with employees, alienation, and less creative or innovative work environments than organizations that are growing.*

It has also been argued that management will respond to decline by centralizing control. Staw et al. (1981) argued that a stressor such as financial adversity can provoke rigid responses in organizations including constriction in control (centralized decision-making). Decision-makers under threat attempt to enhance their control so that subordinates will do as they wish. Also the anxiety that accompanies a crisis can lead leaders to limit participation in decision-making because it reduces uncertainty about outcomes (D'Aunno and Sutton 1992:120). However, there is mixed evidence on the relationship between decline and centralization. Starbuck et al. (1977), D'Aveni (1989), Sutton et al. (1986) found support for this hypothesis, but D'Aunno and Sutton (1992), Cameron, Whetten, and Kim (1987), and Cameron, Kim, and Whetten (1987) did not. Nonetheless, we hypothesize:

H2: *Organizations that experience a decline in resources are more likely to centralize decision-making authority than organizations that are growing.*

### B. The Role That Environmental Context Can Play

In Chapter 3 we argued that growth and decline can only be understood within the context of environmental conditions. For example, Whetten (1980) distinguished between stagnation and cutback and argued that the "meaning" of organizational decline depends upon environmental conditions. Organizations that are in sparsely settled or highly concentrated niches may experience a drop in revenues, employment, or volunteers, but this will not cause alarm. In some instances, it may actually be a welcome relief, as the organization is now able to "catch up" with demand. An organization can have too many customers, donors, employees, and volunteers as well as too few. While a decline in resources may cause some concern, there is the expectation that there will be renewal and growth in the future. In contrast, if organizations are in highly competitive niches, shrinking resources are a signal that the organization is losing ground and having a difficult time competing against its peers. The chances here for recovery and future growth are slim. Organizations in both situations may lose 5 or 10% of their revenues and labor inputs, but the meaning of the shrinkage is very different (see also Greenhalgh 1983; Cameron and Zammuto 1983; Weitzel and Jonsson 1989). In the first case, the organization can simply ride it out; in the second, it may have to think about closing its doors. This gives rise to our third hypothesis.

H3: *Organizations that experience a decline in resources in highly competitive resource niches are more likely to centralize decision-making authority, have disagreements while making decisions, conflict with employees, alien-*

*ation, and a less creative or innovative work environment than organiza-*
*tions that experience a decline in resources in less competitive niches.*

## C. The Role That Tactics Can Play

Alternatively, behavioral outcomes may be influenced more by the tactics that managers employ than by growth and decline per se. Thus far we have assumed that the actions of senior management have no effect on organizational outcomes. Even in periods of decline we assumed that any concerted effort to stymie decline would be futile, that organizational members are only interested in protecting their turf and enhancing their power, and that senior management reacts to crises emotionally instead of rationally. But crises sometimes are created by management as much as by developments in the external environment. Thus while it may appear that a shortage of resources explains negative outcomes, it may be the tactics of managers that are the real cause.

*Retrenchment.* Whether or not they are faced with a decline in resources, management will sometimes go on a cost-cutting binge. This can happen in both utilitarian and normative organizations (Whetten 1981; Hambrick and Schecter 1983). Program delivery staff, fund-raisers, and middle managers can be fired; expense accounts for "wining and dining" donors, executive education and training, subscriptions to trade journals, and business travel can be cut; spending on new emergency room equipment, updating software systems, and capital improvements can be postponed. If the organization faces a decline in resources, these measures are rationalized as efforts to check the drain of resources from the organization and to ensure its solvency (Whetten 1981). Even if other tactics are used and the organization eventually recovers, we expect that most organizations that are experiencing a crisis in funding would pursue these measures to some extent (see Robbins and Pearce 1992). But retrenchment can also be a way of disciplining organizational members, reestablishing authority over rebel forces, and restructuring the organization. That is, it can have nothing to do with cutting costs or fiscal responsibility.

The point is that while a decline in resources presents a challenge to an organization, it is the tactics used by management that results in all the negatives. For example, it has long been argued in sociology that external threats can increase solidarity within groups when the collective identity is challenged (Coser 1956). Faced by an external threat, group members may rally around one another, reaffirm their membership, and work together for the achievement of collective ends. Thus negatives are not inevitable in the face of decline. Rather we would argue that the negatives are the result of management's efforts to reduce costs. This is what mobilizes interest groups, alienates workers, makes every decision a major issue, and encourages grievances and lawsuits. Thus we argue that decline in inputs per se is not that important, but rather it is the tactics of the board and the top management team that produce the negative outcomes. If the leadership decides to retrench operations, i.e., to cut jobs, salaries, benefits, and programs, organizational participants will "dig in their heels," protect their favorite programs and personnel, and even engage in subversive activity (Smith 1990). That is when people will engage in defensive behavior (Ashforth and Lee 1990), and all the negatives will kick in, e.g., disagreements, loss of commitment, increase in selfish or antisocial behavior, enslavement to routines, and less innovation.

H4: *Organizations that retrench operations are more likely to have disagreements while making decisions, conflict with employees, alienation, and a less creative or innovative work environments than organizations that do not retrench operations.*

Earlier we argued that organizations facing a decline in resources will often centralize decision-making, but here we argue that centralization accompanies retrenchment not decline. McKinley (1992) noted that managers who use retrenchment tactics often find themselves having to centralize their power to carry out their charge and coordinate the activity. D'Aveni (1989:581) noted that a typical centralization action is increased supervision of the decision-making process by a central authority like the chief executive officer. Cutting back on services, firing personnel, or lowering pay are decisions that only the top management team can make. They will be the ones responsible for cutting across the board or paring programs selectively. Furthermore, managers now have to restructure the activities within the organization given the reductions in the work force and renegotiate interorganizational activities. All of this requires increased coordination, which can only be achieved by centralizing decision-making.

Retrenchment is also an opportunity to concentrate authority and power. Starbuck et al. (1977:119) noted that cutback management or retrenchment often rids the organization of younger, more maverick types who might call into question the legitimate authority of the current management team. Those who had power are let go or their authority is severely curtailed. Executives and directors also know that they are likely targets for scapegoating, and if they do not wrest power from the board *they* may be the ones to go (Boeker 1992). This perspective is consistent with the view of organizations as arenas of interest group activity. The top management team and board, like every other interest group, vies for power and authority and will exploit every opportunity to advance its interests (Pfeffer 1981; D'Aveni 1989). Thus,

> H5:   *Organizations that retrench operations are more likely to centralize decision-making patterns.*

> H6:   *Organizations that have more centralized decision-making patterns are more likely to have disagreements while making decisions, conflict with employees and clients, alienation, and a less creative or innovative work environments than organizations that have more decentralized decision-making.*

***Political and Managerial Tactics.***   Management can also create problems for itself internally if it employs tactics that take an organization into a new resource niche. At first, this may sound heretical. Changing the strategic direction of the firm is what management is supposed to do. Although innovation and diversification are, in general, sound business strategies (Porter 1991), consultants have warned companies to "stick to the knitting" (Peters and Waterman 1982) and not to move into product lines or markets where they lack core competencies. The information advantages of established players in the market could bury the organization. On top of this, organizations have to make several adjustments, e.g., staff have to be retrained or reassigned, new technologies have to be acquired, board members that represented previous donors and/or clients have to move aside to let in representatives of new donor groups and/or clients, new methods of compensation have to be institutionalized, new control systems have to be put into place, and new lines of authority created. All of this generates uncertainty and anxiety. People's day-to-day routines are disrupted, and the "taken for granted" within the organization is threatened. As McKinley (1992) points out, this can be a very dangerous situation for organizations. Programs, administrative staff positions, and a division of labor are highly institutionalized within organizations (see also Petrie and Alpert 1983). Starbuck et al. (1977) talk about organizations being programmed to behave in certain ways. If organizations change their tactics and ways of doing business, everything in the organization may be up for grabs.

Organizational ecology argues that organizations that radically change their operations reset their organizational clocks and are then again susceptible to the liabilities of newness. Hannan and Freeman (1984) argue that change threatens to undermine two core competencies of organizations. The first is reliability. Stakeholders come to expect certain behaviors and outputs from organizations and are uncomfortable when the quality of outputs or the way they do business varies. As time goes on and organizations come to understand how to produce reliable outcomes, the value of the organization increases in the eyes of those dependent upon it. The second is accountability. Organizations are valued to the extent that they can document how resources have been used and to reconstruct the sequences of how organizational decisions come to be made and implemented. Norms of procedural rationality are especially important when the organization produces symbolic or information-loaded products, when substantial risk exists, or when the goals of the organization are highly political. All of these conditions are especially commonplace among nonprofit organizations. Hannan and Freeman (1984) argue further that reliability and accountability require that organizations are able to reproduce their structures with great regularity. This is achieved as ways of doing business become institutionalized and embodied in rules, regulations, codes, and culture. *Routines* are created, and it is these routines that ensure that the organization is reliable and accountable and thus more likely to survive in the environment. If senior management does anything that undermines these routines, it creates a threat to the organization's persona and thus makes it susceptible to deselection or extinction.

Organizations can also experience difficulties when they try to change their identities. Albert and Whetten (1985) argued that different organizations take on different identities for their stakeholders. While it is obvious that different organizations mean different things to people, Albert and Whetten go further and argue that organizations become a means by which people create meanings. As a consequence, a change in identity can result in a sense of anomie or normlessness among people affiliated with the organization. First, when identities change, the essence of the organization is called into question. Why does the organization exist, why is it important or essential? Second, the criteria that distinguish it from other organizations is changed. Its reference group changes: "We are now to be compared to *them* and not to these others." Or, more basically, "What kind of organization are we now?" Third, a change in identity forces a break with the past, resulting in loss of continuity over time. This refers figuratively to the death and rebirth of the organization. The organization must make a break with its past and contextualize and rationalize that part of its history that is now "dead."

The situation becomes more difficult when the organization is unable to jettison completely its original identity. Not only must the organization be able to square activities with the old identity, but it must also protect the old from being overcome by the new. There are several coping mechanisms that organizations could embrace, e.g., decoupling technical and symbolic components of the organization. In Hall's (1990) description of a museum that attempted to become more businesslike while retaining its old format, we see how this conflict of cultures can result in vicious conflict between an executive director and his or her executive committee, with each fighting for its own "identity."

An especially interesting identify shift takes place when a normative organization attempts to become more utilitarian (see Horch 1992) or even for-profit (see Ginsberg and Buchholtz 1990) or a utilitarian organization attempts to become more normative. There are many reasons why moving from one to the other might cause identity problems. Albert and Whetten (1985:275) identified the differences between business or utilitarian culture and communal or normative culture. Utilitarian organizations value monetarization (cost and revenue considerations are central when decision-makers decide upon alternative courses of action), formalization (there are rules and systems of accountability), internal commercialization (the pricing of services according to market considerations), and externalization (reliance upon income from "investors" through capital markets). The focus is on efficiency (increasing output per unit of input), profitability (maximizing revenues while minimizing costs), return on investment (ROI), and formal accountability. Because of this the organization tailors its activities to fit "market demand." This may mean finding and serving new clientele; it probably means providing new services. In any event, efficiency, profitability, and ROI become the driving forces in the organization and everything else follows. In contrast, being communal or normative is being indifferent to these concerns and focusing on the mission or the domain that the organization is committed to serve. There is more interest in identifying community problems and discovering ways to serve the public interest better.

Albert and Whetten (1985) argue that making nonprofits more businesslike often creates a sense of anomie or normlessness among members, because it calls for a change in identity. Instead of rationalizing itself in terms of some ideal or normative standard, the organization's worth is measured in terms of its output, profitability, and efficiency. This may be a problem especially for volunteers who are motivated to join the organization for normative rather than material reasons (Knoke and Wood 1981). But we suspect that the same identity problems can arise in organizations that are more utilitarian—whether they be nonprofit or for-profit—but decide to become more normative. Instead of focusing on customer satisfaction, quality controls, technological innovation, and internal discipline, the organization worries about its image in the broader community, public relations, whom it may offend, and societal meanings, values, and norms. This can confuse and foster resentment as well.

If the organization is in decline, the situation can be very serious. At the very time when management, employees, staff, volunteers, and members need to "pull together," the organization is moving in a direction that may be foreign to many of them. Quarrelling, conflict, or hostility may arise, because the entire identity of the organization is changing. While changing program activities or going after new funding sources may be a pragmatic response to a decline in resources, it can also mean that previously normative organizations are no longer driven by mission but by norms of efficiency and previously commercial organizations are no longer driven by product innovation and customer service but by public relations. Instead of conflict and withdrawal being the result of losing revenues or personnel, it is the result of losing purpose.

H7a: *Organizations that used managerial tactics are more likely to have disagreements while making decisions, conflict with employees, alienation, and a less creative or innovative work environment, if they were more heavily reliant on donated income and volunteers in the past.*

H7b: *Organizations that used political tactics are more likely to have disagreements while making decisions, conflict with employees, alienation, and a less creative or innovative work environment, if they were more heavily reliant on commercial income and employees in the past.*

### D. The Role That Embeddedness Can Play

What goes on within an organization can also be affected by its network ties to actors outside its borders. It is now fashionable to describe how social networks help to create social capital. According to Coleman (1988), dense social relationships enable or empower actors in a number of different ways. For instance, those in dense social relationships are more likely to gain access to rich, tacit information, to share collective norms with others, and to be trusted.

Coleman also recognized how social relationships exercise a considerable amount of control over actors. In fact, it is this control that enables social capital to accrue. Because alter is somehow under the influence of ego, alter will reciprocate favors, provide true and reliable information, and abide by certain collective norms. In fact, this is the power of social structure. Yet control also implies conformity, deference, hierarchy, and obedience. Ego, under the gaze of alter, feels pressure to moderate her behaviors so as to conform to group expectations. Facing the value judgments of peers, the prospect of incessant gossip over her shortcomings, and the subsequent threat to her reputation, she represses more aberrant impulses.

The implications of network position for the way organizations conduct their affairs are clear. Isolates can pretty much conduct their affairs as they see fit, but those integrated into dense social networks are expected to live up to community norms (Galaskiewicz 1985a, 1997). This includes treating employees and volunteers fairly, treating customers with respect, making decisions without rancor, obeying the law, making charitable contributions, being ethical in relations with donors and/or investors, and maintaining an open, safe, and healthy work environment.

> H8:   *Organizations that are embedded in elite community networks are less likely to have disagreements while making decisions, conflict with employees, alienation, and more likely to have a creative or innovative work environment.*

> H9:   *Organizations that are embedded in community interorganizational resource exchange networks are less likely to have disagreements while making decisions, conflict with employees, alienation, and more likely to have a creative or innovative work environment.*

Finally, the effects we hypothesized may be confounded by the size and industry of the organization. Research has shown that larger organizations are more structurally complex (horizontal differentiation of tasks and vertical hierarchy of control) (Scott 1987:242–46) and decision-making is more decentralized (Haveman 1993; see also Baker and Cullen 1993). Thus we need to control for organizational size. Different nonprofit organizations also have different institutional mandates and provide different kinds of goods and services. Labor unions, business and professional associations, lobbyists, political parties, country clubs, veterans' associations, private and corporate foundations, churches and synagogues, art museums, hospitals, hockey booster clubs, neighborhood improvement organizations, environmental educational groups, rape crisis centers, universities, research institutes, orchestras, and hospital auxiliaries all face different environmental and internal problems. While most all of these organizations could be classified as "services," we suspect that different types of nonprofits will respond to decline very differently, as they have different traditions, subcultures, and histories. Thus we need to control for organizational activities as well.

## DATA, METHODS, AND VARIABLES

The data used in this chapter again come from the panel organizations. The period studied here is from 1988 to 1994. This period was selected because we had data on the internal structure, decision-making patterns, and cultural milieux of the panel organizations for only these two years.

*Size.* The first set of variables measures the growth and decline in total resources. We added up income from donated sources, commercial income, public revenue, and miscellaneous revenues to create a measure of total income for 1979–1980, 1983–1984, 1987–1988, 1991–1992, and 1993–1994. All data were converted into 1994 dollars, and we computed the natural logs. We then used the data on total income (log), total employees (log), and total volunteers (log) to construct an aggregate measure of organizational size. We did a principal components analysis pooling data from 1980, 1984, 1988, 1992, and 1994. We then assigned factor scores to cases. For revenues, employees, and volunteers, the factor loadings were .888, .895, and .556 (the eigenvalue was 1.90 and the construct explained 63.3% of the variance). The factor scores were distributed approximately normal. We then disaggregated the scores by years. In this chapter we use the size constructs for 1987–1988 and 1993–1994. To measure growth and decline, we simply computed the difference in the size scores between the two time points. Values greater than zero indicated that the organizations' revenues and personnel grew; values less than zero showed that the organizations' revenues and personnel shrunk. The mean and standard deviation for the change scores are in Table 5.1.

*Niche Density, Networks, and Tactics.* Almost all the independent variables analyzed in this chapter were introduced in previous chapters. These included the niche density variable measured in 1988, elite support and/or use of the nonprofit in 1988, the log of the number of inter-

*Table 5.1.* Variable Descriptions and Descriptive Statistics

| Variable Descriptions | Mean | SD | N |
|---|---|---|---|
| Total size factor scores, 1988 | .095 | .997 | 173 |
| Total size factor scores, 1994 | .265 | 1.04 | 154 |
| Difference in the total size factor scores, 1994–1988 | .090 | .345 | 154 |
| Decentralized decision-making structure, 1988 | 43.3 | 17.2 | 171 |
| Decentralized decision-making structure, 1994 | 49.6 | 18.2 | 156 |
| Of those making decisions, number of disagreements, 1988 | .843 | 1.01 | 147 |
| Of those making decisions, number of disagreements, 1994 | .607 | .942 | 140 |
| Of those with employees, number of employee strikes/grievances/lawsuits, 1988 | .465 | .664 | 127 |
| Of those with employees, number of employee strikes/grievances/lawsuits, 1994 | .626 | .778 | 115 |
| Creativity and innovation factor scores, 1988 | −.085 | 1.14 | 170 |
| Creativity and innovation factor scores, 1994 | .100 | .802 | 144 |
| Alienation factor scores, 1988 | .115 | 1.04 | 169 |
| Alienation factor scores, 1994 | −.127 | .939 | 153 |

organizational resource / information exchange partners in 1988, and the tactics variables covering the period from 1988 to 1994. The reader will remember that five cases were missing data for the political tactics, and we used mean substitution for this item only.

*Decision-Making Structures.*    In Chapter 3 we described our measure of organizational decision-making structure. In our interviews with the top administrative officers in 1988 and 1994, we asked: "Hypothetically speaking, who would have the final formal authority to make the following decision?" In 1994 we listed five potential decision-makers $i$ (the board, chief administrative officer, professional staff, clients, and volunteers), and cross-tabulated these with seven decisions $j$ (revise mission statement, enter a new service area, approach new funder for contributions, launch a capital campaign, borrow money, dismiss / replace board members, and dismiss / replace professional staff).[1] Respondents then checked as many "cells" as they felt appropriate. If the organization had no employees, volunteers, or clients we assigned a missing value to the respective rows of the table. If the organization never considered a decision, the column was left blank.

Our index measures the degree to which decision-making power was concentrated in the hands of a few or dispersed among many actors. For each organization we scanned the decisions that they would consider. On average, respondents now responded to 4.7 decisions in 1988 and 4.5 in 1994. We then counted up how many different actors had "final authority" across the decisions. We then divided this tally by the number of actors who could have decision-making authority (e.g., not every organization had clients or volunteers) and multiplied by 100. Thus our measure is the percentage of possible decision-makers who had final authority over organizational decisions. The variable ranged in value from 20% (one out of five possible decision-makers) to 100%. Descriptive statistics are in Table 5.1. Before leaving this variable, we should remind the reader that when fewer actors made key decisions, i.e., decision-making was centralized, the *board* dominated. Where more actors made key decisions, i.e., decision-making was decentralized, actors such as the chief administrative officer, professionals, clients, and volunteers came to share power with the board. This was the case both in 1988 and 1994.

*Disagreements.*    The next set of variables measured the extent to which disagreements surrounded organizational decisions. We asked administrators in 1988 and 1994 to tell us if, in the last year or so, their organization had to make any of the following decisions: revise the mission statement, enter a new service area, approach a new funder for contributions, launch a capital campaign, borrow money, dismiss / replace board members, or dismiss / replace professional staff. For each decision that came up, we then asked if there was "none," "some," or "considerable" disagreement within the organization. If there was no disagreement we scored the decision 0; if there was some or considerable disagreement we scored the decision 1. We then counted the number of times that there was some or considerable disagreement. Of the 171 organizations in 1988 that gave us data, only 147 actually made any of these decisions; of the 155 organizations in 1994 that gave us data, only 140 made any of these decisions. Disagreements were also infrequent. In 1988, 44.9% of the 147 organizations that made any decisions said there were no disagreements. In 1994, 62.1% of the 140 organizations that made any decisions said there were no disagreements. Descriptive statistics for these variables are in Table 5.1.

*Conflicts with Employees.* We also wanted to measure the extent to which the organization had problems with its employees. Thus in both 1988 and 1994 we asked respondents if there had been any strikes, employee grievances, or employee lawsuits over the past year or so. Of the 173 organizations that gave us data in 1988, 127 (73.4%) had employees; of the 156 that gave us data for 1994, 115 (73.7%) had employees. Of those with employees, 63.0 and 54.8% said they had no problems with their employees in 1988 and 1994, respectively. The means and standard deviations for this variable are in Table 5.1.

*Morale.* The next set of variables measured morale. In the 1988 interview we handed the top administrator a list of 13 statements that could describe his organization's social milieux (see Table 5.2). We asked administrators to look at each statement and tell us if they "strongly disagreed," "disagreed," "agreed," or "strongly agreed" that a statement described her organization. Thus each item could take on a value of 1 ("strongly disagreed") to 4 ("strongly agreed"). They could also indicate that they did not know, had no opinion on the matter, it was not applicable, or they could refuse to answer. These responses were counted as "missing."

In the 1994 interview we used 11 of the 13 original statements, but proceeded differently.[2] Respondents and reviewers claimed that it was much too crude to have administrators comment on how "people" within the organization felt or behaved. Therefore, for each statement we asked how the board of directors felt or behaved, how the chief administrative officer felt or behaved, how the professional staff felt or behaved, and how volunteers felt or behaved. Thus we had four prefixes for each statement. The problem now was that not all organizations had professional staff or volunteers and thus there were a number of "not applicables" in the data we collected. To derive measures in 1994 that were comparable to measures in 1988, we computed the average score across however many

Table 5.2.  Means, Standard Deviations, and Missing Data for Items Assessing Organizations' Quality of Life (1 = "Strongly Disagree," 2 = "Disagree," 3 = "Agree," 4 = "Strongly Agree")

| Item | 1988 | | 1994 | |
|---|---|---|---|---|
| | Mean (SD) | N (MD) | Mean (SD) | N (MD) |
| In our organization people are almost always willing to listen to new ideas. | 3.40 (.647) | 171 (3) | 3.52 (.426) | 155 (1) |
| People in our organization don't care about one another much. | 1.32 (.600) | 170 (4) | 1.31 (.424) | 156 (0) |
| It's common for people to be angry with one another in our organization. | 1.72 (.690) | 170 (4) | 1.48 (.562) | 154 (2) |
| People in our organization try to avoid risks. | 2.34 (.791) | 166 (8) | 2.38 (.737) | 150 (6) |
| Parties and social functions are a regular feature around this organization. | 2.31 (.930) | 155 (19) | | |
| People from our organization often go out after work and socialize with one another in their free time. | 2.30 (.812) | 148 (26) | | |
| The most creative people in our organization are accorded high status and are well respected. | 3.21 (.718) | 155 (19) | 3.36 (.506) | 153 (3) |
| People are loyal to the organization. | 3.58 (.540) | 172 (2) | 3.69 (.378) | 156 (0) |
| There is considerable emphasis on organizational routines: following rules, guidelines, regulations, etc. | 3.70 (.768) | 169 (5) | 3.15 (.612) | 150 (6) |
| In our organization people work as a team. | 3.36 (.591) | 170 (4) | 3.37 (.490) | 155 (1) |
| People in our organization like to experiment with new ways of doing things. | 2.83 (.745) | 169 (5) | 2.98 (.573) | 151 (5) |
| Everybody in our organization seems to be out for themselves. | 1.42 (.613) | 169 (5) | 1.39 (.489) | 156 (0) |
| People believe in the mission of the organization. | 3.71 (.559) | 172 (2) | 3.74 (.470) | 156 (0) |

actors respondents would comment on. Thus if they reported on the attitudes of board members, the executive officer, and volunteers, we had three scores to average. If they offered opinions on the attitudes of all four actors, we averaged across four answers.[3]

Table 5.2 presents the average scores for each of the statements in 1988 and 1994. As noted above, we coded the data so that a score of 1 corresponded to "strongly disagreed," 2 to "disagreed," 3 to "agreed," and 4 to "strongly agreed." The standard deviations and number of cases are presented as well. The averages are quite similar across the years. For the most part, respondents tended to think well of those in their organizations. One concern was that the standard deviations of the averaged scores in 1994 were considerably smaller than the singular scores in 1988. This, we believe, was due to the way we aggregated responses in 1994.

As we can see, there were considerable missing data for three items in 1988: parties and social functions are a regular feature around here, people go out after work and socialize with one another, and the most creative people are accorded high status and are well respected. Several respondents commented that they did not feel qualified to comment on the social lives of their board, staff, employees, and volunteers. Subsequently we dropped the questions about parties and socializing from the 1994 interview and from our analysis. We are not sure why the other item had so much missing data in 1988. Although we asked it in 1994, we decided to drop this item from our analysis as well.

Although it does not seem like there were much missing data on the other items, there was a problem when we aggregated responses across items into constructs. We decided not to tamper with the missing items for 1994, and thus the number of cases in our subsequent analyses is, for one construct, rather small. However, for 1988, we decided to estimate values for individual missing items using the respondent's responses to the other items. Even disregarding the questions on parties, socializing, and rewarding creative people, 18 different organizations had missing data on at least one of the 10 remaining items and two more organizations gave no response to any of the items. That would be 20 cases that we would lose for 1988. In the 14 cases where respondents answered all but one of the 10 remaining items, we estimated their response to the one missing item by plugging their responses to the other nine items into a regression equation (estimated over the entire sample) and calculating the expected value of the missing item for that case. We still had missing data for two organizations that did not bother to answer any of these questions and the four cases that failed to answer more than one item.

From inspection of these items we identified two possible constructs. The first signaled a climate for innovation and creativity. We expected that a willingness to listen to new ideas, creative people are rewarded, and people like to experiment would load positively and people like to avoid risks and there is an emphasis on routines would load negatively. However, as noted before, because of missing data we had to drop the item on rewarding creative people. The second would describe the degree of alienation within the organization. We expected that people don't care about one another, people tend to be angry, and people tend to be selfish would load positively, and people work as a team, people are loyal, and people believe in the mission of the organization would load negatively.

We created two constructs using principal components analysis. However, before we proceeded we pooled the data across 1988 and 1994. As with the organizational size construct, we were concerned about using standardized scores based on different samples. By pooling the data beforehand, this could be avoided. We estimated the first principal component for each of the two clusters of variables. For the first construct, the eigenvalue equaled 1.68 and it explained 41.9% of the variance in the data. A willingness to experiment (.816), an interest in new ideas (.725), and an interest in avoiding risk (−.693) all loaded as expected. However, an emphasis on organizational routines loaded poorly on this construct (.077). We subsequently eliminated this last item, and the factor loadings of the other variables remained virtually unchanged, while the percentage of variance explained increased to 55.6%. For the second construct, all six items loaded as expected: people are out for themselves (.678), people don't care about one another (.573), people are often angry (.586), people work as a team (−.663), people are loyal (−.589), and people believe in the mission of the organization (−.574). The eigenvalue was equal to 2.25, and the first construct explained 37.4% of the variance. Subsequently we assigned factor scores to our cases. The correlation between the two constructs was −.376, as one might expect. In Table 5.1 we present the means and standard deviations for each construct for 1988 and 1994.[4]

*Controls.* There were several other variables that were used as control variables. We used the data on organizations' primary activities—health / welfare, culture / recreation, and education—in 1988. We also included a dummy variable for public funding in 1988 in several of the analyses, our aggregate measure of commercial income and employees in 1988, and our aggregate measure of donated income and volunteers in 1988. Again, log of expenditures in 1980 and log of organizational age in 1980 were used to estimate the sample selection model.

## ANALYZING THE CONSEQUENCES OF CHANGE

Our ultimate goal was to test if resource decline had a direct effect on outcomes, or tactics and network embeddedness were more important in explaining changes in organizational structure, decision-making, and the cultural milieux of organizations. In this chapter we proceeded differently than in the previous chapters. There we analyzed one dependent variable, e.g., organizational size or tactics, and we reestimated the same equation across several time periods. As we tested different hypotheses we added variables to the equation to see their relative effects. Here we have five dependent variables and only two observations—1988 and 1994. We analyzed one dependent variable at a time and repeated the analysis five times. At the end we will evaluate each hypothesis by presenting and analyzing a summary table of all the variable effects we found in our five separate analyses.

In all the analyses we included a sample selection term, using again the inverse Mills ratio. As noted, in Chapter 3, organizations that had smaller expenditures or were younger were less likely to be in the panel by 1994. We also tested for heteroskedasticity in the OLS models and for multicollinearity in all our models examining the tolerance score for each regressor. Where heteroskedasticity was a problem (at the .10-level), we reestimated the equation using the White (1980) correction. The corrected results are presented in the tables. Of course, with only two observations we could not test for autocorrelation, but the reader should remember that the period is six years in length and autocorrelation should not be a problem.

Before we begin the analysis we should take a moment to examine the dependent variables more closely. Looking first at the means and standard deviations in Table 5.1, we see that, on average, fewer disagreements were cited in 1994 than in 1988, reports of creativity in organizations were more frequent in 1994 than in 1988, and reports of alienation were fewer in 1994 than in 1988. Organizations also tended to have more decentralized decision-making patterns in 1994 than in 1988 and reported more conflicts with employees in 1994 than in 1988.[5] More interestingly, the correlations across years varied remarkably by outcome measure. Organizations that had more conflicts with employees in 1988 had more conflict with employees in 1994 ($r = .376$); organizations that were described as creative and innovative in 1988 were described the same way in 1994 ($r = .251$); organizations that had decentralized decision-making patterns in 1988 also had them in 1994 ($r = .209$); organizations that had more disagreements in 1988 had more disagreements in 1994 ($r = .159$); however, respondents' reports of alienation in 1988 were unrelated to reports of alienation in 1994 ($r = .096$). Finally, the pairwise correlations among the response variables—measured in 1994—were not high. Decentralization was correlated .101, .019, .112, and .259 with creativity, alienation, disagreements, and conflict; creativity was correlated $-.442$, $-.099$, and .037 with alienation, disagreements, and conflict; alienation was correlated .211 and .026 with disagreements and conflict; and disagreements was correlated .262 with conflict. Thus while these may all seem like "quality of life" indicators, they are measuring very different phenomena and thus should be analyzed separately.

## A. Decision-Making Structures

We distinguished between decision-making structures that were highly centralized—one set of actors in the organization made all the decisions—and those which were highly decentralized—many different kinds of actors had decision-making authority over a wide range of issues. We hypothesized that organizations that experienced a decline in resources would centralize their decision-making over time (Hypothesis 2), the effect of decline on centralization would be stronger if the organization was functioning in a more competitive resource environment (Hypothesis 3), and retrenchment tactics would result in organizations becoming more centralized (Hypothesis 5).

We tested these hypotheses estimating the following equation:

$$Y_t = \beta_0 + \beta_1 Y_{t-n} + \beta_2 X_{t-n} + \beta_3 (X_t - X_{t-n}) + \beta_4 W_{t-n} + \beta_5$$
$$[W_{t-n} * (X_t - X_{t-n})] + \Sigma_i \beta_i T_{i,t} + \Sigma_j \beta_j Z_{j,t-n} + \beta\lambda + \epsilon_t \qquad (1)$$

where $Y$ referred to the measure of decentralization described in the methods section; $X$ was the measure of organizational size (total funds and personnel); $W$ was the density variable measuring niche competition; $T_i$ were the three tactics variables (retrenchment, political, and managerial);[6] $Z_j$ were the control variables (health / welfare, educational, and cultural / recreational activities); and $\lambda$ was the sample selection term. We also included a dummy variable indicating if we had used mean substitution for the political tactics variable [not shown in (1)].[7]

It helps in interpreting the results to keep in mind that the dependent variable ranged from 20.0 to 100.0 and had a mean and standard deviation of 49.6 and 18.2. The variable was also approximately normal. We estimated these models using ordinary least squares. We proceeded by estimating components of the model separately—testing each hypothesis, then estimating a reduced model that included all significant and marginally significant effects found in the prior analyses. Only the final model had to be corrected for heteroskedasticity, and in none of the models did tolerance scores associated with any of the regressors dip below .400. To be sure, the $R^2$ and adjusted $R^2$ were modest by social science standards, and we did not account for a significant proportion of change in the dependent variable. The residuals for the four models were distributed approximately normal.

Looking at Table 5.3, we see that Hypothesis 2 received no support. Organizations that grew in size did not become more decentralized and those which shrunk in size did not become more centralized. Larger organizations tended to become more decentralized over time, but the effect of overall size on decentralization decreased when we introduced the tactics variables. In the reduced model, the $p$-value of the size effect was .100. There

Table 5.3. OLS with Decentralization of Decision-Making as the Dependent Variable

| Independent Variables | Dependent Variable: Decentralized Decision-Making Structure$_{94}$ | | | |
| --- | --- | --- | --- | --- |
| | Hyp2 b (SE) | Hyp3 b (SE) | Hyp5 b (SE) | OLS Reduced[a] b (SE) |
| Decentralized Decision-Making Structure$_{88}$ | .149(.090)# | .139(.089) | .169(.089)# | .170(.098)# |
| Tot Inc & Pers$_{88}$ | 6.00(1.83)** | 5.55(1.81)** | 3.88(2.13)# | 3.53(2.15) |
| Tot Inc & Pers$_{94}$ − Tot Inc & Pers$_{88}$ | 1.29(4.03) | 3.81(4.42) | −1.80(4.08) | |
| Niche Density$_{88}$ | | 2.06(.725)** | | 1.97(.713)** |
| ΔTot Inc & Pers * Niche Density$_{88}$ | | −2.07(2.41) | | |
| No. of Retrench Tactics$_{88-94}$ | | | −1.84(.925)* | −1.59(.682)* |
| No. of Managerial Tactics$_{88-94}$ | | | .912(.580) | 1.27(.567)* |
| No. of Political Tactics$_{88-94}$ | | | .997(.861) | |
| Dummy for MD, Political Tactics | | | −6.53(9.93) | |
| Health/Welfare$_{88}$ | 1.13(3.63) | .818(3.59) | .565(3.55) | |
| Education$_{88}$ | .783(3.85) | .459(3.76) | .796(3.77) | |
| Culture/Recreation$_{88}$ | 2.66(4.29) | 4.22(4.23) | .811(4.19) | |
| λ | 18.0(9.35)# | 17.9(9.28) | 15.4(8.85)# | 13.3(7.78)# |
| Constant | 32.8(7.00)*** | 32.8(6.87)*** | 37.2(6.82)*** | 37.9(5.78)*** |
| $R^2$ | .117* | .167** | .169** | .194*** |
| Adj. $R^2$ | .075 | .114 | .102 | .160 |
| N | 152 | 151 | 150 | 151 |
| White test for heteroskedasticity | 5.84(7) | 11.7(9) | 14.3(11) | 13.4(6)* |

*** $p < .001$; ** $p < .01$; * $p < .05$; # $p < .10$.

[a] Standard errors corrected for heteroskedasticity using White (1980).

183

was no support for Hypothesis 3 either. Organizations in denser niches became more decentralized over time ($p < .01$), but being in a more competitive niche did not exacerbate the effect of decline on decision-making patterns as we had expected. Organizations that experienced decline between 1988 and 1994 simply did not become more centralized.

Hypothesis 5 received strong support. Organizations that utilized more retrenchment tactics between 1988 and 1994 became more centralized in their decision-making over time ($p < .05$ in the OLS reduced model). Unexpectedly, we also found that organizations that utilized more managerial tactics between 1988 and 1994 became more *de*centralized over time ($p < .05$ in the OLS reduced model). Evidently, the use of managerial tactics empowered a greater variety of actors in the organization, while the utilization of retrenchment tactics led to the concentration of decision-making in the hands of fewer actors.

## B. Creativity and Innovativeness

We distinguished between organizations that more or less valued creativity and innovativeness. We used the perceptions of administrators— and not interviews with directors, staff, volunteers, and clients—for this item, and thus the results need to be interpreted with some caution. We hypothesized that organizations that experienced a decline in resources would come to value creativity and innovativeness less over time (Hypothesis 1), the negative effect of decline on creativity and innovativeness would be stronger if the organization was functioning in a more competitive resource environment (Hypothesis 3), retrenchment tactics would result in organizations becoming less creative and innovative (Hypothesis 4), more centralized organizations would become less creative and innovative over time (Hypothesis 6), organizations that relied more heavily on donations and volunteers but implemented a large number of managerial tactics would become less creative and innovative over time (Hypothesis 7a) and organizations that relied more heavily on commercial income and employees but implemented a large number of political tactics would become less creative and innovative over time (Hypothesis 7b), and organizations that were more heavily embedded in elite networks would be more creative and innovative over time (Hypothesis 8) as would organizations more embedded in community resource exchange networks (Hypothesis 9).

We tested these hypotheses estimating the following equations using models similar to Equation (1):

$$Y_t = \beta_0 + \beta_1 Y_{t-n} + \beta_2 X_{t-n} + \beta_3 (X_t - X_{t-n}) + \beta_4 W_{t-n} + \beta_5 [W_{t-n} * (X_t - X_{t-n})] + \beta_6 S_{t-n} + \Sigma_i \beta_i T_{i,t} + \Sigma_j \beta_j Z_{j,t-n} + \Sigma_k \beta_k N_{k,t-n} + \beta\lambda + \epsilon_t \quad (2)$$

$$Y_t = \beta_0 + \beta_1 Y_{t-n} + \beta_2 C_{t-n} + \beta_3 D_{t-n} + \beta_4 P_{t-n} + \beta_5 (D_{t-n} * T_{3,t})$$
$$+ \beta_6 (C_{t-n} * T_{2,t}) + \Sigma_i \beta_i T_{i,t} + \Sigma_j \beta_j Z_{j,t-n} + \beta\lambda + \epsilon_t \qquad (3)$$

where $Y$ now referred to the perceptual measure of creativity and innovation described in the methods section; $X$ was an overall measure of organizational size (total funds and personnel); $C$ was our measure of commercial income and employees; $D$ was the measure of donated income and volunteers; $P$ was a dummy variable indicating if the organization had public funding or not; $W$ was the density variable measuring competition; $S$ was the organization's decision-making structure (decentralized vs. centralized); $N_k$ were the two network variables (proximity to the community elite and interorganizational network ties); $T_1$, $T_2$, and $T_3$ were retrenchment, political, and managerial tactics, respectively; $Z_j$ were the control variables (health/welfare, educational, and cultural/recreational activities); and $\lambda$ was the sample selection term. We again included a dummy variable indicating if we had used mean substitution for the political tactics variable.

The dependent variable ranged from $-1.39$ to $1.96$ with a mean of $.100$ and a standard deviation of $.802$. It was distributed approximately normal. The only problem was that there were considerable missing data on the dependent variable. Of the 156 survivors in the panel, only 144 provided us with data on the three indicators used to construct this variable. We estimated these models using ordinary least squares. We proceeded as before, estimating components of the model separately for each hypothesis, then estimating a final model that included all significant and nearly significant effects. None of the models had to be corrected for heteroskedasticity, and in only one model did tolerance scores associated with any of the regressors dip below $.400$. In the fourth model, the tolerance score for total income and personnel was $.398$. The $R^2$ and adjusted $R^2$ were again modest. The residuals for the five models were approximately normal.

Testing Hypotheses 1 and 3 together (see Table 5.4), we found no support for either. Organizations that grew in size did not become more creative and innovative and those that shrank in size did not become less so. In fact, in organizations that experienced decline, creativity and innovativeness became more highly valued, not less: however, this effect was not statistically significant at the .10-level ($p = .160$ in the reduced model). Neither size, niche density, nor the interaction combining change in size and niche density had any effect on the dependent variable.

There was support for Hypothesis 4. Organizations that utilized more retrenchment tactics between 1988 and 1994 came to value creativity and innovativeness less ($p < .10$ in the reduced model). There was support for Hypothesis 6 as well. Organizations that were more decentralized in 1988 became more innovative and creative over time, while more centralized

*Table 5.4.*  OLS with Creativity and Innovativeness as the Dependent Variable

| Reduced Independent Variables | Dependent Variable: Creativity & Innovativeness$_{94}$ | | | | |
| --- | --- | --- | --- | --- | --- |
| | Hyps1&3 $b$ (SE) | Hyps4&6 $b$ (SE) | Hyps7a&7b $b$ (SE) | Hyps8&9 $b$ (SE) | OLS Reduced $b$ (SE) |
| Creativity & Innovativeness$_{88}$ | .183(.061)** | .159(.059)** | .158(.060)** | .175(.060)** | .163(.056)** |
| Tot Inc & Pers$_{88}$ | −.022(.086) | −.056(.100) | | −.054(.108) | −.044(.087) |
| Tot Inc & Pers$_{94}$ − Tot Inc & Pers$_{88}$ | −.255(.211) | −.320(.195) | | | −.257(.183) |
| Niche Density$_{88}$ | .024(.035) | | | | |
| ΔTot Inc & Pers * Niche Density$_{88}$ | .039(.115) | | | | |
| No. of Retrench Tactics$_{88-94}$ | | −.074(.041)# | −.079(.040)* | | −.069(.040)# |
| No. of Managerial Tactics$_{88-94}$ | | −.012(.028) | −.006(.029) | | |
| No. of Political Tactics$_{88-94}$ | | .057(.041) | .039(.041) | | |
| Dummy for MD, Political Tactics | | −.393(.446) | | | |
| Donated Inc & Vols$_{88}$ | | | −.039(.097) | | |
| Donated Inc & Vols$_{88}$ * Managerial Tactics$_{88-94}$ | | | .009(.027) | | |
| Commercial Inc & Empl$_{88}$ | | | −.066(.093) | | |
| Commercial Inc & Empl$_{88}$ * Political Tactics$_{88-94}$ | | | .026(.027) | | |
| Gov't Grants & Contracts$_{88}$ | | | .051(.149) | | |
| Elite Network Contacts$_{88}$ | | | | .191(.081)* | .168(.072)* |
| Interorganizational Network Centrality$_{88}$ | | | | −.068(.101) | |
| Decentralized Decision-making Structure$_{88}$ | | .009(.004)* | .008(.004)# | | .007(.004)# |
| Health/Welfare$_{88}$ | −.110(.180) | −.023(.180) | −.006(.181) | −.096(.179) | |
| Education$_{88}$ | −.195(.179) | −.105(.184) | −.071(.191) | −.178(.179) | |
| Culture/Recreation$_{88}$ | −.038(.205) | −.072(.204) | −.060(.206) | −.199(.212) | |
| λ | −.336(.418) | −.338(.405) | −.383(.425) | −.124(.408) | −.051(.391) |
| Constant | .444(.259)# | .105(.320) | .047(.330) | .418(.273) | −.017(.257) |
| $R^2$ | .088 | .140# | .128 | .114* | .152** |
| Adj. $R^2$ | .024 | .056 | .029 | .059 | .106 |
| N | 138 | 136 | 138 | 139 | 137 |
| White test for heteroskedasticity | 9.21(9) | 12.1(12) | 10.2(15) | 7.58(8) | 7.36(7) |

*** $p < .001$; ** $p < .01$; * $p < .05$; # $p < .10$.

organizations in 1988 came to value creativity and innovativeness less ($p$ < .10 in the reduced model).

There was no support for Hypothesis 7a or 7b. Creativity and innovativeness did not come to be valued less as organizations that relied heavily on donated income and volunteers utilized more managerial tactics or as organizations that relied heavily on earned income and employees utilized more political tactics over time. Hypothesis 8 was confirmed. Organizations that had more elites using their services and/or serving their organization tended to become more creative and innovative over time, while more isolated organizations tended to value creativity and innovativeness less ($p$ < .05 in the reduced model). Finally, Hypothesis 9 was not confirmed. Creativity and innovativeness were unaffected by an organization's linkages to other local organizations.

## C. Reported Alienation

We also drew the distinction between organizations that had high levels of alienation and those which had more commitment and less anger. Relying again on the perceptions of top administrators—always a risky strategy—we asked about people being angry, selfish, in touch with the mission of the organization, and working as a team within the organization. The major problem with this construct is that we are now trying to explain *individuals'* behaviors and attitudes—not something about the organization—using organizational- not individual-level variables. Thus the reader should be skeptical in reviewing the results.

We hypothesized that, in organizations that experienced a decline in resources, people would become alienated over time (Hypothesis 1), the positive effect of decline on alienation would be stronger if the organization was functioning in a more competitive resource environment (Hypothesis 3), retrenchment tactics would result in people withdrawing and becoming more alienated over time (Hypothesis 4), in more centralized organizations people would become more alienated (Hypothesis 6), in organizations that relied more heavily on donations and volunteers but implemented a large number of managerial tactics alienation would increase (Hypothesis 7a) and in organizations that relied more heavily on commercial income and employees but implemented a large number of political tactics alienation would increase (Hypothesis 7b), and finally in organizations that were more heavily embedded in elite networks people would become less alienated over time (Hypothesis 8) as would people in organizations more embedded in community resource exchange networks (Hypothesis 9). We tested these hypotheses estimating Equations (2) and (3) but substituting our measure of alienation for the indicator of creativity and innovativeness discussed above. Otherwise the models were exactly the same.

The dependent variable ranged from $-1.30$ to $1.92$ with a mean of $-.127$ and a standard deviation of $.939$. It was somewhat skewed to the right (skewness $= .401$), because respondents typically saw people in their organization as less alienated and more satisfied. We estimated these models using ordinary least squares. We proceeded as before, estimating components of the model separately for each hypothesis, then estimating a reduced model that included all significant and nearly significant effects. There are two reduced models, because we could not include our measure of overall size and the indicator of earned income and employees in the same equation because they were collinear. However, the interaction term in the first reduced model was not statistically significant, so we will only discuss the results of the second model. None of the models had to be corrected for heteroskedasticity, and in only one model did tolerance scores associated with any of the regressors dip below $.400$. In model four, the tolerance score for total income and personnel was $.397$. The $R^2$ and adjusted $R^2$ were very modest. The residuals for the five models were approximately normal with slight skewness to the right.

We found no support for Hypothesis 1 (see Table 5.5). In organizations that shrank in size people did not become more alienated and in those which grew in size people did not become less alienated. However, in larger organizations people's alienation increased over time ($p < .10$ in the reduced model). Hypothesis 3 received some support. The $p$-value of the interaction term was equal to $.100$ in the reduced model. In more dense organizational niches, decline affected people's attitudes toward their organization negatively. The negative coefficient tells us that in more competitive niches, people in shrinking organizations became more alienated, while those in growing organizations became less so. Looking at the simple slopes, we learn that in niches with average density, the effect of change on people's attitudes was minimal ($b = -.158$; $p = .535$), but in niches one standard deviation above the mean, growth had a weak negative effect on alienation ($b = -.572$; $p = .115$). In niches one standard deviation below the mean, the effect of change on attitudes was nil ($b = .256$; $p = .440$).

There was no support for Hypothesis 4. Organizations that utilized more retrenchment tactics between 1988 and 1994 did not report an increase in the level of alienation. There was, however, a tendency for organizations that employed more political tactics to have higher levels of alienation ($p < .10$ in the reduced model). There was no evidence that organizations that were more decentralized in 1988 had less alienation in 1994 than in 1988.

Table 5.5. OLS with Alienation as the Dependent Variable

| Reduced Independent Variables | Dependent Variable: $Alienation_{94}$ | | | | | |
|---|---|---|---|---|---|---|
| | Hyps1&3 b (SE) | Hyps4&6 b (SE) | Hyps7a&7b b (SE) | Hyps8&9 b (SE) | OLS Reduced b (SE) | OLS Reduced b (SE) |
| $Alienation_{88}$ | .075(.073) | .043(.073) | .041(.073) | .076(.073) | .036(.071) | .078(.071) |
| Tot Inc & $Pers_{88}$ | .210(.090)* | .134(.112) | | .204(.124)# | | .196(.104)# |
| Tot Inc & $Pers_{94}$ – Tot Inc & $Pers_{88}$ | .056(.245) | .219(.227) | | | | -.158(.239) |
| Niche $Density_{88}$ | -.008(.040) | | | | | -.034(.041) |
| ΔTot Inc & Pers * Niche $Density_{88}$ | -.207(.135) | | | | | -.217(.132) |
| No. of Retrench $Tactics_{88-94}$ | | .064(.049) | .062(.048) | | .068(.048) | |
| No. of Managerial $Tactics_{88-94}$ | | -.004(.031) | -.013(.032) | | | |
| No. of Political $Tactics_{88-94}$ | | .051(.047) | .065(.046) | | .069(.038)# | .072(.040)# |
| Dummy for MD, Political Tactics | | -.113(.526) | | | | |
| Donated Inc & $Vols_{88}$ | | | .061(.107) | | | |
| Donated Inc & $Vols_{88}$ * Managerial $Tactics_{88-94}$ | | | | -.011(.027) | | |
| Commercial Inc & $Empl_{88}$ | | | .169(.101)# | | .139(.090) | |
| Commercial Inc & $Empl_{88}$ * Political $Tactics_{88-94}$ | | | -.040(.029) | | -.029(.027) | |
| Gov't Grants & $Contracts_{88}$ | | | -.080(.168) | | | |
| Elite Network $Contacts_{88}$ | | | | -.121(.094) | -.137(.092) | -.211(.096)* |
| Interorganizational Network $Centrality_{88}$ | | | | .017(.115) | | |
| Decentralized Decision-Making $Structure_{88}$ | -.007(.193) | -.009(.005)# | -.007(.005) | | -.007(.005) | |
| Health/$Welfare_{88}$ | .057(.198) | -.112(.193) | -.150(.191) | -.011(.198) | | |
| $Education_{88}$ | .396(.227)# | .072(.204) | .029(.199) | .055(.200) | | |
| Culture/$Recreation_{88}$ | .159(.436) | .379(.228)# | .372(.225)# | .471(.239)* | .542(.202)** | .521(.200)** |
| λ | | | .280(.441) | .087(.444) | .024(.415) | -.073(.428) |
| Constant | -.378(.283) | -.044(.357) | .055(.358) | -.336(.309) | -.024(.284) | -.250(.223) |
| $R^2$ | .088 | .103 | .117 | .063 | .119* | .128* |
| Adj. $R^2$ | .029 | .023 | .023 | .009 | .061 | .070 |
| N | 148 | 146 | 147 | 147 | 148 | 146 |
| White test for heteroskedasticity | 8.18(9) | 14.8(12) | 16.2(14) | 7.21(8) | 11.0(9) | 8.00(9) |

*** $p < .001$; ** $p < .01$; * $p < .05$; # $p < .10$.

189

There was again no support for Hypothesis 7a or 7b. Reports of alienation did not increase as organizations that relied heavily on donated
income and volunteers utilized more managerial tactics or as organizations that relied heavily on earned income and employees utilized more
political tactics over time. There was strong support for Hypothesis 8. In
organizations that had more elites using their services and/or serving
their organization, people were reported to be less alienated over time,
while in more isolated organizations people were reported to become
more alienated ($p < .05$ in the reduced model). Hypothesis 9 was not
confirmed. Reported alienation was unaffected by an organization's linkages to other local organizations. Finally, the dummy variable indicating
if the organization provided cultural and/or recreational services was
statistically significant at the .01-level in the reduced model. This tells us
that reports of alienation among workers, staff, and volunteers increased
dramatically between 1988 and 1994 if the organization provided primarily cultural or recreational services in 1988.

## D. Disagreements

We also wanted to see if organizational growth and decline, environment, and tactics affected the number of disagreements within an organization. In the methods section we described how we tallied up the
number of disagreements in 1988 and 1994 as reported by the chief administrative officer. Again we relied heavily on the perceptions of top
administrators. We hypothesized that, in organizations that experienced a
decline in resources, the number of disagreements would increase (Hypothesis 1), the positive effect of decline on disagreements would be
stronger if the organization was functioning in a more competitive resource niche (Hypothesis 3), retrenchment tactics would result in an increase in the number of disagreements within the organization
(Hypothesis 4), in more centralized organizations the number of disagreements would increase (Hypothesis 6), in organizations that relied more
heavily on donations and volunteers but implemented a large number of
managerial tactics disagreements would increase (Hypothesis 7a) and in
organizations that relied more heavily on earned income and employees
but implemented a large number of political tactics disagreements would
increase (Hypothesis 7b), and finally in organizations that were more
heavily embedded in elite networks people would have fewer disagreements over time (Hypothesis 8) as would people in organizations more
embedded in community resource exchange networks (Hypothesis 9).

We wanted to test these hypotheses estimating Equations (2) and (3) as
before but substituting the number of disagreements for the other depen-

dent variables. However, this dependent variable and its lagged counterpart were not without their problems. Each organization could either have had one or more disagreements, no disagreements, or they could have made no decisions at all. As noted in the methods section, in 1988 and 1994, of the 171 and 155 organizations providing us with data, 24 and 15 made no decisions. Of the 147 and 140 organizations that made decisions, 81 and 53 reported one or more decisions. Another consideration was that the distributions of these count variables were highly skewed to the right.

With respect to the lagged dependent variable, we ignored the fact that some organizations did not make any decisions and coded their response to this item as zero, just as if they made decisions but had no disagreements. We treated the dependent variable differently. If the case made no decisions in 1994, it was simply assigned a missing data code and dropped from the analysis. This, of course, reduced our *N* sharply. Before proceeding with our analysis, however, we did a logistic regression where having made decisions or not in 1994 was the response variable and organizational expenditures (ln), age (ln), and activities (health/welfare, culture/recreation, and education) were the regressors (all measured in 1994).[8] The only variable that was statistically significant was log expenditures ($p < .001$), telling us that larger organizations were more likely to make decisions than smaller organizations. Thus by categorically excluding cases that did not make decisions in 1994, we excluded smaller nonprofits from this analysis. Because the number of disagreements are count data, we utilized a Poisson regression as well as ordinary least squares.

We proceeded as before, estimating components of the model separately for each hypothesis, then estimating a final model that included all significant and nearly significant effects. The first model and the OLS reduced model had to be corrected for heteroskedasticity, but in none of the models did tolerance scores drop below .400. The $R^2$ and adjusted $R^2$ were a bit higher than in the previous models, although still modest. The residuals for the five models were approximately normal with slight skewness to the right. The Poisson regression was estimated only with variables from the reduced OLS model. Overall, the effects were weaker than the OLS results.

Again Hypothesis 1 received no support (see Table 5.6). The number of disagreements in 1994 was unaffected by the growth or decline of the organization. Interestingly, size had a modest effect on the number of disagreements ($p = .100$ in model 1), but it was not included in the reduced model because it was collinear with other regressors. Similarly Hypothesis 3 received no support. Niche conditions did not moderate the effect of growth and decline on the number of disagreements within an

Table 5.6.  OLS and Poisson Regressions with Disagreements as the Dependent Variable

|  | Dependent Variable: No. of Disagreements94 | | | | | | | |
|---|---|---|---|---|---|---|---|---|
| Independent Variables | Hyps1&3[a] b (SE) | Hyps4&6 b (SE) | Hyps7a&7b b (SE) | Hyps8&9 b (SE) | OLS Reduced[a] b (SE) | Poisson b (SE) | OLS Reduced b (SE) | Poisson b (SE) |
| No. of Disagreements88 | .068(.091) | .026(.084) | .046(.079) | .122(.081) | .069(.083) | .087(.093) | .074(.081) | .075(.098) |
| Tot Inc & Pers88 | .190(.116) | .077(.112) |  | .152(.123) |  |  |  |  |
| Tot Inc & Pers94 | −.013(.232) | −.094(.232) |  |  |  |  |  |  |
| Tot Inc & Pers88 |  |  |  |  |  |  |  |  |
| Niche Density88 | .033(.046) |  |  |  |  |  |  |  |
| ΔTot Inc & Pers * Niche Density88 | −.204(.169) |  |  |  |  |  |  |  |
| No. of Retrench Tactics88–94 |  | .030(.049) |  |  |  |  |  |  |
| No. of Managerial Tactics88–94 |  | .012(.032) | .033(.033) |  |  |  | .077(.028)** | .125(.044)** |
| No. of Political Tactics88–94 |  | .094(.045)* | .101(.044)* |  | .108(.039)** | .184(.061)** |  |  |
| Dummy for MD, Political Tactics |  | .020(.616) |  |  |  |  |  |  |
| Donated Inc & Vols88 |  |  | −.165(.108) |  |  |  | −.118(.110) | −.260(.170) |
| Donated Inc & Vols88 * Managerial Tactics88–94 |  |  | .034(.028) |  |  |  | .056(.028)* | .059(.037) |
| Commercial Inc & Empl88 |  | −.013(.102) |  |  | −.001(.089) | −.074(.156) |  |  |

| | (1) | (2) | (3) | (4) | (5) | (6) |
|---|---|---|---|---|---|---|
| Commercial Inc & Empl$_{88}$ * Political Tactics$_{88-94}$ | | | | .060(.031)# | .069(.032)* | .055(.044) |
| Gov't Grants & Contracts$_{88}$ | | -.039(.166) | | | | |
| Elite Network Contacts$_{88}$ | | | .010(.092) | | -.775(.667) | -.814(.475)# |
| Interorganizational Network Centrality$_{88}$ | | | -.048(.112) | | -.453(.383) | -1.53(.739) |
| Decentralized Decision-Making Structure$_{88}$ | -.004(.005) | | | | | |
| Health/Welfare$_{88}$ | .069(.161) | .049(.195) | .107(.192) | .077(.198) | | |
| Education$_{88}$ | -.108(.170) | -.086(.208) | -.135(.206) | -.136(.209) | | |
| Culture/Recreation$_{88}$ | .153(.235) | .142(.231) | .069(.228) | .103(.244) | | |
| λ | -.582(.359) | -.521(.449) | -.679(.468) | -.533(.461) | -.456(.343) | -.089(.374) |
| Constant | .692(.252)** | .889(.361)* | .765(.310)* | .746(.319)* | .678(.247)** | .838(.258) |
| $R^2$ | .141* | .179* | .225** | .108# | .196*** | .147*** |
| Adj. $R^2$ | .079 | .097 | .149 | .051 | .164 | .114 |
| N | 134 | 133 | 135 | 135 | 135 | 135 |
| White test for heteroskedasticity | 22.4(9)** | 17.1(12) | 15.2(12) | 8.13(6) | 15.2(5)** | 8.34(5) |
| Log Likelihood | | | | | -135.6 | -138.3 |

*** $p < .001$; ** $p < .01$; * $p < .05$; # $p < .10$.

[a] Standard errors corrected for heteroskedasticity using White (1980).

organization. Hypothesis 4 received no support; retrenchment tactics had little effect on disagreements. Similarly, Hypothesis 6 received no support. Organizations that were more centralized did not have more disagreements.

We did find support for Hypotheses 7a and 7b in the OLS results. As we did in our previous analyses, on the right-hand side of the equation we entered the number of managerial tactics used between 1988 and 1994, commercial income and employees in 1988, the product term for managerial tactics and commercial income/employees, the number of political tactics used between 1988 and 1994, donated income and volunteers in 1988, the product term for political tactics and donated income/volunteers, whether or not the organization received government grants or contracts in 1988, the activities variables, and the sample selection term. Column 3 in Table 5.6 shows that only the number of political tactics used between 1988 and 1994 and the product term for political tactics and commercial income/employees were statistically significant. However, because of the strong correlation between our product terms ($r = .399$), we redid the analysis, first dropping the political tactics × commercial income/employees product term and then the managerial tactics × donated income/volunteers product term.[9] We found that when only one product term was in the equation, it was statistically significant. The managerial tactics × donated income/volunteers had a $p$-value of .049; the political tactics × commercial income/employees had a $p$-value of .014. We therefore estimated two reduced OLS models and two Poisson regressions analyzing each product term separately. In columns 5, 6, 7, and 8 we see that the more political and managerial tactics employed between 1988 and 1992 the greater the increase in disagreements. Both effects in both the OLS and Poisson regressions were significant at the .01-level. We also see that both interaction terms were significant in the reduced OLS models, but not in the Poisson regressions. In the latter set of results, the $p$-value for the political tactics × commercial income/employees product term was .208, and the $p$-value for the managerial tactics × donated income/volunteers product term was .115.

To get a flavor for what is going on here, we computed the simple slopes from our OLS interaction terms. For organizations with an average amount of donated income and volunteers, there was an increase in the number of disagreements between 1988 and 1994 with the implementation of an additional managerial tactic ($b = .077; p = .005$). For organizations that were one standard deviation above the mean, the effect got stronger ($b = .125; p = .001$). For organizations one standard deviation below the mean, managerial tactics had no effect on the number of disagreements ($b = .029; p = .386$).

The interaction between commercial income and the use of political tactics worked about the same. Among organizations with average amounts of commercial income and employees, the more political tactics used, the greater the increase in disagreements ($b = .108; p = .006$). As dependency upon commercial income and employees increased, the effect of political tactics on disagreements got stronger. At one standard deviation above the mean, $b = .178$ ($p = .000$). At one standard deviation below the mean, $b = .039$ ($p = .476$), political tactics no longer had an impact on disagreements.

Finally, there was no support for Hypothesis 8 or 9 in the OLS analysis. Organizations that had more elites using their services and/or serving their organization did not have fewer disagreements than organizations that were isolated. Similarly, the number of disagreements within an organization was unrelated to the number of ties to other organizations in the community.

## E. Conflict with Employees

Finally, we wanted to see if organizational growth and decline, environment, and tactics affected the number of conflicts with employees. Our measure was an additive index where we summed whether or not the organization had employee grievances, employee lawsuits, or strikes in the last year or so. This was also reported by the chief administrative officer. We hypothesized that, in organizations that experienced a decline in resources, the number of employee conflicts would increase (Hypothesis 1), the positive effect of decline on conflicts would be stronger if the organization was functioning in a more competitive resource niche (Hypothesis 3), retrenchment tactics would result in an increase in the number of employee conflicts within the organization (Hypothesis 4), in more centralized organizations the number of conflicts would increase (Hypothesis 6), in organizations that relied more heavily on donations and volunteers but implemented a large number of managerial tactics conflicts would increase (Hypothesis 7a) and in organizations that relied more heavily on earned income and volunteers but implemented a large number of political tactics employee conflicts would increase (Hypothesis 7b), and finally organizations that were more heavily embedded in elite networks people would have fewer conflicts with their employees (Hypothesis 8) as would organizations more embedded in community resource exchange networks (Hypothesis 9).

We proceeded as we did in the preceding section but substituted the number of conflicts with employees for the number of disagreements in the organization. This dependent variable and its lagged counterpart had problems similar to the disagreements variable. Each organization could have had either one or more incidents, no incidents, or it could have no employees. In 1988 and 1994, of the 173 and 156 organizations providing us with data, 46 (26.6%) and 41 (26.3%) had no paid workers. Of the 127 and 115 organizations that had employees, 47 and 52 reported one or more incidents. Another consideration was that the distribution of this count variable was highly skewed.

If the organization had no employees in 1994, it was dropped from the analysis, which again reduced our $N$ considerably. If the organization had no employees in 1988, it was assigned a value of zero for conflict in 1988. Like we did with disagreements, we created a dichotomous variable— having employees or not in 1994—and regressed it on organizational expenditures (ln), age (ln), and activities in a logistic regression.[10] Again, the only variable that was statistically significant was log expenditures ( $p$ < .001), telling us that larger organizations were more likely to have employees. Thus by assigning missing data codes to organizations that had no employees in 1994, we eliminated a large number of smaller organizations. We proceeded as before, estimating components of the model separately for each hypothesis, then estimating a reduced model that included all significant and nearly significant effects. We again presented results from a Poisson regression replicating the reduced OLS model, because these are count data.

The first, third, and fourth OLS results had to be corrected for heteroskedasticity, and in all but the first, multicollinearity was a concern. In the second, fourth, and fifth set of results, the tolerance score for our overall measure of organizational size dipped below .400 (.327, .317, and .336, respectively), and in the third model the tolerance score associated with the number of political tactics was .391. The $R^2$ and adjusted $R^2$ were much higher than in our previous analyses. The residuals for the five OLS models were approximately normal with slight skewness to the right. The Poisson regression again only included variables from the reduced OLS results, and, as we found in the previous analysis, the effects were generally weaker than in the OLS models.

Here growth and decline were related to changes in conflict, but in a way opposite to what Hypothesis 1 predicted (see Table 5.7). The number of incidents increased between 1988 and 1994 in organizations that experienced *growth* in both the OLS results ( $p$ < .05) as well as the Poisson regression ( $p$ < .10). At the same time, larger organizations had more incidents in 1994 than in 1988, while smaller organizations had fewer. In the OLS model the effect was significant at the .01-level; it was not statistically significant in the Poisson regression ( $p$ = .133). Hypothesis 3 received no support. Evidently niche conditions did not moderate the effect of growth and decline on the number of incidents within an organization. However, organizations that were in more dense niches in 1988 saw an increase in the number of incidents with their employees, while organizations in more sparse niches saw a decrease ($p < .05$ in both the OLS and Poisson regression).

Hypothesis 4 received strong support. Organizations that utilized more retrenchment tactics between 1988 and 1994 saw an increase in the number of incidents of conflict with their employees in 1994 ($p < .01$ in the OLS and $p < .10$ in the Poisson results). Furthermore, organizations that utilized more political tactics between 1988 and 1994 had more incidents in 1994 than in 1988 ($p < .05$ in OLS and $p = .142$ in the Poisson regression). Hypothesis 6 received no support. Organizations with more decentralized structures did not see an increase in conflict over the six-year period.

There was no support for Hypotheses 7a and 7b in the OLS analyses. Conflict did not increase in organizations that relied heavily on donated income/volunteers and utilized more managerial tactics nor did it increase in organizations that relied heavily on earned income/employees and utilized more political tactics. There was no support for Hypothesis 8 or 9 either. Organizations that had more elites using their services and/or serving their organization did not see a decrease in conflict. Similarly, the changes in the number of labor conflicts within an organization were unrelated to the number of ties to other organizations in the community. Finally, we note that organizations that had public funding in 1988 tended to have more conflict with employees in 1994 than in 1988 ($p < .01$ in both the OLS and in Poisson results).

## DISCUSSION

Now it is time to evaluate our hypotheses and reflect on the consequences of change. To aid us in interpreting our results we present Table 5.8. Across the top are the dependent variables; the rows are the independent variables in our models. The cell entries show the sign and $p$-value of the effects from the OLS reduced models. Turning back to our hypotheses what can we conclude? If we take the standard .05-level as our cutoff, we must conclude that none of our hypotheses received much support. If we liberalize our criteria to the .10-level, we can identify some patterns in our data. Given the exploratory nature of the analysis in this chapter, we beg the reader's indulgence but also warn that many of the conclusions are very tentative.

Overall, we conclude that growth and decline in resources had very little impact on changes in decision-making structures or the quality of life within our panel of organizations. Hypothesis 1 said that organizations experiencing decline would have more disagreements, conflicts with employees, alienation, and less value placed on creativity. Hypothesis 2

Table 5.7. OLS and Poisson Regressions with Conflicts with Employees as the Dependent Variable

| Independent Variables | Dependent Variable: Conflicts with Employees94 | | | | | |
| --- | --- | --- | --- | --- | --- | --- |
| | Hyps1&3[a] b (SE)12 | Hyps4&6 b (SE)12 | Hyps7a&7b[a] b (SE)12 | Hyps8&9[a] b (SE)12 | OLS Reduced b (SE)12 | Poisson b (SE)12 |
| No. of Conflicts88 | .107(.126) | .103(.112) | .277(.116)* | .170(.129) | .171(.109) | .199(.209) |
| Tot Inc & Pers88 | .434(.095)*** | .362(.109)*** | | .279(.118)* | .245(.109)* | .346(.230) |
| Tot Inc & Pers94 – Tot Inc & Pers88 | .471(.236)* | .444(.192)* | | | .438(.211)* | .868(.528)# |
| Niche Density88 | .051(.033) | | | | .074(.030)* | .155(.068)* |
| ΔTot Inc & Pers * Niche Density88 | −.135(.155) | | | | | |
| No. of Retrench Tactics88–94 | | .093(.034)** | .097(.034)** | | .086(.033)** | .124(.065)# |
| No. of Managerial Tactics88–94 | | −.041(.026) | −.026(.029) | | −.040(.025) | −.037(.059) |
| No. of Political Tactics88–94 | | .092(.037)* | .093(.036)* | | .087(.036)* | .125(.085) |
| Dummy for MD, Political Tactics | | −.606(.429) | | | | |
| Donated Inc & Vols88 | | | .014(.096) | | | |
| Donated Inc & Vols88 * Managerial Tactics88–94 | | | −.002(.023) | | | |

| | | | | | |
|---|---|---|---|---|---|
| Commercial Inc & Empl$_{88}$ | | | | | | −.010(.112) |
| Commercial Inc & Empl$_{88}$ * Political Tactics$_{88-94}$ | | | | | | .018(.033) |
| Gov't Grants & Contracts$_{88}$ | | −.003(.004) | .358(.118)** | | .324(.125)** | .986(.351)** |
| Elite Network Contacts$_{88}$ | | | | .075(.087) | | |
| Interorganizational Network Centrality$_{88}$ | | | | .125(.094) | | |
| Decentralized Decision-Making Structure$_{88}$ | | | | | | |
| Health/Welfare$_{88}$ | .188(.156) | .198(.142) | .153(.151) | .184(.156) | | |
| Education$_{88}$ | .026(.172) | .057(.161) | .027(.185) | −.052(.183) | | |
| Culture/Recreation$_{88}$ | .068(.182) | .051(.184) | −.073(.211) | −.127(.169) | | |
| $\lambda$ | .239(.365) | .328(.328) | −.060(.406) | .226(.369) | .203(.310) | .370(.627) |
| Constant | .054(.231) | .055(.280) | .035(.273) | .082(.268) | −.085(.185) | −2.27(.520)*** |
| $R^2$ | .347*** | .424*** | .400*** | .309*** | .452*** | |
| Adj. $R^2$ | .289 | .352 | .321 | .256 | .402 | |
| N | 111 | 109 | 112 | 112 | 109 | 109 |
| White test for heteroskedasticity | 23.1(9)** | 16.3(12) | 24.5(13)* | 17.8(8)* | 13.0(9) | |
| Log Likelihood | | | | | | −91.0 |

*** $p < .001$; ** $p < .01$;* $p < .05$; # $p < .10$.
[a] Standard errors corrected for heteroskedasticity using White (1980).

Table 5.8. Summary of Variable Effects across Five Dependent Variables, P-Values from OLS Reduced Equation in Parentheses

| | Hypotheses | Decentralized Decision-Making Structure$_{94}$ | Creativity & Innovation$_{94}$ | Alienation$_{94}$ | Disagreements$_{94}$ | Conflicts with Employees$_{94}$ |
|---|---|---|---|---|---|---|
| Tot Inc & Pers$_{88}$ | | +($p$ = .10) | | +(<.10) | | +(<.05) |
| Tot Inc & Pers$_{94}$ – Tot Inc & Pers$_{88}$ | H1,H2 | | | | | +(<.05) |
| Niche Density$_{88}$ | | +(<.01) | | | | +(<.05) |
| ΔTot Inc & Pers * Niche Density$_{88}$ | H3 | | | –($p$ = .10) | | |
| No. of Retrench Tactics$_{88–94}$ | H4,H5 | –(<.05) | –(<.10) | | | +(<.01) |
| No. of Managerial Tactics$_{88–94}$ | | +(<.05) | | | +(<.01)[a] | |
| No. of Political Tactics$_{88–94}$ | | | | +(<.10) | +(<.01)[b] | +(<.05) |
| Decentralized Decision-Making Structure$_{88}$ | H6 | — | +(<.10) | | | |
| Donated Inc & Vols$_{88}$ | | — | | | | |

| | | | | | |
|---|---|---|---|---|---|
| Donated Inc & Vols$_{88}$ * Managerial Tactics$_{88-94}$ | H7a | — | | | +(<.05)[a] |
| Commer Inc & Empl$_{88}$ | H7b | — | | | +(<.05)[b] |
| Commer Inc & Empl$_{88}$ * Political Tactics$_{88-94}$ | | — | | | |
| Gov't Grants & Contracts$_{88}$ | | — | | +(<.01) | |
| Elite Network Contacts$_{88}$ | H8 | — | +(<.05) | −(<.05) | |
| Interorganizational Network Centrality$_{88}$ | H9 | — | | | |
| Health/Welfare$_{88}$ | | | | | |
| Education$_{88}$ | | | | | |
| Culture/Recreation$_{88}$ | | | | +(<.01) | |

[a] These effects were estimated in a model that did not include political tactics or the product term, political tactics × commercial income and employees.

[b] These effects were estimated in a model that did not include managerial tactics or the product term, managerial tactics × donated income and volunteers.

said that organizations experiencing decline would have more centralized decision-making patterns. Hypothesis 3 said that the effect of decline on organizational outcomes would be stronger under more competitive conditions. Using either conservative or liberal criteria, we must conclude that there was no support for either Hypothesis 1 or 2. We found that *growing* organizations tended to have more conflicts with their employees in 1994 than in 1988, but this is the opposite of what we predicted. In only one case did we find support for Hypothesis 3, and the $p$-level was only .100. Coming out of more competitive niches, organizations that were in decline had higher levels of alienation in 1994 than in 1988. Although this does support our hypothesis, we must remember that this effect was found in only one of the five outcomes.

While decline and growth in resources had little impact on organizations' quality of life, if managers utilized more retrenchment tactics, they created problems in the organization. Hypotheses 4 and 5 stated that organizations utilizing more retrenchment tactics would have more disagreements, conflicts, alienation, and less value placed on creativity and innovation. Also patterns of decision-making would become more centralized. Of all our hypotheses, this received the strongest support. Retrenchment led to more conflicts with employees, more centralized decision-making patterns, and less value placed on creativity and innovativeness. However, retrenchment tactics had little effect on alienation or disagreements.

Decision-making structures had little effect on changes in the organization's quality of life. Hypothesis 6 said that organizations with more centralized decision-making structures would have more disagreements, conflicts, alienation, and less value placed on creativity and innovation over time. Independent of whether organizations experienced decline or retrenched operations, we only found that more centralized patterns in 1988 resulted in less emphasis on creativity and innovativeness by 1994. Decision-making structures had no significant effect on any of the other dependent variables. Thus we cannot say that there was much support for Hypothesis 6.

Changing the organization's strategic direction only affected disagreements within the organization, but had no impact on the other outcome measures. Hypotheses 7a and 7b addressed the proposition that changes in tactics have a negative effect on decision-making patterns and the quality of life within organizations. More specifically, Hypothesis 7a said that if organizations were heavily dependent upon donated income and volunteers, but utilized lots of managerial tactics, decision-making would become more centralized, creativity and innovation would come to be valued less and alienation would increase, and the incidence of disagreements and conflicts with employees would increase. Hypothesis 7b said that if organizations were heavily dependent upon commercial and employees, but utilized lots of political tactics, again decision-making would become more centralized, creativity and innovation would come to be valued less and alienation would increase, and the incidence of disagreements and conflicts with employees would increase. In only one of the five analyses did we find support for these hypotheses. They were borne out in the case of disagreements at the .05-level in the OLS results. However, neither interaction effect came close to being significant in the other models.

Having network ties to local elites had a positive, but limited effect on the quality of life within organizations. Hypotheses 8 and 9 focused on network contacts between the organization and local elites and other nonprofits in the community. We speculated that organizations that were more isolated from these social influences (or social controls), would be more likely to have disagreements, conflicts, alienation, and to value creativity and innovation less. Although interorganizational ties had no effect in our models, we did find that organizations with more elites as clients or patrons in 1988 increasingly valued creativity and innovation and became less alienated over time. Proximity to the elite had no effects on disagreements or conflicts. Perhaps having influential outsiders looking in on the organization did temper tempers and contribute to a more healthy work environment.

Finally, several miscellaneous results surfaced that we did not anticipate, but that are of interest. Larger organizations were different than smaller organizations. Larger organizations tended to become more decentralized in their decision-making over time ($p = .100$), i.e., power was shared by the board with other functionaries in the organization. Second, in larger organizations administrators reported that their organizations became more alienated over time. And, third, conflicts with employees increased in larger organizations. In contrast, smaller organizations became more centralized and less alienated (if we can believe administrators) over time, and the number of conflicts with employees diminished. None of these findings were especially surprising and simply confirmed that life is a little looser, more complicated, and rougher in larger organizations.

We also found that niche conditions had a direct effect on patterns of decision-making and the amount of conflict with employees. In more competitive niches, organizations tended to become more decentralized in their decision-making patterns and incidents of conflict with employees were greater. We are not quite sure how to interpret these results, since there has been scant theorizing on the effects of niche conditions on internal organizational conditions. Yet allowing different actors autonomy to make decisions in more competitive environments may be highly adaptive, and the intensity of being in a highly competitive niche may take its toll in relations with employees. However, this is all speculation and more research is needed.

A more provocative set of findings was related to the direct, independent effects of managerial and political tactics. Although we did not hypothesize that either of these tactics should have a direct effect on decision-making patterns or the quality of life, they did. Managerial tactics led to organizations becoming more decentralized and to having more disagreements. They also resulted in fewer conflicts with employees, although the effect was not significant at the .10-level ($p = .110$ in the OLS results). Managerialism appears to have its good and bad points (Froelich 1993; Middleton-Stone and Crittendon 1993). In contrast, political tactics had all sorts of negative repercussions. Organizations that utilized more political tactics between 1988 and 1994 had more alienation in 1994 than in 1988, had more disagreements in 1994 than in 1988, and had more conflicts with employees in 1994 than in 1988. Doing things to make themselves politically correct and legitimate seems to have taken its toll on our organizations.

We also found that organizations with more public funding had more conflicts with employees in 1994 than in 1988, and the administrators of cultural and recreational organizations reported higher levels of alienation in 1994 than in 1988. Other than that, the control variables had no effect on organizations' decision-making patterns or quality of life.

This chapter did not provide as good a set of tests of organizational theory as the previous chapters. First, our hypotheses were more ad hoc, focusing on the more general organizational policy question of whether or not tactics or decline had more influence on what goes on within organizations. In this respect our findings may have more relevance to applied researchers than to organizational theory. If any theory was tested, we looked to see if change in strategic direction resulted in the kind of dire consequences anticipated by ecologists and if network embeddedness had any warm and snuggly benefits for organizations. While we found little evidence to support either set of hypotheses, it is unfair to present these hypotheses as critical tests of organizational ecology and embeddedness theory. Thus, at best, we have gleaned a set of provocative statistical anecdotes on our panel of organizations.

Second, the outcome variables were undertheorized and to test our effects properly we should have developed a fully specified model based on what we know to date about what causes each individual outcome. The fact that the correlations among our five dependent variables were not high indicated that we were not tapping into a single quality of life construct—which was our original intent. At that point, we realized that different factors would probably give rise to different outcomes. For instance, what caused disagreements over policy matters was probably much different than what caused strikes, employee grievances, and employee lawsuits. Thus we should not be surprised that our $R^2$ were so low. Unfortunately, we did not have the variables to test fully specified models and elected to do a more exploratory analysis instead.

Finally, the data left something to be desired. Our measures of alienation and creativity/innovativeness were based on the responses of administrators who had a vested interest in presenting their organization in a positive light. Furthermore, there were serious questions about whether they could even know what members, staff, clients, and volunteers thought and felt. Thus all the results associated with these two variables have to be looked at with some skepticism.

This chapter was more exploratory in nature, but still we believe that it unearthed some important findings that shed light on changes that took place in Twin Cities nonprofit organizations. Now it is time to consolidate the research presented in Chapters 3 through 5 and see how it speaks to the theoretical issues raised in Chapter 1.

## ACKNOWLEDGMENTS

We would like to acknowledge funding for this chapter from the University of Minnesota's Center for the study of Conflict and Change and its former director, John Clark.

## NOTES

1.   In 1988 we inquired about six potential decision-makers (see Chapter 3). We did not inquire about program directors in the 1994 interview. Thus for this chapter we recomputed our scores for 1988 omitting program directors from our measure. This makes the 1988 and 1994 scores comparable.

2.   We dropped the items: parties and social functions are a regular feature around here and people go out after work and socialize with one another. We will discuss the reasons why below.

3.   Many readers may still feel uneasy about using reports from organizational administrators on the feelings, attitudes, and behaviors of people in the organization. Ideally, we would have surveyed multiple respondents for each organization (e.g., Knoke 1990) or even done fieldwork within the organization (e.g., Ostrander 1995). However, we did not have the resources to do either.

4.   We again did an exploratory factor analysis entering all ten items at once. In the single-factor solution, all but one item (we emphasize organizational routines) loaded highly ($>.48$ and $<-.42$). People are willing to listen to new ideas,

are loyal to the organization, work as a team, like to experiment, and believe in the mission of the organization loaded positively, and people don't care about others, are often angry, try to avoid risks, and seem to be out for themselves loaded negatively. In the two-factor solution (excluding emphasis on organizational routines), people are loyal, work as a team, and believe in the mission loaded positively and people don't care about others, are often angry, and seem to be out for themselves loaded negatively on the first factor. People listen to new ideas, like to experiment, and work as a team loaded positively and people avoid risks loaded negatively on the second factor. We decided to use separate constructs instead of just one, because of the number of cases we would lose due to missing data in a listwise analysis.

5.   The patterns persisted when we looked only at the 1988 and 1994 scores of the 1994 survivors. Thus organizations with more problems were not "selected out" of the panel between 1988 and 1994.

6.   The reason for including all three tactics variables was that we were curious about the impact of managerial and political tactics on organizational well-being. This also laid the groundwork for our later analysis of what happened when organizations used tactics that were not congruent with their patterns of resource dependency.

7.   The dummy variable was coded 1 if we substituted the mean for missing data and 0 otherwise. The results are presented in the tables, but in none of the analyses was the dummy statistically significant at the .10-level.

8.   The model $\chi^2$ statistic equaled 26.6 (df = 5) and 92.3% of the cases were correctly predicted.

9.   We did this for every other table in this chapter, but neither product term—alone or in the same model—was significant at the .10-level.

10.   The model $\chi^2$ statistic equaled 97.4 (df = S), and 88.5% of the cases were predicted correctly with the model.

# 6

# Summary and Conclusions

The purpose of this monograph was to see how well different theories developed in the fields of organizational sociology and management science could explain changes in a panel of nonprofit organizations in a single case community. Ideally the book has been read as a contest of ideas, with different theories coming out ahead depending upon the analysis. We identified some change phenomena, e.g., a change in organizational size, a change in tactics, or a change in decision-making structures, and anticipated how different theories would explain these changes. We then tried to formulate empirical statements or hypotheses that would provide a credible test of each theory and to collect data that would enable us to operationalize concepts validly. Finally, we utilized quantitative methods to test our hypotheses and summarized our results. At the end of each chapter we tried to evaluate each theory and how well it did in explaining organizational change. Now it is the time to bring all our results together and to assess the relative utility of the different theories.

Another goal was to motivate applied researchers to look more closely at organizational theory for guidance when studying nonprofit organizations. Economic theory has become the dominant paradigm in research on nonprofits, and economists have made major contributions to our understanding of how nonprofits behave and change over time (e.g., see Ben-Ner and Anheier 1997). Yet we felt that economists ignored many of the factors that organizational theorists, particularly in sociology and the management sciences, were looking at. There was little attention to conditions in the environment, social networks, cultural and institutional forces, and strategy or tactics. We certainly are not the first organizational theorists to look at the nonprofit sector—organizational sociologists studied nonprofit organizations long before economists became interested in the topic (Lipset, Trow, and Coleman 1956; Sills 1957; Perrow 1961; Zald and Denton 1963)—and much of current organizational theory, e.g., resource dependency and institutional theory, was built using studies of nonprofits. But we wanted to see what organizational theory could do today to explain change in a panel of nonprofits. Indeed, our findings were not always as strong as some of our colleagues in the field would have liked. Yet we found enough results to convince us of the utility of organizational theory in helping scholars understand changes in the not-for-profit organization, and we hope that applied researchers will pay more attention to this literature and body of work in the future.

To ensure that all the theories we tested receive a fair hearing, we now summarize our findings from the previous chapters and present an evaluation of the different theories we considered. We then conclude by reminding the reader of the shortcomings of our research and encouraging others to continue the work we begun.

## EXPLAINING ORGANIZATIONAL CHANGE: A CONTEST OF IDEAS

The bottom line is that no one theory of organizational change dominated our results. There was something to say for each of them, and, in all likelihood, they all will survive to see another day. Both selection theory as well as adaptation theory received support. We also found support for embeddedness theory. We found enough evidence to still believe that public charity organizations are resource driven, but in several instances organizations did not behave as if they were—which speaks for theories that emphasize the importance of mission, morality, and ideals (e.g., Rothschild-Whitt 1979).

We discuss each theory in turn and the relevant results. We recount what we thought we should find if the theory was correct (i.e., we give hypotheses). Figures 6.1a, 6.2a, and 6.3a summarize the hypotheses presented in Chapters 3, 4, and 5, respectively. These models more fully develop the theoretical statement in Figure 1.1. Then we look at our results to see if the hypotheses were supported. Figures 6.1b, 6.2b, and 6.3b summarize all effects that were statistically significant at the $p < .10$ level in our tables. The signs attached to the arrows represent the direction of the relationship, positive or negative. A zero represents a nonsignificant effect. In Figures 6.1b and 6.2b, more than one sign is attached to an arrow. This was because we analyzed more than one period and the signs represent the effects for the respective years. For example, in Figure 6.1b there are four signs, one for each of the four periods analyzed in Chapter 3: 1980–1984, 1984–1988, 1988–1992, and 1988–1994. In Figure 6.2b, there are two signs, one for each period analyzed in Chapter 4: 1984–1988 and 1988–1992. In Figure 6.3b, there is only one sign because we analyzed

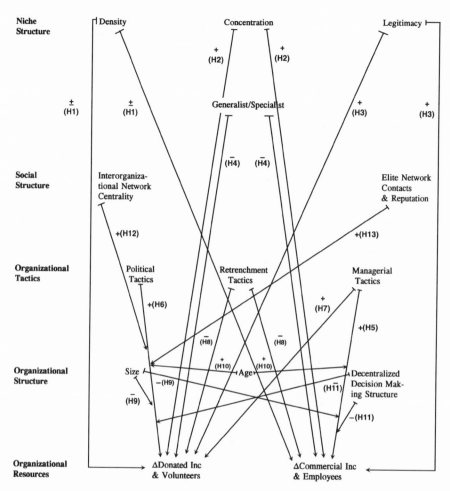

*Figure 6.1a.* Summary of hypotheses in Chapter 3 on changes in organizational resources.

only one period in Chapter 5: 1988–1994. If a hypothesized effect was not significant in any period, we did not draw an arrow representing that effect. On occasion, variables in the models that we had not hypothesized were significant. In these cases we included the effect in our summary of results. We should caution the reader that only variables of theoretical interest are included in Figures 6.1b, 6.2b, and 6.3b. Control variables that were significant regressors were not included. We advise readers to keep these figures handy as we go through our summary and discussion.

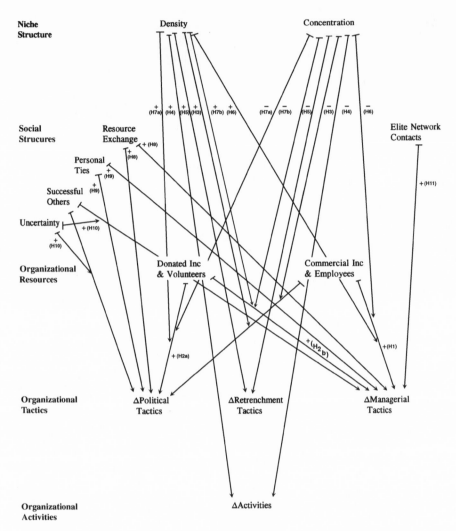

*Figure 6.2a.* Summary of hypotheses in Chapter 4 on changes in tactics and activities.

## A. Selection Models

Selection refers to a change in the composition of a set of organizations as one form is replaced by another simply because the former is unable to reproduce itself while the latter can (Hannan and Carroll 1995a). Organizations and their managers, however, do not have much say in the matter.

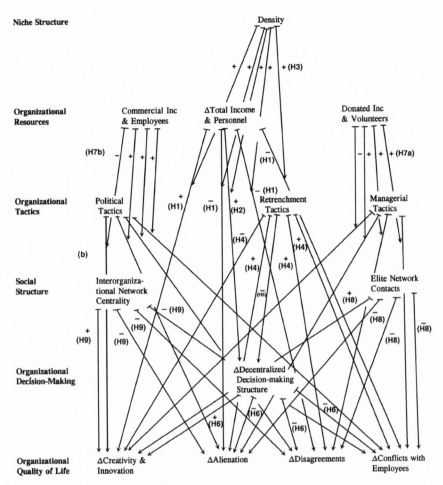

*Figure 6.3a.* Summary of hypotheses in Chapter 5 on changes in organizational quality of life & decision-making.

Depending upon conditions in the larger environment, some organizations will grow and prosper, while others will decline and wither away. Most selection models are formulated at the population level of analysis, predicting changes within populations, e.g., birth and death rates, using variables that are also measured at the population level, e.g., density. Sometimes these theories focus on industries (e.g., Carroll and Hannan 1995); other times they study organizational fields (e.g., Powell and Di-Maggio 1991). This is true for both organizational ecology and institutional theory in organizational sociology. Our goal was to test selection theory

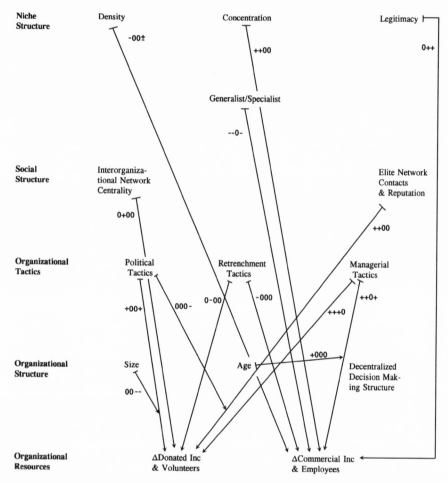

**Niche Structure** · Density · Concentration · Legitimacy
-00‡ · ++00 · 0++

Generalist/Specialist
--0-

**Social Structure** · Interorganiza-tional Network Centrality · Elite Network Contacts & Reputation
0+00 · ++00

**Organizational Tactics** · Political Tactics · Retrenchment Tactics · Managerial Tactics
+00+ · 000- · 0-00 · -000 · ++0+ · +++0

**Organizational Structure** · Size · Age · +000 · Decentralized Decision Making Structure
00-- · 

**Organizational Resources** · ΔDonated Inc & Volunteers · ΔCommercial Inc & Employees

*Figure 6.1b.*    Summary of results in Chapter 3 on changes in organizational resources.

using individual organizations as the units of analysis and environmental conditions as contextual effects.

To aid us in bridging the gap between the environmental and the organizational levels, we focused on organizational niches. We defined a niche as that arena of action in which organizations competed for scare resources, e.g., money, information, support, authority, and focused on the competition among incumbents. However, one could also study actors in the broader organizational field or ecological community that provided the resources (e.g., customers and/or grantmakers), regulated the competi-

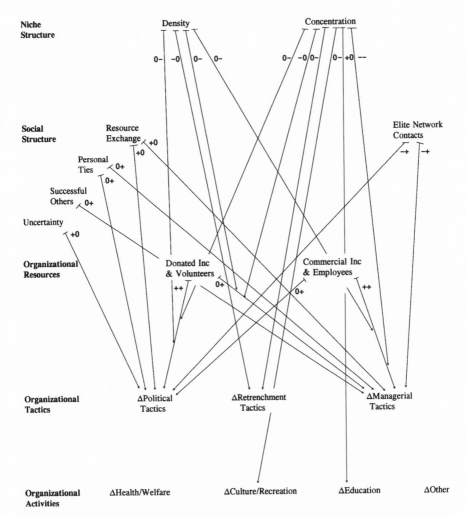

*Figure 6.2b.* Summary of results in Chapter 4 on changes in tactics and activities.

tion (e.g., government agencies and the courts), and observed the action (e.g., community and environmental groups). These players are as crucial in understanding what goes on within niches as those who compete against one another. However, we we focused only on competitors.

Examples of recent research on niches include Baum and Singh (1994a, 1994b; see also Baum and Oliver 1996) and Podolny and Stuart (1995; see also Podolny et al. 1996). Most built in some way on the work of McPher-

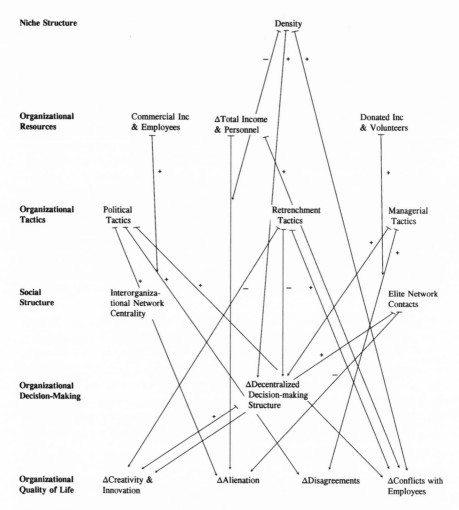

*Figure 6.3b.* Summary of results in Chapter 5 on changes in organizational quality of life and decision-making.

son (1983; see also Popielarz and McPherson 1995) and Burt (1982, 1983). Niches were conceptualized as structurally equivalent action sets that emerged out of the day-to-day competition for scarce resources. The niche could be defined in terms of products, types of revenue sources, organizational capabilities (e.g., organizational size), types of labor inputs, client/consumer/member characteristics (i.e., market segment), technology, or locale. We delimited our niche boundaries focusing on products (or activities), revenue sources, size of organization, and labor imputs.

There is a duality to all niches. One could talk about a niche space (McPherson 1983) where we get an overview of where organizational competition is concentrated at the field level. After delimiting niche boundaries, one could focus on several characteristics of the niche that might affect an organization's chances for survival, e.g., the level of competition or legitimacy. One could also try to locate individual organizations within the niche space and describe their microniche, i.e., the various arenas in which they compete for resources. Clearly some organizations have only one product line, a simple technology, and procure revenues from one source. These we called specialists. Most organizations, however, operate in several niches at once, competing in several arenas (or structurally equivalent sets) against different organizations at the same time. These we called generalists. Thus at the same time that we can talk about the niche structure of an organizational field, e.g., identify structurally equivalent sets of nonprofit organizational competitors in a community like the Twin Cities, we can also talk about the unique microniche that the Guthrie Theater, Minnesota Public Radio, or the Armstrong Hockey Boosters occupied within this larger structure.

We measured several features of organizational niches. We proceeded to operationalize the niche space of nonprofits in the Twin Cities using data from four random samples of public charities in 1980, 1984, 1988, and 1992. We focused on where organizations received their revenues (donations, commercial income, government grants and contracts, and miscellaneous income), their type of labor inputs (employees, volunteers), their products (welfare/health, cultural/recreational, educational, other), and their capabilities (size measured as expenditures) and created structurally equivalent sets from these data (see Appendix B).[1] Looking at the organizations within each segment of the niche space we computed density scores and measured the level of resource concentration within each segment or subset within the space. These were our indicators of niche competition and the former also enabled us to measure constitutive legitimacy. We also computed the average status or prestige of organizations within each niche. This was our indicator of the niche's sociopolitical legitimacy.

The hypotheses we tested were all operational at the organizational— not population—level. We focused only on the panel organizations that were first selected for our study in 1979. We treated the panel organization's position in the niche space and conditions that it faced in its various niches as explanatory variables. Our goal was to test for contextual effects on organizational change. We computed measures of how much competition panel organizations faced and the legitimacy they enjoyed based upon where they were situated in the niche space in 1980, 1984, and 1988. We also measured the extent to which organizations were in one niche or occupied several (specialists vs. generalists).

Now is the time to see how well selection theory did in explaining organizational change in our panel of nonprofits. Our strategy is to state the hypotheses derived from the theory and then review the findings. The more hypotheses supported, the more confidence we can have in the theory. The fewer hypotheses supported, the less confidence.

*Growth and Decline.* In Chapter 3 we offered four hypotheses that used ecological and institutional variables to explain the growth and decline of nonprofits in our panel (see Figure 6.1a). To summarize briefly,

> *Organizations in more dense niches are likely to increase commercial income, donated income, employees, and volunteers, up to a point, after which they are likely to lose commercial income, donated income, employees, and volunteers over time. (Chapter 3, H1)*
>
> *Organizations in more concentrated niches are likely to increase commercial income, donated income, employees, and volunteers over time. (Chapter 3, H2)*
>
> *Organizations in niches with greater sociopolitical legitimacy are likely to increase commercial income, donated income, employees, and volunteers over time. (Chapter 3, H3)*
>
> *Organizations that are specialists are likely to increase commercial income, donated income, employees, and volunteers over time, while organizations that are generalists should lose resources over time. (Chapter 3, H4)*

The effects of density on growth and decline were evident in only three of the eight OLS models that we tested in Chapter 3 (see Figure 6.1b).[2] Density had negative effects on growth in earned income and employees between 1980 and 1984 ($p < .05$).[3] Density had a nonmonotonic effect on changes in earned income and employees between 1988 and 1994 in the shape of an inverted U ($p < .10; p < .10$), but this was the only evidence of density dependence in the eight models.

Concentration, legitimacy, and our generalist/variable performed much better in the OLS models. Organizations in niches that were marked by high levels of resource concentration increased their commercial income and employees between 1980 and 1984 ($p < .10$) and between 1984 and 1988 ($p < .05$), but concentration had little effect on changes between 1988 and 1992 or between 1988 and 1994. Organizations in niches occupied by highly legitimate actors were likely to increase their commercial income and employees between 1988 and 1992 ($p < .01$) and 1988 and 1994 ($p < .05$).[4] Furthermore, specialists increased their commercial income and employees between 1980 and 1984 ($p < .10$), 1984 and 1988 ($p < .01$), and 1988 and 1994 ($p < .001$). However, these three variables had no statistically significant effect on changes in donated income and volunteers in any of the periods.

***Tactics.*** In Chapter 4 we argued that niche conditions would be important in the selection of tactics. Two competing models were offered (see Figure 6.2a). The first said that competition would drive organizations out of their niche. This we borrowed from contingency theory. Operationally this meant that under competitive conditions organizations would embrace new tactics, change their products or activities, and retrench operations.

> *In more competitive niches, organizations that are more dependent on commercial income and employees are likely to increase their use of political tactics over time. (Chapter 4, H3)*

> *Organizations that reside in more competitive niches are more likely to change their products and services over time. (Chapter 4, H4)*

> *Organizations that reside in more competitive niches are likely to increase their use of retrenchment tactics over time. (Chapter 4, H5)*

The second model derived from organizational ecology (inertia theory) said that competition would prompt organizations to step up their efforts, i.e., increase their use of resource tactics, but organizations would stay in their niche, not venture into other niches.

> *In more competitive niches, organizations that are more dependent on commercial income and employees are likely to increase their use of managerial tactics over time. (Chapter 4, H6)*

> *In more competitive niches, organizations that are more dependent on donated income and volunteers are likely to increase their use of political tactics over time. (Chapter 4, H7a)*

> *In more competitive niches, organizations that are more dependent on donated income and volunteers are likely to increase their use of managerial tactics over time. (Chapter 4, H7b)*

We found little evidence that niche conditions prompted organizations to change niche position (See Figure 6.2b). In neither our OLS nor our Poisson regressions did we find niche conditions having an effect on the relationship between commercial income and employees and increases in the use of political tactics our test of niche flight. In the Poisson regressions, however, we found that if their niche was sparsely populated or resources were less concentrated, organizations that were dependent upon commercial income and employees increased their managerial tactics (in three out of four tests), and organizations that were dependent upon donated income and volunteers increased their political and managerial tactics (in four out of eight tests). This happened both between 1984 and 1988 and between 1988 and 1992. We had not expected that sparsely settled niches would bring forth such a defensive response; however, the lack of constitutive legitimacy in a sparsely settled niche may be more threatening to an organization than the presence of many competitors. In sum, there was some evidence that hostile environments now assuming sparsely settled niches are hostile led organizations to compete harder within their domain rather than to flee their niche and find a new home.

We also found that between 1984 and 1988 and between 1988 and 1992 organizations were very reluctant to change their products or services— even when facing a hostile or competitive environment. However, in niche conditions had some effect on the use of retrenchment tactics. In our Poisson analysis, organizations in less concentrated niches in 1988 increased their retrenchment tactics between 1988 and 1992 ($p < .05$), and between 1984 and 1988, organizations that were in less dense niches tended to increase their retrenchment tactics ($p < .10$). In our OLS results we found no niche effects on changes in the use of retrenchment tactics.

We had sketched out two scenarios. Facing competitive environments, organizations could respond either by escalating commitments to the tactics employed in the past or by changing their niche position. Our results showed that in less legitimate or less concentrated niches, organizations increased their efforts to extract resources from familiar sources and did not change their mix of products and services. However, some did downsize their operations. Thus when faced with hostile niche conditions, organizations continued to do what they had done in the past but on a somewhat smaller scale.

*Quality of Life.* In our exploratory analysis in Chapter 5 there was only one hypothesis that linked niche conditions to the quality of life within organizations. However, it was an important hypothesis (see Figure 6.3a). We argued that the effect of growth and decline on conditions within an organization would be contingent on niche conditions. In particular, decline in a competitive environment should result in more "negatives" than decline in a noncompetitive context.

> *Organizations that experience a decline in resources in highly competitive resource niches are more likely to centralize decision-making authority, have disagreements while making decisions, conflict with employees, alienation, and a less creative or innovative work environment than organiza-*

*tions that experience a decline in resources in less competitive niches. (Chapter 5, H3)*

Testing this hypothesis required that we estimate five models and test for five interaction effects, since there were five dependent variables. We only used the measure of niche density in our analysis. In only one of the five analyses was the interaction statistically significant and our hypothesis supported (see Figure 6.1b).[5] Coming out of more competitive niches, organizations that were in decline had higher levels of alienation in 1994 than in 1988 ($p = .100$). In niches with average or below average densities, change in size had no effect on change in alienation. But for the most part, growth and decline were neither important, nor contingent upon conditions in local niches, in explaining changes in the quality of organizational life. We did find, however, that organizations in more crowded niches decentralized their decision-making between 1988 and 1994 ($p < .01$) and had more conflicts with employees in 1994 than in 1988 ($p < .05$), but reasons for this remain unclear.

*Discussion.* Clearly ecological theory worked better explaining changes in arenas where organizations competed for customers and employees than in arenas where they competed for donors and volunteers (see Figure 6.1b). In all periods niche conditions explained growth and decline in commercial income and employees but not donated income and volunteers. Perhaps we should not be surprised, since competition is an important value in market arenas. Yet extensive research on nonprofits found density dependence effects (e.g., Baum and his associates, and Singh and his associates), so we had thought that donative transactions (i.e., donations and volunteering) would also be affected by niche conditions. Perhaps the organizations studied by the ecologists were heavily dependent upon fees and program service revenues. We do not know. But if we can trust our results, they suggest that organizations in niches with strong process controls were immune to selection. This, of course, implies that selection theories have limited utility for studying nonprofit organizations, as many rely heavily on donations and volunteers.

Although restricted to explaining growth and decline in commercial income and employees, we were surprised that specialists so decidedly outcompeted generalists. This was perhaps one of the most consistent ecological effects we found. It is noteworthy, because it goes against common sense. Oftentimes organizations are told to diversify, spread their risks, and ensure that they do not become too dependent on any one source of funds. Yet we found that organizations that drew their resources from a narrower range of sources and had fewer products grew at a faster rate than those that had funding from multiple sources and provided many different products. Here ecological theory clearly won out over common sense.

Selection theory clearly scored points in the flight vs. fight debate, but it did not record a knockout. As inertia theory would predict, niche conditions did not prompt organizations to change their funding source or go into new product lines; as adaptation theory would predict, niche conditions resulted in some retrenchment. For the most part (although not in all periods), hostile environmental conditions prompted organizations to fight back and do more of what they were doing but on a smaller scale. Thus niche conditions had a modifying effect on the relationship between funding source and tactics. Apparently the ecologists—and two streetwise business consultants—were right. Smart organizations "stick to the knitting" and don't stray too far from home.

## B. Adaptation Models

The adaptation approach argued that organizations could and would take measures to achieve their goals or ensure their survival. The adaption model is more proactive and finds expression in what has come to be called the "strategy" literature in management science. Whereas selection models are often criticized for being overly deterministic, ignoring the agency of organizational actors, adaptation theories are often criticized for being "undersocialized," that is, too willing to make managers and administrators omnipotent. Reality probably resides somewhere between these two extremes, and organizations are both affected by the environment and formulate strategies and implement tactics that help to ensure their well-being.

For adaptation theory, the unit of analysis is the organization and thus this theory is more appropriate to our study than selection theory, yet there are still problems. The analyst observes what policies management implements and then waits to see the results. Of course, results will be weak when the outcome is measured at the organizational or corporate level (e.g., return on investment), while strategy is formulated and tactics implemented at the division level or business subunit. Multinational conglomerates present a special challenge to adaptation theory. Many of the standard problems that plague organizational analysis plague adaptation theory as well. Organizational goals are often in conflict, interest groups and coalitions sometimes displace organizational goals with their own agendas, and at times the survival (or systems) needs of the organization seem to mitigate any effort to pursue organizational goals in a rational manner (Scott 1998). Still when asked why organizations change—for better or worse, most would reply that it is because management has done something different (Barnett and Carroll 1995:220). It seems obvious and responds to our need to make someone accountable.

In order to pit variables derived from the selection and adaptation literatures against one another in an empirical contest, we returned to the niche. Our general theoretical argument (recall Chapter 1) was that resources were allocated through different kinds of mechanisms across niches. For example, in some segments of a niche space, resources were allocated on the basis of output controls. Those who get ahead have a better product and could sell it at a lower price. This constituted the market arena. In other segments, those who got ahead were able to convince institutional gatekeepers of their normative purity, political correctness, and the righteousness of their mission. This constituted the grants arena. The upshot of all this was that the dynamics—or you could say processes—within each segment of a niche space were going to be different depending upon the type of controls. For example, organizations that were seeking to attract donors or contributors to their organization went about it differently than organizations that were trying to attract customers. The incentives offered each were different; the meaning of the relationship was different; the obligations of the organization to funding sources were different.

The basic assumption behind our discussion was that organizations and their leaders were striving to optimize resources or inputs. This is implicit in selection theory and explicit in adaptation theory. Some sought more resources to better attain organizational goals (e.g., world peace, social equality, shareholder return on equity), others sought more resources to ensure organizational survival (even if at the expense of goals), some sought more resources to serve managerial utilities, and some sought more resources just to accumulate more resources. Whatever the motivation, the assumption was that organizations would do what they had to do in order to accumulate more inputs.

Clearly this relates directly back to the above discussion. If an organization was in a niche segment where it sought donations from wealthy philanthropists, it would do what it had to, e.g., demonstrate its public regardingness or trustworthiness, to get those donations. If an organization was in a niche segment where it taught English as a second language to immigrants who paid their own tuition, it would do what it had to do to get their business, e.g., advertise its services or improve teaching techniques. In other words, depending upon where they were situated in the resource space, organizations had to do certain things to procure the resources they needed.

To link this argument to the strategy literature, we then argued that organizations, their boards, and their managers have different orientations. Some were oriented toward growth, others toward consolidation.

We next moved to the level of tactics, which we defined as operational initiatives or techniques aimed at achieving certain strategic ends. Here we called efforts to consolidate operations, retrenchment tactics. We then distinguished between tactics geared at achieving growth in niches with strong output controls and tactics oriented toward realizing growth in niches with strong process controls. We called the former managerial tactics, the latter political or legitimation tactics.

Managerial tactics were institutionally approved techniques to realize growth in niches where resources were procured through competitive bidding, the pursuit of self-interest, and exchange processes. We further distinguished between internal tactics aimed at reducing overhead and production costs, improving product quality, and making systems more reliable without reducing organizational capabilities, and external tactics aimed at reducing transaction costs, marketing products better, and competing more effectively against other providers. These tactics were standard for business organizations, but we argued that they were appropriate for any type of organization—for-profit or nonprofit—that sold its products to customers, secured its labor inputs from the marketplace, and produced easy-to-evaluate goods and services.

Political tactics were institutionally approved techniques to realize growth in niches where resources were procured by supplicants demonstrating commitment to collective or public interest goals, institutional gatekeepers evaluating their sincerity and trustworthiness, and resources being allocated through donative processes. We again distinguished between internal and external tactics. The former aimed at strengthening the organization's moral capital, ensuring loyalty to mission, and safeguarding its integrity. External tactics included convincing key stakeholders of the organizations' credibility, changing stakeholders' perceptions and priorities, and getting others to testify on behalf of the organization. These tactics were standard for charitable or communal organizations, but we argued that they were useful for any organization that relied on donations and volunteer help, sold hard-to-evaluate trust goods and services, or provided collective or public goods.

As noted above, a central argument in this book was that an organization would do whatever it thought necessary—within institutional bounds—to procure the resources it needed. If it found itself dependent upon sales to consumers, employees, and selling easy-to-evaluate goods and services, it would utilize more managerial tactics and, in turn, it would increase its commercial income and employees. On the other hand, if it found itself dependent upon donors (or grantmakers) and volunteers, and either sold hard-to-evaluate trust goods or produced collective or public goods, it would utilize more political tactics and, in turn, increase its donated income and volunteers. This was why organizations—

whether for-profit or nonprofit—would come to look more like proto-typical business organizations over time, if they were heavily dependent upon market transactions; and why organizations—whether for-profit or nonprofit—would come to look more like prototypical charitable organizations over time, if they were heavily dependent upon donative transfers for their resources. In other words, we hypothesize competitive isomorphism (DiMaggio and Powell 1983).

Now again it is time to see how well the theory did. As we did for selection theory, we will present the various hypotheses derived from extant theory and review our results. More empirical support for the hypotheses strengthens our faith in adaptation theory; less weakens it.

*Growth and Decline.* The first set of hypotheses closely mirrored the arguments made above, focusing on the employment of certain tactics and the subsequent increases or decreases in different types of resources (see Figure 6.1a). The first two are a restatement of basic adaptation theory. The third came from DiMaggio and Powell's (1983) discussion of how institutional gatekeepers often regard managerial tactics as indicators of organizations' accountability, reliability, and trustworthiness. It demonstrates a commitment to rationality. We introduced the fourth as a further test of adaptation theory, where organizations intentionally attempted to reduce their scale of operations.

*Organizations that employ more managerial tactics are likely to increase commercial income and employees over time. (Chapter 3, H5)*

*Organizations that employ more political tactics are likely to increase donated income and volunteers over time. (Chapter 3, H6)*

*Organizations that employ more managerial tactics are likely to increase donated income and volunteers over time. (Chapter 3, H7)*

*Organizations that employ more retrenchment tactics are likely to lose commercial income, donated income, employees, and volunteers over time. (Chapter 3, H8)*

The results were straightforward (see Figure 6.1b). The use of more managerial tactics increased commercial income and employees between 1980 and 1984 ($p < .05$), 1984 and 1988 ($p < .001$), and 1988 and 1994 ($p < .01$). Managerial tactics also led to an increase in donated income and volunteers between 1980 and 1984 ($p < .10$), 1984 and 1988 ($p < .05$), and 1988 and 1992 ($p < .05$). Thus our position and that of DiMaggio and Powell (1983) were both strongly supported by the data. We also saw that political tactics increased donations and volunteers between 1980 and 1984 ($p < .05$) and between 1988 and 1994 ($p < .01$)

and in a later analysis political tactics led to an increase in commercial income and employees between 1980 and 1984 ($p < .05$). Thus the recent attention given to political or legitimation tactics (e.g., Suchman 1995; Oliver 1991) is well deserved.

Retrenchment sometimes resulted in a decline in resources (commercial revenues and employees between 1980 and 1984 ($p < .05$) and donated income and volunteers between 1984 and 1988 ($p < .05$)), but most of the time it did not. This was a remarkable finding: One of two things was happening. First, organizations were reducing their costs without hurting their income streams. That is, they fired staff, reduced pay, eliminated programs, or did all those other ugly things without jeopardizing either their commercial income or their donated income. They created for themselves a windfall situation that may have returned some of these organizations to solvency and feathered the nest of others. Alternatively, retrenchment was simply a process that organizations routinely engaged in as part of their day-to-day housekeeping. They eliminated programs but started others; they cut some people's pay and benefits but later gave raises to others; they reduced service delivery staff and hired more administrators; or they fired administrators and hired more service delivery staff. Needless to say, this nonfinding was intriguing and worthy of further investigation.

*Tactics.* We also offered several hypotheses that speculated on when organizations would utilize different tactics (see Figure 6.2a). There were certainly irrational explanations for why organizations selected the tactics they did, and these will be discussed in our discussion of embeddedness effects. Here we present and evaluate hypotheses aimed at explaining the use of tactics from the adaptation perspective.

> *Organizations that are more dependent on commercial income and employees are likely to increase their use of managerial tactics over time. (Chapter 4, H1)*

> *Organizations that are more dependent on donated income and volunteers are likely to increase their use of political and managerial tactics over time. (Chapter 4, H2a and H2b)*

All three hypotheses were supported (see Figure 6.2b). We found that between 1984 and 1988 and between 1988 and 1992, organizations that were more dependent upon fees and employees increased their use of managerial tactics ($p < .01$; $p < .01$) and that organizations more dependent upon private donations and volunteers increased their use of political tactics ($p < .01$; $p < .001$). We also saw that organizations more dependent upon private donations and volunteers increased their use of managerial tactics between 1988 and 1992 ( $p < .05$) (but not between 1984 and 1988). Thus organizations took on the appropriate trappings of the arenas upon which they were heavily dependent for resources. Those dependent upon fees and employees came to look more "businesslike" over time, while those dependent upon donations and volunteers came to look more "charitable" and "businesslike."

The anomaly was that between 1988 and 1992 we also found that organizations that were more dependent upon commercial income and employees in 1988 increased their use of political tactics as well ( $p < .01$). This could be driven by resource needs, but it is unclear. In a reanalysis of Chapter 3 results, presented at the end of Chapter 4, we discovered that political tactics led to an increase in commercial income and employees between 1980 and 1984 ( $p < .05$) but not in any other period. Perhaps we overestimated the importance of niche identities and the different effects they have on the procurement of different kinds of resources and that now large organizations—regardless of their funding type—are becoming more managerial *and* more political. Needless to say, more research is needed to address this issue.

*Quality of Life.* In our exploratory analysis we offered four hypotheses linking the use of different tactics with the various quality of life indicators that we identified (see Figure 6.3a). The first two dealt with retrenchment tactics. This time we wanted to see if they affected organizational behaviors. The second two addressed a very interesting proposition that came out of both the ecological and management literatures. Did organizations that employed tactics that were incongruent with their current niche position suffer any negative behavioral consequences?

*Organizations that retrench operations are more likely to have disagreements while making decisions, conflict with employees, alienation, and a less creative or innovative work environments than organizations that do not retrench operations. (Chapter 5, H4)*

*Organizations that retrench operations are more likely to centralize decision-making patterns. (Chapter 5, H5)*

*Organizations that use managerial tactics are more likely to have disagreements while making decisions, conflict with employees, alienation, and a less creative or innovative work environment, if they were more heavily reliant on donated income and volunteers in the past. (Chapter 5, H7a)*

*Organizations that use political tactics are more likely to have disagreements while making decisions, conflict with employees, alienation, and a less creative or innovative work environment, if they were more heavily reliant on commercial income and employees in the past. (Chapter 5, H7b)*

The analysis showed that retrenchment had a much greater impact on decision-making patterns and quality of life than growth and decline (see Figure 6.3b). Retrenchment led to more conflicts with employees ($p <$ .01), less value being placed on creativity and innovativeness ($p < .10$), and more centralized decision-making patterns ($p < .05$) between 1988 and 1994. These findings, of course, were especially impressive because they were independent of growth and decline in resources. One of the reasons we tested these hypotheses was that we wanted to see if growth and decline or the use of retrenchment tactics were more important in deciding organizational behavioral outcomes. The data suggest the latter, not the former. Decline per se had no negative effects on the organizations we studied, although it did interact with niche density and alienation, as noted earlier. In fact, it led to *fewer* conflicts with employees ($p <$ .05). Retrenchment was another matter. These findings were also important in light of our earlier findings that retrenchment had no consistent negative effect on growth in resources and was a seemingly favorite tactic of nonprofits reliant on commercial income and employees. Managers who employed more retrenchment tactics did not jeopardize the flow of resources into the organization, but they surely opened themselves up to problems nonetheless.

Support for the other two hypotheses was much weaker. We found that organizations that utilized more political tactics had more disagreements if they were more heavily dependent upon fees and employees ($p < .001$), and organizations that utilized more managerial tactics had more disagreements if they were more heavily dependent upon donations and volunteers ($p < .01$). We only found these effects for disagreements, but then it may only be in decision-making that the problems caused by switching identities come out. Indeed, it was in policymaking situations that Hall (1990) saw the conflict between an executive director who wanted to protect what he felt to be the mission and integrity of the organization and a board chair and his executive committee that was pushing the organization to be more businesslike.[6]

In a spate of findings that we had not anticipated, we found that organizations that utilized more managerial tactics between 1988 and 1994 became more decentralized in their decision-making ($p < .05$) and had more disagreements ($p < .01$) over the same period. Also, and more surprisingly, organizations that utilized more political tactics between 1988 and 1994 reported higher levels of alienation ($p < .10$), more disagreements ($p < .01$), and more conflicts with employees ($p < .05$) in 1994 than in 1988.

*Discussion.*   What can we say about adaptation theory and its contribution to our understanding of organizational change among nonprofits?

(See Figure 6.1.) Of all three theoretical perspectives, it garnered the most support. Perhaps the popular perception is accurate that administrative initiatives are important in explaining organizational behavior and change.

Retrenchment tactics were intriguing. While having only limited impact on the growth/decline in resources, they produced negative behavioral outcomes. These latter findings were crucial, because they substantiated our theoretical argument that administrative tactics or choices, i.e., the use of retrenchment tactics, had more to do with the quality of life within organizations than the growth or decline in resources. It also placed the blame for the negative externalities on managers' tactics instead of on the lack of resources.

With a few notable exceptions, organizations adopted tactics that were appropriate for the resource niche in which they were dependent for resources, and, if they utilized more of these tactics, they were rewarded with more resources from that arena. First, receiving donated income and having more volunteers led an organization to become more charitablelike in the sense of employing more political tactics, and employing more political tactics garnered an organization more donations and volunteers. We also found some evidence (between 1980 and 1984) that they increased commercial income and employees as well. However, they produced some nasty externalities in the process. Second, receiving commercial income and having more employees led an organization to become more businesslike, and employing more managerial tactics garnered one more earned income/employees and donated income/volunteers. It produced both positive and negative externalities.

Earlier we talked about the possibility of their being a dedifferentiation of the market and grants economies. That is, to get either commercial income or donations may require hefty doses of managerialism *and* politics. Yes, normative charities were coming to look more like business organizations; but nonprofits heavily dependent upon commercial income were coming to look more like charities (i.e., by increasing their political tactics). The bottom line is that by the end of our study, large, successful organizations now did both, regardless of their funding source.

While this may have been driven simply by the resource needs of organizations, the spread of political tactics could be replacing the spread of managerial tactics as an institutional process (DiMaggio and Powell 1983). This could be attributed to a creeping politicalization of all organizational life. Fombrun (1996) argued that all organizations have to worry about their legitimacy and reputation. It is in their enlightened self-interest. He argues that an organization's reputational capital is a valuable asset that has an impact on the bottom line either in the short term or long term. This is also the implicit lesson to managers in the work of the neoinstitutionalists (e.g., W. R. Scott 1995) and made explicit in the work of their students (Suchman 1995). Indeed, someday we may find managerial tactics decoupled from earned income and employees but still coupled to donated income and volunteers, while political tactics are tightly coupled to earned income and employees but decoupled from donated income and volunteers. In all likelihood, however, we expect the differentiation between managerial and political tactics to become less, a higher correlation between earned income/employees and donated income/volunteers, and simply a "tactics" effect on growth and decline of all kinds.

## C. Structural Embeddedness Models

The structural embeddedness perspective was the least developed of the three general models we reviewed, and it produced fewer clear-cut hypotheses. In fact, most of the hypotheses mused on how social structural variables could modify the effect of either environmental conditions or tactics on organizational changes. At this point in its development the embeddedness perspective lacks a strong action component (for an exception, see Burt 1992), and thus its contribution is to identify constraints and opportunities that influence selection and adaptation processes. This is good, for it splashes a healthy dose of reality onto the organizations literature noting that transformative processes—which selection and adaptation theory often ignore with a certain aplomb—are vulnerable to social structural influences.

The attractiveness of the embeddedness approach lies in the identification of "clutter" within an otherwise sterile and sanitized organizational world. The social structural factors identified in this monograph included formal properties of the organization—its size, age, and pattern of decision-making—as well as informal structures—social networks. We equated social structure with clutter, because sometimes it gets in the way and sometimes it is quite useful. For example, large organizations are often difficult to manage or communicate with, but they can be quite useful when fighting off a hostile takeover attempt and one is trying to garner political support at the state legislature (e.g., Davis and Thompson 1994). Age can also be an asset or liability depending upon the circumstances, as can decision-making structures. We focused on two types of social networks. The first was the network of linkages among nonprofit organizations in the community. The second was the use and support of the organization by local or community elites. Maintaining the organization's position in both networks is costly in terms of time and sometimes money, but the possible benefits of drawing on network contacts in crisis situations far outweighs the costs. Yet the organization may never have a crisis, so it is not clear that attending all those breakfast meetings or hosting those receptions for local celebrities will ever pay off. One is never too sure how much to invest in their social networks.

Informal social structures or networks are especially attractive to both scholars and practitioners today (see, for example, Mackay 1997), since they seem to hold some "secrets to success" that we have not yet discovered. It is now fashionable to find value in the network itself (e.g., Powell 1990). It is not something that might come in handy some day, but is a valuable asset in its own right. Coleman (1988) and Putnam (1995) told us that social networks are the basis for the development of social capital and that the latter is crucial in building and sustaining community. Burt (1992) told us that the entrepreneurial organization survives and thrives in networks rich in structural holes. The network is the tool that strategic actors use to realize competitive advantage over their foes. And micro and macro theorists from Krackhardt and Hanson (1993) to Powell (1990) described how the virtual organization of the future will be built on social networks rather than rule books, administrative procedures, and other bureaucratic paraphernalia.

Our view of social networks was more modest, for we viewed them as auxiliary features—maybe even "clutter"—within and between organizations. The hypotheses tested in this monograph reflected this more temperate perspective on social structure.[7]

***Growth and Decline.*** All the hypotheses looked for modifying effects (see Figure 6.1a). That is, social structure was seen as either facilitating strategy implementation or blocking it. The first two focused on the impact of size and age. Larger organizations were assumed to be more bureaucratized with a more elaborate set of rules and regulations, control systems, and more established routines. Older organizations were assumed to have more wisdom or, at least, more accumulated knowledge. Both fit the image of structure as clutter. Bureaucracy could get in the way of change, but having some extra knowledge and experience around could help an organization get through some tough times and over some new terrain.

*The effects of managerial tactics on increases in commercial income and employees and political tactics on increases in donated income and volunteers will be stronger, the smaller the organization. (Chapter 3, H9)*

*The effects of managerial tactics on increases in commercial income and em-
ployees and political tactics on increases in donated income and volunteers
will be stronger, the older the organization. (Chapter 3, H10)*

We also developed a hypothesis that focused on decision-making
structures. We derived a measure of how centralized or decentralized
decision-making authority was within the organization. Our inspection of
these scores showed us that within organizations where few positions
had authority to make formal decisions, the board of directors dominated. This was the centralized organization. Where decision-making was
decentralized, many different functionaries (e.g., administrators, professional staff, volunteers, even clients) had to be consulted before decisions
could become policies. Again, we viewed social structure as clutter. Once
the board decided on a tactic to implement, it could proceed without
delay if other folks in the organization did not have to be listened to or co-
opted or brought on board.

*The effects of managerial tactics on increases in commercial income and em-
ployees and political tactics on increases in donated income and volunteers
will be stronger, the more centralized decision-making authority. (Chapter
3, H11)*

The third set of embedded effects involved interorganizational network ties as well as ties to local elites. However, they only addressed the
coupling of political tactics to increases in donated income and volunteers. The argument was that organizations that had ties to many other
organizations and/or more members of the local community elite were
able to realize greater returns on their efforts to convince others of their
public regardingness and trustworthiness. They had more folks to tap for
favors, more folks to make introductions, and more folks to be references,
i.e., actors who would vouch for them and back up their claims.

*The effects of political tactics on increases in donated income and volunteers
will be stronger, the greater the number of network ties to other organizations. (Chapter 3, H12)*

*The effects of political tactics on increases in donated income and volunteers
will be stronger, the greater the number of network ties to the local community elite and the more the elite values the organizations. (Chapter 3, H13)*

The results were simple to summarize (see Figure 6.1b). Among
middle-aged and older organizations, the use of managerial tactics increased commercial income and employees between 1980 and 1984, but

not among younger organizations ($p < .10$). Among medium-size and smaller organizations, the use of political tactics increased donated income and volunteers between 1988 and 1992 ($p < .05$), and between 1988 and 1994 ($p < .01$). But that was all. We tested for twenty interaction effects that involved size, age, and decision-making structures as modifying variables, and only found three significant effects. We tested an additional eight models where network ties to the elites and to other organizations in the panel were the modifying variables, and only one was statistically significant and in a direction opposite of what we hypothesized (more on this later). Thus, for the most part, large organizations were as successful as small organizations, young organizations were as successful as old organizations, decentralized organizations were as successful as centralized organizations, and socially isolated organizations were as success as heavily networked organizations in implementing tactics. There was not enough support to argue that strategy implementation was contingent or modified by social structural variables.

However, the network variables did have some independent effects on growth in donated income and volunteers. Organizations more embedded in interorganizational networks in 1984 increased their donated income between 1980 and 1984 ($p = .133$) and between 1984 and 1988 ($p < .10$). Organizations more embedded in elite networks in 1980 increased their donated income between 1980 and 1984 ($p < .10$) and between 1984 and 1988 ($p < .05$). Also, if organizations utilized fewer political tactics, elite network ties had a significant effect on growth in donated income and volunteers between 1988 and 1994 ($p < .05$). Thus there was some evidence that social networks did have a direct effect on the growth and decline of donated income and volunteers.

*Tactics.* The hypotheses offered here were drawn from the literature on social influence and network diffusion processes (Marsden and Friedkin 1993) (see Figure 6.2a). They also drew heavily on DiMaggio and Powell's (1983) discussion of mimetic isomorphism within organizational fields. Here we posit direct effects of social structure on organizational change. Basically the thesis was that the choice of tactics was a function of the tactics of one's social network contacts and role models. That is, organizations would adopt the tactics of those whom they knew and trusted. They would also mimic the tactics of those they thought were successful especially under conditions of environmental uncertainty.

*Organizations are likely to increase their use of political and/or managerial tactics, if they had direct resource exchanges with other organizations that used political and/or managerial tactics extensively in the past. (Chapter 4, H8)*

*Organizations are likely to increase their use of political and/or managerial tactics, if managers knew personally other managers who used political and/or managerial tactics extensively in the past. (Chapter 4, H9)*

*Under conditions of uncertainty, organizations are likely to increase their use of political and/or managerial tactics, if managers perceived other organizations as successful who used political and/or managerial tactics extensively in the past. (Chapter 4, H10)*

Organizations increased their managerial tactics between 1984 and 1988, if organizations with which they exchanged resources or information utilized more managerial tactics in 1984 ($p < .05$) (see Figure 6.2b). Organizations also increased their political tactics between 1984 and 1988 if organizations with which they exchanged resource or information utilized more political tactics in 1984 ($p < .10$). Organizations increased their managerial tactics between 1988 and 1992 if organizations where they knew someone personally utilized more managerial tactics in 1988 ($p < .05$). And organizations increased their political tactics between 1988 and 1992 if organizations where they knew someone personally utilized more political tactics in 1988 ($p < .05$). Except in one single case,[8] organizations did not mimic the tactics of those whom they believed were more successful; and the interaction term, which included a measure of funding uncertainty, was not statistically significant.

We also offered a hypothesis that stated that contact with more members of the local community elite would result in the organization utilizing more managerial tactics (see Figure 6.2a). The argument also borrowed from DiMaggio and Powell (1983), who described the role of coercive isomorphism in homogenizing organizational fields. The gist of our argument was that elites, as champions of the "business model," coerced organizations into adopting this management style with the implicit threat that they would abandon the organization if it refused (e.g., Hall 1990).

*Organizations are likely to increase their use of managerial tactics, if more members of the community elite personally used or supported their organizations with donations, volunteer help, board memberships, and consulting services. (Chapter 4, H11)*

We found that organizations increased their use of both managerial ($p < .10$) and political tactics ($p < .05$) between 1988 and 1992, if more members of the community elite used their services or supported their efforts with time and money (see Figure 6.2b). However, in the OLS analysis we found no such effect between 1984 and 1988, and the Poisson regressions uncovered a negative relation between elite proximity and changes in managerial ($p < .10$) and political tactics ($p < .10$).

*Quality of Life.* In our exploratory study we speculated that organizations that were embedded in social network ties would have less "rancorous" disruptions and become better work environments over time (see Figure 6.3a). Here we posit a direct social structural effect on change. The argument was that organizations deeply embedded in a network of interorganizational or elite ties would be more moderate or temperate and might even be more benevolent toward participants, because "others" were watching. This was a crude test of Coleman's (1988) thesis that networks are vehicles that exercise social control over participants.

> *Organizations that are embedded in elite community networks are less likely to have disagreements while making decisions, conflict with employees, and alienation, and more likely to have a creative or innovative work environment. (Chapter 5, H8)*

> *Organizations that are embedded in community interorganizational resource exchange networks are less likely to have disagreements while making decisions, conflict with employees, and alienation, and more likely to have a creative or innovative work environment. (Chapter 5, H9)*

Centrality in community interorganizational resource exchange networks had no effect whatsoever on any of the quality of life indicators (see Figure 6.3b). We found, however, that having more members of the elite supporting and / or using the organization for services resulted in organizations becoming more creative and receptive to innovations ($p < .05$) and less alienated ($p < .05$). Elite presence had no affect on the number of disagreements or conflicts with employees.

*Discussion.* What can we now say about embeddedness theory? Were we unfair in equating social structure with clutter? Probably. The clutter hypotheses received little support. With a few exceptions, social structures did not modify the effect of tactics on growth and decline. Thus organizational size, age, decision-making structures, and network ties did not increase or decrease the chances of successfully implementing tactics.

Did social structure then have an independent effect on organizational change? For the most part, yes. For example, proximity to the elite had a positive effect on growth in donations / volunteers between 1980 and 1984, between 1984 and 1988, and between 1988 and 1994 (if the organization utilized few political tactics). Also organizations increased their use of managerial and political tactics between 1988 and 1992, if more elites used their services or supported them in 1988. However, there was no effect between 1984 and 1988 in the OLS results, and the Poisson regressions cited a negative effect.

These findings suggest that there was a complicated interaction between elite contacts, political and managerial tactics, donations and volunteers, and time. Our suspicion is that the elite's role in nonprofit organizations changed over time. In the earlier period the elite was a market signal that nonprofits used to show funders that they were reliable, accountable, and worthy of support. Ties to the elite were rewarded with more donations and volunteers. In turn, it was the elite's job to monitor the organization. The negative effects that we found in the Poisson regressions suggest that earlier in the study period, nonprofits may have felt they could shed both political and managerial tactics, if they had strong ties to the local elite. In the 1990s things changed. Instead of being a market signal and watchdog for the rest of the donor community, elites became more like extension agents, spreading the gospel of strategic management. Their presence was important to procure donations and recruit volunteers, if the organization did not employ political tactics, but was no longer important if they did. Rather the elite was there to teach nonprofit boards and managers how to behave proactively—both in a managerial and political way.

The sociological literature has often taken a dim view of elite participation in nonprofits (for an exception, see Ostrander 1995). Maybe this position should be reevaluated. Over the fifteen years of our study, elite contacts resulted in more donations and volunteers, an increase in the use of political and managerial tactics (which, in turn, resulted in an increase in donated and commercial income), less alienation among participants, and a work environment more sympathetic to creativity and innovation. Of course, this does not speak to what happened to organizations' mission, outputs, or client base with greater elite involvement. This is still an empirical question. Yet, in all fairness to our data, contact with the elite had numerous beneficial effects on organizations.

We also found that interorganizational networks influenced the choice of organizational tactics, independent of organizations' patterns of resource dependencies. Organizations adopted tactics that were used by organizations in their resource exchange networks and managers in their acquaintanceship networks. Social influence effects were present both between 1984 and 1988 and between 1988 and 1992. This was not good news for rational choice theorists and those who believe that tactics should be tightly coupled to the resource needs of organizations. The social influence findings were impressive precisely because they were independent of the organization's dependency upon different resource streams, mimetic variables, and funding uncertainty. This suggested that these effects were important and played an ongoing role in influencing the tactics used by organizations. Whether this is a "problem" or not is something others can decide.

This brings us to our final point. Earlier we argued that we might better interpret social network effects using selection theory rather than adaptation theory. Network ties tend to be unobtrusive and "taken for granted." A manager and/or her organization interact with other managers and other organizations on a day-to-day basis. Not much thought goes into these exchanges, yet our data suggested that these network ties had subtle influences over growth and decline, the selection of tactics, and even the quality of organizational life. In addition to seeing elites as a kind of resource tactic used by organizations, in Chapter 3 we interpreted the effect of elite ties on donated income and volunteers as a kind of inertial effect where organizations that received donations and volunteer support in the past would receive donations and volunteer support in the future. Similarly we would say that organizations that do things certain ways, say, employ managerial or political tactics, cluster together and reinforce one another's choices and habits. The network did not so much bring about change as it may have "bonded" actors that tended to do things similarly. In this respect network effects are longstanding and difficult to dislodge and may have long-term (and unanticipated) positive and negative effects on organizations.

## CONCLUSION

It is difficult to write the conclusion to a study that was as complex and difficult to do as this one. Should we make grand claims? Should we give a summary of our summaries? Should we make policy recommendations? Or, should we repeat our gratitude to those who helped us in the research and supported us throughout the years? At this point, it would be most useful to address the utility of organizational theory for studying the nonprofit sector and some of the study's shortcomings.

Is organizational theory useful for studying nonprofit organizations and particularly public charities, or can we simply rely on economic theory for our understanding of nonprofit behavior? None of our theories were supported in their entirety, and we certainly cannot claim to have discovered the "silver bullet" that can answer all the questions surrounding changes in nonprofit organizations today. We did, however, have a number of results, and they are summarized in Figures 6.1b, 6.2b, and 6.3b. Niche conditions were important in explaining growth and decline in earned income and employees. The use of certain tactics, e.g., managerial and political, did result in organizational growth and affected behavioral patterns within organizations. Patterns of resource dependencies did explain the choice of tactics. And social network variables had an independent effect on the growth in donated income and volunteers, the choice of tactics, and the quality of life within organizations. To view organizations simply as production functions, to explain productivity in terms of incentives, or to focus exclusively on efficiency is to miss an awful lot of what is happening in these organizations. But note: this is not to say that economizing is unimportant, that organizations are not interested in maximizing incomes, and that folks are indifferent to incentives. All of these are central, and in our study we tried to incorporate all these factors in one way or another. However, it is also true that organizations do not operate in a vacuum but are integrated into organizational fields in complicated and sophisticated ways. Also organizations may act rationally (e.g., try to become more efficient) but for reasons that are irrational (e.g., people are simply friends of one another and imitate what their friends do). Using economic theory in conjunction with organizational theory and management science holds the greatest promise for future work.

A more important question is whether our distinction between normative and utilitarian organizations was useful and would it "wipe out" any differences we might observe between nonprofit and for-profit behavior. That is, economists may attribute differences in nonprofit and for-profit behavior to the nondistribution constraint. However, might these differences be explained better by organizations' funding sources, e.g., dependency upon commercial income versus donated income? Of course, we cannot give a definitive answer to that question, because we did not include any for-profits in our study, but we can at least raise the question.

In some respects there were meaningful differences between organizations heavily reliant on commercial income and employees and those heavily reliant on donated income and volunteers. For example, organizations that were more utilitarian were more vulnerable to changing structural conditions within their niches (e.g., density, resource concentration, and legitimacy) than normative organizations.[9] In contrast, organizations that wished to increase their donated income and volunteers fared much better, if members of the local community elite used, supported, and thought well of them. Elite contacts and reputation had no effect on the growth and decline of commercial income and employees. Perhaps more importantly, the growth and decline of donated income and volunteers and changes in commercial income and employees were independent of each other.

There were, however, many similarities. Organizations heavily reliant on commercial income and employees, and organizations heavily reliant on donated income and volunteers embraced both managerial and political tactics by the end of the study period. Both managerial and political tactics led to an increase in commercial income, employees, donated income, and volunteers during various phases of our study. Furthermore, utilitarian and normative nonprofits had neither more or less creative and innovative work environments, more or less alienation, more or fewer disagreements, nor more or fewer conflicts with employees. Needless to say, our inability to identify clear-cut differences between these two types of charity organizations leaves some doubt in our mind as to the usefulness of this distinction. Also, simply controlling for patterns of resource dependency will probably not eliminate differences between nonprofit and for-profit behavior found in other studies (e.g., Weisbrod, 1988, 1998).

If nothing else, the research adds balance to some of the more sensational accounts in the mass media and nonfiction press that the sector has succumbed to commercialism (e.g., Glaser 1994; Gaul and Borowski 1993). Indeed the sector has its share of rascals and enormous pockets of wealth (note, we are not suggesting correlation here). In retrospect, we should have gathered data on executive compensation, perquisites, and chiseling. However, we approached the problem in a different way, focusing on conventional measures of "commercial" activity, e.g., earned income and employees, but we did look at the concentration of wealth as well. There was no question that a smaller percentage of organizations came to control a larger percentage of the resources in the Twin Cities (and we suspect elsewhere, e.g., Salamon, Altschuler, and Myllyluoma 1990), but the sector has not "gone commercial" in that earned income and employees have come to displace donated income and volunteers. We found a slight increase in the percentage of organizational revenues coming from fees and program service revenue (and a decrease in the percentage received from government sources). But we found no change in the percentage of funds from private donations and grants, and we even found an increased dependency upon volunteers in both the cross-section and panel surveys.

More importantly, we shed some understanding on where the "business model" fits into the sector, when it makes sense, and why organizations came to adopt this approach. For some nonprofits the business model was essential to compete against others for customers; for others it was a symbolic display for institutional gatekeepers and a way to get donations; for others it resulted from contacts with elites and contacts with other nonprofit and managers in their network. Our research did not unearth any sexy scandals, but we do think it gave us a better understanding of what is behind the commercialism in the sector and what are the consequences for organizations.

In the hope that this research will be repeated elsewhere in the future, we will focus on three major shortcomings of this research that future researchers need to redress. First, researchers have to pay attention to context. Second, researchers have to pay attention to the why and how questions. Third, researchers have to gather data on beneficiaries. All three require different methodological approaches than the one presented here, but they are absolutely necessary if we are to appreciate fully how public charities—as organizations—change over time.

As noted earlier in the research, we proceeded as if the changes we were describing were ahistorical and ageographical. We ignored the fact that the period from 1980 to 1994 was a very tumultuous time in the history of nonprofit organizations and that the study was done in Minneapolis–St. Paul. Major changes took place in the sector and we touched upon many in the course of the monograph. However, none of these changes were brought into our analysis in any systematic way. Our discussion of changes in governmental funding and priorities was particularly weak, yet many accounts tell a convincing story that this contingency had an enormous impact on some of the very issues we were studying—growth and decline, changes in tactics, and changes in organizational cultures (e.g., Gibelman and Demone 1990). For example, we saw how organizations with government funding in 1984 increased their managerial, political, and retrenchment tactics between 1984 and 1988. We also saw how organizations with more government funding in all periods tended to increase their commercial income and employees—but not their donated income and volunteers. We interpreted these findings as examples of niche flight in the face of a coarse-grained (i.e., long-term) change in the funding environment. Indeed, by 1992 and 1994 organizations were less dependent upon government grants and contracts than in 1980. There is provocative material here that we did not explore fully but that needs to be examined more closely to get a more complete understanding of change among these organizations.

We also were deeply concerned that we did not fully answer the questions why and how organizations changed. We derived hypotheses from extant theory and when the facts did not fit the theory, we were left with "making up" theories to explain what we found. In-depth case studies can provide the rich, detailed explanation for why organizations *really* grew or shrank, adopted one tactic or another, or became more or less hostile working environments. Hall's (1990) study of the conflict between an executive director and board members in the case he studied is an example of the kind of work we need. Our approach also made it difficult to know how change came about. We spoke in crude terms about "selection" and "adaptation," but the way we went about our research did not allow us to get into the organization and understand both the processes of change and social reproduction. Hager's (1998) qualitative comparative case analysis of how organizations disbanded in the course of our 15-year period will add greatly to our understanding of change processes. Again, we strongly encourage researchers to go this route.

Probably the biggest shortcoming was the inattention to beneficiaries. As noted in Chapter 1, public service is a major part of the charity sector and some of the most important research in the field over the last ten years has looked at this issue, e.g., Gray (1991), Wolpert (1993a, 1996), and Clotfelter (1992). In the first and second wave of the panel (1980 and 1984) we asked about beneficiaries and often were told that the community benefits. We asked for numbers served and some organizations had duplicated numbers while other had unduplicated numbers. Other responded that they provided services to other organizations, and it was not fair to compare their "numbers" to others—and they were right. For those which served clients, we asked about the latter's demographics. But even those which had numbers had a difficult time recalling the race, gender, socioeconomic status, or residence of those they served. After that we gave up, but this was a grave mistake. We should have gone back to our workshop and devised better instruments. Any study of organizational change that does not answer the question, Who benefits? and how that changed is simply incomplete. We admonish future research to be attentive to these issues.

Even after putting on the hair-shirt and acknowledging the work's shortcomings, we hope that this monograph makes a contribution both to theory and research on organizations and public charities in particular. Hopefully, it will stimulate others to get into the field and do the same. As you discover whenever you do research, there always are more questions after you are finished than before you started. With the progress we made, we hope to lay the groundwork for more research on non-profits and organizational change in the future.

## NOTES

1. We regret that we were unable to include demographic characteristics of clients, students, members, and audiences (e.g., Baum and Singh 1994a, 1994b). We attempted to collect these data, but found that many organizations did not keep records of these statistics or were unable (or unwilling) to provide us with estimates.

2. Effects are regarded as statistically significant of they were significant at the $p \leq .10$ level in either our OLS, or Poisson regressions.

3. Density also had a negative effect on changes in donated income and volunteers between 1988 and 1992 in our initial analysis. However, this effect weakened when we controlled for the network variables.

4. Note that we included niche legitimacy in only three analyses: 1980–1984, 1988–1992, and 1988–1994, because we did not have data on niche legitimacy for 1984.

5.  We repeated the analyses substituting niche dispersion/concentration for density but again found no effects.

6.  Even if political tactics resulted in growth in commercial income and employees and managerial tactics resulted in growth in donated income and volunteers, this does not mean that everyone in the organization would be happy about it. It's a cultural and not a resource argument that we proffer here.

7.  Perhaps one reason that both academics and practitioners get so excited about networks and social capital imagery is that some of that clutter (or social inventory) that the organization has had to carry can finally be valuated and thus rationalized as part of the asset base of the organization.

8.  In one Poisson regression, measuring change in tactics between 1988 and 1992, we did find that organizations increased their use of managerial tactics if those which they perceived to be successful utilized more managerial tactics in 1988 ($p < .10$).

9.  To be more precise, growth and decline in donated income and volunteers appeared to be indifferent to selection processes, but the coupling of donated income and volunteers to the use of political and managerial tactics was affected by niche conditions.

# Appendix A

## Original Sample, 1980

### Recreational

Armstrong Hockey Boosters, Inc.
Bloomington Gymnastics Club
Brooklyn Park Ski Racing Club
Buck Hill Ski Racing Club
Camp Patmos, Inc.
Cedar Athletic Association
Crystal Little League, Inc.
Eden Prairie Gymnastics Club
Edina Swim Club
Girl Scout Council of St. Croix Valley
Highland Groveland Recreational Association
Linwood Park Booster Club
Metropolitan Park Foundation
Minnesota Babe Ruth League, Inc.
Minnesota Parks Foundation
Northend Youth Hockey Association
North St. Paul Hockey Boosters Club
Orono–Long Lake Baseball Association
Phelps Field Boosters
Robbinsdale District Traveling Baseball
St. Anthony Village AAU Swim Club
St. Paul Turners
Twin City Yoga Society
White Bear Lake Babe Ruth League

### Media

Daytons Bluff News, Inc.
Minnesota Public Radio, Inc.
Twin Cities Public Television

## *Legal*

Crime Stoppers of Minnesota
Golden Valley Crime Prevention Fund
Legal Assistance of Minnesota
Legal Assistance of Ramsey County
Minnesota Citizens Rights Fund
Southern Minnesota Regional Legal Services, Inc.

## *Housing*

American Indian Business Development Corporation
Common Space
Loring Nicollet Development Corporation
Maple Hills of Red Wing, Inc.
Minnesota Multi-Housing Institute, Inc.
Old Town Restorations, Inc.
Southside Neighborhood Housing Service of Minneapolis
Twin Cities Center For Urban Policy, Inc.
2nd Southeast Corporation

## *Health and Welfare*

Abbott Northwestern Hospital
Afton Lakeland Preschool Center
Airmans Nantambu Memorial Foundation
Alpha Kappa Epsilon Society Foundation
American Citizens Concerned for Life, Inc. Ed Fund
American Indian Health Care Association
Applied Cardio-Pulmonary Research Foundation
Association of Radio Reading Services
Augustana Lutheran Homes
Beltrami Health Center
Big Brothers
Bloomington Child Development
Building Block Nursery School & Day Care
Carr for the George Washington University Hospital
Central Health Services, Inc.
Childbirth Education Association
Child Care Parents of Anoka County
Childrens Center, Inc.

Childrens Home Society of Minnesota
Childrens Oncology Service Upper Midwest
Christian Union Home
City, Inc.
Community Emergency Assistance Program
Community Retreat Corporation
Concern: Community Organized for Nutritional Concerns of East
    Side Residents
Covenant Living Centers—Minnesota
Dakota County Receiving Center
Dakotas Adults, Inc.
Dakotas Children Benefit Association
Dental Home Care
Divine Redeemer Memorial Hospital Auxiliary
Door of Hope
East Communities Youth Service Bureau
Edina Special Childrens Group
Emerge Counseling Center
Episcopal Group Homes
Fairview Community Hospitals
Faith Fund Charitable Trust
Family Service
Forest Lake Area Youth Service Bureau
Foundation of the Minnesota Medical Association
Fremont Community Health Services
Fremont Connection
Genesis II for Women
Good Shepherd Residence
Great Plains Organization for Perinatal Health Care, Inc.
Greenvale Place of Northfield
Guadalupe Service Center, Inc.
Harriet G. Olson Trust Fund
Harriet Tubman Women's Shelter, Inc.
Harrington Trust U/W Paris 14 Item 630
Harrington Trust U/W Paris Item 10
Hidden Ranch, Inc.
HIRED: Helping Industry Resolve Employment Disabilities
Hopkins Nursery School
Human Aging Attitude Reassessment Program
Institute on Healing of the Whole Person
International Heart Relief
Jack and Jill Preschool
Jesus Peoples Free Store

Jewish Marriage Encounter of Minnesota
Judson Family Center
KOPE: Keep Older Persons Employed
Lakeview Memorial Hospital Women's Auxiliary
Learn and Grow Playhouse
Loring-Nicollet Meals on Wheels
Lutheran Social Services Auxiliary
McIntyres Center for Gifted Children
Messiah Willard Day Care Center, Inc.
Metro Affiliated Senior Entertainment Program
Midway Hospital Foundation
Minneapolis Hearing Society
Minneapolis Youth Diversion Program
Minnesota American Legion & Auxiliary Heart Research Foundation
Minnesota Behavioral Institute
Minnesota Council for Ex-Offender Employment
Minnesota Dental Research Foundation
Minnesota Diversified Industries, Inc.
Minnesota Human Genetics League
Minnesota Hundred Club
Minnesota Law Enforcement Memorial Association
Minnesota Marriage Encounter
Minnesota Power Mikes, Inc.
Minnesota Society for Crippled Children & Adult
Minnesota State Dental Association Relief Foundation
Minnesota Vikings Children's Fund
National Association of Women Helping Offenders
National Council on Family Relations
Nativity Lutheran Church Women's Nursery Schools
NE Learning Center for Persons with Developmental Disabilities
New Life Homes
North East Senior Citizen Resource Center
North Metro Developmental Achievement Center
Northside Child Development Center
North Suburban Day Activity Center
NW Suburban Youth Service Bureau
Opportunity Workshop, Inc.
Ours, Inc.
Owobapte Industries, Inc.
People, Inc.
Person Education—Developmental Education
Pilgrim Rest Child Development Center
Presbyterian Homes, Inc.

Prodigal House
Project Life
Redeemer Corporation
Resident Council Services, Inc.
Riverview Memorial Hospital Auxiliary
Sabathani Community Center
Schizophrenia Association of Minnesota
Senior Federation Services
Seward Nursery School, Inc.
Shalom Home, Inc. Auxiliary
Social Opportunities and Resources
Southern Anoka Community Assistance
Southside Life Care Center
St. Anthony Park Nursery School
St. Croix Area United Way
St. Louis Park Medical Center Research Foundation
St. Mary's Rehabilitation Center
St. Paul Ostomy Association
Suburban North Alano
Summit-University Senior Outreach & Advocacy Program
Tac Two, Inc.
Trinity Health Care
Twin City Home Economists in Home-Making
United Blind of Minneapolis.
Unity Settlement Association
University Hospitals Auxiliary of Faculty Women's Club
Vanderlip Trust
VEAP: Volunteers Enlisted to Assist People
Victory House, Inc.
Wakota Life-Care, Inc.
Warm World Child Development Center
Washington County Association for Senior Citizens
Wilder Foundation
Willows Inner Community Center
Worldwide Eye Care & Research Foundation
Youth Emergency Services
Youthcraft Industries

## *Environmental/Natural Resources*

Environmental Balance Association of Minnesota
The Intersociety Consortium for Plant Protection

Izaak Walton League of America
Midwest Environmental Education & Research Association
Minnesota River Valley Audubon Club
Natural Resources Corporation
9th International Congress for Plant Protection
Quetico Superior Foundation
Tree Trust U/A (Twin Cities Tree Trust)


## *Education*

ABC Montessori School
Alpha Tau Omega Foundation of Minnesota
Anoka Junior Great Books
Augsburg College
Bloomington Scholarship Foundation
Calvin Christian School
Career Development and Evaluation Services
Challenge Research Institute, Inc.
Community Resources for Education, Alternative Treatment &
    Evaluation
Dial-Logue, Inc.
Edison Scholarship & Memorial Fund
Emma Willard Task Force on Education
Environmental Agribusiness Resources Technologies & Horticulture
    Association of Minnesota
Flight Unlimited
Golden Valley Lutheran College
Greater Gustavus Fund
Higher Education & Development, Inc.
Institute for Continuing Education
Kenneth Hall School
Kinderhaus Montessori School
Lightening and Transients Research Institute
Macalester College
Metropolitan Medical Center Alumna
Minneapolis Better Jobs for Women
Minnesota Alumni Association, University of Minnesota
Minnesota Association of Continuing Education
Minnesota Bible College
Minnesota Consulting Group, Inc.
Minnesota Office Education Foundation
Minnesota Private College Research Foundation

Minnesota State Horticultural Society
Minnesota Women in Higher Education
Mrs. Liisles Montessori Schools
Native American Theological Association
Newgate Education & Research Center
Northwestern College of Chiropractic Foundation
Parkview Alumni Association
Plymouth Montessori
Psyche, Inc.
Rainbow Research
Richard Spruce Foundation for the Study of Ethnobotany
Scientists & Engineers Tech Assessment Council
Sister Joseph Endowment Fund for Nursing Education
Spanish Evangelical Educational Crusade
St. Paul Educational Foundation
Survival Skills Institute, Inc.
Twin Cities Creation-Science Association
United Ministries in Higher Education
University Student Telecommunication Corp
Voluntary Action Center of St. Paul
Washington County Foundation

### *Cultural*

African American Cultural Center
Artspace Reuse Project
Bach Society of Minnesota
Bloomington Historical Society
Centre for Internationalizing the Study of English
Choreogram Dance Studio
Colonial Dames of American in Minnesota
Cooperating Libraries in Consortium
Cricket Theatre Corporation-Phoenix Theatre Corporation
Edina Historical Society
Film in the Cities
Fine Arts Society of Dakota County
Greater Twin Cities Youth Symphonies
Guild of Performing Arts
Hennepin County Historical Society
International Center of Medieval Art
Jo Lechay Dance Company
Land O' Lakes Theatre Organ Society

Metro Boys Choir
Midwest Libertarian Library Association
Minneapolis Chamber Symphony
Minnesota Archeological Society
Minnesota Chorale
Minnesota Dance Theatre and School
Minnesota Historical Society Trust 3892
Minnesota Jazz Dance Company
Minnesota Orchestral Association—Minneapolis Symphony
   Orchestra
Minnesota Theatre Federation
Minnesota Zoological Garden Foundation
Minnetonka Orchestra Association
New Hope Musical Theatre, Inc.
Park Square Theatre
Plymouth Historical Society
Richfield Historical Society
Sarah Hughes American Holiday for Irish Children
Space Theatre Consortium
St. Andrews Society of Minnesota
Suburban Symphony Association
Theatre Studio
Thursday Musical
Trinity Films
Twin Cities Catholic Chorale
Twin Cities Choirmasters Association
Weavers Guild of Minnesota
Women Historians of the Midwest
Womens Auxiliary of Minneapolis Musicians Association Local #73


*Civic*

Anoka County Community Action Program
Board of W. Central Area Council of YMCA
CHARGE: Citizens of Hanover Advocating Responsible Government
Council of Community Councils
District Community Council
Friends of Cue
Good Helps, Inc.
Lexington-Hamline Community Council
Midway Club
Minneapolis Kiwanis Foundation

Minnesota Council American Youth Hostels
National Fly the Flag Crusade
National Foundation for Philanthropy
Nokomis Planning District Citizens Council
Northeast Kiwanis Foundation
Powderhorn Residents Group
St. Louis Park Rotary Foundation
Weesner Charitable Trust Fund 6107
World Trade Week, Inc.
YMCA Illinois Area Council

## Miscellaneous

Board of Trustees, Mt. Zion Cemetery
Brain Rudd Trip Beyond
Brorby, Thea Charitable Trust
Community Research Associates
Dunwoody Trust 775, Kate L.
Evaluation Systems
Good News for Israel
Hudson Trust U/AZ 1541-1, Laura Bell
Masterton Memorial Trust, William J.
Miller Peace Memorial, James
National Distillers Distributors Foundation
O'Brien Trust 8451, Hannah F.
Ramsey Charitable Trust
Religion and Society
St. Mary's Hall, Ethel M. Vanderlip Fund Trust U/A
St. Paul Lutheran Friends of Israel
Wells, Frederick B., Jr., Trust Fund
Yeshuah Hamashiach Fellowship

# Appendix B

## Niche Analysis

Our goal was to derive measures that would give us an estimate of the amount of crowding in an organization's niche, the degree of resource concentration, and the legitimacy of organizations in the niche. Once the niche spaces were constructed for 1980, 1984, 1988, and 1992 using the cross-sectional data, we assigned niche density, concentration, and legitimacy scores to each nonprofit in our panel depending upon its pattern of income, labor inputs, size, and services/activities.

We needed to construct the niche spaces for 1980, 1984, 1988, and 1992. We used data from four cross-sectional surveys. The first was the original sample of 229 nonprofits drawn from a population of Twin Cities charities current for October 1979; the second was a new cross-sectional survey of 266 nonprofits drawn from a population of Twin Cities charities current for October 1983; the third was a cross-sectional survey of 230 nonprofits current for October 1987; and the fourth was a survey of 252 nonprofits drawn from a population current for October 1991. Because of the distortions introduced by the presence of a large community foundation and a United Way in 1984 and 1992, these two organizations were excluded from the sample, reducing the $N$ from 266 to 264 and from 252 to 250 for these two years. See Chapter 2 for a detailed description of all four surveys.

There were four sets of data that we needed from each survey. First, for each organization we computed the proportion $r_j$ of total revenue that came from private donations, public sources, commercial venues (which included program service fees), and other sources, where $j$ is the source of income, ranges from one to four, and $\Sigma r_j = 1.0$. In 1980 six organizations reported no income, and two organizations were missing data on income streams. In 1984 six reported no income, and three were missing data on income streams. In 1988 three reported no income, and ten were missing data on income. In 1992 three reported no income, and three were missing data. Second, for each organization we computed the proportion $w_k$ of total workers who were employees (part-time and full-time) and volunteers, where $k$ is the type of labor input, ranges from one to two, and $\Sigma w_k$ = 1.0. In 1980 three organizations were missing data for this item, and 32 organizations reported no employees or volunteers. In 1984 five were missing data on personnel and 17 had neither employees nor volunteers. In 1988, 20 reported no personnel, and three were missing data on these items. In 1992, 14 reported no personnel and one was missing data.[1]

We also coded organizations on the basis of their primary activity. Respondents were handed a list of eight ($l$ = 1, 8) activity areas: health/welfare, education, legal, recreational, culture, science, housing/urban development, and other. We asked them to rank-order these in terms of how important they were for the organization, $a_l$. We recoded responses so that $a_l$ was coded 1 if the activity was identified as primary and 0 otherwise. We subsequently collapsed these activities into four types: (1) health/welfare, (2) education, (3) recreational/culture, and (4) legal/science/housing/urban development/other (subsequently, $l$ = 1, 4).[2] In 1980, 17 organizations cited more than one activity area as primary (one, in fact, cited all four areas) and 6 cited no activities.[3] In 1984 25 organizations cited more than one activity as primary (again one cited all four) and none cited no activities. In 1988, 24 organizations cited more than one activity as primary (again, one cited all four) and one cited no activities. In 1992, 26 cited more than one activity as primary and none cited no activities. If $t$ activity areas were cited as primary, each primary activity area $a_l$ = 1 was divided by $t$. Thus $\Sigma a_l/t$ = 1.0.

Finally, we coded the size of the organization using average operating expenditures in 1979–1980, 1983–1984, 1987–88, and 1991-92 (converted to 1994 dollars). We divided the sample into thirds and coded organizations as being small, medium, and large.[4] Instead of using one variable to indicate size, we used three binary variables: $e_1$ = 1 if the organization had few expenditures, $e_2$ = 1 if it had medium-size expenditures, and $e_3$ = 1 if it had large expenditures. Of course, $\Sigma e_m$ = 1.0. In 1980 three organizations were missing data for expenditures; in 1984 two were missing data; in 1988 nine were missing data; and in 1992 three were missing data.

Due to our relatively small $N$, we decided to create two niche spaces for each year instead of one megaspace. The first was dimensioned 4 (donations, public, commercial, other) by 4 (health/welfare, education, cultural/recreational, other) by 3 (small, medium, large). The second was dimensioned 2 (employees, volunteers) by 4 (health/welfare, education, cultural/recreational, other) by 3 (small, medium, large). Assigning cases to the cells of the space was not trivial. For example, if an organization received all its funding from, say, donations, provided only educational services, and was small, then it could be assigned to niche (1, 2, 1): row one, column two, and level one. However, if it received funding from multiple sources and/or engaged in more than one activity, it had to be split proportionately across the respective cells in the table. For example, if it received 90% of its funding from commercial income and 10% from government sources and engaged in both educational and legal activities, it had to be distributed proportionately across four cells in the space.

More formally the total count in each cell of the revenue by activity by expenditure niche space can be expressed as follows:

$$f_{JLM} = \Sigma_i \, (r_{ij} * (a_{il}/t_i) * e_{im}) \qquad (1)$$

where the sum is across all the valid cases in the sample, $i$. Table B.1, Panel A, illustrates the process presenting the revenue $(J)$ by activity $(L)$ by expenditure $(M)$ niche table for 1980. The total count is $229 - 13 = 216$, because 13 organizations either had no income, missing data on the income item, no activities, or missing data on the expenditure item in 1979–1980. Table B.2, Panel A, is the revenue by activity by expenditure niche table for 1992. $N$ here is $250 - 7 = 243$, because seven organizations either had missing data or no income or no activities in 1992.

Similarly the count in each cell of the labor-by-activity-by-expenditure niche can be expressed as follows:

$$f_{KLM} = \Sigma_i \, (w_{ik} *(a_{il}/t_i) * e_{im}) \qquad (2)$$

where the sum is again across all the valid cases in our sample. Table B.1, Panel B, presents the labor $(K)$ by activity $(L)$ by expenditures $(M)$ niche table for 1980. The total count is $229 - 38 = 191$, because 38 organizations either had no workers, missing data on the worker item, no activities, or missing data on the expenditure item in 1979–1980. Table B.2, Panel B, presents the labor-by-activity-by-expenditures niche table for 1992. The count is $250 - 17 = 233$, because of missing data, and no labor or activities.

*Niche Density/Sparsity.*   To determine the density of these niches, we treated the eight niche tables as contingency tables, estimated a loglinear model with main effects only, and computed the adjusted residuals.[5] The adjusted residuals $q_{JLM}$ and $q_{KLM}$ were used as our indicators of niche density.[6] Positive residuals were interpreted as signaling denseness, while negative residuals were interpreted as signaling sparseness. Table B.3 summarizes the $\chi^2$ statistics for the eight models we estimated and presents the descriptive statistics for the adjusted residuals, our measure of niche density. The large $\chi^2$ statistics indicate poor fits to the data, suggesting that there is considerable crowding and sparseness in several of the cells or niches.[7]

The next step is to see where the crowding was the greatest. We could do this by inspecting the eight niche tables visually, looking for unusually large and small residuals.[8] To identify crowded and sparse niches we

Table B.1. Niche Table for 1980, Frequency Counts and Adjusted Residuals in Parentheses

Panel A (N = 216)

| Activities (L): | Health/Welfare | | | Educational | | | Recreational/Cultural | | | Other | | |
|---|---|---|---|---|---|---|---|---|---|---|---|---|
| Funding (J) Expenditures (M): | Small | Med | Large | Small | Med | Large | Small | Med | Large | Small | Med | Large |
| Donations | 9.6 | 12.5 | 5.2 | 12.7 | 3.7 | 3.6 | 6.6 | 5.4 | 4.4 | 5.5 | 7.5 | 2.8 |
| | (.04) | (.52) | (−1.8) | (2.4) | (−1.8) | (−1.6) | (1.4) | (.31) | (.05) | (.82) | (1.4) | (−.78) |
| Public | 0.5 | 6.4 | 15.4 | 1.3 | 2.3 | 8.1 | 3.1 | 2.5 | 1.9 | 1.8 | 3.6 | 3.9 |
| | (−2.5) | (−.29) | (4.0) | (−1.6) | (−1.4) | (1.7) | (.29) | (−.35) | (−.56) | (−.54) | (.39) | (.75) |
| Commercial | 0.8 | 9.0 | 10.7 | 6.6 | 9.1 | 6.9 | 2.1 | 6.4 | 2.4 | 3.1 | 0.2 | 1.4 |
| | (−2.7) | (.36) | (1.4) | (.71) | (1.4) | (.65) | (−.58) | (1.7) | (−.51) | (.07) | (−1.9) | (−1.1) |
| Other | 6.1 | 5.9 | 1.0 | 3.9 | 1.7 | 1.7 | 0.2 | 0.5 | 0.5 | 3.1 | 1.2 | 1.2 |
| | (1.8) | (1.2) | (−1.5) | (1.0) | (−.72) | (−.55) | (−1.0) | (−.95) | (−.87) | (1.6) | (−.32) | (−.22) |

Panel B (N = 191)

| Activities (L): | Health/Welfare | | | Educational | | | Recreational/Cultural | | | Other | | |
|---|---|---|---|---|---|---|---|---|---|---|---|---|
| Labor (K) Expenditures (M): | Small | Med | Large | Small | Med | Large | Small | Med | Large | Small | Med | Large |
| Employees | 2.9 | 13.1 | 22.5 | 5.8 | 7.1 | 13.3 | 0.2 | 5.4 | 6.4 | 4.0 | 8.8 | 4.8 |
| | (−2.6) | (−.42) | (3.0) | (−.31) | (−1.1) | (1.5) | (−2.3) | (−.71) | (−.13) | (.52) | (2.1) | (.07) |
| Volunteer | 9.1 | 18.7 | 9.7 | 11.2 | 7.7 | 7.0 | 12.0 | 9.4 | 3.8 | 3.0 | 2.6 | 2.5 |
| | (−.24) | (1.3) | (−1.5) | (2.1) | (−.89) | (−1.0) | (3.7) | (1.0) | (−1.4) | (−.19) | (−1.2) | (−1.2) |

254

*Table B.2.* Niche Table for 1992, Frequency Counts and Adjusted Residuals in Parentheses

**Panel A (N = 243)**

| Activities (L): | Health/Welfare | | | Educational | | | Recreational/Cultural | | | Other | | |
|---|---|---|---|---|---|---|---|---|---|---|---|---|
| Funding (J) \ Expenditures (M): | Small | Med | Large | Small | Med | Large | Small | Med | Large | Small | Med | Large |
| Donations | 7.8 (−1.6) | 9.3 (−.95) | 10.2 (−1.1) | 18.4 (2.5) | 17.0 (2.1) | 7.6 (−1.6) | 23.4 (4.5) | 10.7 (.08) | 6.2 (−2.0) | 7.9 (.27) | 4.6 (−1.1) | 5.1 (−1.2) |
| Public | .7 (−1.5) | 2.6 (−.31) | 13.3 (5.9) | .2 (−1.7) | 1.0 (−1.2) | 1.2 (−1.2) | .1 (−1.7) | .1 (−1.7) | 2.0 (−.65) | 1.3 (−.46) | 6.1 (3.4) | 4.1 (1.6) |
| Commercial | .9 (−2.4) | 4.0 (−.92) | 17.9 (4.9) | 4.4 (−.63) | 6.3 (.37) | 4.9 (−.59) | 4.6 (−.44) | 7.8 (1.2) | 6.0 (.08) | 0.4 (−1.9) | 3.0 (−.30) | 3.9 (.02) |
| Other | 3.1 (1.0) | 1.6 (−.05) | .5 (1.1) | 3.0 (1.2) | 1.3 (−.24) | .8 (−.76) | .5 (−.91) | .3 (−.99) | 1.3 (−.31) | 3.4 (2.5) | 1.3 (.37) | .9 (−.22) |

**Panel B (N = 233)**

| Activities (L): | Health/Welfare | | | Educational | | | Recreational/Cultural | | | Other | | |
|---|---|---|---|---|---|---|---|---|---|---|---|---|
| Labor (K) \ Expenditures (M): | Small | Med | Large | Small | Med | Large | Small | Med | Large | Small | Med | Large |
| Employees | 1.0 (−2.4) | 3.2 (−1.4) | 23.4 (6.6) | 2.2 (−1.6) | 6.1 (.23) | 3.4 (−1.4) | 2.0 (−1.7) | 3.8 (−.89) | 6.5 (−.03) | 1.2 (−1.5) | 5.3 (.86) | 9.8 (2.8) |
| Volunteer | 9.5 (−2.0) | 14.3 (−.47) | 18.6 (.09) | 20.8 (2.5) | 18.4 (1.6) | 10.1 (−1.9) | 24.5 (3.8) | 15.2 (.51) | 9.0 (−2.3) | 11.8 (1.1) | 7.7 (−.62) | 5.2 (−2.1) |

Table B.3. Statistics for the Main-Effects-Only Model for the Eight Niche Spaces and for Niche Density, Niche Concentration, and Niche Legitimacy, 1980, 1984, 1988, and 1992

| | Model Statistics | | | | Niche Density | | | | Niche Concentration | | | | Niche Legitimacy | | | | |
|---|---|---|---|---|---|---|---|---|---|---|---|---|---|---|---|---|---|
| | $\chi^2$ | df | p | N | Mean | SD | Min | Max | Mean | SD | Min | Max | Mean | SD | Min | Max | N |
| Funding by Activities by Expenditures | | | | | | | | | | | | | | | | | |
| 1980 | 75.3 | 39 | .000 | 216 | −.01 | 1.36 | −2.70 | 4.03 | .64 | .21 | .00 | 1.0 | 6.90 | 8.45 | .000 | 38.4 | 48 |
| 1984 | 88.6 | 39 | .000 | 255 | .00 | 1.67 | −2.28 | 7.68 | .64 | .18 | .00 | 1.0 | — | — | — | — | 48 |
| 1988 | 85.3 | 39 | .000 | 213 | .00 | 1.60 | −2.36 | 6.03 | .71 | .16 | .45 | 1.0 | 5.12 | 6.21 | .000 | 28.1 | 48 |
| 1992 | 109.6 | 39 | .000 | 243 | .01 | 1.83 | −2.40 | 5.87 | .63 | .21 | .00 | 1.0 | — | — | — | — | 48 |
| Labor by Activities by Expenditures | | | | | | | | | | | | | | | | | |
| 1980 | 43.5 | 17 | .000 | 191 | .00 | 1.62 | −2.57 | 3.73 | .65 | .20 | .00 | .90 | 6.64 | 7.27 | .890 | 32.1 | 24 |
| 1984 | 84.2 | 17 | .000 | 240 | −.01 | 2.34 | −2.87 | 7.16 | .64 | .17 | .25 | .92 | — | — | — | — | 24 |
| 1988 | 46.8 | 17 | .000 | 197 | −.01 | 1.82 | −2.17 | 5.99 | .63 | .23 | .00 | .93 | 4.11 | 4.26 | .140 | 17.6 | 24 |
| 1992 | 71.9 | 17 | .000 | 233 | −.01 | 2.22 | −2.40 | 6.64 | .69 | .16 | .33 | .94 | — | — | — | — | 24 |

256

could inspect Tables B.1 and B.2 visually, looking for unusually large and small residuals. Alternatively, we could estimate hierarchical loglinear models eliminating nonsignificant effects until we find a model for each table that best fits the data. Looking then at the interaction parameters we could identify the dense and sparse cells in our four niche spaces.

Table B.4 presents the best fitting models for the four funding-by-activities-by-expenditures niche tables. We derived these models by eliminating higher order effects one at a time, based on the change in the model $\chi^2$ statistic. To save space, we present the statistics and the estimated parameters for the interaction effects from the reduced or "best fitting" model only. The effect parameters tell us which niches were most crowded and which were least. To expedite our discussion, we focus on effects that were twice their standard error (indicated by *).

First, we see that the funding-by-expenditures effect was found in all four years. In general, smaller organizations tended to rely heavily on donations and have relatively few public dollars, while larger organizations tended to rely heavily on public funding and depend relatively little on donations and grants. In 1988 and 1992 larger organizations were relatively more dependent upon commercial or earned income, while smaller organizations depended relatively little on commercial income. In 1980, 1988, and 1992, smaller organizations were more dependent upon "other" income, while larger organizations depended very little on other sources. Thus in all four years we see that smaller and larger organizations are in very different funding niches and do not compete against one another.[9] However, medium-size organizations are caught in between. They are not especially dependent on any one source and, in this respect, are more diversified, but the result of this is that they have no niche of their own and have to compete against both large and small organizations.

Moving on, we see that the activity-by-expenditure effect was significant in 1984, 1988, and 1992. In all three years we see that health/welfare organizations tended to be larger (as opposed to smaller). In 1984 and 1988 cultural/recreational organizations tended to be smaller (as opposed to larger). We also see that in 1988, educational organizations tended to be smaller. Finally, the funding-by-activity effect was significant only in 1992. Cultural/recreational organizations were more dependent upon donated and earned income, while other types of nonprofits (i.e., organizations that produce collective goods) were heavily reliant on public support and had significantly less donated income and commercial income.

Table B.5 presents the best fitting models for the four labor-by-activities-by-expenditures niche tables. Again the models were derived using hierarchical loglinear analysis, eliminating nonsignificant higher order effects. First, we see that the labor-by-expenditures effect was

Table B.4. Estimated Effect Parameters for Reduced Model, 1980, 1984, 1988, 1992: Funding (Fund) by Activities (Activ) by Expenditures (Expn)[a]

### 1980

Model: Fund by Expn, Activ ($\chi^2$ = 44.4; df = 33; p = .089)

Effects:

A. Fund by Expn ($\Delta\chi^2$ = 30.9; $\Delta$df = 6; p = .000)

|  | Small | Med | Large |
|---|---|---|---|
| Don | .398* | -.004 | -.394* |
| Pub | -.666* | -.107 | .773* |
| Com | -.310 | .127 | .182 |
| Oth | .577* | -.016 | -.562* |

### 1984

Model: Fund by Expn, Activ by Expn ($\chi^2$ = 25.7; df = 27; p = .534)

Effects:

A. Fund by Expn ($\Delta\chi^2$ = 30.0; $\Delta$df = 6; p = .000)

|  | Small | Med | Large |
|---|---|---|---|
| Don | .365* | .129 | -.495* |
| Pub | -.512* | -.325 | .836* |
| Com | -.121 | .215 | -.094 |
| Oth | .267 | -.019 | -.248 |

B. Activ by Expn ($\Delta\chi^2$ = 32.9; $\Delta$df = 6; p = .000)

|  | Small | Med | Large |
|---|---|---|---|
| H/W | -.395* | -.294 | .690* |
| Edu | .192 | -.177 | -.015 |
| C/R | .347* | .397* | -.744* |
| Oth | -.143 | .075 | .068 |

### 1988

Model: Fund by Expn, Activ ($\chi^2$ = 26.8; df = 27; p = .475)

### 1992

Model: Fund by Expn, Activ by Expn ($\chi^2$ = 13.6; df = 18; p = .754)

Effects:

A. Fund by Expn ($\Delta\chi^2 = 29.1$; $\Delta df = 6$; $p = .000$)

|       | Small   | Med    | Large   |
|-------|---------|--------|---------|
| Don   | .582*   | -.240  | -.342*  |
| Pub   | -.572   | .038   | .534*   |
| Com   | -.545*  | .092   | .453*   |
| Oth   | .536*   | .110   | -.646*  |

B. Activ by Expn ($\Delta\chi^2 = 29.3$; $\Delta df = 6$; $p = .000$)

|       | Small   | Med    | Large   |
|-------|---------|--------|---------|
| H/W   | -.621*  | -.107  | .728*   |
| Edu   | .427*   | -.309  | -.118   |
| C/R   | .354*   | .176   | -.530*  |
| Oth   | -.160   | .240   | .080    |

Effects:

A. Fund by Expn ($\Delta\chi^2 = 32.8$; $\Delta df = 6$; $p = .000$)

|       | Small   | Med    | Large   |
|-------|---------|--------|---------|
| Don   | .475*   | -.046  | -.428*  |
| Pub   | -.880*  | .206   | .673*   |
| Com   | -.463*  | .067   | .396*   |
| Oth   | .869*   | -.227  | -.641   |

B. Activ by Expn ($\Delta\chi^2 = 18.3$; $\Delta df = 6$; $p = .006$)

|       | Small   | Med    | Large   |
|-------|---------|--------|---------|
| H/W   | -.436*  | -.181  | .617*   |
| Edu   | .113    | .182   | -.295   |
| C/R   | .329    | -.080  | -.250   |
| Oth   | -.007   | .080   | -.073   |

C. Fund by Activ ($\Delta\chi^2 = 26.3$; $\Delta df = 9$; $p = .002$)

|       | HW     | Edu    | C/R    | Oth     |
|-------|--------|--------|--------|---------|
| Don   | -.378  | .371   | .497*  | -.490*  |
| Pub   | .468   | -.715  | -.535  | .781*   |
| Com   | -.121  | .161   | .592*  | -.632*  |
| Oth   | .031   | .183   | -.554  | .340    |

[a] Starred effects are twice their standard error.

Table B.5. Estimated Effect Parameters for Reduced Model, 1980, 1984, 1988, 1992: Labor (Labr) by Activities (Activ) by Expenditures (Expn)[a]

## 1980

Model: Labr by Expn, Labr by Activ ($\chi^2$ = 15.8; df = 12; p = .199)

Effects:

A. Labr by Expn ($\Delta\chi^2$ = 19.2; $\Delta$df = 2; p = .000)

|     | Small  | Med   | Large  |
| --- | ------ | ----- | ------ |
| Emp | -.433* | .010  | .423*  |
| Vol | .433*  | -.010 | -.423* |

B. Labr by Activ ($\Delta\chi^2$ = 8.4; $\Delta$df = 3; p = .038)

|     | HW    | Edu   | C/R    | Oth    |
| --- | ----- | ----- | ------ | ------ |
| Emp | .004  | -.006 | -.380* | .382*  |
| Vol | -.004 | .006  | .380*  | -.382* |

## 1984

Model: Labr by Expn, Activ by Expn ($\chi^2$ = 13.1; df = 9; p = .160)

Effects:

A. Labr by Expn ($\Delta\chi^2$ = 39.6; $\Delta$df = 2; p = .000)

|     | Small  | Med   | Large  |
| --- | ------ | ----- | ------ |
| Emp | -.757* | .189  | .568*  |
| Vol | .757*  | -.189 | -.568* |

B. Activ by Expn ($\Delta\chi^2$ = 31.5; $\Delta$df = 6; p = .000)

|     | Small  | Med   | Large  |
| --- | ------ | ----- | ------ |
| H/W | -.416* | -.268 | .683*  |
| Edu | .222   | -.144 | -.078  |
| C/R | .391*  | .344* | -.735* |
| Oth | -.197  | .068  | .130   |

## 1988

Model: Labr by Expn, Activ by Expn ($\chi^2$ = 9.1; df = 9; p = .425)

Effects:

A. Labr by Expn ($\Delta\chi^2$ = 16.6; $\Delta$df = 2; p = .000)

|     | Small  | Med   | Large  |
| --- | ------ | ----- | ------ |
| Emp | -.340* | -.099 | .439*  |
| Vol | .340*  | .099  | -.439* |

B. Activ by Expn ($\Delta\chi^2$ = 21.1; $\Delta$df = 6; p = .002)

|     | Small  | Med   | Large  |
| --- | ------ | ----- | ------ |
| H/W | -.645* | .008  | .637*  |
| Edu | .289   | -.243 | -.047  |
| C/R | .375*  | .151  | -.526* |
| Oth | -.019  | .084  | -.064  |

## 1992

Model: Labr by Expn, Activ by Expn ($\chi^2$ = 8.4; df = 9; p = .499)

Effects:

A. Labr by Expn ($\Delta\chi^2$ = 35.4; $\Delta$df = 2; p = .000)

|     | Small  | Med   | Large  |
| --- | ------ | ----- | ------ |
| Emp | -.597* | .022  | .574*  |
| Vol | .597*  | -.022 | -.574* |

B. Activ by Expn ($\Delta\chi^2$ = 28.2; $\Delta$df = 6; p = .000)

|     | Small  | Med   | Large  |
| --- | ------ | ----- | ------ |
| H/W | -.574* | -.122 | .697*  |
| Edu | .216   | .218  | -.433* |
| C/R | .348*  | -.046 | -.303  |
| Oth | .010   | -.049 | .039   |

[a] Starred effects are twice their standard error.

significant in all four years and the effects were consistent. Smaller organizations were more dependent upon volunteers (and had a smaller percentage of employees), while larger organizations had a greater percentage of employees (and relatively small percentage of volunteers). Medium-size organizations had about as many employees and volunteers as one would expect given the marginal distributions. Again we have a pattern of segmentation. Smaller organizations are heavily dependent upon volunteers while larger organizations are heavily dependent on employees. Medium-size organizations are again diversified but caught in the middle, competing against both small and large organizations.

The activity-by-size effect was significant in 1984, 1988, and 1992 and this mirrors our findings in Table B.4. The pattern of effects was also similar: health/welfare organizations were larger and cultural/recreational organizations were smaller. The only other significant effect was in 1980: labor-by-activities. Here cultural/recreational organizations tended to rely on volunteers (and have fewer employees), while other types of organizations (i.e., collective goods–type nonprofits) were more dependent upon employees (and had relatively fewer volunteers).

Although our qualitative comparisons across years suggests that there were some changes in the niche space of Twin Cities nonprofits, we also noted a number of stable patterns. To test if changes in the niche space were statistically significant we pooled the 1980 and 1992 data sets, creating two new cross-tabulations: a funding source-by-activity-by-expenditure-by-year cross-tabulation and a labor source-by-activity-by-expenditure-by-year cross-tabulation. The $N$ for the first table was 459; the $N$ in the second was 424.[10] We estimated a hierarchical loglinear model for each table, and the best fitting model for each is presented in Table B.6.

Note that in neither panel were the four-variable interactions nor any of the three-variable interactions statistically significant. This means that although many more effects were significant in 1992, these effects were not *that much more pronounced* in 1992 than in 1980. Thus the field really did not become that much more segmented—although the earlier qualitative analysis might suggest this. Examining the significant two-factor interactions, we see two changes in the marginal distributions over time. Organizations in 1992 were more reliant on donated income than in 1980, and organizations were more reliant on volunteers and less reliant on employees in 1992 than in 1980. Dependence upon government income was less—although not statistically significant—and there was no real change in the dependence upon earned or commercial income. This is pretty much what we found looking at the marginals in Chapter 2.

Moving on to the other effects, we see that when we looked at the pooled sample, smaller organizations tended to be more reliant on do-

Table B.6. Estimated Effect Parameters for Reduced Model, 1980–1992 Pooled: Funding (Fund) by Activities (Activ) by Expenditures (Expn) and Labor (Labr) by Activities (Activ) by Expenditures (Expn)[a]

### 1980–1992 Fund by Activ by Expn

Model: Fund by Year, Fund by Expn, Fund by Activ, Activ by Expn ($\chi^2 = 67.9$; df = 62; $p = .285$)

Effects:

A. Fund by Year ($\Delta\chi^2 = 16.0$; $\Delta$df = 3; $p = .001$)

|     | 1980 | 1992 |
| --- | --- | --- |
| Don | -.274* | .274* |
| Pub | .186 | -.186 |
| Com | -.078 | .078 |
| Oth | .166 | -.166 |

B. Fund by Expn ($\Delta\chi^2 = 63.4$; $\Delta$df = 6; $p = .000$)

|     | Small | Med | Large |
| --- | --- | --- | --- |
| Don | .406* | -.020 | -.387* |
| Pub | -.725* | -.000 | .725* |
| Com | -.425* | .100 | .325* |
| Oth | .743* | -.080 | -.663* |

C. Fund by Activ ($\Delta\chi^2 = 29.0$; $\Delta$df = 9; $p = .001$)

|     | HW | Edu | C/R | Oth |
| --- | --- | --- | --- | --- |
| Don | -.306* | .050 | .443* | -.188 |
| Pub | .092 | -.325 | -.164 | .396* |
| Com | -.134 | .225 | .449* | -.580* |
| Oth | .347 | .050 | -.768* | .371 |

D. Activ by Expn ($\Delta\chi^2 = 20.6$; $\Delta$df = 6; $p = .002$)

|     | Small | Med | Large |
| --- | --- | --- | --- |
| H/W | -.466* | .027 | .439* |
| Edu | .183 | -.053 | -.131 |
| C/R | .236 | -.026 | -.211 |
| Oth | .046 | .051 | -.097 |

### 1980–1992 Labr by Activ by Expn

Model: Labr by Year, Labr by Expn, Labr by Activ, Activ by Expn ($\chi^2 = 32.3$; df = 28; $p = .263$)

Effects:

A. Labr by Year ($\Delta\chi^2 = 18.3$; $\Delta$df = 1; $p = .000$)

|     | 1980 | 1992 |
| --- | --- | --- |
| Emp | .217* | -.217* |
| Vol | -.217* | .217* |

B. Labr by Expn ($\Delta\chi^2 = 47.2$; $\Delta$df = 2; $p = .000$)

|     | Small | Med | Large |
| --- | --- | --- | --- |
| Emp | -.499* | .029 | .469* |
| Vol | .499* | -.029 | -.469* |

C. Labr by Activ ($\Delta\chi^2 = 10.6$; $\Delta$df = 3; $p = .014$)

|     | HW | Edu | C/R | Oth |
| --- | --- | --- | --- | --- |
| Emp | .020 | -.062 | -.263* | .305* |
| Vol | -.020 | .062 | .263* | -.305* |

D. Activ by Expn ($\Delta\chi^2 = 22.0$; $\Delta$df = 6; $p = .001$)

|     | Small | Med | Large |
| --- | --- | --- | --- |
| H/W | -.526* | .049 | .477* |
| Edu | .163 | -.033 | -.130 |
| C/R | .206 | -.036 | -.170 |
| Oth | .157 | .020 | -.177 |

[a] Starred effects are twice their standard error.

nated and other income and volunteers, while larger organizations were more dependent upon public money and commercial income and employees. Our data also show that health/welfare organizations tended not to be dependent on donations. Cultural/recreational organizations tended to rely on donated income, commercial income, and volunteers, but were unlikely to have income from other sources or employees. "Other" nonprofits (public goods organizations) tended to be heavily dependent upon government funds and employees and tended not to rely on volunteers or, as one might expect, commercial income. Finally, health/welfare organizations were more likely to be larger than smaller.

Although this exercise was mostly methodological, the empirical findings speak to some issues in the literature. First, it is clear that the public charity sector is not becoming more commercial if this is operationalized in terms of commercial income and paid employees. Our findings tell us that over time the population of public charities has come to be more reliant on donated income and volunteers *controlling for organizational size and activities* instead of less. Dependency upon employees dropped and there was no significant or even apparent change in dependency upon commercial or earned income.

Second, Hannan and Freeman's (1977) insight that large and small organizations do not compete against one another—even within the same industry—was borne out by our analysis. Controlling for activities, we found that large organizations are dependent upon public revenues, commercial income, and employees, while smaller organizations are dependent upon donated income and volunteers. Larger and smaller organizations are in very different funding arenas—however, medium-size organizations compete against both. Of course, another implication of these findings is that large organizations do not have much competition from other large organizations if they are seeking private sector grants and/or volunteers, and smaller organizations seeking public funding, service fees, or employees do not have much competition from other smaller organizations. Furthermore, health/welfare organizations seeking private grants/donations do not have much competition from other health/welfare organizations. Thus this set of findings not only tells us where organizations are constrained; it also tells us where the opportunities lie.

*Niche Resource Concentration.* To measure the degree to which resources were concentrated within a niche we computed the proportion of actors in the niche that accounted for 75% of the resources in the niche and subtracted this proportion from 1.[11] In the funding-by-activities-by-expenditures niche space we focused on income; in the labor-by-activities-by-expenditures niche space we focused on number of personnel. It is important to remember that within a niche we are focusing on the total amount of resources of a given kind. For example, in the donations-education–small organization niche we take as our denominator all donated revenues to small educational organizations.[12] Once we have the total and the amount attributable to any one actor, we can compute the proportion of the total attributable to a single organization and the proportion of organizations in a niche that account for 75% of the total. The larger the proportion, the less concentrated the niche. Because we wanted a measure of concentration, we subtracted the proportion from 1, resulting in $c_{JLM}$ and $c_{KLM}$. Thus there is a score for each niche or cell in the niche space. The concentration scores range from values of 0 (which meant that nothing less than 100% of organizations in the niche were needed to account for 75% of the total income or labor in a niche) to 1 (which meant that a very small fraction of the organizations accounted for 75% of the total income or labor inputs). The anomaly, where there was only one organization in a niche, was recoded to a 1.00 although its score would be computed as 0. Thus a low value meant low concentration (and high competition) and a high value meant high concentration (or low competition). The means and standard deviations of the concentration scores across the 48 cells of the funding-by-activities-by-expenditures niche space and the 24 cells of the labor-by-activities-by-expenditures niche space are also in Table B.3.

*Niche Legitimacy.* To measure the legitimacy of a niche, we used data on the status of organizations in the niche. We obtained this from our interviews with prominent citizens. Because we did not do a cross-sectional survey of elites in 1985 or 1993, we had data only for 1981 and 1989. During the interviews with prominent citizens in 1981 and 1989, we asked respondents to circle those cross-section organizations that they thought were providing essential services to the community; then, going through the list again, we asked them to underline those which they thought had achieved outstanding accomplishments in their respective fields. We then computed the percentage of respondents who said that the nonprofit was either essential *or* had achieved outstanding accomplishments. These percentages were our measures of organizational status.

To measure the status of a niche we computed the average status of organizations in a niche as follows:

$$p_{JLM} = \Sigma_i \, (s_{i,JLM}) / f_{JLM} \tag{4}$$

$$p_{KLM} = \Sigma_i \, (s_{i,KLM}) / f_{KLM} \tag{5}$$

where $p_{JLM}$ and $p_{KLM}$ are the status scores assigned to niches $J$, $L$, $M$ and $K$, $L$, $M$, $s_{i,JLM}$ and $s_{i,KLM}$ are the status scores for actor $i$, who is a resident of niches $J$, $L$, $M$ and $K$, $L$, $M$, and $f_{JLM}$ and $f_{KLM}$ are the raw frequencies for niches $J, L, M$ and $K, L, M$. Essentially we tally the total status of actors in the niche and then divide this by the number of organizations in the niche. The amount of status that an actor contributes to the niche is proportional to its dependency upon a particular funding or labor source, the number of its activities, and its expenditures. In 1980 the means and standard deviations of the average status scores across the 48 cells of the funding-by-activities-by-expenditures niche space were 6.90 and 8.45 and across the 24 cells of the labor-by-activities-by-expenditures niche space were 6.64 and 7.27.

Before we move on, we note that although the density scores were supposed to indicate high competition and the concentration scores low competition, the correlations between these scores tended to be positive—not negative. For the funding-by-activities-by-expenditures niche space, the correlations were .245 in 1980, .266 in 1984, −.050 in 1988, and .113 in 1992; for the labor-by-activities-by-expenditures niche space, the correlations were .324 in 1980, .504 in 1984, .407 in 1988, and .304 in 1992. Also we often hear that more dense niches are allegedly more legitimate. However, we found that the zero order correlations between our density scores and our legitimacy scores were weakly correlated and negative: −.079 in 1980 and −.191 in 1988 for the funding-by-activities-by-expenditures niche space and −.151 and −.229 in 1980 and 1988 for the labor-by-activities-by-expenditures niche space. We should remember, though, that ours is a measure of sociopolitical legitimacy, not constitutive legitimacy. We did find, however, that the correlation between our legitimacy scores and our resource concentration scores was positive for both the funding-by-activities-by-expenditures niche space (.447 in 1980 and .312 in 1988) and the labor-by-activities-by-expenditures niche space (.341 in 1980 and .470 in 1988). Thus niches where high-status organizations resided tended to be niches that were highly concentrated, while low-status organizations tended to reside in niches where resources were more evenly distributed and thus more competitive.

*Organizational Level Variables.* The final step was to assign niche density, concentration, and legitimacy scores to each panel organization depending upon where it sat in our niche space. Since most organizations spanned more than one cell, we had to assign weighted scores. That is, we assigned scores to each panel organization that took into account the proportion of funding (or labor) from each source, the activities cited as primary, and organizational expenditures. More formally,

$$d_i^{JLM} = \Sigma_J \Sigma_L \Sigma_M q_{JLM} \left( r_{ij} * (a_{il}/t_i) * e_{im} \right) \tag{6}$$

$$d_i^{KLM} = \Sigma_K \Sigma_L \Sigma_M q_{KLM} \left( w_{ik} * (a_{il}/t_i) * e_{im} \right) \tag{7}$$

where $d_i^{JLM}$ and $d_i^{KLM}$ are the organization's density scores based on the funding-by-activities-by-expenditures and labor-by-activities-by-expenditures niche spaces, respectively; the sums are across the cells of the niche space; $q_{JLM}$ is the adjusted residual for cell $J, L, M$; $q_{KLM}$ is the adjusted residual for cell $K, L, M$; $r_{ij}$ is the proportion of an organization's funding from funding source $j$; $w_{ik}$ is the proportion of an organization's labor force from labor source $k$; $a_{il}$ is equal to one if the organization cited activity $l$ as primary; $t_i$ is the number of activity areas cited as primary; and $e_{im}$ equals 1 if the organization has expenditures of size $m$. We followed a similar set of procedures in assigning concentration and legitimacy scores. The descriptive statistics for the several niche measures that we operationalized are in Table 3.1.

Finally, we should note that we had missing niche data for several panel organizations, because either a panel organization was missing data on funding activities or labor inputs in a given year, or it had no funding activities or labor inputs that year (see Table 3.1). In 1980 alone, we were unable to assign density, concentration, or status scores derived from the funding-by-activities-by-expenditures niche table to 13 organizations, and we could not assign density, concentration, or status scores derived from the labor-by-activities-by-expenditures niche space to 38 organizations. This seriously limited the utility of density, concentration, and legitimacy scores derived from the labor-by-activities-by-expenditures niche tables, and in the book we only used scores derived from the funding-by-activity-by-expenditures niche tables.

## NOTES

1. When we asked for data on volunteers we specified that the respondent *not* include board members. In the organizations that reported no volunteers or employees, we surmised that the board did the work of the organization.

2. We collapsed activities because eight different activities were too many for our subsequent niche analysis and also for the regression analysis. Recreation was collapsed with cultural because both provided separable goods that were relatively easy to evaluate in terms of quality; and science, housing, urban development, legal, and other were lumped together because these provided, for the most part, collective goods to community residents. Our coding rules were simple. If, say, a respondent ranked cultural activities as its number one priority, but not recreation, it received a rank of 1 for the collapsed category recreational/cultural. Thus we assigned a value of 1 to a collapsed category if the respondent indicated that any of the activities in the collapsed category was her number one priority.

3. Although the boards of these organizations were still meeting and they were not disbanded, they were inactive for all practical purposes.

4. The size categories were under $25,000, $25,000 to $200,000, and $200,000 and above for 1980; under $23,000, $23,000 to $230,000, and $230,000 and above for 1984; under $20,000, $20,000 to $200,000, and $200,000 and above for 1988; and under $32,000, $32,000 to $250,000, and $250,000 and above for 1992.

5. We obviously relaxed the assumption that cell counts were independent, since "bits and pieces" of organizations were in different cells. Since our purpose was to identify crowding in the niche space rather than draw inferences about relationships between variables, we felt that our strategy was justified.

6. The adjusted residuals are calculated by dividing each standardized residual by an estimate of its standard error. Standardized residuals are computed by dividing each residual by the square root of the expected count.

7. If one were to speculate, the increase in the value of $\chi^2$ from 1980 to 1992 could indicate that over time the sector was becoming more structurated. By this we mean that distinct niches—very densely or very sparsely populated— emerged. In contrast to 1980 when organizations were more evenly spread across the niche space, by 1992 distinct types of organizations were emerging, leading to a more fragmented and sophisticated organizational field.

8. One attractive feature of adjusted residuals is that values greater than 1.96 or less than $-1.96$ can be interpreted as statistically significant at the .05-level. This is because for large samples the distribution of the adjusted residuals is approximately standard normal.

9. Pratt and Sullivan (1995:10) did a similar analysis of IRS Form 990 data for public charities in Minnesota. The data were current for 1995. They found essentially the same pattern. Smaller nonprofits relied heavily on direct public support, dues, and "other revenue," while larger organizations relied mostly on program service revenue and governmental grants.

10. The reader should be reminded that the number of organizations in 1980 and 1992 that had no labor inputs, beyond the board, was quite large. Because we treated these as missing data, we analyzed niche spaces for revenue and labor inputs separately.

11. The choice of 75% as our criterion was arbitrary, and researchers are encouraged to use other criteria. We found consistent patterns as we experimented with different criteria, e.g., 80% or 90% resources.

12. If a small organization named two areas as primary, e.g., education and health/welfare, then its contribution of private donations to the donations-education-small total would be half the amount otherwise.

# References

Akers, R. and F. Campbell. 1970. "Size and the Administrative Component in Occupational Associations." *Pacific Sociological Review* 13:241–51.

Albert, Stuart and David A. Whetten. 1985. "Organizational Identity." Pp. 263–95 in *Research in Organizational Behavior*, Volume 7, edited by Barry M. Staw and Larry L. Cummings. Greenwich, CT: JAI.

Alchian, Armen and Harold Demsetz. 1972. "Production, Information Costs and Economic Organization." *American Economic Review* 62:777–95.

Aldrich, Howard, Udo Staber, Catherine Zimmer, and John J. Beggs. 1990. "Minimalism and Organizational Mortality: Patterns of Disbanding Among U.S. Trade Associations, 1900–1983." Pp. 21–52 in *Organizational Evolution: New Directions* edited by Jitendra Singh. Newbury Park, CA: Sage Publications.

Alexander, Victoria D. 1996. *Museums and Money: The Impact of Funding on Exhibitions, Scholarship, and Management.* Bloomington: Indiana University Press.

Arnove, Robert F. (Ed.). 1980. *Philanthropy and Cultural Imperialism: The Foundations at Home and Abroad.* Boston: G.K. Hall.

Ashforth, Blake E. and Raymond T. Lee. 1990. "Defensive Behavior in Organizations: A Preliminary Model." *Human Relations* 43:621–48.

Bacharach, Samuel and Edward J. Lawler. 1980. *Power and Politics in Organizations.* San Francisco: Jossey-Bass.

Baker, Douglas and John B. Cullen. 1993. "Administrative Reorganization and Configurational Context: The Contingent Effects of Age, Size, and Change in Size." *American Management Journal* 36:1251–77.

Barnett, William P. and Glenn R. Carroll. 1987. "Competition and Mutualism among Early Telephone Companies." *Administrative Science Quarterly* 32:400–21.

Barnett, William P. and Glenn R. Carroll. 1995. "Modeling Internal Organizational Change." *Annual Review of Sociology* 21:217–36.

Barney, Jay B. and William G. Ouchi (Eds.). 1986. *Organizational Economics.* San Francisco: Jossey-Bass.

Baum, Joel A. C. and Jane E. Dutton. 1996. "The Embeddedness of Strategy." Pp. 1–15 in *Advances in Strategic Management*, Volume 13, edited by Paul Shrivastava, Anne S. Huff, and Jane E. Dutton. Greenwich, CT: JAI.

Baum, Joel A. C. and Heather A. Haveman. 1997. "Love Thy Neighbor? Differentiation and Agglomeration in the Manhattan Hotel Industry, 1898–1990." *Administrative Science Quarterly* 42:304–38.

Baum, Joel A. and Stephen J. Mezias. 1993. "Competition, Institutional Linkages, and Organizational Growth." *Social Science Research* 22:131–64.

Baum, Joel A. C. and Christine Oliver. 1991. "Institutional Linkages and Organizational Mortality." *Administrative Science Quarterly* 36:187–218.

Baum, Joel A. C. and Christine Oliver. 1992. "Institutional Embeddedness and the Dynamics of Organizational Populations." *American Sociological Review* 57:540–59.

Baum, Joel A. C. and Christine Oliver. 1996. "Toward an Institutional Ecology of Organizational Foundings." *Academy of Management Journal* 39:1378–1427.

Baum, Joel A. C. and Walter W. Powell. 1995. "Cultivating an Institutional Ecology of Organizations." *American Sociological Review* 60:529–38.

Baum, Joel A. C. and Jitendra V. Singh. 1994a. "Organizational Niche Overlap and the Dynamics of Organizational Mortality." *American Journal of Sociology* 100:346–80.

Baum, Joel A. C. and Jitendra V. Singh. 1994b. "Organizational Niche Overlap and the Dynamics of Organizational Founding." *Organization Science* 5:483–502.

Baum, Joel A. C. and Jitendra V. Singh. 1996. "Dynamics of Organizational Response to Competition." *Social Forces* 74:1261–97.

Ben-Ner, Avner and Helmut K. Anheier. 1997. "Economic Theories of Non-profit Organizations: A Voluntas Symposium." *Voluntas* 8:93–96.

Ben-Ner, Avner and Theresa Van Hoomissen. 1991. "Nonprofit Organizations in the Mixed Economy: A Demand and Supply Analysis." *Annals of Public and Cooperative Economics* 62:519–50.

Benson, J. Kenneth. 1977. "Organizations: A Dialectical View." *Administrative Science Quarterly* 22:1–21.

Berk, Richard A. 1983. "An Introduction to Sample Selection Bias in Sociological Data." *American Sociological Review* 48:386–98.

Bibeault, Donald B. 1982. *Corporate Turnaround: How Managers Turn Losers into Winners.* New York: McGraw-Hill.

Bielefeld, Wolfgang. 1992a. "Funding Uncertainty and Nonprofit Strategies in the 1980s." *Nonprofit Management and Leadership* 2:381–401.

Bielefeld, Wolfgang. 1992b. "Nonprofit-Funding Environment Relations: Theory and Application." *Voluntas* 3:48–70.

Bielefeld, Wolfgang. 1994. "What Affects Nonprofit Survival?" *Nonprofit Management and Leadership* 5:19–36.

Bielefeld, Wolfgang and John J. Corbin. 1996. "The Institutionalization of Nonprofit Human Service Delivery: The Role of Political Culture." *Administration and Society* 28:362–89.

Bielefeld, Wolfgang, Joseph Galaskiewicz, and Bryant Hudson. 1998. "Cooperation and Competition between Nonprofit Organizations: Organizational, Dyad, and Niche Effects." Paper presented at the Annual Meetings of the American Sociological Association, San Francisco.

Bielefeld, Wolfgang, Jim Murdoch, and Paul Waddell. 1997. "The Influence of Demographics and Distance on Nonprofit Location." *Nonprofit and Voluntary Sector Quarterly* 26:207–25.

Bielefeld, Wolfgang, Richard K. Scotch, and G. S. Thieleman. 1995. "National Mandates and Local Nonprofits: The Sharing of a Local Delivery System for HIM/AIDS Services." *Policy Studies Review* 14:127–36.

Bigelow, Barbara, Melissa Middleton Stone, and Margarete Arndt. 1996. "Corporate Political Strategy: A Framework for Understanding Nonprofit Strategy." *Nonprofit Management and Leadership* 7:29–43.

Blau, Peter M. 1972. "Interdependence and Hierarchy in Organizations." *Social Science Research* 1:1–24.

Blegen, Theodore C. 1975. *Minnesota: A History of the State*, 2nd edition. Minneapolis: University of Minnesota Press.

Bloomfield, Kim. 1994. "Beyond Sobriety: The Cultural Significance of Alcoholics Anonymous as a Social Movement." *Nonprofit and Voluntary Sector Quarterly* 23(1):21–40.

Boeker, Warren. 1992. "Power and Managerial Dismissal: Scapegoating at the Top." *Administrative Science Quarterly* 37:400–21.

Bordt, Rebecca L. 1997. "How Alternative Ideas Become Institutions: The Case of Feminist Collectives." *Nonprofit and Voluntary Sector Quarterly* 26:132–55.

Borger, Judith Yates. 1997. "Health Care Premiums Rising 5%–15%." *St. Paul Pioneer Press*, July 9, p. 1A.

Bowen, William G., Thomas I. Nygren, Sarah E. Turner, and Elizabeth A. Duffy. 1994. *The Charitable Nonprofits*. San Francisco, CA: Jossey-Bass.

Breusch, T. 1978. "Testing for Autocorrelation in Dynamic Linear Models." *Australian Economic Papers* 17:334–55.

Burt, Ronald S. 1982. *Toward a Structural Theory of Action: Network Models of Social Structure, Perception, and Action*. New York: Academic Press.

Burt, Ronald S. 1983. *Corporate Profits and Cooptation: Networks of Market Constraint and Directorate Ties in the American Economy*. New York: Academic Press.

Burt, Ronald S. 1992. *Structural Holes: The Social Structure of Competition*. Cambridge, MA: Harvard University Press.

Burt, Ronald S. and Ilan Talmud. 1993. "Market Niche." *Social Networks* 15:133–49.

Bush, Richard. 1992. "Survival of the Nonprofit Spirit in a For-Profit World." *Nonprofit and Voluntary Sector Quarterly* 21(4):391–410.

Cameron, Kim and Raymond Zammuto. 1983. "Matching Managerial Strategies to Conditions of Decline." *Human Resource Management* 22(Winter):359–75.

Cameron, Kim S., Myung U. Kim, and David A. Whetten. 1987. "Organizational Effects of Decline and Turbulence." *Administrative Science Quarterly* 32:222–40.

Cameron, Kim S., Robert I. Sutton, and David A. Whetten (Eds.). 1988. *Readings in Organizational Decline: Frameworks, Research and Prescriptions*. Boston: Ballinger.

Cameron, Kim S., David A. Whetten, and Myung U. Kim. 1987. "Organizational Dysfunctions of Decline." *Academy of Management Journal* 30:126–38.

Carroll, Glenn R. 1984. "Organizational Ecology." *Annual Review of Sociology* 10:71–93.

Carroll, Glenn R. 1985. "Concentration and Specialization: Dynamics of Niche Width in Populations of Organizations." *American Journal of Sociology* 90:1262–83.

Carroll, Glenn R. and Michael T. Hannan (Eds.). 1995. *Organizations in Industry: Strategy, Structure and Selection*. New York: Oxford University Press.

Chandler, Alfred D., Jr. 1962. *Strategy and Structure: Chapters in the History of the American Industrial Enterprise*. Cambridge, MA: MIT Press.

Chang, Cyril F. and Howard P. Tuckman. 1990. "Why Do Nonprofit Managers Accumulate Surpluses, and How Much Do They Accumulate?" *Nonprofit Management and Leadership* 1(2):117–35.

Chang, Cyril F. and Howard P. Tuckman. 1991. "A Methodology for Measuring the Financial Vulnerability of Charitable Nonprofit Organizations." *Nonprofit and Voluntary Sector Quarterly* 20:445–60.

Child, J. 1972. "Organizational Structure, Environment and Performance: The Role of Strategic Choice." *Sociology* 6:1–22.

Clarke, Lee and Carroll L. Estes. 1992. "Sociological and Economic Theories of Markets and Nonprofits: Evidence from Home Health Organizations." *American Journal of Sociology* 97:945–69.

Clarkson, Kenneth. 1972. "Some Implications of Property Rights in Hospital Management." *Journal of Law and Economics* 15:363–85.

Clotfelter, Charles T. (Ed.). 1992. *Who Benefits From the Nonprofit Sector?* Chicago: University of Chicago Press.

Cnaan, Ram A., Amy Kasternakis, and Robert J. Wineburg. 1993. "Religious People, Religious Congregations, and Volunteerism in Human Services: Is There a Link?" *Nonprofit and Voluntary Sector Quarterly* 22(1):33–51.

Cohen, Michael D., James G. March, and Johan P. Olsen. 1972. "A Garbage Can Model of Organizational Choice." *Administrative Science Quarterly* 17:1–25.

Coleman, James. 1968. "The Mathematical Study of Change." Pp. 428–78 in *Methodology in Social Research*, edited by Hubert Blalock, Jr., and Ann B. Blalock. New York: McGraw-Hill.

Coleman, James S. 1974. *Power and the Structure of Society.* New York: Norton.

Coleman, James S. 1986. "Social Theory, Social Research, and a Theory of Action." *American Journal of Sociology* 91(6):1309–35.

Coleman, James S. 1988. "Social Capital in the Creation of Human Capital." *American Journal of Sociology* 94(Supplement):S95–S120.

Corbin, John J. 1995. *Analysis of Economic and Non-Economic Determinants of the Division of Labor Among Social Service Providers.* Ph.D. dissertation, School of Social Sciences, University of Texas at Dallas.

Coser, Lewis. 1956. *The Functions of Social Conflict.* New York: Free Press.

D'Aunno, Thomas and Robert I. Sutton. 1992. "The Response of Drug Abuse Treatment Organizations to Financial Adversity: A Panel Test of the Threat-Rigidity Thesis." *Journal of Management* 18:117–31.

D'Aveni, Richard A. 1989. "The Aftermath of Organizational Decline: A Longitudinal Study of the Strategic and Managerial Characteristics of Declining Firms." *Academy of Management Journal* 32:577–605.

Daft, R. L. 1989. *Organization Theory and Design*, 3rd edition. St Paul, MN: West.

Davis, Gerald F. and Tracy A. Thompson. 1994. "A Social Movement Perspective on Corporate Control." *Administrative Science Quarterly* 39:141–73.

Delacroix, Jacques and Anand Swaminathan. 1991. "Cosmetic, Speculative, and Adaptive Change in the Wine Industry: A Longitudinal Study." *Administrative Science Quarterly* 36:631–61.

Dill, William R. 1958. "Environment as an Influence on Managerial Autonomy." *Administrative Science Quarterly* 2:409–43.

DiMaggio, Paul. 1988. "Interest and Agency in Institutional Theory." Pp. 3–21 in

*Institutional Patterns and Organizations: Culture and Environment*, edited by Lynne G. Zucker. Cambridge, MA: Ballinger.

DiMaggio, Paul and Helmut Anheier. 1990. "The Sociology of Nonprofit Organizations and Sectors." *Annual Review of Sociology* 16:137–59.

DiMaggio, Paul and Walter W. Powell. 1983. "The Iron Cage Revisited: Institutional Isomorphism and Collective Rationality in Organizational Fields." *American Sociological Review* 48:147–60.

DiMaggio, Paul and Walter W. Powell. 1991. "Introduction." Pp. 1–38 in *The New Institutionalism in Organizational Analysis*, edited by Walter W. Powell and Paul J. DiMaggio. Chicago: University of Chicago Press.

Downey, H. K., D. Hellriegel, and J. W. Slocum. 1975. "Environmental Uncertainty: The Construct and Its Application." *Administrative Science Quarterly* 20:613–29.

Downey, H. K. and R. D. Ireland. 1979. "Quantitative Versus Qualitative: Environmental Assessment in Organizational Studies." *Administrative Science Quarterly* 24:630–37.

Duncan, R. B. 1972. "Characteristics of Organizational Environments and Perceived Environmental Uncertainty." *Administrative Science Quarterly* 17:313–27.

Eckel, C. and Richard Steinberg. 1993. "Competition, Performance, and Public Policy Towards Nonprofits." Pp. 57–81 In *Nonprofit Organizations in a Market Economy*, edited by David Hammack and Dennis Young. San Francisco: Jossey-Bass.

Elazar, Daniel J. 1972. *American Federalism: A View from the Streets*. New York: Crowell.

Evan, William E. and R. Edward Freeman. 1988. "A Stakeholder Theory of the Modern Corporation: Kantian Capitalism." Pp. 97–106 in *Ethical Theory and Business*, 3rd edition, edited by Tom L. Beauchamp and Norman E. Bowie. Englewood Cliffs, NJ: Prentice Hall.

Feigenbaum, S. 1987. "Competition and Performance in the Nonprofit Sector: The Case of U.S. Medical Research Charities." *Journal of Industrial Economics* 35(3):241–53.

Ferris, James and Elizabeth Grady. 1989. "Fading Distinctions Among the Nonprofit, Government and For-Profit Sectors." Pp. 123–39 in *The Future of the Nonprofit Sectors*, edited by Virginia Hodgkinson and Richard Lyman. New York: Jossey-Bass.

Fienberg, Stephen E. 1977. *The Analysis of Cross-Classified Categorical Data*. Cambridge, MA: MIT Press.

Fligstein, Neil. 1985. "The Spread of the Multidivisional Form Among Large Firms, 1919–1979." *American Sociological Review* 50:377–91.

Fligstein, Neil. 1996. "Markets as Politics: A Political-Cultural Approach to Market Institutions." *American Sociological Review* 61:656–73.

Fombrun, Charles J. 1996. *Reputation: Realizing Value from the Corporate Image*. Boston: Harvard University Business School Press.

Ford, Jeffrey D. 1980. "The Occurrence of Structural Hysteresis in Declining Organizations." *Academy of Management Review* 5:589–98.

*Fortune*. 1990a. "The Fortune 500." April 23, pp. 346–65.

*Fortune.* 1990b. "The Service 500." June 4, pp. 304–31.

*Fortune.* 1994a. "Fortune 500 Ranked within States." April 18, p. 298.

*Fortune.* 1994b. "Fortune's Service 500 Ranked within State." May 30, pp. 252, 254.

Fox, John. 1991. *Regression Diagnostics.* Quantitative Applications in the Social Sciences Series. Newbury Park, CA: Sage.

Frank, Ove. 1978. "Sampling and Estimation in Large Social Networks." *Social Networks,* 1:91-101.

Freeman, Edward R. 1984. *Strategic Management: A Stakeholder Approach.* Marshfield, MA: Pitman.

Freeman, John and Michael Hannan. 1975. "Growth and Decline Processes within Organizations." *American Sociological Review* 40:215–28.

Friedland, Roger and Robert R. Alford. 1991. "Bringing Society Back In: Symbols, Practices, and Institutional Contradictions." Pp. 232–63 in *The New Institutionalism in Organizational Analysis,* edited by Walter W. Powell and Paul J. DiMaggio. Chicago: University of Chicago Press.

Froelich, Karen A. 1993. "Commercial Activity, Organizational Process and Performance in Not-For-Profit Organizations." Ph.D. dissertation, Carlson School of Management, University of Minnesota.

Froelich, Karen A. and Terry W. Knoepfle. 1996. "Internal Revenue Service 990 Data: Fact or Fiction?" *Nonprofit and Voluntary Sector Quarterly* 25(1):40–52.

Galaskiewicz, Joseph. 1985a. *Social Organization of an Urban Grants Economy: A Study of Business Philanthropy and Nonprofit Organizations.* Orlando, FL: Academic Press.

Galaskiewicz, Joseph. 1985b. "Interorganizational Relations." *Annual Review of Sociology* 11:281–304.

Galaskiewicz, Joseph. 1997. "An Urban Grants Economy Revisited: Corporate Charitable Contributions in the Twin Cities, 1979–81, 1987–89." *Administrative Science Quarterly* 42:445–71.

Galaskiewicz, Joseph and Barbara Rauschenbach. 1988. "The Corporation-Culture Connection: A Test of Interorganizational Theories." Pp. 119–35 in *Community Organizations: Studies in Resource Mobilization and Exchange,* edited by Carl Milofsky. New York: Oxford University Press.

Galaskiewicz, Joseph and Stanley Wasserman. 1989. "Mimetic Processes within an Interorganizational Field: An Empirical Test." *Administrative Sciences Quarterly* 34:454–79.

Gaul, Gilbert and Neill M. Borowski. 1993. *Free Ride: The Tax-Exempt Economy.* Kansas City: Andrews and McMeel.

Gibelman, Margaret and Harold W. Demone, Jr. 1990. "How Voluntary Agency Networks Fared in the 1980s." *Journal of Sociology and Social Welfare* 17:3–19.

Ginsberg, Ari and Ann Buchholtz. 1990. "Converting to For-Profit Status: Corporate Responsiveness to Radical Change." *Academy of Management Journal* 33:445–77.

Glaser, John. 1994. *The United Way Scandal: An Insider's Account of What Went Wrong and Why.* New York: Wiley.

Godfrey, L. 1978. "Testing Against General Autoregressive and Moving Average Error Models When the Regressors Include Lagged Dependent Variables." *Econometrica* 46:1293–1302.

Goldberger, Arthur S. 1981. "Linear Regression After Selection." *Journal of Econometrics* 15:357–66.

Goodman, Leo A. 1972. "A Modified Multiple Regression Approach to the Analysis of Dichotomous Variables." *American Sociological Review* 37:28–46.

Goodman, Leo A. 1973. "Causal Analysis of Data from Panel Studies and Other Surveys." *American Journal of Sociology* 78:1135–91.

Granovetter, Mark. 1985. "Economic Action and Social Structure: The Problem of Embeddedness." *American Journal of Sociology* 91:481–510.

Gray, Bradford H. 1991. *The Profit Motive and Patient Care: The Changing Accountability of Doctors and Hospitals.* Cambridge, MA: Harvard University Press.

Greene, William H. 1997. *Econometric Analysis,* 3rd edition. Upper Saddle River, NJ: Prentice-Hall.

Greenhalgh, Leonard. 1982. "Maintaining Organizational Effectiveness During Organizational Retrenchment." *Journal of Applied Behavioral Science* 18:155–70.

Greenhalgh, Leonard. 1983. "Organizational Decline." Pp. 231–76 in *Research in the Sociology of Organizations,* Volume 2, edited by Samuel B. Bacharach. Greenwich, CT: JAI.

Gronbjerg, Kirstin A. 1991a. "How Nonprofit Human Service Organizations Manage Their Funding Sources: Key Findings and Policy Implications." *Nonprofit Management and Leadership* 2:159–76.

Gronbjerg, Kirstin A. 1991b. "Managing Grants and Contracts: The Case of Four Nonprofit Social Service Organizations." *Nonprofit and Voluntary Sector Quarterly* 20:5–24.

Gronbjerg, Kirstin A. 1993. *Understanding Nonprofit Funding: Managing Revenues in Social Service and Community Development Organizations.* San Francisco: Jossey-Bass.

Hage, Jerald and Michael Aiken. 1967. "Program Change and Organizational Properties." *American Journal of Sociology* 72(5):503–19.

Hager, Mark A. 1998. "Explaining Demise among Nonprofit Organizations." Ph.D. dissertation, Department of Sociology, University of Minnesota, Minneapolis.

Hager, Mark A., Joseph Galaskiewicz, Wolfgang Bielefeld, and Joel J. Pins. 1996. "Tales From the Grave: Organizations' Accounts of Their Own Demise." *American Behavioral Scientist* 39(8):975–94.

Hall, Peter D. 1990. "Conflicting Managerial Cultures in Nonprofit Organizations." *Nonprofit Management and Leadership* 1:153–65.

Halliday, Terrence, Michael Powell, and M. Granfors. 1987. "Minimalist Organizations: Vital Events in State Bar Associations." *American Sociological Review* 52:456–71.

Hambrick, Donald C. and Steven M. Schecter. 1983. "Turnaround Strategies for Mature Industrial-product Business Units." *Academy of Management Journal* 26:231–48.

Handy, Femida. 1995. "Reputations as Collateral: An Economic Analysis of the Role of Trustees of Nonprofits." *Nonprofit and Voluntary Sector Quarterly* 24(4):293–305.

Hannan, Michael T. and John Carroll. 1992. *Dynamics of Organizational Populations.* New York: Oxford University Press.

Hannan, Michael T. and Glenn R. Carroll. 1995a. "An Introduction to Organizational Ecology." Pp. 17–31 in *Organizations in Industry: Strategy, Structure and Selection*, edited by Glenn R. Carroll and Michael T. Hannan. New York: Oxford University Press.

Hannan, Michael T. and Glenn R. Carroll. 1995b. "Theory Building and Cheap Talk about Legitimation: Reply to Baum and Powell." *American Sociological Review* 60:539–44.

Hannan, Michael T. and John Freeman. 1977. "The Population Ecology of Organizations." *American Journal of Sociology* 82:929–64.

Hannan, Michael T. and John Freeman. 1984. "Structural Inertia and Organizational Change." *American Sociological Review* 49:149–64.

Hannan, Michael T. and John Freeman. 1988. "The Ecology of Organizational Mortality: American Labor Unions, 1836–1985." *American Journal of Sociology* 94:25–52.

Hannan, Michael T. and John Freeman. 1989. *Organizational Ecology*. Cambridge, MA: Harvard University Press.

Hannan, Michael T. and Alice A. Young. 1977. "Estimation in Panel Models: Results on Pooling Cross-Sections and Time Series." Pp. 52–83 in *Sociological Methodology, 1977*, edited by David R. Heise. San Francisco: Jossey-Bass.

Hansmann, Henry B. 1980. "The Role of Nonprofit Enterprise." *Yale Law Journal* 89:835–98.

Hansmann, Henry B. 1981. "Nonprofit Enterprise in the Performing Arts." *Bell Journal of Economics* 12:341–61.

Hansmann, Henry B. 1987. "Economic Theories of Nonprofit Organization." Pp. 27–42 in *The Nonprofit Sector: A Research Handbook*, edited by Walter W. Powell. New Haven, CT: Yale University Press.

Haunschild, Pamela R. and Anne S. Miner. 1997. "Modes of Interorganizational Imitation: The Effects of Outcome Salience and Uncertainty." *Administrative Science Quarterly* 42:472–500.

Haveman, Heather A. 1992. "Between a Rock and a Hard Place: Organizational Change and Performance Under Conditions of Fundamental Environmental Transformation." *Administrative Science Quarterly* 37:48–75.

Haveman, Heather A. 1993. "Organizational Size and Change: Diversification in the Savings and Loan Industry after Deregulation." *Administrative Science Quarterly* 38:20–50.

Hawley, Amos. 1950. *Human Ecology*. New York: Ronald.

Heckman, James J. 1976. "The Common Structure of Statistical Models of Truncation, Sample Selection and Limited Dependent Variables and a Simple Estimator for Such Models." *Annals of Economic and Social Measurement* 5:475–92.

Heckman, James J. 1979. "Sample Bias as a Specification Error." *Econometrica* 45:153–62.

Herman, Robert D. and David O. Renz. 1997. "Multiple Constituencies and the Social Construction of Nonprofit Organizations Effectiveness." *Nonprofit and Voluntary Sector Quarterly* 26:185–206.

Hirsch, Paul M. 1997. "Sociology without Social Structure: Neoinstitutional Theory Meets Brave New World." *American Journal of Sociology* 102:1702–23.

Hodgkinson, Virginia A. and Murray S. Weitzman. 1996. *Nonprofit Almanac, 1996–1997,* 5th edition. San Francisco, CA: Jossey-Bass.

Hodgkinson, Virginia A., Murray S. Weitzman, Christopher M. Toppe, and Stephen M. Noga. 1992. *Nonprofit Almanac, 1992–1993.* San Francisco, CA: Jossey-Bass.

Holtman, A. G. 1983. "A Theory of Non-Profit Firms." *Economica* 50:439–49.

James, Estelle. 1983. "How Nonprofits Grow: A Model." *Journal of Policy Analysis and Management* 2:350–66.

Jensen, Michael C. and William H. Meckling. 1976. "Theory of the Firm: Managerial Behavior, Agency Costs, and Ownership Structure." *Journal of Financial Economics* 3:305–60

Jepperson, Ronald L. and John W. Meyer. 1991. "The Public Order and the Construction of Formal Organizations." Pp. 204–31 in *The New Institutionalism in Organizational Analysis,* edited by Walter W. Powell and Paul J. DiMaggio. Chicago: University of Chicago Press.

Kahn, Faith S. 1996. "Pandora's Box: Managerial Discretion and the Problem of Corporate Philanthropy." Working paper, New York Law School.

Kim, Jae-On and G. Donald Ferree, Jr. 1981. "Standardization in Causal Analysis." Pp. 22–43 in *Linear Models in Social Research,* edited by Peter V. Marsden. Beverly Hills, CA: Sage.

Kimberly, John R. and Robert A. Miles and Associates. 1980. *The Organizational Life Cycle.* San Francisco: Jossey Bass.

Kingma, Bruce R. 1993. "Portfolio Theory and Nonprofit Financial Stability." *Nonprofit and Voluntary Sector Quarterly* 22(2):105–19.

Kirkpatrick, David. 1989. "Fortune's Top Ten Cities." *Fortune,* October 23, p. 79.

Knoke, David. 1990. *Organizing for Collective Action: The Political Economies of Associations.* Hawthorne, NY: Aldine de Gruyter.

Knoke, David and Robert Guilarte. 1994. "Networks in Organizational Structures and Strategies." Pp. 77–115 in *Current Perspectives in Social Theory, Supplement 1.* Greenwich, CT: JAI.

Knoke, David and James R. Wood. 1981. *Organized for Action: Commitment in Voluntary Associations.* New Brunswick, NJ: Rutgers University Press.

Kotler, Philip. 1980. *Marketing Management: Analysis, Planning and Control,* 4th edition. Englewood Cliffs, NJ:Prentice-Hall.

Kraatz, Matthew S. and Edward J. Zajac. 1996. "Exploring the Limits of the New Institutionalism: The Causes and Consequences of Illegitimate Organizational Change." *American Sociological Review* 61:812–36.

Krackhardt, David and Jeffrey R. Hanson. 1993. "Informal Networks: The Company Behind the Chart." *Harvard Business Review* (July–August):104–11.

Krashinsky, Michael. 1998. "Does Auspice Matter? The Case of Day Care for Children in Canada." Pp. 114–123 in *Private Action and the Public Good,* edited by Walter W. Powell and Elisabeth Clemens. New Haven, CT: Yale University Press.

Kretchmar, Laurie. 1991. "The Best Cities for Business." *Fortune,* November 4, p. 52.

Labich, Kenneth. 1993. "The Best Cities for Knowledge Workers." *Fortune,* November 15, p. 50.

Lawrence, Paul R. and Jay W. Lorsch. 1967. *Organizational and Environment: Man-*

*aging Differentiation and Integration.* Boston: Harvard University, Graduate School of Business Administration.

Lee, Maw Lin. 1971. "A Conspicuous Consumption Theory of Hospital Behavior." *Southern Economics Journal* 38:48–58.

Levine, Charles H. 1978. "Organizational Decline and Cutback Management." *Public Administration Review* 38(July–August):316–25.

Levine, Sol and Paul White. 1961. "Exchange as a Conceptual Framework for the Study of Interorganizational Relationships." *Administrative Science Quarterly* 5:583–601.

Lipset, Seymour Martin, Martin A. Trow, and James S. Coleman. 1956. *Union Democracy.* Glencoe, IL: Free Press.

Lohmann, Roger A. 1992. *The Commons: New Perspectives on Nonprofit Organizations and Voluntary Action.* San Francisco: Jossey-Bass.

Mackay, Harvey. 1997. *Dig Your Well Before You're Thirsty: The Only Networking Book You'll Ever Need.* New York: Currency/Doubleday.

March, James and Herbert Simon. 1958. *Organizations.* New York: Wiley.

Markus, Gregory B. 1979. *Analyzing Panel Data.* Sage University Paper series on Quantitative Applications in the Social Sciences, series no. 07-018. Newbury Park, CA: Sage.

Marsden, Peter V. and Noah E. Friedkin. 1993. "Network Studies of Social Influence." *Sociological Methods & Research* 22:127–51.

Mauser, Elizabeth. 1998. "The Importance of Organizational Form: Parent Perceptions Versus Reality in the Day-Care Industry." Pp. 124–133 in *Private Action and the Public Good,* edited by Walter W. Powell and Elisabeth Clemens. New Haven, CT: Yale University Press.

McCormack, Patrick J. 1996. "Nonprofits at the Brink: Lean Budgets, Growing Needs, and the Fate of Nonprofits." *Northwest Report* (April):2–9.

McKinley, William. 1992. "Decreasing Organizational Size: To Untangle or Not to Untangle." *Academy of Management Review* 17:112–23.

McPherson, J. Miller. 1983. "An Ecology of Affiliation." *American Sociological Review* 48: 519–35.

McPherson, J. Miller and Thomas Rotolo. 1996. "Testing a Dynamic Model of Social Composition: Diversity and Change in Voluntary Groups." *American Sociological Review* 61:179–202.

Messer, John G. 1994. "Emergent Organization as a Practical Strategy: Executing Trustee Functions in Alcoholics Anonymous." *Nonprofit and Voluntary Sector Quarterly* 23(4):293–307.

Meyer, John W. and Brian Rowan. 1977. "Institutionalized Organizations: Formal Structure as Myth and Ceremony." *American Journal of Sociology* 83:340–63.

Middleton-Stone, Melissa and William Crittendon. 1993. "A Guide to Journal Articles on Strategic Management in Nonprofit Organizations, 1977 to 1992." *Nonprofit Management and Leadership* 4:193–214.

Miles, Raymond E. and Charles C. Snow. 1978. *Organizational Strategy, Structure, and Process.* New York: McGraw-Hill.

Milliken, F. J. 1987. "Three Types of Perceived Uncertainty about the Environment: State, Effect, and Response Uncertainty." *Academy of Management Review* 12:133–43.

Minkoff, Debra. 1997. "The Sequencing of Social Movements." *American Sociological Review* 62:779–99.

Mintzberg, Henry. 1983. *Power in and around Organizations.* Englewood Cliffs, NJ: Prentice-Hall.

Mintzberg, Henry. 1987. "The Strategy Concept I: Five Ps for Strategy." Pp. 7–20 in *Organizational Approaches to Strategy,* edited by Glenn R. Carroll and David Vogel. Cambridge, MA: Ballinger.

Mizruchi, Mark and Joseph Galaskiewicz. 1994. "Networks of Interorganizational Relations." Pp. 239–53 in *Advances in Social Network Analysis: Research in the Social and Behavioral Sciences,* edited by Stanley Wasserman and Joseph Galaskiewicz. Thousand Oaks, CA: Sage.

National Council of the Churches of Christ in the U.S.A. 1995. *Yearbook of American and Canadian Churches,* 1995 edition. Nashville, TN: Author.

Newhouse, Joseph P. 1970. "Toward a Theory of Nonprofit Institutions: An Economic Model of a Hospital." *American Economic Review* 60:64–73.

Niskanen, W.A., Jr. 1971. *Bureaucracy and Representative Government.* Hawthorne, NY: Aldine de Gruyter.

Nohria, Nitin and Robert Eccles (Eds.). 1992. *Networks and Organizations: Structure, Form, and Action.* Boston: Harvard University Business School Press.

O'Neill, Michael. 1994. "Philanthropic Dimensions of Mutual Benefit Organizations." *Nonprofit and Voluntary Sector Quarterly* 23:3–20.

Ocasio, William. 1994. "Political Dynamics and the Circulation of Power: CEO Succession in U.S. Industrial Corporations, 1960–1990." *Administrative Science Quarterly* 39:285–312.

Oliver, Christine. 1991. "Strategic Responses to Institutional Processes." *Academy of Management Review* 16:145–79.

Oliver, Christine. 1996. "The Institutional Embeddedness of Economic Activity." Pp. 163–86 in *Advances in Strategic Management,* Volume 13, edited by Paul Shrivastava, Anne S. Huff, and Jane E. Dutton. Greenwich, CT: JAI.

Olson, Mancur. 1965. *The Logic of Collective Action: Public Goods and the Theory of Groups.* Cambridge, MA: Harvard University Press.

Onyx, Jenny and Madi Maclean. 1996. "Careers in the Third Sector." *Nonprofit Management and Leadership* 6:331–45.

Ostrander, Susan A. 1995. *Money for Change: Social Movement Philanthropy at Haymarket People's Fund.* Philadelphia, PA: Temple University Press.

Ostrower, Francie. 1996. *Why the Wealthy Give: The Culture of Elite Philanthropy.* Princeton, NJ: Princeton University Press.

Palmer, John L. and Isabel V. Sawhill (Eds.). 1982. *The Reagan Experiment: An Examination of Economic and Social Policies under the Reagan Administration.* Washington, DC: Urban Institute Press.

Pauley, Mark and Michael Redisch. 1973. "The Not-for-profit Hospital as a Physicians Cooperative." *American Economic Review* 63:87–99.

Pennings, Johannes M. 1985. "Introduction: On the Nature and Theory of Strategic Decisions." Pp. 1–34 in *Organizational Strategy and Change,* edited by Johannes M. Pennings. San Francisco: Jossey-Bass.

Perrow, Charles. 1961. "Organizational Prestige: Some Functions and Dysfunctions." *American Journal of Sociology* 66:335–41.

Peters, Thomas J. and Robert H. Waterman, Jr. 1982. *In Search of Excellence: Lessons from America's Best-Run Companies*. New York: Harper and Row.

Petrie, Hugh G. and Daniel Alpert. 1983. "What Is the Problem of Retrenchment in Higher Education?" *Journal of Management Studies* 20:97–119.

Pfeffer, Jeffrey. 1981. *Power in Organizations*. Marshfield, MA: Pitman.

Pfeffer, Jeffrey and Anthony Leong. 1977. "Resource Allocations in United Funds: Examination of Power and Dependence." *Social Forces* 55:775–790.

Pfeffer, Jeffrey and Gerald R. Salancik. 1974. "Organizational Decision Making as a Political Process: The Case of a University Budget." *Administrative Science Quarterly* 19:135–51.

Pfeffer, Jeffrey and Gerald R. Salancik. 1978. *The External Control of Organizations*. New York: Harper & Row.

Podolny, Joel M. and Toby E. Stuart. 1995. "A Role-Based Ecology of Technological Change." *American Journal of Sociology* 100:1224–60.

Podolny, Joel M., Toby E. Stuart, and Michael T. Hannan. 1996. "Networks, Knowledge, and Niches: Competition in the Worldwide Semiconductor Industry, 1984–1991." *American Journal of Sociology* 102:659–89.

Popielarz, Pamela A. and J. Miller McPherson. 1995. "On the Edge or In Between: Niche Position, Niche Overlap, and the Duration of Voluntary Association Memberships." *American Journal of Sociology* 101:698–720.

Porter, Michael. 1991. "Towards a Dynamic Theory of Strategy." *Strategic Management Journal* 12:95–117.

Powell, Walter W. 1990. "Neither Market nor Hierarchy: Network Forms of Organization." Pp. 295–336 in *Research in Organizational Behavior*, Volume 12, edited by Larry L. Cummings and Barry M. Staw. Greenwich, CT: JAI.

Powell, Walter W. and Peter Brantley. 1992. "Competitive Cooperation in Biotechnology: Learning through Networks?" Pp. 366–94 in *Networks and Organizations: Structures, Form, and Action*, edited by Nitin Nohria and Robert G. Eccles. Boston: Harvard University Business School Press.

Powell, Walter W. and Paul J. DiMaggio (Eds.). 1991. *The New Institutionalism in Organizational Analysis*. Chicago: University of Chicago Press.

Powell, Walter W., Kenneth W. Koput, and Laurel Smith-Doerr. 1996. "Interorganizational Collaboration and the Locus of Innovation: Networks of Learning in Biotechnology." *Administrative Science Quarterly* 41:116–45.

Powell, Walter W. and Laurel Smith-Doerr. 1994. "Networks and Economic Life." Pp. 368–402 in *The Handbook of Economic Sociology*, edited by Neil Smelser and Richard Swedberg. Princeton, NJ: Princeton University Press.

Pratt, Jon and Chris Sullivan. 1995. *Minnesota's Nonprofit Economy: Structuring a New Partnership with Government and Communities*. St. Paul: Minnesota Council of Nonprofits.

Preston, A. E. 1988. "The Nonprofit Firm: A Potential Solution to Inherent Market Failures." *Economic Inquiry* 26:493–506.

Provan, Keith G., Janice M. Beyer, and Carlos Kruytbosch. 1980. "Environmental Linkages and Power in Resource-Dependence Relations between Organizations." *Administrative Science Quarterly* 25:200–25.

Putnam, Robert. 1995. "Bowling Alone: America's Declining Social Capital." *Journal of Democracy* 6:65–78.

Renz, Loren, Shaista Qureshi, and Crystal Mandler. 1996. *Foundation Giving, 1996 Edition*. New York: Foundation Center.

Robbins, D. Keith and John A. Pearce II. 1992. "Turnaround: Retrenchment and Recovery." *Strategic Management Journal* 13:287–309.

Roller, Robert H. 1996. "Strategy Formulation in Nonprofit Social Services Organizations: A Proposed Framework." *Nonprofit Management and Leadership* 7:137–53.

Rothschild-Whitt, Joyce. 1979. "The Collectivist Organization: An Alternative to Rational Bureaucratic Models." *American Sociological Review* 44:509–27

Salamon, Lester M. 1987. "Partners in Public Service: The Scope and Theory of Government-Nonprofit Relations." Pp. 99–117 in *The Nonprofit Sector: A Research Handbook*, edited by Walter W. Powell. New Haven, CT: Yale University Press.

Salamon, Lester M. 1997a. *Private Action/Public Good: Maryland's Nonprofit Sector in a Time of Change*. Baltimore: Maryland Association of Nonprofit Organizations.

Salamon, Lester M. 1997b. *Holding the Center: America's Nonprofit Sector at a Crossroads*. New York: Nathan Cummings Foundation.

Salamon, Lester M., David M. Altschuler, and Jaana Myllyluoma. 1990. *More than Just Charity: The Baltimore Area Nonprofit Sector in a Time of Change, Executive Summary*. Baltimore, MD: Johns Hopkins University Institute for Policy Studies.

Saporito, Bill. 1992. "The Best Cities for Business." *Fortune*, November 2, p. 40.

Schiff, J. and Burton Weisbrod. 1991. "Competition between For-Profit and Nonprofit Organizations in Commercial Activities." *Annals of Public and Cooperative Economics* 62:619–40.

Schneider, John C. 1996. "Philanthropic Styles in the United States: Toward a Theory of Regional Differences." *Nonprofit and Voluntary Sector Quarterly* 25:190–210.

Scott, Jacquelyn T. 1995. "Some Thoughts on Theory Development in the Voluntary and Nonprofit Sector." *Nonprofit and Voluntary Sector Quarterly* 24(1):31–40.

Scott, W. Richard. 1987. *Organizations: Rational, Natural, and Open Systems*, 2nd edition. Englewood Cliffs, NJ: Prentice-Hall.

Scott, W. Richard. 1992. *Organizations: Rational, Natural, and Open Systems*, 3rd edition. Englewood Cliffs, NJ: Prentice-Hall.

Scott, W. Richard. 1995. *Institutions and Organizations: Theory and Research*. Thousand Oaks, CA: Sage.

Scott, W. Richard. 1998. *Organizations: Rational, Natural, and Open Systems*, 4th edition. Upper Saddle River, NJ: Prentice-Hall.

Sellers, Patricia. 1990. "The Best Cities for Business." *Fortune*, October 22, p. 48.

Selznick, Philip. 1949. *TVA and the Grass Roots*. Los Angeles and Berkeley: University of California Press.

Sewell, William H., Jr. 1992. "A Theory of Structure: Duality, Agency, and Transformation." *American Journal of Sociology* 98(1):1–29.

Sills, David L. 1957. *The Volunteers: Means and Ends in a National Organization*. New York: Free Press.

Simon, Herbert. 1957. *Administrative Behavior,* 2nd edition. New York: Macmillan.

Simon, John. 1987. "The Tax Treatment of Nonprofit Organizations: A Review of Federal and State Policies." Pp. 67–98 in *The Nonprofit Sector: A Research Handbook,* edited by Walter W. Powell. New Haven, CT: Yale University Press.

Singer, M. I. and J. A. Yankey. 1991. "Organizational Metamorphosis: A Study of 18 Nonprofit Mergers, Acquisitions, and Consolidations." *Nonprofit Management and Leadership* 1:357–69.

Singh, Jitendra V. 1986. "Performance, Slack, and Risk Taking in Organizational Decision-Making." *Academy of Management Journal* 29(September):562–85.

Singh, Jitendra V., Robert J. House, and David J. Tucker. 1986. "Organizational Change and Organizational Mortality." *Administrative Science Quarterly* 31:587–611.

Singh, Jitendra V. and Charles J. Lumsden. 1990. "Theory and Research in Organizational Ecology." *Annual Review of Sociology* 16:161–95.

Singh, Jitendra V., David J. Tucker, and Robert J. House. 1986. "Organizational Legitimacy and the Liability of Newness." *Administrative Science Quarterly* 31:171–93.

Singh, Jitendra V., David J. Tucker, and Agnes G. Meinhard. 1991. "Institutional Change and Ecological Dynamics." Pp. 390–422 in *The New Institutionalism in Organizational Analysis,* edited by Walter W. Powell and Paul J. DiMaggio. Chicago: University of Chicago Press.

Smith, David H. 1993. "Public Benefit and Member Benefit Nonprofit, Voluntary Groups." *Nonprofit and Voluntary Sector Quarterly* 22(1):53–68.

Smith, David H. 1994. "Determinants of Voluntary Association Participation and Volunteering: A Literature Review." *Nonprofit and Voluntary Sector Quarterly* 23(3):243–63.

Smith, David H. 1995. "Some Challenges in Nonprofit and Voluntary Action Research." *Nonprofit and Voluntary Sector Quarterly* 24(2):99–101.

Smith, David H. 1997. "Grassroots Associations Are Important: Some Theory and a Review of the Impact Literature." *Nonprofit and Voluntary Sector Quarterly* 26:269–306.

Smith, Tom and Vikki Kratz. 1996. "The Nonprofit 100: Minnesota's Largest Nonprofits, and the Compensation of the People Who Run Them." *Corporate Report Minnesota* 27(November):64.

Smith, Vicki. 1990. *Managing in the Corporate Interest: Control and Resistance in an American Bank.* Berkeley: University of California Press.

Staber, Udo. 1989. "Organizational Foundings in the Cooperative Sector in Atlantic Canada: An Ecological Perspective." *Organizational Studies* 10:383–405.

Stanley, Mary B. 1993. "The Rich Are Always with Us." *Nonprofit and Voluntary Sector Quarterly* 22(3):267–70.

Starbuck, William H. 1965. "Organizational Growth and Development." Pp. 451–533 in *Handbook of Organizations,* edited by James G. March. Chicago: Rand-McNally.

Starbuck, William H., Arent Greve, and Bo L. T. Hedberg. 1977. "Responding to Crisis." *Journal of Business Administration* 9:111–37.

Staw, Barry M., Lance E. Sandelands, and Jane E. Dutton. 1981. "Threat-Rigidity

Effects in Organizational Behavior: A Multilevel Analysis." *Administrative Science Quarterly* 26: 501–24.

Stebbins, Robert A. 1996. "Volunteering: A Serious Leisure Perspective." *Nonprofit and Voluntary Sector Quarterly* 25(2):211–24.

Steinberg, Richard. 1993. "Public Policy and the Performance of Nonprofit Organizations: A General Framework." *Nonprofit and Voluntary Sector Quarterly* 22(1):13–31.

Steinberg, Richard and Bradford H. Gray. 1993. " 'The Role of Nonprofit Enterprise' in 1993: Hansmann Revisited." *Nonprofit and Voluntary Sector Quarterly* 22(4):297–316.

Stevens, Susan K. 1994. *Refocusing on Community: The 1994 Report on the Financial Health of Minnesota's Nonprofits.* Minneapolis: Minnesota Nonprofits Assistance Fund.

Stevenson, David R., Thomas H. Pollak, and Linda M. Lampkin. 1997. *State Nonprofit Almanac, 1997: Profiles of Charitable Organizations.* Washington, DC: Urban Institute Press.

Stinchcombe, Arthur. 1965. "Social Structure and Organizations." Pp. 142–93 in *Handbook of Organizations*, edited by James G. March. Chicago: Rand McNally.

Stolzenberg, Ross M. and Daniel A. Relles. 1997. "Tools for Intuition about Sample Selection Bias and Its Correction." *American Sociological Review* 62:494–507.

Stromsdorfer, Ernst W. and George Farkas. 1980. "Methodology." Pp. 32–41 in *Evaluation Studies Review Annual*, volume 5, edited by Ernst W. Stromsdorfer and George Farkas. Beverly Hills, CA: Sage.

Suchman, Mark C. 1995. "Managing Legitimacy: Strategic and Institutional Approaches." *Academy of Management Review* 20:571–610.

Sundeen, Richard A. 1992. "Differences in Personal Goals and Attitudes Among Volunteers." *Nonprofit and Voluntary Sector Quarterly* 21(3):271–91.

Sundeen, Richard A. and Sally A. Raskoff. 1995. "Teenage Volunteers and Their Values." *Nonprofit and Voluntary Sector Quarterly* 24(4):337–57.

Swaminathan, Anand. 1995. "The Proliferation of Specialist Organizations in the American Wine Industry, 1941–1990." *Administrative Science Quarterly* 40:653–80.

Tassie, Bill, Vic Murray, James Cutt, and Denise Bragg. 1996. "Rationality and Politics: What Really Goes on When Funders Evaluate the Performance of Fundees." *Nonprofit and Voluntary Sector Quarterly* 25(3):347–63.

Thompson, James D. 1967. *Organizations in Action.* New York: McGraw-Hill.

Tolbert, Pamela S., and Lynne G. Zucker. 1983. "Institutional Sources of Change in the Formal Structure of Organizations: The Diffusion of Civil Service Reform." *Administrative Science Quarterly* 28:22–39.

Tullock, Gordon. 1966. "Information without Profit." *Papers on Non-Market Decision-making* 1:141–59.

Tushman, Michael L., William H. Newman, and Elaine Romanelli. 1986. "Convergence and Upheaval: Managing the Unsteady Pace of Organizational Evolution." *California Management Review* 29:29–44.

Tushman, Michael L. and Elaine Romanelli. 1985. "Organizational Evolution: A

Metamorphosis Model of Convergence and Reorientation." Pp. 171–222 in *Research in Organizational Behavior,* Volume 7, edited by Barry M. Staw and Larry L. Cummings. Greenwich, CT: JAI.

Tyson, James L. 1996. "How Minneapolis Became a Start-up City." *Christian Science Monitor,* August 1, p. 9.

U.S. Department of Commerce. 1991. *State and Metro Area Data Book, 1991.* Washington, DC: U.S. Government Printing Office.

U.S. Department of Commerce. 1992. *1990 Census of Population. General Population Characteristics, Minnesota.* Washington, DC: U.S. Government Printing Office.

U.S. Department of Commerce. 1993. *U.S. Census of Population. Social and Economic Characteristics, Minnesota.* Washington, DC: U.S. Government Printing Office.

U.S. Department of the Treasury. 1983. *List of Organizations.* Washington, DC: U.S. Government Printing Office.

Van de Ven, Andrew H. and Raghu Garud. 1993. "Innovation and Industry Development: The Case of Cochlear Implants." Pp. 1–46 in *Research on Technological Innovation, Management and Policy,* Volume V, edited by Richard S. Rosenbloom. Greenwich, CT: JAI.

Van de Ven, Andrew H. and Marshall Scott Poole. 1995. "Explaining Development and Change in Organizations." *Academy of Management Review* 20(3):510–40.

Warren, Roland L. 1967. "The Interorganizational Field as a Focus for Investigation." *Administrative Science Quarterly* 12:396–419.

Weisbrod, Burton A. 1988. *The Nonprofit Economy.* Cambridge, MA: Harvard University Press.

Weisbrod, Burton A. 1998. "Institutional Form and Organizational Behavior." Pp. 69–84 in *Private Action and the Public Good,* edited by Walter W. Powell and Elisabeth Clemens. New Haven, CT: Yale University Press.

Weitzel, William and Ellen Jonsson. 1989. "Decline in Organizations: A Literature Integration and Extension." *Administrative Science Quarterly* 34:91–109.

Wernet, S. P. and S. A. Jones. 1992. "Merger and Acquisition Activity Between Nonprofit Social Service Organizations: A Case Study." *Nonprofit and Voluntary Sector Quarterly* 21:367–80.

Whetten, David A. 1980. "Sources, Responses, and Effects of Organizational Decline." Pp. 342–74 in *The Organizational Life Cycle,* edited by John R. Kimberly and Robert H. Miles. San Francisco: Jossey-Bass.

Whetten, David A. 1981. "Interorganizational Relations: A Review of the Field." *Journal of Higher Education* 52:1–28.

Whetten, David A. 1987. "Organizational Growth and Decline Processes." Pp. 335–55 in *Annual Review of Sociology,* Volume 13, edited by W. Richard Scott and James F. Short, Jr. Palo Alto, CA: Annual Reviews.

White, H. 1980. "A Heteroskedasticity-Consistent Covariance Matrix Estimator and a Direct Test for Heteroskedasticity." *Econometrica* 48:817–38.

*Who's Who in America, 1980–81 edition.* 1980. Chicago: A. N. Marquis.

*Who's Who in America, 1988–89 edition.* 1988. Chicago: A. N. Marquis.

Williamson, Oliver E. 1975. *Markets and Hierarchies: Analysis and Antitrust Implications.* New York: Free Press.

Williamson, Oliver E. 1981. "The Economics of Organization: The Transaction Cost Approach." *American Journal of Sociology* 87(3):548–77.

Wilson, E. K. 1985. "What Counts in the Death or Transformation of an Organization?" *Social Forces* 64:259–80.

Winship, Christopher and Robert D. Mare. 1992. "Models for Sample Selection Bias." *Annual Review of Sociology* 18:327–50.

Wolpert, Julian. 1993a. *Patterns of Generosity in America: Who's Holding the Safety Net?* New York: Twentieth Century Fund.

Wolpert, Julian. 1993b. "Decentralization and Equity in Public and Nonprofit Sectors." *Nonprofit and Voluntary Sector Quarterly* 22(4):281–96.

Wolpert, Julian. 1996. *Half a Loaf: The Limits of Charity in the Nineties.* New York: Twentieth Century Fund.

Wuthnow, Robert. 1991. *Acts of Compassion: Caring for Others and Helping Ourselves.* Princeton, NJ: Princeton University Press.

Yuchtman, Ephraim and Stanley E. Seashore. 1967. "A System Resource Approach to Organizational Effectiveness." *American Sociological Review* 20:206–10.

Zald, Mayer. 1969. *Power in Organizations.* Nashville, TN: Vanderbilt University Press.

Zald, Meyer N. and Patricia Denton. 1963. "From Evangelism to General Service: The Transformation of the YMCA." *Administrative Science Quarterly* 8:214–34.

Zucker, Lynne. 1983. "Organizations as Institutions." Pp. 1–47 in *Research in the Sociology of Organizations,* Volume 2, edited by Samuel B. Bacharach. Greenwich, CT: JAI.

# Index

Adaptation theory, 1, 8–15, 20–24, 36, 89–92, 117–118, 120, 128, 145, 155, 220–223, 227, 235
Administrative component, 165
Alienation, 166–167, 169–170, 173–174, 176–177, 181, 190–195, 202–204, 219, 226, 234, 237
Amenity goods, 33
Anomie, 171–172
Authority, (see Decision-making structures)

Bureaucracy, 16–17, 165, 229

Charitable organizations, 26–27, 32, 239
Churches, 26, 37–38, 52, 77
Clubs, 26–27, 31–32, 38
Coercive isomorphism, 223, 232
Collective goods, 26–27, 29, 31, 38
Commercial income, 26, 36, 38, 223, 227–228, 234–238, 240
  and growth or decline, 80–89, 91–95, 216–217, 224, 230
  and organizational milieux, 173, 184–185, 187–188, 190, 194–195, 197, 203, 219, 226
  and strategies, 127, 129–130, 139, 143–5, 147, 155–157, 160–161, 218, 225
  of study nonprofits, 64–65, 70–71
Communitarian organizations, 30
Competition, 4–5, 13, 15, 23, 36, 39, 215, 237
  and growth or decline, 85, 87–88, 90–91

and organizational milieux, 176, 184, 187–188, 195, 203, 219
and strategies, 128–130, 143–5, 147, 157–158, 160–161, 218
Concentration, 4, 23, 36, 69, 85–88, 117, 128, 143–4, 157, 161, 167, 215–216, 218, 237
  operationalization of, 263–264
Conflict with employees, 166–167, 169–170, 173–174, 177, 181, 195–197, 202–204, 219, 226, 237
Contingency theory, 1, 89, 217
Contributions, see Donated income
Creativity and innovation, 131, 166–167, 169–170, 173–174, 177–181, 184–187, 202–204, 226, 233–234, 237

Decision-making structures, 17–18, 36, 92–93, 119
  centralization, 166–167 169–170, 174, 176, 181–182, 185, 187–188, 190, 194–195, 202–204, 219, 226, 230–231
  operationalization of, 103–104
Density, 3–4, 7, 23, 36, 86–88, 117, 128, 144–147, 157, 184–185, 188, 196, 215–216, 218–219, 226
  operationalization of, 253–263
Disagreements, 166–167, 169–170, 173–174, 176–177, 181, 190–195, 202–204, 226–227, 237
Donated income, 26–27, 29, 36, 37, 223, 227–228, 233–238, 240